Perfectly Legal

Perfectly Legal

THE COVERT CAMPAIGN TO RIG OUR TAX SYSTEM TO BENEFIT THE SUPER RICH— AND CHEAT EVERYBODY ELSE

David Cay Johnston

Portfolio

PORTFOLIO

Published by the Penguin Group

Penguin Group (USA) Inc., 375 Hudson Street, New York, New York 10014, U.S.A.

Penguin Books Ltd, 80 Strand, London WC2R 0RL, England

Penguin Books Australia Ltd, 250 Camberwell Road, Camberwell, Victoria 3124, Australia

Penguin Books Canada Ltd, 10 Alcorn Avenue, Toronto, Ontario, Canada M4V 3B2

Penguin Books India (P) Ltd, 11 Community Centre, Panchsheel Park, New Delhi – 110 017, India

Penguin Books (N.Z.) Ltd, Cnr Rosedale and Airborne Roads, Albany, Auckland, New Zealand

Penguin Books (South Africa) (Pty) Ltd, 24 Sturdee Avenue, Rosebank, Johannesburg 2196, South Africa

Penguin Books Ltd, Registered Offices: 80 Strand, London WC2R 0RL, England

First published in 2003 by Portfolio, a member of Penguin Group (USA) Inc.

9   10   8

Library of Congress Cataloging-in-Publication Data

Johnston, David Cay
Perfectly legal : the covert campaign to rig our tax system to benefit the super rich—
and cheat everybody else / David Cay Johnston.
p.   cm.
ISBN 1-59184-019-8
1. Taxation—United States.   2. Tax evasion—United States.   3. Taxation—Law and legislation—
United States.   4. Rich people—United States.   I. Title.

HJ2362.J64 2003
336.2'00973—dc22   2003061660

This book is printed on acid-free paper. ♾

Printed in the United States of America
Set in Bembo
Designed by Erin Benach

For
Jennifer Leonard
who serves the common good every day

Acknowledgments

Hundreds of people contributed to this book in ways small and large by giving of their time and knowledge. To each of them I am indebted. My apologies to those I will surely overlook in the words that follow.

The Internal Revenue Service has long been considered impenetrable by journalists, yet—like all large institutions—it can be explored when the basic tools of inquiry are persistence, document reading and a gentle ear. The vast majority of my sources are people I identified, but within the IRS many of those who proved helpful wish to remain anonymous. To those revenue agents and revenue officers, tax auditors, clerks, branch chiefs, appeals officers, specialists and executives who gave freely of their time and in many cases shared with me important documents, my deep appreciation for helping advance my knowledge of the IRS. Likewise, many people inside accounting and law firms and corporations helped me with documents and interviews, but asked not to be identified. To all of you who remain anonymous, I hope that after reading these pages you feel your time was well spent. To those sources I never met because they only sent raw documents my way, I also express thanks, along with a plea that next time you enclose an explanation or contact me directly so that what is so vital to you will make better sense to me.

Among the many others to whom I am indebted:

Some of the wealthiest and most generous residents of Rochester, New York, provided me with practical observations about business and taxes that added an important dimension to my understanding of the degree to which both parties in Congress are out of touch. I am especially grateful to Joe Briggs, Ron Fielding, Marvin and Nancy Yanes Hoffman, Tom Hubbard, Mike Millard, John McMath, John Summers and I.C. Shah.

The reporters for *Perfectly Legal* (Stephanie Mencimer in Washington, D.C., Kate Berry in Southern California, Gary Craig in Rochester and Ruth Ford and Jarrett Murphy in New York City) conducted many interviews for this book and ferreted out important facts. Jarrett, a graduate student in economics when we met, prepared many of the economics tables and charts I relied on. Donald Holland organized my files.

The great editor Gene Roberts brought me into *The New York Times* in the belief that I could show a new and better way to cover taxes and their impact on America. Joe Lelyveld, Bill Keller and Howell Raines, like Roberts all of strong spines that are too rare in journalism today, gave faithful support. I also thank each of them for recruiting the tough and talented editors who challenged and encouraged my reporting.

Many editors in the "Business Day" section of *The Times* polished my work, especially Dan Niemi, Winnie O'Kelley, Tom Redburn, Jim Schachter and Judith H. Dobrzynski (now managing editor of CNBC), as well as Brent Bowers, Fred Brock, Donna Cartwright, Vicki Epstein, Deidre Leipziger, Mickey Meece, Jim Norman, Steven Rosenfeld, Doug Ward and Bill Wellman. Alain Delaqueriere and Donna Anderson, diligent researchers, found many hidden details.

Many fellow reporters provided help, especially Daniel Altman, Christopher Drew, Geraldine Fabrikant, Jonathan Fuerbringer, Ken Gilpin, Jonathan D. Glater, Diana B. Henriques, David Leonhardt, Patrick McGeehan, Gretchen Morgenson, the great Floyd Norris, Joe Treaster, Mary Williams Walsh and Michael Weinstein, now at the Robin Hood Foundation.

No serious coverage of taxes is possible without reading the journal *Tax Notes,* published by Tax Analysts, a nonprofit enterprise whose beneficiaries include reporters. I am especially thankful to Chris Bergin, George Guttman, Amy Hamilton, Sheryl Stratton, Joseph Thorndike, their former colleague Ryan Donmoyer and, most of all, the acerbic tax critic Lee Sheppard. Don Barlett and Jim Steele of *Time* magazine, who pioneered serious coverage of the IRS when they were at *The Philadelphia Inquirer,* offered sage advice and continuing encouragement once I started my running investigation of our tax system.

Brian Foley, Robert Salwen, Pearl Meyer, Frederic W. Cook, Alan Johnson, Graef Crystal and others taught me many nuances of executive compensation. JJ MacNab, Jay D. Adkisson and Robert L. Sommers, who make a hobby out of tracking tax scams, kept me abreast of new developments while Paul Thomas, Mike Wellman and Daniel Evans, among others, defended my work as they jousted with tax protesters on the Internet. Many of the tax protesters were impressively cooperative, including Nick Jesson, Larken Rose, Irwin Schiff and Al Thompson. David Burnham, one of America's great reporters on matters of substance, and his Syracuse University colleague Susan Long showed me how to use their Web site, trac.syr.edu, to analyze IRS data.

While the political side of tax is rife with people who will say anything to advance ideology, some sources demonstrated their intellectual integrity at every turn. Among those whose principled conduct I especially admire are William A. Niskanen of the Cato Institute, David Keating of the Club for Growth and, earlier, the Tax Foundation, Bob McIntyre of Citizens for Tax Justice, former IRS commissioners Don Alexander and Sheldon Cohen, as well as tax lawyers Alan Halperin, Dan Halperin, Elliott H. Kajan, Henry Lowett, Robert E. McKenzie and Paul J. Sax.

My friends David Crook, founding editor of *The Wall Street Journal Sunday,* his wife, the witty writer Lauren Lipton, and the author Dennis McDougal, the toughest reporter to ever investigate Hollywood, provided wise counsel and support.

Danelle Morton, hilarious author and dear friend, showed the depth of her serious side in the brilliant proposal she crafted from my ideas. My longtime agent, Alice Fried Martell, again showed why she is everything a serious journalist could want in an agent. Adrian Zackheim, the founder of Portfolio, enthusiastically embraced my proposal, and Stephanie Land showed great skill at weeding out the extraneous and polishing my words. Thanks also to Megan Casey, editorial assistant, Bruce Sylvester, copy editor, and Betty Lukas.

As always my family was drawn into my work. My wife, Jennifer Leonard, the president and executive director of the Rochester Area Community Foundation, lovingly gave unvarnished criticism. Our daughter Molly Leonard, whose study of Latin and Greek has enriched her own talents as a writer, gave rigor to my early drafts and asked youthful questions that reminded me how esoteric even simple *tax-*

speak can be. Another daughter, Amy E. Boyle Johnston, also known as the photographer Bonk Johnston, did yeoman library research, while my son Marke Johnston created www.perfectlylegalthebook.com and even my youngest, Kate Leonard, helped keep my home office in shape.

Finally, there is no one in my 37 years of reporting whom I have come to admire more than Glenn Kramon, business editor of *The New York Times*. Glenn is a model editor, creating an environment where reporters are rewarded only for the quality of their work. He also manages to encourage collaboration among highly competitive journalists, an extraordinary achievement that serves readers well. Glenn's integrity, fearlessness and natural sense of fairness to subject and reader alike were essential to my pursuit of the real story of how the American tax system works.

Contents

Acknowledgments   vii

Prologue   1

Chapter 1   Taxes—They're Not for Everyone   5

Chapter 2   A Nickel an Hour More   20

Chapter 3   The Rich Get Fabulously Richer   30

Chapter 4   Big Payday   45

Chapter 5   Plane Perks   59

Chapter 6   When the Old Man Is Dead and Buried   71

Chapter 7   The Stealth Tax   92

Chapter 8   How Social Security Taxes Subsidize the Rich   117

Chapter 9   Preying on the Working Poor   129

Chapter 10   Handcuffing the Tax Police   145

Chapter 11   Mr. Rossotti's Customers   157

Chapter 12   For Want of a Keystroke   169

Chapter 13   Mr. Kellogg's Favorite Loophole   186

Chapter 14   Mass Market Tax Evasion   194

Chapter 15   Getting off the Hook   207

Chapter 16   Profiting off Taxes   217

Chapter 17   Profits Trump Patriotism   229

Chapter 18   Letters to Switzerland   251

Chapter 19   Gimme Shelter   262

Chapter 20   Only the Rich Deserve a
                Comfortable Retirement   274

Chapter 21   Is Reform Possible?   292

Conclusions   305

Notes   319

Index   329

Perfectly Legal

Prologue

When *The New York Times* hired me early in 1995, friends and fellow reporters around the world called to congratulate me. But as soon as I told them my assignment, the enthusiasm drained from their voices. A few offered condolences. My beat was to be taxes. The callers assumed that I would be covering taxes the way they always had been covered: tips on saving a few bucks, reports on the pronouncements of politicians, the occasional story of an indictment for tax evasion.

That was not what I had in mind.

I believe that taxes are at the core of our democracy. Americans pay heavy taxes, and most of us complain about them. Many live in fear of the IRS, a fear skillfully exploited by some politicians. What I wanted to do at *The New York Times* was to apply the techniques of investigative reporting to beat coverage, to launch a running investigation. So did Gene Roberts, who was then the managing editor. A skeptical John M. Geddes, who was then business editor, agreed to let me try, and his successor, Glenn Kramon, pushed me to deepen my inquiry.

If you have heard about companies using a Bermuda mailbox to escape American taxes or that the IRS audits the poor more than the rich or that Enron paid no taxes or that executives have amassed untaxed fortunes or that the retired chief executive of General Electric had a free corporate jet, then you have already had a taste of some of the more shocking stories I came across. As you can see, this is not just about facts, figures and statistics.

In covering taxes for *The New York Times* much of my work is translating the arcane language of tax into plain English. My sources for this book, from coast to coast, are tax lawyers, accountants, preparers and members of the tax protest movements. Some are deep in the IRS.

Much of what I learned surprised me, especially the degree to which the sound bytes of politicians in both parties bear as much connection to the reality of the tax system as my third grandson's belief in Santa. I was surprised to find how many working-class Americans blame the tax system for their loss of faith in democracy, and how many wealthy Americans believe they should be heavily taxed. I was especially surprised to find that some of the biggest tax breaks for the rich are not even in the tax code and that the IRS was completely unaware of many widely used tax fraud schemes. But what surprised me more than anything was the realization that our tax system now levies the poor, the middle class and even the upper middle class to subsidize the rich, as you will see in the pages ahead.

Our Constitution says we can have pretty much any kind of tax system we want. Today we have one designed for a national, industrial, wage-based economy, but we are moving into a global, services, asset-based world.

A good tax system flows from the economic order and greases the wheels of commerce. Taxes make it possible to do business through the enforcement of contracts, maintenance of the infrastructure, protection provided by the military and education of the populace, among other functions. In every place where there is no real tax system, such as Honduras or Afghanistan, there is no widespread wealth. All rich countries have high taxes because wealthy societies have high demands for public goods. As Supreme Court Justice Oliver Wendell Holmes said, "Taxes are what we pay for civilized society." Today, though, many want their civilization at a deep discount. Some want a free ride. There are politicians who spout law and order, but vote to handcuff the tax police.

Taxes have an impact far beyond the amounts each of us pay or fail to pay. What we tax, and how we tax it, shapes our society from how money is invested to how much people can save to what services government provides.

Perfectly Legal will expose how the majority of Americans are being duped into supplementing the incomes and extravagant lifestyles of the rich and powerful. In the nine years that I have researched this story, I have met hundreds of people whose very livelihoods have been threatened because of the blatantly unfair, even prejudiced, way that our current tax system is manipulated for profit by the wealthy and well positioned. These are their stories.

In a democracy we should not be surprised by these moves. But neither should we accept them. Democracy is about each of us pursuing our self-interest in the belief that our society can achieve a common goal. Yet those who wash their hands of politics, do not vote, do not make the effort to be informed and do not talk about public issues with our familes, friends and neighbors cede to others the shaping of society and the conditions of our lives. It is this apathy that has allowed certain individuals to contort, or even to remake, rules that work for their benefit at the expense of the average American taxpayer. We must fight these manipulations if we are to, as the preamble to our Constitution says, "establish justice, insure domestic tranquility, promote the general welfare and secure the blessing of liberty to ourselves and our posterity." It is my hope that the truths revealed in this book will serve as a wake-up call to everyone who believes as much as I do in the principles our country was founded on.

David Cay Johnston
Rochester, New York
July 2003

Taxes—They're Not for Everyone

1

Jonathan Blattmachr walked swiftly toward the Park Avenue curb, eager to find his driver so he could be whisked away from Manhattan to a waiting plane. A small man with the gait of a military officer and a reassuring voice, Blattmachr counsels tax avoidance to people who hold more wealth than anyone else in America. On this sunny morning in July 2002, a grateful client had put his personal jet at Blattmachr's disposal, making it possible for him to visit rich clients in eight cities over three days. Then Blattmachr would head to Alaska for some fishing with his brother Douglas, owner of the Alaska Trust Company, which, because of laws that Blattmachr wrote, offers the wealthy new ways to escape taxes today and forever, shifting the burden of supporting government onto everyone else.

Blattmachr is a partner at Milbank, Tweed, Hadley & McCloy, the New York City law firm that drafted the will of Jacqueline Kennedy Onassis, represents oil companies in Washington and Riyadh and has long had intimate ties to the Central Intelligence Agency. While many tax lawyers are expert at their craft, only one other practicing attorney, Carlyn S. McCaffrey of Weil, Gotshal and Manges in New York, is in Blattmachr's league as a prolific creator of perfectly legal ways for wealthy Americans to escape taxes on their fortunes.

Few Americans have heard of Blattmachr (pronounced BLOT-mach-ur). But among the 16,000 other lawyers in America who specialize in trusts and estates, which is to say in the passing of wealth from one generation to the next, he enjoys the status of some Hollywood stars—his first name alone prompts recognition.

The likes of Bill Gates, the Gettys and the Rockefellers seek Blattmachr's counsel on how to make taxes shrink—and sometimes even vanish. His roster of clients reads like the Forbes 400 list, supplemented by the names of people whose vast wealth is little known because they avoid controlling interests in companies whose shares trade on Wall Street.

Men (and a few women) of great wealth confide in Blattmachr. Because his specialty is maintaining wealth across time, he needs to know more than just the size and shape of his clients' fortunes. Happy families are easy to work with. But each unhappy family is unhappy in its own way, requiring custom tailoring of tax plans depending on whether a marriage is an enduring bond of love or a commercial relationship, on whether heirs can be trusted with fortunes or only allowed a stream of income to support their idleness. He knows of prodigal sons and promising granddaughters, of executives at family-owned businesses who will not learn for years that the brass ring is never going to be theirs. Sometimes men of great wealth whisper secrets they would never share with their wives, like how much a mistress costs or whether, if health fails, they trust their spouse with the power to pull the plug.

What makes Blattmachr invaluable to the super rich, however, is not so much his attentive ear or his sound counsel on familial relations. What the wealthy pay him for are the secret routes he has charted through the maze of the tax code. Over the years Blattmachr has found dozens of ways to navigate huge sums of money around government's many levies. He knows how to make a man who appears as a Midas before his bankers look like a pauper to the taxman.

While Blattmachr is the partner in charge of trusts and estates, his work is not limited to advice about what some opponents call "the death tax." Unlike the politicians who parrot slogans, Blattmachr knows what lies beneath the surface of the tax laws. Part of his genius is his understanding that the taxes on income, gifts and estates are not discrete levies. Rather, these taxes intersect and interact in subtle ways. Line up seemingly unrelated sections of these different tax laws in a certain way and vast sums can flow with only a widow's mite going to taxes. Find gaps between the levies and vast fortunes can be passed tax-free. His genius is in seeing the whole and the holes in the whole.

Once, Blattmachr devised a way that Bill Gates, the richest man in America, could reap $200 million in profits on Microsoft stock without paying the $56 million of capital gains taxes that federal law required at the time. The plan was so lucrative that Gates would not have to pay a single dollar in tax and would even be entitled to an income tax deduction of $6 million or so. And that was just the initial plan. The concept could be applied endlessly, allowing Gates to convert billions of dollars in Microsoft stock gains into cash over the years. So long as the Internal Revenue Service did not challenge the deals, then Gates could realize unlimited capital gains without the pain of taxes.

The trick was in manipulating charitable trusts, a common enough device used by generous people who own an asset, such as stock or a building that has appreciated in value. Instead of selling the asset and investing the after-tax proceeds, an individual or a married couple can donate the asset to a charitable trust that they control. The trust sells the asset tax-free and invests the proceeds, giving the donating individual or couple a lifetime income, typically 6 percent per year. When the donors die, what remains in the trust, typically half its value, goes to charity.

Blattmachr's plan was to take back not 6 percent annually for life, but 80 percent per year for two years. Gates could have pocketed at least $192 million without paying any tax. Then the trust would fold and a charity would get the remaining sum, less than $8 million. Under the plan Gates could have converted into cash more than 96 percent of gains on the Microsoft shares he donated, not the 72 percent he was entitled to after federal capital gains taxes. The charity would get less than four cents on each donated dollar. The government would collect nothing.

The scheme even created a tax deduction that was enough to reduce Gates's income taxes by about $2 million.

Whether Gates took advantage of such a plan is not known for sure because the law makes individual income tax records confidential. What is known is that when Blattmachr made this route available to others, it sold like a treasure map where X marks the tax-free spot. Billions of dollars of assets poured into these short-term charitable trusts and their super-rich owners took many millions of dollars of income tax deductions that further cut into the flow of revenue to the government.

The technique was so outlandish that when some other tax lawyers got their hands on the map in March 1994, they sent it to the Department of the Treasury in a plain brown envelope. That July, Treasury blocked the route to newcomers and said that it would pursue those who used the device. However, the Internal Revenue Service never announced whether it collected any of the taxes. One hint that the IRS may not have acted against those who used the technique can be found in the records of United States Tax Court, which is where taxpayers challenge the IRS. There are no Tax Court cases in which taxpayers fought for a court blessing on the device, known in taxspeak as an "accelerated charitable remainder trust."

The Treasury rules shutting down this route to tax-free investment profits were not the end of stretching charitable trusts in ways never anticipated by Congress. So facile is Blattmachr's mind that from those 1994 rules he divined a new route to tax-free gains. He started selling a new treasure map and billions of dollars more in capital gains passed untaxed into the bank accounts of his clients before the government blocked that second path, known in taxspeak as "son of accelerated charitable remainder trust."

That few Americans know of the routes that Blattmachr has charted through the tax code is not surprising. Blattmachr rarely talks to journalists, and his clients sign confidentiality agreements.

Blattmachr charges hefty fees, but he has also walked away from opportunities to make many more millions of dollars. He is wealthy by any standard, but compared to his clients his personal fortune is so small as to be lost in their rounding. Of course, money is not the only way in which people get paid. For Blattmachr the knowledge that it is his smarts that direct how many of the richest people in history arrange their fortunes is an enormous psychic paycheck. It is also an important insight into how Blattmachr came to his occupation, a story rich with significance for taxpayers because it goes to the heart of our tax system's flaws and their threat to our democracy.

Jonathan Blattmachr grew up on Long Island after World War II, exploring its woods and streams. He was good with numbers and his father, a lawyer, encouraged his dreams of becoming a mathematics professor. In 1963, Blattmachr enrolled at Bucknell University in Pennsylvania, studying math and economics and distinguishing himself in the Reserve Officer Training Corps just as ROTC was becoming a four-letter word on many campuses.

At Columbia University Law School, Blattmachr distinguished himself again with his easy grasp of complicated theoretical concepts. At a time when Communism posed a very real threat to liberty, Blattmachr set out to make a name for himself by showing Americans that in Moscow some comrades were more equal than others because Soviet law was unprincipled, written only to advance the interests of the ruling elite. To discredit the Soviets, Blattmachr immersed himself in Russian law books, only to conclude that "on paper Soviet law was very well drafted, grounded in sound principles." It was, he came to realize, the administration of Soviet law that was so often monstrous, not the statutes themselves.

Next Blattmachr turned his well-ordered mind to examining the laws of European countries he considered socialist, but searched in vain for law weak on principles. Finally, he came upon Title 26 of the United States Codes, commonly known as our Internal Revenue Code.

"The U.S. tax code is the most political law in the world," Blattmachr said on a summer morning in his second office, a sunny Park Avenue aerie from which one can look down on the great wealth machine that is Manhattan. His soft, soothing voice filled with the energy he must have felt more than three decades earlier when he finally found the holy grail he had sought: law based on politics, not principles. As Blattmachr told of his journey, it seemed as if he were still living in that moment when he realized that he would never teach mathematics, but only apply its principles every day to the politically motivated law he found in our tax code.

The story of how the American tax system really works, of who benefits and who pays, extends far beyond Blattmachr and his cadre of super-rich clients. Understanding what Blattmachr does, whom he does it for and how the government reacts, however, are keys to unlocking the secret of how the tax system in America is being rigged to benefit the super rich. And understanding that, in turn, can help explain the ways in which Democrats and Republicans alike have turned the tax system into a vehicle not just to finance government but to finance social change. For the past three decades, it is a system that has been weighing down the already deep pockets of the super rich while just weighing down everyone else.

When governments set tax rates, they are making decisions about who will prosper and by how much. A government that takes 90 cents out of each dollar above a threshold, as the United States did in the Eisenhower years, is deciding to limit the wealth that people can accumulate from their earnings. Likewise, a government that taxes the poor on their first dollar of wages, as the United States does with the Social Security and Medicare taxes, is deciding to limit or eliminate the ability of those at the bottom of the income ladder to save money and improve their lot in life.

The rules that governments set for their tax systems, and the degree to which they enforce them, also affect who prospers. Congress lets business owners, investors and landlords play by one set of rules, which are filled with opportunities to hide income, fabricate deductions and reduce taxes. Congress requires wage earners to operate under another, much harsher set of rules in which every dollar of income from a job, a savings account or a stock dividend is reported to the government, and taxes are withheld from each paycheck to make sure wage earners pay in full.

Our federal tax laws are often voted on without any public hearing, without any disclosure of who introduced this or that provision. Members of Congress routinely vote on tax bills they have never read, much less understood even on a superficial level.

Sanford J. Schlesinger, a prominent estate tax lawyer in New York whose clients included the trusts of tobacco heiress Doris Duke, says that "there hasn't been a member of Congress with a comprehensive understanding of the tax laws since Wilbur Mills, and I'm not a fan of Wilbur Mills." Mills left Congress in 1977 after a drunken romp in the Tidal Basin in Washington with a stripper known as the Argentine Firecracker. The result of having the ill-informed writing tax laws, Schlesinger believes, is that "we have a patchwork of taxes and when you put it all together we have what is pretty much a flat tax."

• • •

While he is a hero to his clients, other Americans may see Blattmachr's work differently. Each time his clients escape paying tax, everyone else in America has to bear the burden of those untaxed dollars. Sometimes the price is paid in higher taxes. More often it is paid by fewer government services or by more borrowing to maintain government services. But the bill is always paid. As all economists are taught, there is no free lunch. Blattmachr's clients just leave part of their bill on your table.

Blattmachr's navigation charts do more than just lighten the burden of taxes for his clients. Often his strategies allow money to pass from one person to another without showing up in the official statistics on wealth and income. Were these transactions counted in the official government reports, then the share of taxes paid by the rich would be smaller than the official statistics now show.

Add to this the reductions in tax rates on the rich that started in 1981 and a picture begins to emerge of why wealth in America today is more highly concentrated than at any time since 1929. In recent years the richest 1 percent of Americans, the top 1.3 million or so households, have owned almost half of the stocks, bonds, cash and other financial assets in the country. The richest 15 percent control nearly *all* of the financial assets.

This does not mean that the rich pay little or no tax. As a group the richest Americans pay significant taxes. The richest 1 percent, those with adjusted gross incomes of more than $313,000 in 2000, earned almost 21 percent of all reported income and paid more than 37 percent of individual federal income taxes.

However, when all federal taxes are considered—from those on gasoline and beer to Social Security taxes as well as income and estate taxes—the top 1 percent's share drops to about a fourth of the total tax bill. That is not much more than their share of reported income.

If you tally up the economic benefits to the top 1 percent that do not show up in income statistics—for reasons of written law and because of tax tricks fashioned by lawyers like Blattmachr—then the richest 1 percent are taxed more lightly than the middle class. The same data show that the poor are taxed almost as heavily as the rich are—and even more heavily than the super rich.

In the years ahead the super rich will pay less, shifting the burden onto those with less means. Using techniques developed by Blattmachr and many others, the richest Americans and most large corporations are arranging their affairs in ways that Congress seems to only dimly understand.

Corporations, for example, lowered the portion of their profits that go to federal income taxes from 26 cents of each dollar in 1993 to 22 cents in 1998, even though the official corporate income tax rate remained unchanged at 35 percent. For almost three decades corporate profits have been growing one third faster than corporate income taxes.

In the years ahead the people and businesses that benefit most from operating in the United States will pay a dwindling share of their income to sustain government, even if tax rates remain the same as they are today. That means they will be able to accumulate even more wealth—and the political power that goes along with that wealth.

A few companies, like Ingersoll-Rand, have made Bermuda their tax home, while keeping the real company headquarters in America. Renouncing America for tax purposes allows these corporations to earn tax-free profits in the United States, an issue that has divided Congress and highlighted much of the mendacity on taxes inside the Capitol dome.

Much more common are other techniques that slash corporate tax bills for companies that keep their official, and tax, headquarters in the United States. Corporations are busy moving intellectual property such as patents, trademarks and the title to the company logo to entities organized in tax havens like Bermuda. These corporations then pay royalties to use their own intellectual property, allowing them to convert taxable profits in the United States into tax-deductible payments sent to Bermuda and other havens that impose little or no tax. You pay for this through higher taxes, reduced services or your rising share of our growing national debt. You also pay for it through incentives in the tax system for companies to build new factories overseas and to reduce employment in America.

These trends to lower taxes on wealthy people and on corporations are aided by new rules allowing capital and goods to flow freely around the world, while immigration and employment laws limit any mass movements of workers and ever-tougher rules against union organizing give capital an advantage over labor in setting wages.

These trends are also encouraged by many little-noticed changes in the laws, including that Alaskan law drafted by Blattmachr which breaks with four centuries of tradition and allows trusts to exist in perpetuity. The old rule limited trusts to the life of the youngest living beneficiary plus 21 years. Right now is when some of the trusts created after the Robber Baron era a century ago are facing termination in the foreseeable future. Legislative relief in the form of new rules to maintain these trusts is being sought along with special tax breaks and elimination of the estate tax.

At the same time, state legislatures starting in 1991 have passed laws that, however unintentionally, took away the most powerful incentive for self-policing by the corporate professions of law and accounting. These laws, allowing "limited-liability" partnerships and corporations, help explain the wave of corporate cheating that swept the country in the past decade and brought good times to a crashing end in 2000. Congress also has passed a series of little-noticed laws that shift risks off corporations and the super rich and onto most Americans. Among these are laws governing retirement accounts that both encourage misconduct by corporations and their top executives and put workers at risk of losing their retirement savings.

That some of these issues, other than the scandals in Corporate America, have been little reported in the news is not surprising. Most news is a report of the official version of events, including what politicians said the day before. Few politicians, however, mention how the tax system is being rigged to benefit the super rich at the expense of everyone else. Many journalists rely for expert quotes on a dozen well-financed nonprofits that exist in Washington to promote policies that primarily benefit their rich donors. Their aim is to convince us that these policies are actually in everyone's best interest. The rise of marketing posing as policy is one of the great and subtle advances in the never-ending effort to manipulate the news media.

Most Americans depend on wages for their income, wages that are tracked closely by the government and leave little opportunity to escape taxes. The super rich are different. They largely control what the government knows about their incomes. And their friends in Congress have slashed budgets for inspecting the tax returns of the rich and super rich. Many of the rich own businesses, creating opportunities to charge a portion of their lifestyles to the company and, if it is privately held, to organize companies so that profits for tax purposes are held close to zero. By holding taxable profits down, owners can build up wealth within their business, wealth that will be taxed only when they die, assuming there is an estate tax.

A host of law and accounting firms are busy marketing devices to make taxes that are still on the books shrink or vanish. Most of the super rich invest in complicated, often multilayered partnerships, which are rarely audited by the IRS. Ernst & Young, BDO Seidman and the other major accounting firms that sell these partnership deals insist they are perfectly legal. But the use of layered partnerships raises questions about escaping taxes by merely hiding questionable deals from the IRS. It also recalls a line sometimes used by judges about efforts to hide misconduct: truth needs no disguise.

Under our tax system the IRS can easily nab a wage earner whose tax return shows only 95 percent of his wages. But an investor who overstates what he paid for stock he sold at a profit is unlikely to be caught even if he pays only half the taxes due. If the overstatement is by a decimal point or results from forgetting a stock split, the risk of paying anything more than interest on the additional tax is next to nil. That is to say, when it comes to taxes, it often pays to cheat so long as your income is not from wages.

Politicians seldom look into these things. Blattmachr, for example, has never been hauled before a Congressional committee and grilled about his tax avoidance schemes. Instead, Congress has developed a studied hostility to enforcement of the tax laws. The tax police—and that is what the IRS is—are treated with disrespect by Congress for reasons that will become clear.

When Congress did look into the tax system, it didn't go after the tax cheats. It went after the IRS. At the dramatic Senate Finance Committee hearings in 1997 and 1998, IRS workers testified behind curtains like Mafia dons to conceal their identity. The senators denounced several armed raids on the homes and offices of suspected tax cheats. Senator Frank Murkowski of Alaska denounced "Gestapo-like tactics" and said, "You don't need to send in armed personnel in flak jackets." No one at the hearings mentioned the fact that in the previous several years IRS agents had been shot at, beaten, and threatened with death and that bombs exploded outside two IRS offices. No IRS agents were killed, but in Arizona a sheriff's deputy, whom a tax protester evidently mistook for a tax agent, was shot and nearly died. Also unmentioned at the hearings, which generated loose talk of jackbooted thugs from the IRS, was the fact that despite having an arsenal of weapons, no IRS agent has ever fired a single shot at anyone.

How the system really works is not at all like the descriptions that politicians from both parties offer, their sound bytes filling news reports that accurately recount what the politicians said even as the deeper truths are missed. Lawmakers tailor their remarks to how the average person understands the tax system: what you make is reported to the government and so is the biggest deduction, for home mortgage interest.

The politicians talk about how taxes affect employment rates and fairness to families with children. They talk about how the top 1 percent earns 20.8 percent of the income and pays 37.4 percent of the income taxes and suggest this burden is excessive. Seldom mentioned is that for many at the top the primary object is to take income in forms that, like the device that Jonathan Blattmachr invented for people like Bill Gates, do not have to be reported on income tax returns. Just as there is an underground economy of gardeners and handymen and petty merchants who get paid in cash and pay little or no tax, there is also an underground economy among the super rich that lets them understate their true income and overstate their tax deductions.

The American tax system is, as Blattmachr discovered, malleable. For those who wield the most influence on who gets elected, a narrow and rich group we shall call the political donor class, the system is being remade to serve their interests while disguising the changes as benefits for every American.

The major change taking place is a shifting of burdens off the super rich and onto everyone below them. It is a shift that began with the Democrats in 1983 and that has been increased dramatically since the Republicans won control of the House in 1995. The evidence of this shift in burdens is already showing up in the official government statistics.

To cite one telling example, the Internal Revenue Service in 2003 released its first public analysis of tax returns filed by the 400 highest income Americans each year from 1992 to 2000, the years of both the Clinton administration and the stock market bubble. The minimum to make the top 400 more than tripled from $24.4 million to $86.6 million. About 2,200 different names appeared on the 3,600 tax returns that were analyzed. Only 21 taxpayers made the list each year and only a few times was an income of a billion dollars reported.

In the year 2000 the top 400 taxpayers received 1.1 percent of all the income in America, more than double their 0.5 percent share in 1992.

On average their income was nearly $174 million, nearly quadruple the $46.8 million average in 1992. They paid an average of $38.6 million each in federal income taxes in 2000. That is a lot of money. However, the share of their income going to federal income taxes was another matter. It fell. Federal income taxes consumed just 22.2 cents on each dollar of their income in 2000, down from 26.4 percent eight years earlier and a peak of 29.9 percent in 1995.

The 400's tax burden was not much more in 2000 than the overall federal income tax burden of 15.3 cents on each dollar of income. And the overall effective tax rate had increased from 13 cents on the dollar in 1992.

So during years when the federal income tax burden on Americans overall rose by 18 percent, it fell by 16 percent for the top 400, whose incomes soared. The share of income going to taxes for the top 400 in 2000 was about the same as that paid by a single person making $123,000 or a married couple with two children earning $226,000— and it was smaller than that paid by many in the upper middle class.

The top 400 saw their tax burden fall beginning in 1997. That year Congress passed what its sponsors promoted as a tax cut for the middle class and especially for families with children. Buried in that law were many tax breaks for the rich, some subtle and some huge, notably a sharp reduction in the tax rate on long-term capital gains, the source of two thirds of the incomes of the top 400.

Another law that year also contained a feature that favored tax cheats who might well have incomes large enough to qualify for the top 400, but were not on the list because they reported far less on their tax returns. For years the IRS found big tax evaders by looking into people whose reported income did not seem sufficient to support their lifestyle, the technique used to convict Al Capone. If a taxpayer's address was a mansion and she owned a private jet, but her tax return showed a middle-class income, the IRS might investigate. But the 1997 law stopped such inquiries. Congress said that lifestyle was no longer grounds for an audit. Lee Sheppard, a tax lawyer who critiques tax law for the magazine *Tax Notes,* said the law "should be called the mobsters and drug dealers tax relief act of 1997."

But even the 1997 tax cuts for the rich were not enough for them or their friends in Congress. Under the first round of tax cuts sponsored by President Bush in 2001, the share of their income going to taxes would slip further, to about 21 percent of their incomes. Had the third round of Bush tax cuts in 2003 been in effect in the year 2000, the 400 richest Americans would have saved an average of $8.3 million each. They would have paid 17.5 cents on the dollar of income in 2000, not much more than the average paid by all Americans. Six years of tax cut bills, all promoted as promoting the interests of the middle class, were in fact primarily a boon to the super rich.

It hasn't always been this way. After the Sixteenth Amendment was adopted in 1913, the federal government in short order enacted a regime to tax incomes, gifts and estates. These taxes came with the explicit promise that the basic means of sustaining life would not be taxed. The original tax regime applied only to the economic elite, to what were then called "surplus" incomes. Back then income from capital was taxed more heavily than income from wages in the belief that it was morally offensive to take more from money earned by the sweat of one's brow than from money obtained by clipping coupons.

To pay for World War I, in which young men were conscripted, it was said that the "conscription of wealth" was also necessary and fair. One of the leading economists of the day, Edwin R. A. Seligman, a proponent of taxes based on ability to pay, said that "patriotism can often be translated into dollars and cents—in fact, the material side of patriotism is often quite as important as the spiritual side." The estate tax and the gift tax, which apply to wealth, were expanded and the income tax came to apply to a larger, but still minute, percentage of Americans.

Just a third of a century after the war to end all wars, the costs of a second global conflict ended the promise that only surplus incomes would be taxed. While only a minority of people was taxed during World War II, the politicians got a taste of the huge revenues they could control by expanding the tax base. After the war, primarily at the behest of Democrats, but with support from many Republicans, the income tax was steadily expanded until it applied to most Americans and to most of what they earned. Much of this money was poured into the military and the Korean conflict, but funds were also used to expand education, build highways and finance technological breakthroughs that improved lives. Throughout the fifties and sixties, Congress also let inflation erode the value of exemptions for taxpayers and their children, causing them to pay a growing share of their incomes in taxes.

By the late seventies, this system was becoming untenable as sales of tax shelters flourished. Once the province of the rich, tax shelters were being mass marketed to doctors, dentists and even cops and working journalists. Many of these shelters did nothing to grow the economy, but were instead a drag on it, and not a few were pure scams. Inflation, combined with an end to real growth in wages beginning in 1973, created a phenomenon known as "bracket creep" that moved people into higher tax brackets even if their real incomes were unchanged. Government through this era kept growing, especially military spending to prosecute the war in Vietnam and state and local spending to pay for schools, professionalize police departments and provide welfare for those unable or unwilling to compete in the job market.

Now, less than a century after its adoption, the tax system is being turned on its head. Since at least 1983 it has been the explicit, but unstated, policy in Washington to let the richest Americans pay a smaller portion of their incomes in taxes and to defer more of their taxes, which amounts to a stealth tax cut, while collecting more in taxes from those in the middle class.

The Democrats embraced this in 1983, when they controlled Congress. They voted to raise Social Security taxes, changing it from a pay-as-you-go system to one in which people were required to pay 50 percent more than the retirement and disability program's immediate costs, to build a trust fund to pay benefits more than three decades into the future. Those taxes were not, however, locked away but instead were spent to help finance tax cuts for the super rich that began in 1981.

Under the Republicans, beginning in 1997, this policy of taxing the poor and the middle class to finance tax cuts for the super rich was expanded through changes in the income tax system. The changes were subtle and hardly reported in the news media, but they were also substantial. Under the first round of Bush tax cuts enacted in 2001 the middle class and the upper middle class will subsidize huge tax cuts for the top 1 percent and, especially the top one tenth of 1 percent, the 130,000 richest taxpayers.

For a nation that has debated for years whether the tax rate cuts begun by President Reagan in 1981 are "trickle-down economics," it may be startling to read that the reality of these changes has been just the reverse. The tax system is causing the benefits of American society to flow up and pool at the top. As we shall see in the chapters ahead, the official government statistics show just that. And the critics who have decried the growing concentration of wealth and power at the top have been wrong—because they have seriously understated the transformation now taking place.

The tax system is becoming a tool to turn the American dream of prosperity and reward for hard work into an impossible goal for tens of millions of Americans and into a nightmare for many others. Our tax system is being used to create a nation with fewer stable jobs and less secure retirement income. The tax system is being used by the rich, through their allies in Congress, to shift risks off themselves and onto everyone else. And perhaps worst of all, our tax system now forces most Americans to subsidize the lifestyles of the very rich, who enjoy the benefits of our democracy without paying their fair share of its price.

A Nickel an Hour More

2

In the 1960s, America was becoming so rich that economists, sociologists and the crystal-ball gazers called futurists warned of a looming crisis. Just about now, they predicted, Americans would have become so fabulously wealthy that they would never have to work hard again. With productivity rising, science making ever more useful discoveries and technology driving down the costs of manufacturing, the worry was that by the dawn of the new millennium, Americans would be making too much money for their own good.

The experts envisaged 28-hour workweeks plus vacations six weeks long. Moralists fretted about the prospect of too many rich and idle hands finding occupation in the "devil's workshops." Corporate advisers mused about how to motivate these new workers. Would too much leisure time undermine Americans' self-image as the industrious and enterprising people whose forefathers had brought the world freedom and, with it, prosperity? What would Americans do with both money and free time in abundance?

As the experts predicted, the economy grew. From 1970 to 2001, the American economy more than doubled in size even after adjusting for inflation. The total value of all the goods and services that Americans produced, from automobile tires to Hollywood movies to the hours that lawyers billed their clients, also outpaced the population. The number of Americans increased over those three decades by less than 40 percent, growing from 203 million to 283 million. As a result, productivity per person shot up. For each dollar per individual the American economy generated in 1970, it produced about $1.40 in 2001.

This economic growth financed many high-visibility symbols of greater national wealth. For example, in 2002, Mercedes-Benz sold more than 213,000 vehicles in America, seven times its 1970 sales, when the luxury car market did not yet include competitors such as Lexus, Infiniti and Acura.

Americans also built bigger houses. At 2,200 square feet, the average new home in 2000 was 50 percent larger than the average 1970 house. Many of these new homes had amenities like whirlpool baths in the master bedroom suite, three-car or larger garages and central air conditioning that made the hot states of the South and West hospitable to millions of newcomers. The extra floor space and luxuries were encouraged by tax breaks that Congress had created decades earlier. These subsidies, in the form of the mortgage interest deduction, were supposed to help people buy a roof over their heads. By 2000, they had become the middle class's most cherished tax break. But because home buyers could afford to purchase bigger houses with these subsidies, over the years housing prices had artificially risen, discouraging first-time home buyers.

Therefore, paradoxically, the strategy to broaden home ownership had instead morphed into a vast subsidy for the best-off Americans. The design of the mortgage interest deduction meant that the more a house cost, the bigger the tax subsidy. And the more owners earned, and thus the higher their tax rates, the bigger the subsidies. Combining these two factors created a huge benefit for highly affluent Americans but only a minuscule one for those most in need of help to buy their own homes.

In 2000, for each dollar of tax saved by home owners earning $30,000 to $40,000, the mortgage interest deduction lopped $50 on average off the tax bills of those making $200,000 or more. At the extreme, those making more than $200,000 saved $29,000 in federal income taxes for each dollar of tax savings going to the poorest Americans, those making less than $10,000. This subsidy was so valuable to the affluent that the National Association of Realtors estimated that eliminating the ability to deduct home mortgage interest on individual income tax returns would cause housing prices to fall by about a third, with the biggest declines among the more expensive houses.

In economic terms, the mortgage interest deduction created an upside-down subsidy. Instead of those with abundance being forced to help out the poor, the tax subsidy for housing was redistributing income up, making the poor and the middle class help those who were much better heeled.

Overhead another symbol of greater national wealth could be seen—and heard. By 2003, the skies were filled with more than 9,000 privately owned jets. The boom was again due to favorable tax breaks, including rules that allowed chief executives and business owners to use company planes as personal taxis for as little as half a cent per dollar of the actual cost. (This issue will be explored in a later chapter.)

During the past three decades the price of many consumer goods fell, although at the cost of many manufacturing jobs in America. Prod-

The Upside Down Home Owner Subsidy

People who make the most get
the biggest subsidy because
they borrow more and are in
higher tax brackets

Income Categories	Percent Who Claim Deduction	Average Deduction	Average Tax Savings at Marginal Tax Rate
$10,000 to $25,000	11%	$ 432	$ 65
$25,000 to $50,000	33%	$ 1,704	$ 256
$50,000 to $75,000	63%	$ 4,028	$ 1,128
$75,000 to $100,000	81%	$ 5,991	$ 1,677
$100,000 to $200,000	90%	$ 8,430	$ 2,613
$200,000 to $500,000	93%	$ 12,845	$ 4,624
$500,000 to $1 million	91%	$ 16,863	$ 6,678
$1 million to $5 million	68%	$ 21,928	$ 8,684
$5 million and above	62%	$ 25,528	$ 10,109
Average Deduction	27%	$ 2,319	$ N/A

Source: IRS Statistics of Income for year 2000

uct quality often improved, too, enabling families to buy more with less, especially electronic devices built overseas. By 2002, when color television sets were no longer built in America, brands with American names like Zenith and RCA sold for a small fraction of their 1970 price. The price tags on the televisions looked the same in both years, but the real price of the 2002 set was 78 percent lower. Back in 1970, only one in four households with a television owned a color set. Today, nearly all households have two or more color televisions, with better pictures and bigger screens.

The cost of food and clothing fell by so much that in 2001 they took up just 18 cents on each dollar of the average family's income, down from 26 cents in 1972. The removal of trade barriers brought down the price of clothes, creating new jobs in China, Honduras and other countries desperate for work, even at sweatshop wages. The government stimulated lower food prices through tax breaks and subsidies, especially to sugar, corn and cattle operations. These policies encouraged overproduction that filled the supermarkets, fast-food joints and school cafeterias with so much cheap sugar, grease and starch that Americans spent a shrinking portion of their incomes on food, but obesity and diseases associated with them became common.

During these decades the numbers on paychecks grew, too. Incomes tend to increase with age because experience makes most workers more valuable to their employers, and the American population was aging. Pay also rose for those who won promotions or who moved from lightly financed small employers on the fringe of the economy to well-capitalized major companies that paid higher wages to attract the most productive workers. For those with a college degree, wages rose in real terms 16 percent between 1973 and 2001; for those with a postgraduate education, they rose by almost a fifth, the equivalent of getting six days of 1973 pay for working five days in 2001.

This was also an era of rising debt. For every dollar of debt Americans owed on credit cards in 1975, they owed $53 ($16.50 when adjusted for inflation) in 2000. Much of the 2000 debt was at interest rates that would have been criminal violations of the law in 1975, before a federal court effectively voided the nation's usury laws in a decision that also urged Congress to protect consumers. Congress ignored the advice. One result was a huge rise in bankruptcies. Between 1980 and

2002 more than 18 million couples and individuals filed for bank-ruptcy. That means one in every eight households went bankrupt at least once during those years. Each year since 1996 more than a mil-lion households a year have sought refuge from creditors in bankruptcy court, including 1.5 million consumers in 2002, more than five times as many as in 1980.

The social seers of the 1960s got it partly right when they envi-sioned American riches at the dawn of the twenty-first century. The economy created vast new wealth, and age and experience made many individuals better off, especially those with college degrees and post-graduate study. What the futurists missed was that these riches would be highly concentrated: that those with the least education and skills would actually be worse off and the middle class would be squeezed on every front—stagnant wages, rising taxes and increased economic risks. And they failed to predict the way that tax policies would bring about this massive, undeclared transfer of the fruits of opportunity to a relative handful of its citizens.

Indeed, most Americans did not get ahead during the last three decades of the twentieth century. Four out of five Americans had more only because they worked more hours. So many women who had stayed at home joined the workforce, most of them full time, that today the average family does 20 more weeks of paid labor than it did in 1975. It is this added labor, more than anything else, that explains why Amer-icans can afford more now than three decades ago. The two-income family comes at a price paid by children who get 800 fewer hours of parenting each year, not counting all the time diverted to commuting, clothes shopping and other activities necessary to support one's job.

Furthermore, in contrast to some who did better with the growing economy, others fared far worse, their pay growing more slowly than inflation. The poorly educated, especially men who had dropped out of high school, had the biggest declines in earnings. Their wages, ad-justed for inflation, fell by more than $2 an hour from 1973 to 2001, the equivalent of working five days in 2001 for four days of 1973 pay. Wages fell slightly for high school graduates and were flat for those with some college but not a four-year degree.

The young were hit hard, too. Someone who was under 25 years old at the end of the century made about $2 less per day, on average, than someone of the same age in 1973. And the economic indicators pointed to a future in which today's twentysomethings would make less when they reached their fifties than those who are in their fifties today.

The growing numbers on paychecks created an illusion for many people. Years of inflation not only erode the value of money; they also make it difficult for most Americans to calculate whether their higher gross pay is really more than they used to earn. And inflation's effect varies from year to year, making it harder still to compare one year to the next. But the impact over time is substantial. A dollar earned in 2002 was worth not quite as much as a quarter in 1973. Or, looked at the other way, for every dollar earned in 1973 it took $4.04 in 2002 just to keep even with inflation. The average American salary did little more than that.

In fact, in real dollars, the average American salary rose so minimally from 1970 to 1999 that it would be easy to miss the increase. First, nearly all of the increase came in the beginning of that period, from 1970 to 1972. Adding up all the wages and salaries paid and dividing by the number of jobs, and adjusting for inflation to 2003 dollars, showed that the average American salary increased from $36,573 in 1970 to $38,529 in 1972, a real gain of more than 5 percent in just two years. The year 1972 is significant because it marked the end of the economic glow that warmed the American economy after World War II, which had left industrial Europe and East Asia in ruins. America had built new factories to fight the war and that gave it global dominance in manufacturing for the next 28 years, when Americans gained across the board as the standard of living doubled. The American economy also expanded because of massive public investments that greased the wheels of commerce. The GI Bill increased our store of educated minds. The interstate highway system, built to ensure mobility for a future war, allowed goods to be trucked quickly and reliably over great distances. And the development of the 30-year mortgage, combined initially with veterans' benefits, allowed people to buy a home with little or no money down.

Then, from 1973 to 1997, average incomes for the bottom 99 percent of Americans declined or were flat. But in 1998 wages jumped and by 2000 average income for 99 percent of Americans had grown only 8.3 percent—after three decades. Had pay risen steadily over those years, the average raise for 99 percent of Americans would have been just $90 per year. That is the sum total in wage increases across three decades of growing American prosperity: a real pay raise, before taxes, for 30 years averaging less than a nickel an hour each year. The raise, though, came in two clusters: 1970 to 1973 and then, following a long trough of flat or falling real income, from 1998 through 2000. Since then wages have been close to flat, preliminary government reports show, in part because many employers sought wage concessions from those who kept their jobs.

Three factors contributed to the surge in wages that began in 1998. (Some other government data show that wages started rising in the mid-1990s.) The first factor was the brief end to federal budget deficits, which have been continuous from 1969 except for the years 1998 through 2001. When the government spends more than taxes bring in, it runs a deficit, which must be closed by borrowing money in the bond markets. That borrowing soaks up money that otherwise could have been invested by individuals and businesses to make the economy grow. The second factor was a surge in productivity, as companies finally figured out how to make efficient and effective use of computers for everything from designing automobile engines to calculating down to the dollar the performance of each Taco Bell. Third was the Internet bubble, in which hundreds of billions of dollars chased after a supposed New Economy in cyberspace where costs would fall and profits soar.

Many people, including young people with college degrees, made big incomes in the late 1990s because of the dot.coms. People spent freely on personal trainers, foaming cups of designer coffee and other luxuries, creating jobs servicing their desires. Those who socked some of their bread away in 401(k) plans saw the values rise like dough with too much yeast. It was a time when airlines jacked fares up and still flew with record numbers of their seats occupied. Millions of people, who in the long trough of flat or falling wages had either quit looking for work or had been forced to settle for part-time jobs, suddenly found employers begging them to work and at better wages than they had previously received. And as the reserves of underemployed labor were drawn down, companies started paying bounties to employees who could find more workers.

Then the bubble burst. Within a matter of months more dot.coms

Average Wages Have Been Flat for 3 Decades

In 2003 dollars

1970	$ 36,573
1971	$ 37,325
1972	$ 38,529
1973	$ 38,475
1974	$ 37,226
1975	$ 36,844
1976	$ 37,297
1977	$ 37,395
1978	$ 37,292
1979	$ 36,329
1980	$ 35,145
1981	$ 34,794
1982	$ 35,117
1983	$ 35,737
1984	$ 35,901
1985	$ 36,282
1986	$ 37,054
1987	$ 37,322
1988	$ 37,635
1989	$ 37,029
1990	$ 36,857
1991	$ 36,809
1992	$ 37,475
1993	$ 37,353
1994	$ 37,299
1995	$ 37,315
1996	$ 37,449
1997	$ 38,194
1998	$ 39,499
1999	$ 40,330

Source: Piketty & Saez

folded than this chapter has periods, some revealed as "dot.cons," which had been promoted with the help of highly paid liars on Wall Street. The effects of this collapse did not trickle down; they cascaded through the economy. At Enron, Global Crossing and other companies where workers had their life savings invested in their employer's stock, the 401(k) plans turned to dust. These were not new problems, but ones that Congress had been warned about and had ignored, as it continues to do today because our lawmakers, like most Americans, do not fully grasp the economics of 401(k) plans, which will be explained in later chapters. With trillions of dollars lost in the sinking stock market, new investments withering along with profits and fears of terrorist attacks strangling travel and tourism, the nation quickly switched from full employment to the highest jobless rate in eight years.

By the end of 2002, a disturbing trend, one that had begun back in the 1970s, had moved to a higher rung on the income ladder. Blue-collar workers had lost jobs in the 1970s and 1980s, when *Rust Belt* became a household term as American factories closed and new ones were built overseas. In the 1990 recession, the erosion of jobs moved up to middle managers, especially older ones. The 2000 recession hit hard at very well-paid workers, including airline pilots, computer programmers and marketing vice presidents. By the end of 2002, half the people who had run through their six months of unemployment benefits were managers, technical workers and professionals, the highest proportion of the jobless ever for these occupations.

So far we have discussed the state of the American economy mostly in terms of averages, which (like any other single measure) can be misleading. When Bill Gates walks into a café where a dozen people are already eating, the average wealth in the room rises to billions of dollars, hardly a reasonable picture of the situation.

There are many ways to measure the economy and people's incomes. Various agencies such as the Bureau of Labor Statistics, the Federal Reserve, the Internal Revenue Service and the Department of Commerce provide official measures of wages per hour, with and without fringe benefits, of salaries alone and of salaries plus government benefits like Social Security and welfare. There are measures that combine salaries with income from investments: dividends, interest, rents and capital gains. Incomes are also measured both before taxes and after, a crucial difference to those who are focused on building wealth. There are statistical reports based on the flow of funds through the banking system, on surveys of people and their employers and on analyzing income tax returns.

Because each of these techniques samples a different piece of the economic pie, the specific numbers they generate do not match perfectly. But just as the eastern edge of South America still aligns neatly with the West Coast of Africa millions of years after they split apart, the overall findings in the government's many economic reports are consistent. And the key fact that aligns all of these reports is this: from 1973 until 1997, the wages and salaries of 99 percent of Americans either declined or stagnated. Then they started rising again in the mid- to late 1990s, while through most of these three decades the incomes of those at the very top soared. The evidence of this is so overwhelming that not a single mainstream economist in America has questioned these facts in recent years. Opinions vary greatly, however, on what caused these trends and what they mean.

It will be several years before definitive economic data produce a firm answer on what happened to average wages in 2002 and 2003, but it is unlikely that the average salary continued to grow. It may well have fallen back. One reason is that many people depended on a rising stock market for part of their higher incomes in the late 1990s, as stock options and cash bonuses and even some 401(k) matches relied on the price of company stock. But just as important as the sharp fall in the stock market is the loss of 2.3 million jobs in 2001 and 2002. In those two years, nearly one in every 50 jobs in America vanished and many other job holders saw their wages frozen or cut. People drawn back into the labor force during the bubble economy held many of those lost jobs. But many were also high-paying positions, the kind that were largely immune to cuts before the erosion of jobs moved its way up from blue collar to white collar to wool suit.

Over the past three decades most Americans have struggled and many have made ends meet only by becoming two-income households. But some people have prospered to a degree unprecedented in our nation's history. The story of how the rich really did get richer while the poor got poorer, and the role of our tax system, is the story of how income is distributed, like money on the rungs of a ladder, an unstable ladder. Many of the lower rungs are growing thinner. Those near the top are almost in the same position as they were three decades ago, while on the very topmost rung a rapidly growing share of the nation's income is piling up, weighing ever more heavily on everyone below.

The Rich Get Fabulously Richer

3

In 1977, the richest 1 percent of Americans had as much to spend after taxes as the bottom 49 million. Just 22 years later, in 1999, the richest 1 percent—about 2.7 million people—had as much as the bottom 100 million Americans. Few figures derived from the official government data on incomes present more starkly the growing chasm between the rising incomes at the top and the falling incomes at the bottom.

Those in the top 1 percent saw their average income, adjusted for inflation to 1999 dollars and after income taxes were paid, more than double from $234,700 in 1977 to $515,600 in 1999. Meanwhile, the 55 million Americans in the poorest fifth of the population lived in households whose average income fell from $10,000 in 1977 to $8,800 in 1999. The Center for Budget and Policy Priorities, a liberal group that advocates for the poor, calculated these figures from the sophisticated income data that the Congressional Budget Office began collecting in 1977. Studies by other economic research and advocacy organizations made similar findings using other official data. Across the political spectrum, economists found the same basic trend: the rich really are getting richer and the poor really are getting poorer.

Looking more closely at the top fifth gives a hint as to how incomes were changing in the last three decades of the twentieth century. Think of a ladder with 100 rungs. The poorest person in America stands at the bottom and the person with the biggest income stands at the top, with everyone else taking their place on the rungs in between.

Between 1973 and 2001, those whose income ranked them above

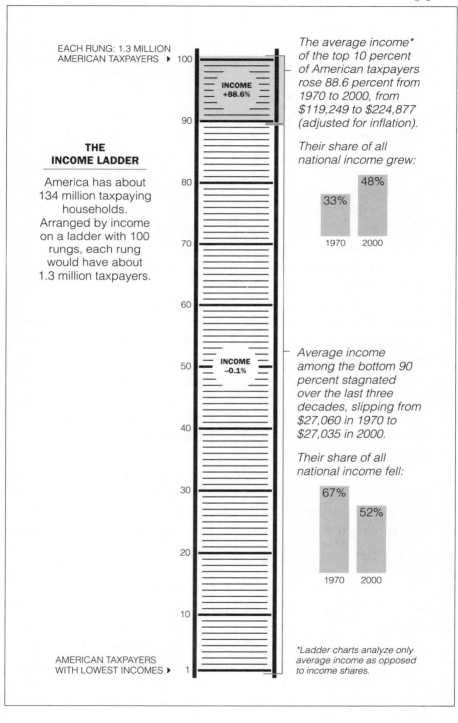

EACH RUNG: 1.3 MILLION
AMERICAN TAXPAYERS ▸ 100

INCOME
+88.6%

**THE
INCOME LADDER**

America has about
134 million taxpaying
households.
Arranged by income
on a ladder with 100
rungs, each rung
would have about
1.3 million taxpayers.

INCOME
–0.1%

AMERICAN TAXPAYERS
WITH LOWEST INCOMES ▸ 1

The average income
of the top 10 percent
of American taxpayers
rose 88.6 percent from
1970 to 2000, from
$119,249 to $224,877
(adjusted for inflation).*

*Their share of all
national income grew:*

48%

33%

1970   2000

*Average income
among the bottom 90
percent stagnated
over the last three
decades, slipping from
$27,060 in 1970 to
$27,035 in 2000.*

*Their share of all
national income fell:*

67%

52%

1970   2000

**Ladder charts analyze only
average income as opposed
to income shares.*

80 percent of Americans but below the richest 5 percent—those on the eightieth up to the ninety-fifth rungs—saw their share of national income rise almost imperceptibly. The Bureau of the Census calculated that in 2001 they earned 27.7 percent of all income, up from 27 percent in 1973.

The top 5 percent did much better. Their share of the national income grew by more than a third, from 16.6 percent to 22.4 percent. There is the suggestion of a pattern here, of those at the top of the ladder having so much added income that it is reinforcing their position, holding the middle class in place and squeezing those at the bottom, whose incomes were falling.

While the Bureau of the Census did not break the numbers down further, many others did. The National Bureau of Economic Research, the nonprofit organization that makes the official decisions about whether the country is in recession or expansion, published the most extensive analysis. The bureau's president is Martin S. Feldstein, the Harvard University economics professor who was President Ronald Reagan's chief economics adviser. He is a leading proponent of supply-side economics, the idea that economic growth is most likely if taxes on high earners are lowered and more capital can be invested. Economists of every political view rely on the bureau's data and reports because of its reputation for analysis based on facts.

Thomas Piketty and Emmanuel Saez, both French economists, wrote a paper the National Bureau of Economic Research published in 2002 that examined in fine detail income and wealth data for the years 1917 through 2000. They relied mostly on the National Income and Products Accounts, the most comprehensive economic data the government collects, and on tax data. Their study focused not on all Americans, but on those who made the most and how they fared compared to everyone else.

There are many ways to measure income. First we will consider what Piketty and Saez found about the portion, or share, of income going to people at each income level. That is, how big each income group's slice of the pie was. Then we will examine the average incomes of people.

They drew their first line between the top 10 percent and the bottom 90 percent. Overall the bottom 90 percent lost ground. Their share of national income fell from two thirds to slightly more than half. And their average income, adjusted for inflation, was essentially the same in

Income Shares: The Rich Get a Bigger Slice

The share of all income going to the bottom 90 percent of Americans shrank between 1970 and 2000. Among the top 10 percent, the higher a person ranked the more one's slice of the economic pie grew.

	Bottom 90%	90 to 95	95 to 99	99 to 99.5	99.5 to 99.9	99.9 to 99.99	Top 13,360 Households
1970	67.1%	11.1%	12.7%	2.8%	3.5%	1.8%	1.0%
2000	52.0%	11.1%	15.2%	4.1%	6.6%	5.9%	5.1%
Change	**-22.5%**	**0.4%**	**19.5%**	**47.0%**	**90.0%**	**227.0%**	**412.0%**

Source: Piketty & Saez

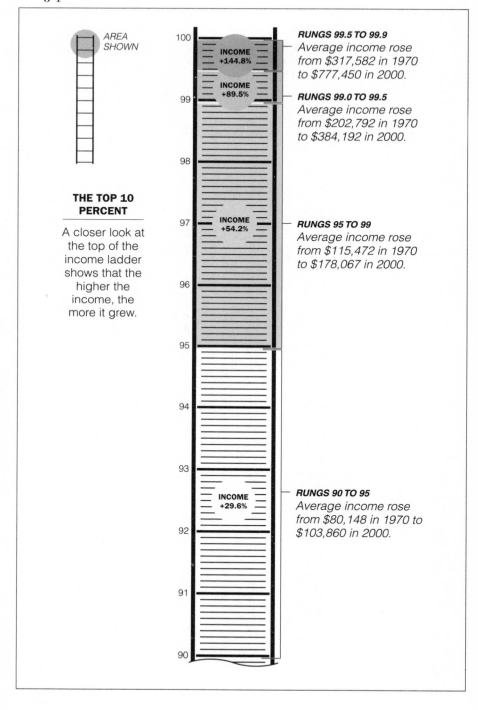

AREA
SHOWN

**THE TOP 10
PERCENT**

A closer look at
the top of the
income ladder
shows that the
higher the
income, the
more it grew.

100

INCOME
+144.8%

INCOME
+89.5%

99

98

97

INCOME
+54.2%

96

95

94

93

INCOME
+29.6%

92

91

90

RUNGS 99.5 TO 99.9
*Average income rose
from $317,582 in 1970
to $777,450 in 2000.*

RUNGS 99.0 TO 99.5
*Average income rose
from $202,792 in 1970
to $384,192 in 2000.*

RUNGS 95 TO 99
*Average income rose
from $115,472 in 1970
to $178,067 in 2000.*

RUNGS 90 TO 95
*Average income rose
from $80,148 in 1970 to
$103,860 in 2000.*

2000 as in 1970. The average income for the bottom 90 percent in 2000 was $27,035, which was $25 less than three decades earlier.

The top 10 percent of Americans had done very well since 1970, or so it seemed at first blush. These 11.3 million households, comprising roughly the population of California, saw their share of national income grow by almost half, from just under 33 percent in 1973 to just above 48 percent in 1998. When examined more closely, however, a curious trend appeared. The figures showed that the higher the income group, the larger the income gains.

Piketty and Saez cut off the top 10 steps on the ladder and divided the top 10 percent into ever-smaller segments of the population.

They examined those on the rungs from 90 to 95. Their share of the national income was flat. Next came the slightly smaller group between rungs 95 and 99. Their share grew by 19.5 percent.

Next the professors sliced off the top rung on the ladder, the top 1 percent or about 1.3 million households, roughly the population of Kentucky. This group earned more than a fifth of all the income in the country. The economists broke the top 1 percent down into ever-finer amounts, into minirungs on the ladder, the smallest of which represented a hundredth of 1 percent, or about 13,400 of the country's 134 million taxpayer households.

They examined the bottom half of the top 1 percent. Their share of national income grew by 47 percent, which was more than twice the rate of the group just below them on the income ladder.

The professors then looked at those on the minirungs from 99.5 to 99.9. Their share of national income grew even more, rising by 90 percent. Next came those on the minirungs from 99.9 to 99.99, just 120,000 households. Their share of national income more than tripled, growing 227 percent.

Finally, the professors examined the very top rung, the richest 13,400 households. These are the people who made more than 99.99 percent of their fellow Americans. They had by far the biggest gains. Their share of national income in the year 2000 was more than five times what it had been in 1970. Back then this elite group received 1 percent of national income, while in 2000 it received more than 5 percent. Even more telling was how it had done compared to those fortunate enough to stand

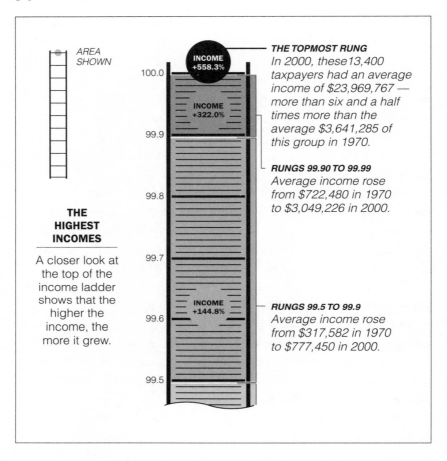

between the ninetieth and ninety-fifth rungs—the top group's share of income had grown almost 1,000 times faster.

The average income of all households in 2000 was $42,700, while the 13,400 households at the very top had an average income of $24 million each or 560 times the average. It was not always this way. In 1970 the very top group had about 100 times the average.

Clearly the only significant income gains over three decades went to a very narrow slice at the top. After adjusting for inflation, for each dollar of income in 1970 the top 13,400 households had four additional dollars plus a dime to spend in 2000, while the average household in the bottom 99 percent had only eight cents more per dollar.

The enormous concentration of income among a very very few

*Bar should continue
off the page for 62 more feet.*

FOR A VERY FEW, EXTRAORDINARY INCOME GROWTH

For every $1 that each taxpayer in the bottom 99 percent of Americans saw in income growth between 1970 and 2000, each of those in the top one-hundredth of 1 percent—some 13,400 taxpayers in 2000—earned $7,500.

**BOTTOM
99 PERCENT**

+$2,710

**TOP 1/100 OF
1 PERCENT**

+$20,328,482

INCOME GROWTH 1970–2000

In 1970, average income was $32,763 (adjusted for inflation). By 2000, it had grown to $35,473, an increase of $2,710.

This elite group had an average income of $3,641,285 in 1970; in 2000 it reached $23,969,767, an increase of $20,328,482.

Incomes Grew Most at the Top

Average incomes for nearly all Americans declined from 1970 to 2000, but the higher a person stood on the income ladder the more that income grew.

Pretax incomes in 2000 dollars

	Bottom 90%	90 to 95	95 to 99	99 to 99.5	99.5 to 99.9	99.9 to 99.99	Top 13,400 Households
1970	$ 27,060	$ 80,148	$ 115,472	$ 202,792	$ 317,582	$ 722,480	$ 3,641,285
2000	$ 27,035	$ 103,860	$ 178,067	$ 384,192	$ 777,450	$ 3,049,226	$ 23,969,767
Percentage Change	**-0.1%**	**29.6%**	**54.2%**	**89.5%**	**144.8%**	**322.0%**	**558.3%**

Source: Piketty & Saez

becomes even clearer with a simple comparison of income growth between 1970 and 2000. How did the top one hundredth of 1 percent compare to the bottom 99 percent? For each dollar of additional income going to each of those in the bottom 99 percent of Americans the richest each averaged an astonishing $7,500.

Applying the National Bureau of Economic Research report to the incomes reported on tax returns in 2000 produces an astonishing result. The 13,400 top households had slightly more income than the 96 million poorest Americans. That is a chasm vastly greater than the liberal Center on Budget and Policy Priorities reported when it said that the top 2.7 million had as much as the bottom 100 million.

The data show that slices of the pie have changed, with a few getting a lot bigger share and many getting less. Now let's look at a second way to analyze the data by examining actual incomes, at what Piketty and Saez found about how much money people at each income level made in 2000 compared to 1970.

What Piketty and Saez showed from the official government data was that two decades after the promise that lowering tax rates and reducing regulation would benefit everyone, the income gains were flowing straight up to the top of the income ladder. Even the derisive description by critics captured in the phrase "trickle-down economics" was not proving out. At the bottom there was less money for food, shelter and clothing. Four out of five Americans were making less or were no better off in 2000 than in 1970.

People in the middle class and even those making more than 95 percent of their fellow Americans were working harder than ever and going nowhere fast. For those on the ninetieth rung of the ladder, average income in 2000 was $90,271, which, after adjusting for inflation, was a one-fourth increase from the $72,320 in 1970. In real terms incomes for those on the ninetieth rung rose at less than 1 percent per year, which was far less than the rate of growth in the economy.

Those at the ninetieth rung saw their incomes rise at an annual average of less than $600 per year, compared to about $4,600 annually at the ninety-ninth rung and more than $672,000 annually for the top group, those 13,400 super-rich families.

Money, it seems, was made to flow uphill. The great majority of Americans were, at least through 2000, having their pockets flattened or even drained, the value created by their labor flowing in a Niagara of greenbacks not to the affluent or even the merely rich, but to the megarich. But just as the liberals at the Center for Budget and Policy Priorities had understated the chasm between rich and poor, so too did Piketty and Saez.

The figures Piketty and Saez used were pretax incomes. But changes in the tax system had vastly expanded the ability of the megarich to save while those making less than $72,000 had their ability to save stripped away by rising Social Security taxes. In 1970, the top income tax bracket was 70 percent. By 2000 it had fallen to 39.6 percent—and it is now just 35 percent. Over those same years, however, the maximum Social Security soared from $327 to $4,724, figures that double if one counts the employer contribution.

Internal Revenue Service reports show that from 1973 to 2000, when the Democrats were mostly in control of Congress, Social Security and Medicare taxes grew 82 percent faster than incomes. Because Social Security taxes applied only to the first $76,200 of wages in 2000 (and lesser amounts in previous years), this rising burden fell mostly on the middle class and the upper middle class.

The rich got a tax break beginning when their wages passed the maximum subject to Social Security. On dollars above the Social Security ceiling an individual pays 6.2 percent less tax because Social Security is no longer deducted from paychecks. Employers get the same tax break. For the rich, the top 1.3 million households, the Social Security tax was inconsequential.

The tax rate on capital gains, the source of more than half of income for the super rich, was 28 percent starting in 1987, fell to 20 percent in 1998 and then was lowered again in 2003 to 15 percent.

Over the last three decades of the twentieth century the average income grew modestly, but the share of earnings going to income and Social Security taxes rose. At the same time the super rich saw their incomes skyrocket and, because their tax rates fell, they kept an even higher percentage than before.

In addition, the rates at which state and local governments levied sales, property and income taxes all rose in those last three decades, eating into incomes. Those taxes tend to be regressive; that is, they tend to hit harder the lower one's income.

Piketty and Saez's facts and figures show us what happened, but they do not say why these changes occurred. Understanding how this happened involves many issues because, in a nation as complex and diverse as America, there are many ways to collar a dollar. Some of these, as we shall see, involved pumping up compensation for those high in the corporate structure, no matter how it affected the company's workers and shareholders. These strategies, in turn, had an important side effect: creating a demand for corporate tax shelters, which helped shift the overall tax burden off capital and onto labor. By 2002, the portion of federal revenues coming from corporations was below 10 percent, down from a third in the Eisenhower years. The demand for tax shelters in turn encouraged an anything-goes morality about hiding money, both corporate profits and individual incomes, from the IRS. Some companies went so far as to renounce America as their headquarters, at least on paper, once they learned that if they used a Bermuda mailbox as their tax headquarters they could earn profits tax-free in the United States.

Arranging to have torrents of money flow to a very few pockets also required putting immense pressure on Corporate America's front lines, the employees, to make the numbers demanded from on high. Even if it meant cheating people out of their wages or disability benefits, or foisting costs off onto the taxpayers, corporate managers were driven to produce the results the home office demanded or else join the ranks of the downsized. The cuts in regulatory agencies, and even in many law enforcement agencies, made such thievery easy. When people complained that they had been cheated out of overtime or even regular pay, the agencies had no resources to pursue the cases, even when there was a pattern of abuse by brand-name companies like Wal-Mart and Taco Bell.

In all of this, both big corporations and those among the very wealthy who wanted to handcuff law enforcement—at least when it came to stealing by business practice—had as allies their good friends in Congress. Corporate America's effort to mold both political parties to do its bidding was increasingly successful as politicians needed ever more contributions to buy the television ads that got them reelected. Politicians insisted that no one bought their vote with their donation and that was true. But what donations did buy, every politician acknowledged, was access. That access meant that every senator and representative was listening primarily to the concerns and ideas of the super rich, of the political donor class. At the same time the forces arrayed on the other side—unions, consumer advocates and social service charities—had little to give and, except for the unions, were barred by law from making campaign donations. These forces were so enfeebled that Congress often behaved as a wholly owned subsidiary of Corporate America, enabling the super rich to use their access to lawmakers to assert that what was good for them was good for the rest of America.

These lawmakers—often passing bills they had not read (some of which came to the floor of the House or Senate without a single public hearing)—may not even have realized how they were systematically undermining the economic welfare of most Americans. Most lawmakers would probably be astonished, for example, to learn that they passed laws that took away the most powerful incentive for accountants to behave with integrity, a change that was behind the accounting scandals at Enron, Global Crossing, Adelphia, Tyco, Waste Management and so many other companies. And yet the lawmakers encouraged these corporate scandals by ending a single legal principle—the policy that each partner in an accounting or law firm was liable for the acts of every other partner. The significance of how this rule eliminated a powerful self-policing mechanism was written about in academic journals and debated by the most thoughtful in the corporate professions, but was unknown to the public because it was ignored in the news media. Significantly, that change represented a triumph of political influence interfering with the market.

Likewise, few lawmakers probably have any idea that they passed another federal law that requires companies to put too little money away in pension plans for younger workers. This law not only contributes to a lack of financial soundness, it also requires that so much extra money be set aside for older workers that it creates an incentive to lay them off. And few lawmakers grasp that the spread of 401(k) plans shifts risks onto investment amateurs. Fewer still understand how 401(k) plans artificially add to a company's balance sheet and generate cash flow by tapping the government's pockets, all with no more work than it takes to electronically move a stock certificate from one computer file to another.

The steady erosion of law enforcement budgets for white-collar crime also emboldened those who would have behaved better if the chances of getting caught were significant. In the area of taxes, especially, cuts in enforcement had a dramatic effect on behavior. A pollster named

Frank Luntz persuaded Republicans that the single best way to get votes was to attack the Internal Revenue Service. He urged them to call for tax relief—being careful not to say "tax cuts"—a campaign that has cost the government tens of billions of dollars and emboldened lawbreakers. The IRS budget has been restrained so severely that only one in five of the tax cheats it identifies is pursued to make him pay. The other four pay nothing. Tax law enforcement became so weak that businessmen were quoted on the front page of *The New York Times* in the year 2000 boasting about how they neither paid taxes nor withheld them from their employees' paychecks. More than two years later, not one of them had been indicted or even forced through civil court action to pay up. Not only did more than 1,500 people, caught red-handed hiding money off-shore when their banker turned over records of their crimes, escape prosecution, but most were not even asked to pay the taxes they had evaded.

The advantages that many of these laws, regulations and budget cuts give to corporations and the rapacious rich went unreported in the major news media. As publishers cut news budgets, junk journalism expanded because covering opinions and official leaks about sex scandals was far less expensive than digging out complicated facts about the economy, budgets and taxes. Fewer reporters were assigned to explain how government policies and administrative practices affected individual lives and the economy. And with stagnant incomes, Americans were working longer hours just to stay even, leaving less time for family, not to mention keeping up with what serious news there was about politics and government.

The executives and investors who wanted these changes were not in a rush. Unlike journalists who think of the next edition and politicians who think of the next election, many of them were patient, spending money for decades to get their way one law, one rule, one fewer regulator at a time. And with their campaign contributions, they wielded enormous influence. In the 2000 elections for Congress, the nonpartisan Center for Responsive Politics found that more than 80 percent of identifiable political contributions came from just one in 625 Americans. By the 2002 elections, the ratio was down to just one in 833, roughly equaling the top tenth of 1 percent.

At the same time the number of Americans who voted continued to decline. In 2000, a majority of those 18 to 21—the age group to whom voting was extended during the Vietnam War years—did not cast ballots. And studies showed that many of those who did cast ballots knew less about even the major issues of the day than the generation or two before them, much less the subtle and complex economic, regulatory and tax matters that affected whether they would ever get ahead.

Active pursuit of self-interest makes democracy work. But democracy also requires vigorous debate and give-and-take. When the great majority of people are not pursuing their own interests, the power of the political donor class grows. And while the wealthy have, and always will have, disproportionate influence over politics, their power can only be held in check by the great mass of voters recognizing and pursuing their own self-interest. The spread of corporate policies that prohibit workers from wearing campaign buttons or discussing politics at work is part of the trend that squelches debate that might pose a threat to the political donor class and its power in reshaping our tax system to benefit their interests.

How the rich arranged to do so much better than everyone else, and the reasons why they took home huge increases in income while many lost ground, were not state secrets. To the extent that government continues to be conducted in the open, many of the answers can be found in the public record. But if no one looks in obvious places and they do not become part of the news, then, like Edgar Allan Poe's "Purloined Letter," those answers can be hidden in plain sight, as we shall see in the next chapter.

Big Payday

4

In March 1992, the news of one executive's big payday fascinated Americans. The story broke on the front page and quickly moved to Johnny Carson's monologue and ABC's *Nightline,* which devoted a show to this one paycheck. In factories and offices, workers debated with awe or outrage whether any one year of work could be worth so much, while in the executive suites the talk was about how to arrange the same sort of deal.

The subject of all this fascination was Roberto C. Goizueta, the son of a Cuban sugar cane grower, who earned a chemical engineering degree at Yale in 1953 and went back home to work for Coca-Cola. Then in 1964 Goizueta took his wife, their children and 100 shares of Coca-Cola stock on vacation to the United States, never to return. At Coca-Cola headquarters in Atlanta, Goizueta became professionally obsessed with how much each of his employer's investments earned after taxes, developing insights that propelled him to chief executive in 1981 and shaped his own views about how he wanted to be paid.

Few people had ever heard of Goizueta until the story about his compensation broke, not even those who cared passionately about his biggest blunder, the 1985 introduction of New Coke, which tasted like Pepsi. So much was written and said about his pay that a month after the news broke, Goizueta himself observed that everyone in America seemed to have an opinion about how much he made and whether he was worth it. What attracted all this attention was not the nearly $5 million in salary, bonus and little extras that had sweetened his pay the year before as chief executive of Coca-Cola. That money alone made him one of the best-paid executives in America. What fascinated people was the other part of his pay, the part the company tried to hide. Goizueta had been given 1,000,000 shares of Coke stock, which at the end of 1991 were worth $81 million.

It was in the 1990s, starting with Goizueta, that rising pay for chief executives would become a defining trend for the economy as compensation grew at such a grand scale that the numbers almost defy comprehension. To many executives Goizueta was the master of pay, the executive to emulate.

Looked at in the way that blue-collar workers contemplate their income, in terms of how much their hourly wage goes up each year, pay raises for CEOs were astronomical. By 1999 the average pay of the 100 top CEOs was $37 million and annual pay of $100 million was no longer news by itself. Analyzing the *Forbes* magazine annual reports on the compensation of chief executives shows that while wages languished for almost everyone, the CEOs won steady pay increases. While the overall annual pay increase for everyone in America averaged a nickel an hour between 1970 and 2000, chief executives won pay raises that averaged $660 per hour per year. If this disparity was turned into a chart in this book and the nickel per hour was shown as a column one inch high, the column for the average annual CEO pay raise would extend almost 1,100 feet beyond the top of this page.

Goizueta's big payday almost went by unnoticed. Instead of listing his 1,000,000 shares of stock along with his salary and bonus in the executive compensation portion of the proxy statement sent to shareholders, the company wrote out "one million shares" and buried it in a dense paragraph of legalese six pages deeper into the proxy. Some reader, perhaps one trying to cure insomnia, spotted the language and the next day it made the news. Still, the strategy to hide the full amount of Goizueta's compensation was a partial success. The year before, in 1990, Goizueta had been given a half million shares and it, too, was buried. That compensation went unnoticed at the time and was not even discovered when the controversy over the million shares arose a year later. The million shares struck a chord, though. One million shares was a nice round figure—one people could remember, especially those who had heard how the value of Coca-Cola shares was rising faster than bubbles in a Coke.

Much better hidden than the grants of stock were features of Goizueta's pay package that made it more valuable than even $86 million and far more relevant to the lives of most Americans. These features were little known outside of a select circle at Coca-Cola, so even those who followed the story closely could not have been aware of them at the time. One of these features allowed him to pay less than 2 percent of his 1991 pay in federal income tax that year.

Goizueta was not alone in paying such a tiny percentage of his income in taxes, a smaller percentage than even many in the working class paid. The year that Goizueta had his big payday, similar deals were made by chief executives John F. Welch Jr. of General Electric, Louis V. Gerstner, Jr. of IBM, Lawrence Bossidy of Allied-Signal Companies and tens of thousands of other executives.

When people read about chief executives making huge incomes, few realize that the executives typically do not pay taxes on all of that money immediately, the way Congress says everyone who makes much less must. The special rules for senior executives also extend to top salespeople as well as to movie stars and athletes, whose outsize pay is promoted as part of a strategy to enhance their career image and to make them even more valuable. Congress lets these Americans put off paying taxes for years or even decades and there is no limit on how much they can set aside untaxed.

These secret features and similar ones at many other companies were significant because they contributed to the economic pain felt by millions of workers whose compensation was squeezed so that the top executives could take a larger share of the compensation budget. These features relate to aspects of the tax system that benefit senior executives and others at the top of the income ladder at the expense of everyone else. Goizueta's role is significant because his pay package neatly encapsulates many of these features, especially widespread efforts to hide the real value of executive pay packages.

Here's how it works and what it means: the executives decline to take delivery of a big chunk of their pay, instead deferring receipt of the money to some future year. No taxes are taken out because, technically, the executives have not been paid. That means that the executive gets to invest the full amount that is deferred, unlike everyone else who can only invest their after-tax income.

The company he works for invests the money that the executive defers. The money may simply be plowed back into the company as part of its working capital. But in most cases the money is set aside in a separate account and cannot be used to finance the company's operations. Money in such separate trusts is often invested in life insurance, mutual funds or, as with Goizueta, the stock of the company. The dividends and interest earned in the deferral account usually keep building up inside the account, untaxed. But a few executives choose to have the dividends paid out, in which case they become immediately taxable. When the executive cashes out, usually at retirement, the company withholds income taxes and pays the executive the balance, usually installments over a period of years.

Such deals to defer compensation amount to an unlimited 401(k) plan. But while Congress limits how much you and I can save in these plans to about $1,000 a month, executives can defer unlimited amounts. But there's a catch to these unlimited plans. They are expensive for shareholders, rank-and-file workers and taxpayers.

Money an executive defers cannot be deducted on the company's tax return. So instead of deducting $86 million from its profits on Mr. Goizueta's pay in 1991, Coca-Cola deducted only the nearly $5 million that it paid to him immediately. As a result Coca-Cola's corporate income tax bill was about $29 million higher than if Mr. Goizueta had not deferred his pay. In effect, Coca-Cola shareholders loaned Goizueta that $29 million, interest-free.

Now think about the entire world of tax deferral for all the executives in America. Many tens of thousands of executives defer part of their pay, from the modest sums put aside by junior executives to the tens of millions of dollars deferred by chief executives like Goizueta. Each year another round of deferrals takes place, adding to the interest-free loans companies grant these executives.

No law requires companies to disclose how much is deferred by their executives or how much they are obligated to pay when the deferrals end. The accounting rules do not require such disclosures, either. Curiously, however, the Securities and Exchange Commission rules do require disclosures of picayune items such as the $2,286 in "all other compensation" paid in 2002 to Sanford I. Weill, chief executive of Citigroup, whose total compensation has run as high as $151 million for a single year. That neither the SEC nor the Financial Accounting Standards Board has required routine and understandable disclosure of deferrals explains one of the reasons that executives are so eager to take advantage of deferral.

While no one knows the total amount of these corporate liabilities, given the size of the economy and the tens of thousands of executives, senior sales agents, movie stars and athletes who make such deferrals year after year, the total surely amounts to hundreds of billions of dollars. Goizueta alone had, by early 1997, built up an untaxed fortune of more than a billion dollars.

If these deferral deals were marketed openly, instead of being treated as corporate secrets, a typical ad might say this:

**Looking to make an investment
using borrowed money?
How do these terms sound?**

- No interest!
- No application forms!
- No credit checks!
- Approval is automatic!
- Borrow up to 40 percent of your pay
  each year!
- Borrow until you retire!
- No repayment until you retire!

**Sound too good to be true?
Congress created this opportunity
for those who qualify.★
Don't delay—borrow today.**

★Available to executives, highly paid salespeople, movie stars and athletes under a 1974 federal law; sorry, but Congress says that no other Americans are eligible for these interest-free loans.

Even that mock ad does not capture it all because some executives even get guaranteed investment returns on the money they defer. When Michael H. Jordan was chief executive of Westinghouse Electric, for example, he deferred $1.8 million in bonuses in 1994 and 1995. The company agreed to pay him interest at a rate equal to the 10-year Treasury notes, about 7 percent at the time. However, if when he retired it turned out that he would have made more money by investing his deferred money in shares of Westinghouse, then he'd be entitled to the higher amount. If the price of Westinghouse stock fell, shareholders would lose, but the chief executive's investment was guaranteed to profit.

Welch, the GE chief executive, worked out an even better deal for himself when he deferred half of his $2 million base salary in 1995. First, GE gave Welch a $35,000 matching contribution, the same 3.5 percent rate that the company gave employees on money they saved in the company's 401(k) plan. But while GE deducted on its corporate tax return the much smaller sums each worker could collect in 401(k) match money, no deduction was allowed on Welch's $35,000 until his deferral ended. GE's taxes thus increased by about $12,000 and the real cost to shareholders of Welch's match was $47,000.

Second, GE agreed to pay Welch 14 percent interest on his money until he retired. At 14 percent, Welch's money would nearly double in five years, when he was scheduled to retire. After paying federal and Connecticut state income taxes, Welch would have more than $1.1 million left to spend.

Had Welch not deferred the million dollars, he would have had to pay his taxes immediately. After taxes he would have been left with about $572,000 to invest. Even if Welch had been lucky enough to earn 14 percent interest on this sum, he would, after five years, have about $810,000 to spend—or about $300,000 less than with the deferral.

At the time, GE was borrowing money in the securities markets for five years at 4.5 percent interest. Thus GE paid its chief executive more than three times the market rate on the million dollars he left on deposit with the company until retirement. Paying three times the market rate of interest is a subsidy from shareholders to the chief executive. It is commonplace for corporations to pay above-market interest to executives on money they defer. Few shareholders know this because the SEC rules allow companies to partially hide this. Companies need only tell shareholders the amount of interest paid to the top five executives each year that is above market rates, which must be taken from a monthly government report, not the rates themselves or the effect of compound interest over the years.

Even when a company pays no interest to an executive on deferred pay, however, there are still huge costs. If the company uses the deferred money to buy bonds, for example, then the executive's gains on the deferral come from the market. Still, the company is making an interest-free loan to the executive on the amount of the taxes that the executive did not have to pay and that the company did because it did not get to deduct the compensation immediately. At the corporate tax rate of 35 percent this means that each million dollars of deferred pay costs the company $1,350,000—the amount of the deferral plus the income taxes that had to be paid.

If the company invests the deferred pay back into the company, then it has some value to shareholders, who want the business to grow. But the more common arrangement is to place the money in a separate account, which the company owns, and to invest it for the executives through a trust. Money in such trusts is working not for the company, but for the executives, although it remains on the company's balance sheet. Money tied up in interest-free loans to executives and then put into a trust for them cannot be used to build new factories, to buy new equipment and to invest in growing the business.

Consider a company in which the deferral accounts of its executives, including the tax cost, totals $1.5 billion and the company has $7 billion of total capital. If the company's board sets a goal of earning 20 percent on capital, then it really must earn more than 25 percent on the capital that remains available to grow the business and is not subsidizing the executives. A factory that is earning 20 percent or even 22 percent on the capital invested in it is at risk of being shut down because of the need to generate a return that masks the subsidy to the deferring executives.

The way in which Goizueta's pay was structured, when multiplied by the tens of thousands of executives at Coke and other companies whose compensation packages were variations on the same theme, directly affected the pay, the benefits and the career prospects of every person working for these enterprises. While these plans were carefully designed to conceal their true costs, that does not change the fact that there is no free lunch. The true price of deferral may be hidden, but it still must be paid somehow and by someone. Those someones included millions of people whose careers were ended prematurely by the forced retirements that began sweeping through Corporate America in the late eighties. They included people who were never hired because payrolls shrank. They even extended to people who instead of solid jobs at big companies had to settle for work at discount wages, with few benefits, at firms created to do the work the big companies outsourced. They extended to people who kept their jobs at big companies, but had their health and retirement benefits trimmed and sometimes eliminated.

At the annual meeting of Coke shareholders in April 1992, Goizueta went on the offensive before anyone among the company's owners could ask any probing questions about his compensation package, questions that might have led to scrutiny of these carefully hidden features in his pay package. Goizueta reminded the assembled shareholders that they had approved the executive compensation plan under which he received the stock. When they approved it in 1989, a million shares were worth only $5 million, he noted. He said the value of those shares had grown 16-fold only because of his stewardship, ignoring the contributions of all the tens of thousands of other Coca-Cola employees. He also noted that he was given the stock so that he would not retire early and that if he quit during the next four years, he had to walk away from those million shares. His strategy of making sure that no one asked a probing question, that no one dug any more deeply into his deal, worked. A little later that morning, when the time came for shareholders to get their brief annual chance to question Coke management, no one asked about Goizueta's pay.

Beyond the Coca-Cola shareholder meeting, however, there was plenty of criticism. The time was ripe for it. The country had just come out of a recession, one that had had an unsettling effect on white-collar workers. They were not used to seeing themselves laid off, like the blue-collar workers who had taken the brunt of job cuts during the previous two decades as imported cars and other goods manufactured overseas flooded the country and shrank the number of well-paying factory jobs. Many white-collar workers were also uneasy because reliable lifetime employers like AT&T, IBM, Delta Airlines and Hallmark, which had always rewarded loyalty with steady work, were, for the first time, laying people off and doing so by the thousands. Companies that had begun thinning the ranks of their better educated workers in an attempt to prop up profits tried to mask the mass firings by coining a new euphemism: *downsizing*. The idea of mutual loyalty between workers and companies was collapsing with the most dire price paid by older workers whose age and specialization gave them few options when their employers suddenly withdrew from the implicit contract on which they had staked their economic futures.

Millions who kept their jobs had their benefits cut. Instead of a pension, which came on top of their salary, they would have to save for their old age in a 401(k) plan with money that came out of their salary. Even with a matching contribution for those who saved, this was a major reduction in the future income for each affected worker. It was also a huge savings for the employer because a 401(k) savings match goes only to those who save, which is to say mostly to the better paid workers. A match often costs employers just a dime for each dollar that would be spent on a much more secure traditional pension. Medical and dental plans were also cut, with growing numbers of workers being shunted into health maintenance organizations (HMOs), which many people found were skilled at erecting obstacles to seeing a doctor or getting needed care. Even those workers who stayed in medical insurance plans that let them pick their doctors found that more and more procedures were excluded from coverage. The trend toward more out-of-pocket expenses like patient co-payments, which advocates said reduced unnecessary medical care, further squeezed paychecks. Companies making these cuts all said they just could not afford to provide the same benefits as before. The question that was not pressed hard at the time was just why this was so, especially at companies that continued to report solid profits.

For weeks after the Goizueta story broke, critical articles and strident opinion columns filled newspapers and magazines. "Gross Pay" was the headline on the *Boston Globe*'s look at rising compensation for the few amid pay freezes and firings for so many. On its weekly page for students, the Long Island newspaper *Newsday* printed Goizueta's compensation and asked "is something wrong here?" Even the editorial page of Coke's hometown newspaper, *The Atlanta Journal–Constitution*, blasted Goizueta's pay as an insult to all the little people at Coca-Cola whose dedication and hard work made the company prosper. "How is anyone worth the compensation being paid to execs who did not invent a product, formulate an idea or start a company from the ground up?" the Atlanta newspaper asked. The question fit with a broadly held American sentiment that founders of companies were due their riches, but hired hands, even top hands, were not. The criticism was so intense and lasting that federal securities regulators, who usually deal with corporate lawyers, even responded to the pleas of Father Leo Conti, a Catholic priest who tended to the elderly and infirm at a nursing home in Evansville, Indiana, work that paid $7,200 a year. Father Conti complained to the SEC that pay on the scale that Goizueta received was "legalized corporate theft." Instead of ignoring his complaint, the Securities and Exchange Commission used it as the basis for deciding that shareholders were entitled to a bit more disclosure about just how deeply executives were being allowed to dig into the corporate treasury for their own benefit.

Among the most informed of the critics of executive compensation was Graef ("Bud") Crystal. He is an aggressively cheerful man who in the sixties, seventies and eighties designed packages that enlarged the pay of executives. Crystal's creativity was legendary among CEOs, and their companies paid well for Crystal's advice on how to make more. Many executives felt they were seriously underpaid, despite a steady stream of articles in business magazines each spring about how overpaid executives were. *Forbes* magazine, whose wealthy readership is comprised of more investors than executives, frequently observed that being a chief executive was the road to great comfort, but not the kind of riches one could earn by starting his own enterprise, which, of course, is also a much riskier way to live. *Forbes* also would remind its investing readers that a chief executive who failed to deliver a rising stock price was overpaid at any salary.

Crystal felt partly responsible for the average compensation of the 100 best-paid chief executives rising from $1.7 million in 1973 to almost $9 million 1991. One day he looked at the society around him and was appalled at what he had done to help chief executives earn so much, especially since his own research showed little relationship between how executives and their shareholders fared. Bud Crystal declared himself a heretic in the House of Mammon and cast himself out. He fashioned a new role for himself as a critic. But rather than analyzing the latest Broadway play or Hollywood movie, he used his knowledge to dissect whether an executive was paid too much or too little. At first he gave his reviews in acerbic columns in *Fortune* magazine, but when the new chairman of its corporate parent tried to block a column describing him as the most overpaid executive in America, that gig ended. Crystal found other outlets for his critiques and he wrote a hard-hitting book called *In Search of Excess* that earned him a reputation as the man CEOs love to hate.

As critical as he was of other executives, Crystal admired Goizueta. "As far as chief executive officers go, they don't come much better than Roberto Goizueta," he wrote in 1992. In the 11 years Goizueta had been at the helm of Coke, shareholders had seen their investment grow at a compound annual rate of 31.7 percent. That was a phenomenal performance, far above the 11 percent shareholders of big companies could expect over the very long haul. If shareholders plowed their dividends back into more Coke shares, it meant that their money was doubling every two years and three months. That was a fabulous improvement over the years before Goizueta, when the price of Coca-Cola shares rose at only about 1 percent annually, less than the shareholders could have made by putting their money in a savings account. With a savings account there was no risk that the price of the stock would fall, creating a loss, so shareholders reasonably demanded bigger returns from stock investments than from savings accounts.

Fantastic as Goizueta's performance was for shareholders, Crystal noted that it was not the best. Coca-Cola shareholders would have done even better holding the shares of 15 other big companies. Investors in the Food Lion supermarket chain, Sara Lee, Gillette, Gerber and Kellogg all earned even higher returns over those 11 years than owners of Coke stock. So had investors in General Mills and Philip Morris. The 15 companies paid their chief executive as little as $3.5 million and as much as $7 million in 1991. Goizueta's salary, bonus and various pay sweeteners alone put him squarely within that range at nearly $5 million. But then he collected that million shares of Coca-Cola stock worth $81 million on top of that, putting him in a league of his own. Crystal concluded that "in short, Roberto Goizueta is worth a lot of money to shareholders, but he isn't worth" his pay plus a million shares of stock.

The public reaction to Goizueta's huge payday was more visceral and mostly critical, even among people unaware of Crystal's careful analysis of the numbers. This popular criticism had enough staying power that it found an audience in two places with the power to do something about executive pay. One was the Securities and Exchange Commission. The other was Congress. The regulators soon imposed new disclosure rules on companies, though to this day they have not extended them to the issues that matter most. But at least they required that numerals, not words, be used to spell out dollar and share amounts and that all executive compensation disclosures be placed together in the section of the proxy concerning executive pay. Congress reacted the following year by voting a cap on how much salary for top executives could be deducted on corporate tax returns.

The law did not limit what executives could be paid. It just said that the maximum base salary that could be deducted on a corporate tax return was $1 million. Any amount above that would be deductible only if it was based on the executive's performance under rules set in advance by the company. A few companies, IBM among them, ignored the million-dollar limit and paid whatever salary the chief executive demanded. On each dollar of salary above the first $1 million (the cap), the shareholders had to pay an extra 35 cents to cover additional corporate income taxes.

Making performance-based pay deductible no matter the amount created a bonanza for pay consultants, who set about designing compensation plans that both were fully deductible and made executives rich even if their shareholders suffered from falling stock prices or if their stock merely rose in tandem with the whole market. All the CEOs needed to rake in millions upon tens of millions of dollars was to pack the compensation committee with people who had an interest in bigger pay. Goizueta, for example, had his pay set by a committee that included Herbert Allen, a New York investment banker whose firm, Allen & Co., raked in millions of dollars in fees for issuing new debt for Coca-Cola. Investment bankers and others on the board who relied on the chief executive to send them business were logical choices. So were other chief executives. It was also a good idea to put gullible, or uninformed, directors on the committee. Since smart CEOs pick who sits on their board, and especially on the board committee that determines their compensation, getting more money was about as hard as reserving a seat in the corporate dining room for lunch. With the compensation committee controlled by someone who depended on the CEO to steer business to her, the sky was still the limit on compensation. These back-scratching arrangements are perfectly legal.

By the dawn of the new millennium, executive compensation had grown so huge that the amounts that were paid out 30 years earlier, which were criticized at the time as too high, were not more than pocket change to the CEOs of big companies. More significant, most Americans would be worse off as a direct result of the explosion in executive compensation, though few would understand the connection, because companies and their pay consultants worked hard to make sure it was not drawn. Instead much of the business press hailed those who earned gigantic paychecks as heroes, only rarely asking hard questions about the trade-offs between each extra dollar for the executives and how that money could have been paid to others or invested to grow the business.

Big as the untaxed fortunes that executives like Goizueta, Welch and others socked away, they are pikers compared with another group of rich tax delayers—the managers of hedge funds. A hedge fund is basically an unregulated mutual fund in which, by law, only the rich may invest because they are risky, offering huge profits but at the risk of huge losses. These funds are run from places like Wall Street, but are legally organized in tax havens offshore. Their managers charge fat fees, sometimes taking a fifth of the investment profits for themselves.

In the summer of 2003, one hedge fund manager had $2.2 billion in his untaxed deferral account offshore, according to a fellow investment adviser who has seen the documents. Another has more than $2 billion. And at least two other managers have more than $1 billion untaxed growing offshore. One of these managers is just 35 years old and he can keep deferring taxes on his fortune until he retires, which could be three decades into the future. During all those years the deferred money, and whatever else he adds to it, will grow with compound interest, without a dollar going to taxes unless he reaches in to spend some on a yacht, a Monet or a divorce.

Much of the money invested in these hedge funds comes not from rich individuals, but from some of the biggest charitable endowments, whose investment income is usually free of tax. The reason giant charitable endowments invest in hedge funds is leverage. Hedge funds borrow against their assets to leverage how much they can invest. This leverage is similar to what home owners do when they make a down payment and take out a mortgage. Federal law says that when otherwise tax-exempt endowments make leveraged investments they have to pay taxes on their investment profits—unless they invest offshore.

Thus hedge funds cost the vast majority of Americans, who by law are barred from investing in them, in two ways: The managers stash untaxed fortunes offshore and the biggest charitable endowments get around a rule that would tax some of their investment gains.

So how many hearings has Congress held in recent years on these huge untaxed fortunes offshore? None. And what steps has Congress taken to make sure that these hedge fund managers only delay paying their taxes and cannot slip away decades from now without paying their taxes? Again, none.

Inflated tax-free salaries and bonuses were not the only way that executives gained and others felt the pain. The best single tax trick actually forced chief executives to pay higher taxes. And why would anyone want to pay higher taxes? Well, imagine for a moment that you paid an extra dollar of tax and that in return you received something worth much more, say 30 to 200 times more. Welcome aboard the corporate jet.

Plane Perks
5

Just as the real value of executive pay can be legally hidden from share-holders, government rules allow executives to hide the costs of their luxury tastes and habits. Suzy Wetlaufer, the editor of the *Harvard Business Review,* unintentionally brought into focus the hidden costs to taxpayers of supporting regal executive lifestyles. The magazine, which had been so influential in helping chief executives make their pay soar through its promotion of stock options a decade earlier, spent months on a package of articles that would celebrate the achievements of John F. (Jack) Welch Jr., who had just retired from General Electric.

Welch had no worry that anything derogatory or negative would appear because, like fan magazines, the *Harvard Business Review* gives the subjects of its articles effective control over what it writes about them. Ms. Wetlaufer took the usual concessions even further, however, prompting a telephone call that inquired about whether she had become too close to her source even for the standards of the *Review.* The caller was Jane Beasley Welch, the wife of Jack Welch, and her call set in motion the most important disclosures ever made about perks and the efforts made to conceal their costs. It was a story of deep signifi-cance for the readership of the *Review,* though none of it would appear under Ms. Wetlaufer's byline.

A few weeks after her call to Wetlaufer, who had become Welch's girlfriend, Jane Beasley Welch filed for divorce. Mrs. Welch, who had been a corporate lawyer before her 1989 wedding ended her career, hired William Zabel of Manhattan, a lawyer well known for his skill at discreetly settling disputes between prominent people, to negotiate a settlement.

Jack Welch left GE in September of 2001 after 41 years. His final salary and bonus totaled $16.7 million. He also left with stock options worth a quarter of a billion dollars and a pension that shareholders were told was worth more than $9 million a year. His net worth, even with the depressed price of GE stock, was north of a half billion dollars. Out of this Welch gave his estranged wife $35,000 a month for living expenses, which was less than he made each day in retirement. He also offered her $10 million to go away. Before their wedding, Jane Beasley had signed a prenuptial agreement that limited what she would receive in a divorce, but it had expired on their tenth wedding anniversary in 1999. So Mrs. Welch pressed for a much larger share of the marital estate. When Zabel could not negotiate privately what he considered a reasonable settlement for Mrs. Welch, he switched to hardball. He had Mrs. Welch prepare a detailed list of all the perks that GE was providing the couple in retirement, including an estimate of their value, and then filed it in divorce court, where Geraldine Fabrikant of *The New York Times* found it.

The list included a sumptuous Manhattan apartment at Trump International Hotel & Tower that overlooked Central Park, as well as all the expenses of maintaining appearances from fresh flowers to the laundering of linens and maids to keep everything perfectly in order. Mrs. Welch estimated the value of the apartment at $80,000 per month. There were memberships at 11 country clubs. And there were box seats on the Grand Tier level of the Metropolitan Opera at Lincoln Center, just four short blocks from the apartment, and luxury box or courtside seats for a long list of professional sports teams and high-profile events. At each of the five Welch homes—two in Connecticut, two in Florida and one on Nantucket Island—GE provided its latest appliances and electronic gadgets. GE also paid for the communications gear at all five residences, including computers, faxes, telephones and the latest in satellite dish connections. It paid for security systems and architectural and landscaping services. Mrs. Welch valued all the home improvements provided by GE at $7.5 million. Everywhere the couple traveled they were provided with GE limousines and helicopters.

If they rented a car, GE covered the tab. Unmentioned in the court papers were observations by neighbors, who saw Welch walk into stores where he regularly did business, like the convenience mart near his Nantucket mansion, gather household items and tell the clerk to put them on GE's tab. But the big item in the court files, the one that captured the nation's attention, was the corporate jet.

GE flew Welch and his wife around during retirement in the most spacious and luxurious corporate jet on the market, one used by governments for heads of state: a Boeing 737 Business Jet, a $50 million aircraft with GE engines. In the space where 130 or so seats would normally go, it offered such luxurious appointments as a conference room and a bedroom suite complete with shower. The $50 million that the Boeing 737 Business Jet cost GE shareholders was capital not employed to enhance the value of their investment, but diverted to provide transportation to a pensioner. It was also an interesting use of capital for a man who, upon becoming GE chief executive, quickly earned himself the nickname "Neutron Jack" for throwing 100,000 employees out of work so that capital could be more efficiently invested to benefit shareholders.

The Boeing 737 Business Jet is so costly to operate that no charter company keeps one in the United States. But an idea of its true costs can be discerned from the $87,000 fee to charter a much smaller Gulfstream IV one-way from New York to Paris. Mrs. Welch estimated the value of using the Boeing jet at $3.5 million a year. Welch later said that the estimate was too high, but never gave an estimate of his own. In terms of total costs to GE, Mrs. Welch's estimate may have been right on the money or even low. But Welch could reasonably say that the value of using the jet was next to nothing because of the way that Congress requires the IRS to value the personal use of company planes.

Welch, like other executives, pays the company nothing when he uses a corporate jet for personal travel. His only expense is an additional income tax he must pay on the value of the flight, which is counted as a form of income just like salary and bonus. This "imputed income" is reported to the IRS. The imputed value of the flight is not based on actual costs, however, but on a formula required by Congress, one that discounts the value so deeply that it makes personal use of a company jet more attractive than any other form of pay. And this discounting, in turn, helps explain why there are more than 9,000 corporate planes flying today.

Abuses of corporate jets abound. When William Agee was running the engineering firm Morrison-Knudsen into bankruptcy, he replaced its one corporate jet, already paid off, with two new ones and boasted about how the way he financed them polished up the company's financial reports. His wife, Mary Cunnigham Agee, used the extra jet as her personal air taxi to hop around the United States and Europe. When F. Ross Johnson ran the cigarette-and-food company RJR Nabisco, which had a fleet of at least a dozen corporate jets, he once had his dog flown home, listed on the manifest as "G. Shepherd." And Kenneth Lay let his daughter take one of Enron's jets to fly across the Atlantic with her bed, which was too large to go as baggage on a commercial flight.

Under the rules set by Congress, flying in the luxury of a company's Boeing 737 Business Jet is often cheaper than the cost of a middle seat in coach on a commercial airliner. If Welch decided on a whim to fly from New York to Paris, for example, he would be out just $486 each way in additional federal income taxes. The cost to GE shareholders, though, would be more than $100,000 each way if the company chartered the plane. Corporations dislike comparisons to charter rates and prefer instead to count what are known as direct costs, which include fuel and landing fees. Left out of the direct-cost calculation are the salaries of the pilots and stewards, insurance payments and the cost of the plane itself. But even when only direct costs are counted, the cost of flying a Boeing 737 Business Jet from New York to Paris is about $14,600 each way. This means that under the rules set by Congress, the expense Welch incurs to fly a Boeing 737 Business Jet works out to less than a half penny on the dollar at charter rates and about three cents on the direct-cost dollar.

Someone must pay the real costs of personal use of company jets. They are borne by shareholders, who may in turn deduct them on the corporate income tax return, forcing all taxpayers to pick up 35 percent of the true costs. And that means that at charter rates the taxpayers get stuck with 72 times the cost in lost revenue that they collect in extra taxes for the New York–to–Paris flight. Counting only direct costs, the taxpayers pay out more than 10 times as much as the executive pays in taxes.

The government rules that allow Welch and other executives to fly in private luxury and force others to pay have their genesis in a 1985 tax law. That law makes no mention of aircraft, however, making it a model of how Congress fashions stealth tax savings for the political donor class and shifts tax burdens onto everyone else.

Robert Packwood, the Oregon Republican who then chaired the Senate Finance Committee, marched onto the Senate floor on April 3, 1985, clutching in his hand what he called "a very, very simple bill." The bill reversed a law, enacted a year earlier, requiring people who took a company car home at night to keep a daily log detailing their usage. The logs made it possible to determine how much personal use was made of company cars so that use could be valued and reported to the IRS as income. Tracking every movement of their company car was the kind of petty annoyance that angered a lot of people, some of whom argued that a simple rule assigning a daily value for personal car use would be simpler. Packwood called on his fellow senators to end "an unjustified and undignified burden." He also said they could vote for the bill without fear of any hidden agenda.

"There is no other change," Packwood said. "There is no other sleight of hand." But there was.

Senator Howard Metzenbaum, an Ohio Democrat rich enough to buy his own jet if he wanted, agreed that detailed trip logs were excessive. But he was not taken in by Packwood's assurances that this was the entirety of the bill because he had read the committee report accompanying it. When a bill becomes law, the bureaucracy relies on committee reports to craft regulations implementing the new law, often lifting the report language verbatim. The committee report on this bill directed the IRS to stop valuing personal use of corporate jets by executives at the rates companies paid to charter planes and to instead apply the much lower value of first-class airfare.

Metzenbaum attacked the corporate jet portion of the committee report as a "giveaway of I do not know how many millions or hundreds of millions of dollars" to executives. Metzenbaum said that the formula in the committee report would reduce the value of a personal trip by an executive from St. Louis to Atlanta and back in a Learjet from $6,470 to just $752. The same flight in a turboprop would be valued at just $218 because the report's formula was based on the weight of the aircraft.

Metzenbaum's solution was simple: just delete the report language on corporate jets. The debate that followed vividly displayed how deeply certain senators cared about the concerns of the political donor class.

First, Metzenbaum tried to shame his fellow senators by comparing this tax break for high-flying executives to the growing number of people who had exhausted their unemployment benefits, but could not find work. "What kind of a U.S. Senate are we when we do not have the money to take care of unemployed workers?" he asked. Yet "We come here on the floor of the U.S. Senate to provide a new way of treating our corporate executives so they do not pay too much taxes?"

Packwood and the acting president of the Senate that day, Senator Rudy Boschwitz, a Minnesota Republican, tried to dissuade Metzenbaum, saying that only the bill itself, and not the committee report, was up for a vote. Metzenbaum was unmoved. "This is a day in which we feel very generous and we are going to take care of the corporate executive. . . . Why? What crying need is there? I do not understand this. . . . I sure have a lot of problems with giving away Treasury dollars. You do not have to fly in a corporate jet if you do not want to. You can take a commercial flight if you want to. . . . [I]s this the day of rip-offs? Every American who files his tax return on April 15 should be concerned about the vote of every Senator here this afternoon because when you reduce the taxes of the corporate executives you have to get the money somewhere else and that means that the rest of the taxpayers of this country are called upon to pay it."

Senator Jesse Helms, a North Carolina Republican whose views were at least as far to the right as Metzenbaum's were to the left, rose to support Metzenbaum. Just that morning, Helms said, he had heard about how the chief executive of CBS had been at the Greenbrier, a West Virginia resort favored by corporate executives, when his golf game was rained out. Helms quoted the executive as saying, "I have my company plane here. Let's fly down to Florida and play a round of golf, and we'll be back here in time for cocktails this evening." Helms said that "the Senator from Ohio and I sometimes differ on legislation, but I think that he and I are equally revulsed by activities such as this."

Metzenbaum resumed his attack. "This is a sheer attempt on the part of the Finance Committee to see to it that the corporate executives of this country are protected; that they can use the corporate aircraft to go the World Series games, to go on a vacation trip, or to take their family wherever they want" at a fraction of the real cost. "This is as wrong as wrong could be. This is just the matter of playing to the corporate executives. This is a matter of treating them as a special group of people. . . . This is the kind of thing that causes Congress to lose respect. This is the kind of thing that does not even come to the floor as an amendment . . . this is not even in the bill. . . . Why is it not in the bill? Why does it not come up and indicate that which it is? Why do we have to dig through the committee report in order to find out what is going on?"

Packwood insisted repeatedly that the committee report was not before the Senate. Senator Robert Dole of Kansas, who arrived late for the floor debate, assumed that it was and began arguing in favor of the report language that would make it cheaper for executives to make personal use of corporate planes. He said the cost to the taxpayers would be only about $10 million a year and that more private use of corporate jets by executives would help create jobs in Wichita, where Cessnas, Learjets and other corporate planes were manufactured.

Then Dole suggested that flying in a corporate plane was less fancy than flying first class. Senator Steven Douglas Symms of Idaho seized on this theme, describing his own travels as a guest on a corporate jet as almost a pain to be endured. "We talk about the lavish comfort of flying in corporate jets, however, I think sometimes we should remember that some of these corporate jets, such as one I am familiar with in Idaho that a food processing company owns, will barely seat eight people," Symms said. "They are jammed in the airplane. I am sure that is one of the types of airplanes that the Senator from Ohio is referring to when he talks about lavish accommodations. Say, for example, the head of Corporation A is taking six of his employees somewhere with him on a business trip and somebody from another company or a 'hitchhiker' rides along. That passenger is then supposed to be imputed at first-class accommodations. I think the Senator should also be reminded that the corporate leader, whether it is the personal owner or head of the company, is in charge of the flight. The people who are riding along have to go at the whim of the other person's schedule. If you are riding on a commercial airliner, you can choose the flight that is most agreeable to your schedule. If you are riding with someone else, you may not be able to control the time."

Metzenbaum said he was confident that the people of Idaho would not agree with Symms and offered to come there to debate the issue. Symms declined. Soon Metzenbaum sat down. Packwood never varied from his claim that there was no sleight of hand, no giveaway. The debate prompted brief reports in a smattering of newspapers the next day reporting vaguely that the Senate had changed some tax rules on corporate travel. Afterward the giveaway to corporate executives that vexed Metzenbaum did indeed take place. But while Metzenbaum had fumed that valuing personal trips in corporate planes at the equivalent of first-class airfares was too good of a bargain, what transpired was a better deal for executives than even Metzenbaum feared.

Following the directive in the committee report, the IRS devised a formula for valuing personal use of corporate planes down to the hundredth of the penny per mile flown. At the end of 2002 the rates were as low as 9 cents a mile for small planes and no more than 83 cents per mile for the biggest jets on short flights. The highest rate was less than half what it costs to ride in a taxi. For a trip from New York to Los Angeles in a Hawker 800, a corporate jet that seats eight in luxury, the official rates valued the trip at $1,347 per person. That is about what a last-minute traveler would pay as the walk-up fare on a commercial jet, where the odds are high that one would be squeezed into a middle seat in coach. It was also far less than the first-class fare of more than $2,200.

An executive making this trip does not pay $1,347, however. He pays nothing. Federal Aviation Administration rules effectively prohibit payment for air travel by executives flying on company planes. Federal rules say that if the company charges for flights, it must meet the stringent operational practices of commercial airlines. (It would be easy to include an exception for executives making personal use of company planes, if there was any popular demand for it.) So to comply with the rule against accepting payment, companies count the value of the executive's personal trips as if it were income, just like the personal use of a company car, and all the executive pays are the income taxes on this amount. For an executive in the top tax bracket, the additional income tax on the cross-country flight in a Hawker corporate jet was $520 in 2002.

But even $520 for an executive to make a personal trip across the country in a private jet is more than Congress makes the executive pay. With one piece of paper an executive can get half off. All that is required is a memo in the corporate files saying that the company finds commercial air travel too dangerous and that for his or her own security the executive must travel in company-provided transportation. That one piece of paper cuts the cost of this personal trip in a corporate jet to $260 in federal income taxes.

The $260 in additional tax revenue that the government takes in from the executive is offset by the value of the tax deduction that the corporation claims on the jet. Even if only the direct costs are counted, on the cross-country trip in the Hawker the company gets a deduction that saves at least $3,500 in taxes. That means the minimum subsidy the taxpayers are providing to the executive is $3,240, the value of what the company saves in taxes offset by the $260 in taxes paid by the executive. Since a first-class ticket coast-to-coast costs about $2,200, it would be cheaper for the taxpayers to give away first-class tickets to executives rather than subsidize their personal use of company jets.

Defenders of this system note that executives usually travel with others who are their guests and that the rates apply for each guest. True enough. An executive who takes his spouse and two children on vacation pays taxes on the value of four passengers. His total expense for the coast-to-coast flight would be $1,040 if the reduced security rates apply to all four and $1,820 if the lower rate applies only to the executive. That is still less than the price of one first-class ticket.

To this day no one knows how much in total this stealth tax cut is worth to all of the country's senior executives or how much their combined personal travel costs shareholders and taxpayers. Indeed, the IRS does not even try to find out. The IRS says it has no policy on whether to examine such executive expenses at large companies. However, in dozens of interviews over the past six years not one IRS auditor who examines corporate tax returns could recall examining the expense accounts of a chief executive. This was despite the fact that chief executive expense accounts can run to millions of dollars per year, and even though it is routine to examine the same expenses in audits of closely held family businesses. Big corporations get a pass on the theory that no matter how large the spoon with which the chief executive sups, the money is not enough to be material to the company's tax bill. One auditor said that a request to look into deductions taken by a Fortune 100 company for a new jet, which according to news reports was used mostly for personal travel by the company's chief executive, was rejected by her superiors without explanation. "My branch chief told me that I was not to raise any questions about it," the auditor said.

The most diligent shareholders, who study the disclosure statements from the companies they own, would have no idea from examining these documents how much personal use of corporate planes costs them. Publicly traded companies are required to disclose salary, bonus and incentives as well as "other compensation" of the chief executive and the next four executives with company-wide responsibilities. Any component that is more than $50,000, or at least a fourth of the "other compensation," must be specified in a footnote. In his last year as GE chief executive, Welch's "other compensation" was $171,772, of which 83 percent was for financial planning advice, according to the company's proxy statement. That leaves little room to pay for personal use of the company's planes that Mrs. Welch valued at $3.5 million annually.

It was perfectly legal for GE to reveal nothing in its annual proxy statements about the value of Welch's use of company planes when he was chief executive. Welch and GE were able to hide these costs because of a Securities and Exchange Commission rule defining "other compensation." The securities regulators require the disclosure to shareholders of "other compensation" only when it involves an "incremental cost." That is, if a perk causes the company to spend additional money, then it must disclose it. But there is a way out of this, too. Welch was one of those executives with a memo in the file saying that for his own safety he was required to travel at all times on GE transportation. By the SEC's circular reasoning, personal use of a corporate jet to protect the executive does not create any incremental costs for the company because the executive has to travel on company planes for his or her own safety and therefore there is no extra expense to disclose.

Even the most careful student of GE's disclosure documents would never have known about the Boeing 737 or its real costs, however, as a personal taxi for the retired chief executive. Here in its entirety is what GE disclosed to shareholders about the retirement perks Welch would get and their cost: The GE board agreed in 1996 to "provide him continued lifetime access to Company facilities and services comparable to those which are currently made available to him by the Company."

Bud Crystal, the pay expert, told reporters who asked that Welch's use of the company plane and his other perks seemed ripe for investigation by both tax auditors and the SEC. Crystal reasoned that since Welch had retired and had left the board of directors, GE no longer had any business purpose in securing his safety through the use of company planes. "Tax deductions require a business purpose," Crystal noted. "What's the business purpose here?"

After the author detailed these issues, GE disclosed that the securities commission had opened an inquiry into Welch's perks and whether they had been properly disclosed. A few days later Welch, in a column for *The Wall Street Journal* editorial page, said that he would pay for the plane and the other perks. Welch said that the GE board in 1996 had offered him a special bonus of tens of millions of dollars if he would stay until the end of 2000, when he would be 65. Welch wrote that instead he asked to keep his executive perks, which he described as a bargain for GE, but without giving any specifics to support his claim. Because "perception matters," he wrote, he would pay GE between $2 million and $2.5 million annually for the use of its planes, the Manhattan apartment and other perks, again without saying what techniques were used to value them. Welch made a series of television appearances that day, where he answered one softball question after another, none of them examining how shareholders and taxpayers were forced to subsidize Welch's lifestyle until he agreed to pay for the perks. There was television chatter about the sanctity of contracts—a reference to Welch's employment agreement with GE, of course, not to his marriage contract.

The Welch divorce disclosures caused a change at GE, too. In its 2003 proxy statement GE was not required to disclose anything about the cost of personal travel on company planes by Jeffrey R. Immelt, Welch's successor. In the "other compensation" box the company listed just $49,093 for Immelt, the majority of which was for financial planning advice. But as a result of the Welch divorce disclosures, GE volunteered to shareholders that it spent $119,191 in incremental costs in 2002 for personal jet travel by Immelt, and a total of $684,820 more on its three vice chairmen. GE was not required to disclose anything about these costs because it required all four men to travel only on GE planes for security reasons. Laudable as this voluntary disclosure was, it did not reveal to shareholders the total costs, and no rule requires any company to do so. There is no serious move currently in Congress to require any additional disclosure of the costs of these perks. And nothing is being done to change the Federal Aviation Administration rule that prohibits companies from charging executives for the true cost of their personal use of company planes. That is a reform that could relieve taxpayers of the burden of subsidizing these executives while also discouraging the diversion of corporate assets for executive benefit.

Meanwhile, the company-car tax break sponsored by Senator Packwood, who is now a lobbyist on tax issues, remains, freeing many Americans from a burdensome rule to note every trip in their company car. Unlike the almost-free travel deal for executives, it is actually in the tax code. But so long as that little-known Senate Finance Committee report stands as policy, the taxpayers will continue to shoulder far more of the costs of personal travel in corporate jets than the executives who profit from this perk.

When the Old Man
Is Dead and Buried

"To keep farms in the family we are going to get rid of the death tax," the second President Bush said shortly after he took office, restating a major theme of his successful campaign. It was a powerful message, resonating with deeply rooted cultural values about the yeoman farmers who long ago cleared the Eastern forests, broke the Midwest sod and herded cattle to market across hostile territory, evoking nostalgia among many for a common experience largely lost to a world of urban and suburban office workers.

Soon after President Bush took office, both the White House and the American Farm Bureau Federation were asked for information identifying families who had lost their farms to the estate tax. After all, both had said repeatedly that to save the family farm, the estate tax had to be killed.

Weeks passed without any answer. The White House could not find one example.

The best that the Farm Bureau could do was R. Elaine Gunlad, whose California grape vineyard was hit hard when her husband died unexpectedly and she had to mortgage the land to pay taxes on his estate. But that case was two decades old—and Congress made sure it could never happen again in 1981 when it voted to defer estate taxes until the death of the second spouse.

Of course, even the White House and the Farm Bureau might have just been unable to find specific cases to support their rhetoric. So a reporter and a photographer from *The New York Times* traveled through the richest corn-growing counties in Iowa, knocking randomly on the doors of farmers, every one of whom turned out to be a Republican who had voted for Bush and many of whom were local elected officials. Not one of them had ever heard of a farm lost to the estate tax. Nearly all of them wanted to keep the estate tax, but with a higher threshold before any tax was due. The most common suggestion was applying the tax only to fortunes greater than $5 million.

One of these farmers was Harlyn Riekena, who started out teaching public school as a young man, but quit to farm, spending four decades growing corn and soybeans with his wife Marilyn and raising their children. The Riekenas worked hard and watched their money, like most farmers who manage to stay in business through bad weather, tight credit and unfavorable prices. Over the years they bought more land until they owned 950 acres of thick loam on the gently rolling hills outside Wellsburg in the best corn-growing region in the state, a comfortable home, several cars and investments. Their land alone was worth $2.5 million in 2001, but with what the couple described as modest tax planning they said that everything they had built up would one day pass to their children untaxed.

"For most farmers around here, the estate tax is not high in their minds," Harlyn Riekena said. "What we need are better crop prices."

At the Marshall County Courthouse, where the county supervisors, farmers all, were having coffee and discussing their community's problems, a reporter's question about how many farms had been lost to estate taxes drew leg-slapping laughter. The supervisors called in the county treasurer, who also farms part-time, and asked a local who was in the hallway, but none of them could recall any farm being lost because of estate taxes.

Many of the farmers said that repealing the estate tax was not about helping them—more per bushel for their corn and soybeans would do that—but about helping billionaires. Repealing the estate tax, they said, was about helping the Mars candy-making family and Bill Gates and, a few volunteered, the leaders of their party, President Bush and Vice President Dick Cheney, both very wealthy men.

Neil Harl, an Iowa State University economist whose tax seminars are so well attended that he is a household name among midwestern

farmers, searched far and wide for three decades for a farm lost to estate taxes without finding a single one. "It's a myth," Harl said.

Harl was aware of one case, from a television newscast, where a
family blamed the estate tax for the sale of their farm. But it turned out
that the widowed father would not prepare a will, would not take advantage of any of the estate tax breaks in the law and was in debt for
unpaid income taxes when he died, a careful viewer of the newscast
could discern. In this one case any loss was the fault of the farmer, not
the law.

That the White House and the Farm Bureau could not find any
examples to substantiate their claims is not surprising because few
farmers in America have the kind of wealth that would even make
them subject to the estate tax. The IRS statistics on estate tax returns
show why. Only 2 percent of the 2.4 million Americans who died in
2000 left an estate that owed any taxes. Of the 52,000 estates that paid
taxes, only 2,765 had any farm assets and their average value was
$149,000, far below the threshold for estate taxes. Compared to other
forms of wealth, farms were almost insignificant, equaling $3.16 out of
every $1,000 of taxable wealth. Art in estates was worth more than
twice as much as farms, but a campaign to save the family Rembrandts
and Picassos would not have won much popular support. Nor would
one to protect bank vaults stuffed with cash and bonds, each worth
more than 20 times as much as farms, or stock portfolios, which totaled 115 times as much as farms. As the farmers in Iowa knew, estate
tax repeal was not about the family farmer.

In 2000, an individual could leave $675,000 to heirs without ow-
ing any federal estate tax. A couple who wrote wills, at a cost of less
than $1,000, partly tax deductible, could pass $1.35 million of assets
tax-free. In Iowa the average farm was worth less than that, $1.3 mil-
lion. Congress also gave extra estate tax breaks for farmers and for small
businesses—and a farm is a business—that boosted the tax exemption
to $4.1 million. There was one hitch to the break for farmers, though.
To qualify, one of the heirs had to farm the land for a decade—that is,
he had to continue farming. But most of today's grown children, the
Riekenas and others said, want city jobs and when they inherit, they
put the family farm up for sale so they can enjoy the cash and a less ar-
duous lifestyle. Still, with the regular and small business exemptions, a

Farmers and Estate Taxes

Only 1 in 8 of the 49,863 taxable
estates in 1999 had any farm assets
and the average value was well under
the threshold to trigger estate taxes.

Size of Total Estate	Number of Taxable Estates with Farm Assets	Average Farm Value
$600,000 to $1 million	2,076	$ 244,974
$1 million to $2.5 million	2,917	$ 374,289
$2.5 million to $5 million	720	$ 649,263
$5 million or more	502	$ 1,335,440
All	**6,215**	$ 440,584

Estate tax exemption:

for any married couple	$ 1,350,000
for working farms owned by married couples	$ 4,100,000

Source: IRS Statistics of Income, Internal Revenue Code

couple could pass $2.6 million tax-free, far more than the value of all but the biggest farms, and with only modest estate planning, several times that amount could be passed on untaxed. A family with two or more children could also give their farm away a bit each year, taking a discount of a third or so on the value of the gifts because no one owner was in control.

A few days after the news hit that Iowa farmers were mocking the idea that estate tax repeal would save the family farm, Bob Stallman, president of the Farm Bureau, sent an urgent message to affiliates. "It is crucial for us to be able to provide Congress with examples of farmers and ranchers who have lost farms . . . due to the death tax," it said. Still, not one example could be found.

A few weeks later President Bush stopped in Iowa and said he had heard that it was being said that "the death tax doesn't cause people to sell their farms. I don't know who they're talking to in Iowa. I've talked to people who were forced to sell their farms in order to pay for the

Major Assets in Estates

Farms account for only a tiny portion
of all assets; liquid assets like stocks,
bonds, cash and retirement accounts
make up nearly two thirds of all assets.

Average value of all estates filing returns in 1999: $1,888,890

Type of Asset	Average Assets	Average Share of Estate Total
Stock, publicly traded	$ 622,448	33%
Cash	$ 209,675	11%
Tax Exempt Bonds	$ 198,025	10%
Investment Real Estate	$ 154,339	8%
Personal Residences	$ 132,114	7%
Stock, closely held	$ 120,481	6%
Retirement accounts	$ 93,359	5%
Federal Bonds	$ 66,885	4%
Farms	**$ 58,418**	**3%**
Insurance	$ 57,576	3%
Other Financial Assets	$ 47,475	3%
Other Assets	$ 44,215	2%
Mortgages and notes owned	$ 38,367	2%
Noncorporate business	$ 38,018	2%

Source: SOI Statistics of Income

death tax." The White House, which a few weeks earlier could not identify one such farmer, did not respond to repeated requests for the names of those the president said had talked with him.

Michael Graetz, the Yale law school professor who was a tax policy adviser in the first Bush administration, said that the Iowa farmers who scoffed at the second President Bush's assertion that farms were being lost to estate taxes had seen through a carefully orchestrated deception. The super rich were using a myth about family farms to get a tax break for themselves, he said. Even assuming for the sake of argument that the estate tax was forcing farms to be sold, Graetz said that the solution was not repeal of the tax but raising the threshold at which the estate tax began to apply.

"Protecting family farms and businesses from having to liquidate to pay estate taxes is no reason for exempting large liquid estates from tax," he said, referring to much greater amounts of wealth held in stocks, bonds and other financial instruments. "Wealth inequality has always been greater than income inequality."

The year before all of this, Congress had voted to repeal the estate tax and had the bill delivered to the White House on a tractor. President Clinton, in vetoing the bill, said, "Half the benefit of that bill that came here on a tractor goes to 3,000 people and I'll bet you not a single one of them ever drove a tractor."

The imagery, however false, was powerful enough that after years of not thinking about the estate tax, the Democrats had started to pay attention. They had let the top estate tax rate reach 55 percent, although the real rate paid by estates in 2000 averaged 24 percent. And while it was not a tax on death, but a tax on the right to transfer property, the phrase *death tax* took hold.

A Gallup poll found that 17 percent of Americans believed that they would pay the estate tax after death, more than eight times the actual figure. The Gallup finding may have uncovered middle-class hopes for their 401(k) accounts when the stock market was rising, as well as

Taxable Estates in 2000 by Size and Tax Paid

Actual estate taxes paid in 2000 were well below the statutory marginal rates of 37 percent to 55 percent; the tax rate of the largest estates is heavily affected by charitable bequests, which are deductible.

Size Category	Number of Taxable Estates	Average Value	Average Tax Paid	Effective Tax Rate
$600,000 to $1 million	18,634	$ 847,947	$ 41,270	4.9%
$1 million to $2.5 million	23,827	$ 1,490,693	$ 230,238	15.4%
$2.5 million to $5 million	5,917	$ 3,424,938	$ 858,768	25.1%
$5 million to $10 million	2,258	$ 6,884,752	$ 1,950,852	28.3%
$10 million to $20 million	814	$ 13,553,285	$ 3,608,721	26.6%
$20 million or more	549	$ 58,667,401	$ 10,418,672	17.8%
Total	**51,999**	**$ 2,507,141**	**$ 469,213**	**18.7%**

Source: IRS Statistics of Income

how deeply the Senate Finance hearings scared people with its bogus tales. Fear of the estate tax even reached down to taxi drivers, especially those who listened to talk radio. In New York, Washington and San Francisco it was easy to find immigrant cabbies who would regale their passenger with tales of how terrible it was that the IRS was going to come when they died and take half of whatever their families had.

There were two other factors that opponents of the estate tax effectively used to stir broad support: housing prices and the shift to retirement plans in which people own their own assets instead of getting a pension check. That year as many as one in 13 households had a net worth of $1 million and close to one in five had a half million dollars of net worth, assets that would be drawn down and spent in old age.

Donald D'Amato, president of the machinists union local at the Stanley Works in New Britain, Connecticut, said he had heard some of his members, who made about $14 an hour, argue for repealing the estate tax. D'Amato thought it was absurd to hear men with lunch buckets worrying about the rich, but as he listened he realized what was motivating such thoughts. "A working man who has never had any stocks or bonds, maybe just a savings account, gets one of these 401(k) plans," D'Amato said. "Then a statement comes every three months and it says he has a few thousand dollars or maybe a few tens of thousands and he starts to think he's a capitalist—until he gets laid off and has to spend the money to keep a roof over his kids' heads."

Congress had not adjusted the amounts of wealth that may be passed free of tax to take into account the spread of retirement plans in which workers owned their own plan instead of collecting a pension check from their employer. More than 40 million people now participate in such plans. The broad rise in residential real estate values also played a role. In the most productive urban centers, someone with a five-figure income who bought a house when she was young can retire as the owner of a house worth a million dollars, pushing her into taxable estate territory.

Trying to head off a stampede to end the estate tax, Representative Charles Rangel, a New York Democrat, introduced legislation that would have immediately raised the amount exempt from tax. Rangel wants to tax the rich and make sure they pay for the bounty they enjoy, but he proposed to exempt up to $4 million for a couple. President

Clinton said he would sign such a bill, but not sign one for outright repeal.

The Republicans were not interested in compromise. Their leaders said the issue was one not of setting higher thresholds, but of moral principle. A dollar saved was a dollar already taxed, the argument went, and the estate tax was double or triple or maybe quintuple taxation of that dollar. The timing of the bill did not suggest it was a moral issue, however. It delayed repeal for nine years into the future, until 2009. That delay meant years of opportunities to raise money from donors who could see the abyss coming and would be eager to speed up the effective date of repeal. And passing the legislation, knowing that Clinton would repeal it, was smart politics. It gave then-Governor Bush and his party a clear-cut issue for the fall elections—death to the death tax!

Sandy Schlesinger, a prominent New York estate lawyer, said the Democrats' offer of immediate relief in 2000 and their willingness to exempt 90 percent of small business owners from the estate tax was a good move. "The fact is that the Democrats are making the better offer—and I'm a Republican saying that," Schlesinger said. He said the estate tax was long in need of an overhaul and business owners who would die before repeal took effect would lose out. And if the threshold for a couple was set at $10 million, only about 1,200 estates each year would be taxed. There would still be plenty of work with trusts for lawyers like Schlesinger, even if the tax was repealed. It was the small-time lawyers who would need to shift their practices.

In Iowa, Professor Harl said that the Democrats were making an offer that would exempt virtually all working farmers, while keeping the tax for "the Ted Turners who own huge ranches and are not working farmers." Harl said he was surprised that farmers were not flooding Capitol Hill with calls demanding that their representatives take the Democrats up on their offer.

Few calls were made because the Democrats' offer of immediate relief for farmers and entrepreneurs received almost no news coverage. The big lobbies for farmers and entrepreneurs, the American Farm Bureau Federation and the National Federation of Independent Business, did not alert their members to the opportunity, either. One could view this as these organizations selling out their members, sacrificing immediate relief for them so that the real beneficiaries of estate tax repeal, the super rich, would ultimately escape the tax. Or maybe it was just a coalition of organizations representing the moderately rich promising to stick together with their partners among the super rich. When asked about this, leaders of both the Farm Bureau and the business federation said such a view was entirely wrong. The two lobbies said that they rejected the bird in the hand because of moral principle.

That Rangel and other Democrats were in a panic would have been unthinkable less than a decade earlier. The story of what changed is an important part of the secretive campaign by the very rich to shift the burden of taxes off themselves and onto everyone else. It begins with Patricia Soldano.

Soldano owns Cymric Family Office Services in Costa Mesa, California, which takes the hassle out of everyday life for the rich extended families whose wealth it manages. Cymric creates budgets for family members, pays their personal bills, manages their investments, keeps track of all the paperwork and prepares their tax returns with a focus on paying as little as possible. The name Soldano gave her firm refers to an ancient breed of pussycat with a double coat of fur that requires special grooming.

A prim middle-aged MBA who maintains a laser focus on the problems and desires of her clients, Soldano decided one day in the early nineties that the best way to serve them better would be to get the estate tax repealed. When Soldano first raised the matter in her intensely private and wealthy circle in Orange County, she encountered doubt. "I was told it couldn't be done, that no one cared about the estate tax except the people paying it," Soldano said. It was at the time the conventional wisdom—no one cared about the estate tax except two groups. One was the very rich, or at least those among the very rich who hated it but figured they had no one with whom they could make common cause. The other group was wonks who believed it was critical to ensuring that America would be a meritocracy and not an aristocracy of inherited privilege and power. Soldano believed she could change that wisdom.

Soldano hired Patton Boggs, a Washington lobbying firm, and built alliances to wealthy families with privately held companies and a public history of hostility to taxes, notably the candy-making Mars and wine-making Gallo families. She founded the Center for the Study of

Taxation. Despite its name there is nothing scholarly about the center. It publishes brochures opposing the estate tax, relying on anecdotes and witty quotes, not scholarship, to make its points. It is a pure marketing organization, no different from the big ad agencies except that it sells ideology instead of detergent.

She also hired Frank Luntz, the Republican pollster and idea man, to examine public attitudes toward the estate tax, along with pollster Peter Hart. Luntz believed that wording was crucial to shaping public opinion, that saying something the right way could sway voters and, if said the wrong way, could turn them off. That politicians did not seem to appreciate this and still got ahead fascinated him, as did the resistance of some of them to his ideas on the effective use of slogans.

"Classic example," Luntz said, "if you ask people, 'Would you be willing to pay more taxes to improve law enforcement?,' 51 percent of Americans would say yes. If you ask people, 'Would you be prepared to pay more taxes to halt the rising crime rates?,' 68 percent say yes. Same thing. Law enforcement is the process. Rising crime rate is the result. Half will pay more for process but two thirds will pay more for results. The key to this is how to wrap the language . . . the difference between a tax cut and tax relief. *Tax cut* is a political term that politicians offer in every election cycle. Tax relief is what the American taxpayer is actually looking for. They want a break. They don't want a political promise. They want their elected officials to give them a break."

Luntz didn't really want to do the Soldano project because he assumed, like her clients, that the estate tax was just a tax for the rich. There'd be no way to sell an effort to repeal it, he said, except to make it the caboose at the end of the tax cut train he was helping assemble in Washington.

But there was one little thing that intrigued Luntz, the phrase *death tax*. That phrase is usually attributed to James Martin, a conservative leader of older Americans. Luntz did not know or care where it came from, only how it played in focus groups and surveys. "I went out and looked at the difference between the estate tax, the inheritance tax and the death tax. And even back in '96, about half of Americans would support a repeal of the estate tax and 58 percent would support repeal of the inheritance tax and about 65 percent would support repeal of the death tax," he said.

After concluding that *death tax* was language he could change attitudes with, Luntz started selling. "I took it to every politician, every journalist, started using it in my own interviews, and right now, the only people who still call it the estate tax are lawyers. Now when you talk about repeal of the death tax, support is somewhere in the mid-70s, because the definition has changed. The same tax, roughly the same rates, but the definition of the tax, the focus of the tax, is no longer on millionaires, it's now on dying and death."

The term *death tax* is a superb example of marketing triumphing over reasoned debate. So thoroughly has the phrase been infused into Washington that many journalists, like White House correspondent David Gregory of the General Electric–owned NBC network, employ this term of advocacy instead of the neutral, and correct, term *estate tax,* without rebuke by their superiors. Even the usually scrupulously straight Dow Jones news wires used the phrase without qualification or explanation.

So had Luntz been advising the Democrats, what advice would he have given them to keep the tax?

"Honestly? They should raise the exemption from $1.5 million, raise it to $10 million, lower the top rate to 25 percent. If you cut the percentage to 25 percent, people think, Well hey, you still get to keep 75 percent. And you raise the exemption to $10 million, because Americans like round numbers."

And, he said, he would have taught the Democrats to always refer to "the billionaire's tax" because that was a fortune beyond the dreams of nearly all Americans. "We all want to be millionaires, but how many of us will actually ever be worth $10 million?" He said that if the Democrats could raise the exemption high enough, the movement to repeal it would collapse because it would affect so few families. Even so, he said, lowering the top rate would also be crucial because his surveys had convinced him that "right now Americans believe that the government shouldn't take half of anything, no matter how rich or successful you've been. Americans consider the 55 percent top rate confiscation."

It was, Luntz said, just the other side of the language he implored Republicans to use to eliminate the capital gains tax—call it the "savings and investment tax"—and to deflect voter concern about making

Social Security partly a private plan. He said the words *Social Security* should never be uttered, only *retirement security.*

"The overall message in all of this is: personalize. That's the key to winning the tax debate."

Another way to encourage repeal has been to raise dubious claims about the tax. One of the biggest is the statement, repeated often by Bush White House officials, that administering the tax and efforts to avoid it cost as much as the tax raises. It is a powerful claim. Soldano's Center for the Study of Taxation made exactly the same claim, but with nothing to back it up but a footnote to a Congressional document. And many news organizations have treated this claim as settled fact.

Charles Davenport and Jay Soled, professors at Rutgers University who teach estate tax law and business management, decided to investigate. They counted up the number of estate tax lawyers and looked at their fees. They examined sales of life insurance, trust company fees and other costs. In an exhaustively detailed report in the journal *Tax Notes* they showed that administering the tax and private efforts to avoid it total about six cents on each dollar of tax collected, not 100 cents. Neither Soldano nor any of her allies have produced evidence to the contrary, but they continue their claim, as does the White House, that the tax costs as much as it brings in.

Soldano and her allies sought to create the impression that opposition to the estate tax was overwhelming. They did so using Luntz polls that measured agreement and disagreement to statements like this: "Inheritance taxes represent double and triple taxation. It is unfair for people to pay taxes on income, and then more taxes on what they save, and a third time when they die."

Given how the statement was worded, it is surprising that only 79 percent of those surveyed agreed with it. Indeed, an earlier poll using almost the same language found 89 percent in agreement. The value of such loaded survey questions is that they allow politicians to appear authoritative when they tell voters on Sunday morning talk shows, "A survey shows that four out of five Americans oppose inheritance taxes."

There is a small problem with the question. It is based on a false premise. Some of the biggest fortunes in America have never been taxed, not even once. They have never shared in paying the price of civilization, as Justice Oliver Wendell Holmes defined taxes.

Without an estate tax and the related gift tax, huge untaxed fortunes could be built and passed on generation after generation tax-free. No one knows it better than the richest man in America, Bill Gates.

Microsoft began with a gift from his parents, Bill Sr. and the late Mary Gates. And in significant ways it was the taxpayers who made that gift possible. The father went to college on the GI Bill. The couple bought their first house with a VA loan. Those investments by the taxpayers paid off for the Gates family, as they did for millions of other Americans. The father became a successful Seattle lawyer. The couple had money to give their son to start his business, after he dropped out of Harvard, because the taxpayers also paid a salary to Mrs. Gates when she taught public school. So not only did the country's largest fortune begin with a gift that was tax-free, but also the gift money was there because of the taxpayers.

Many wealthy Americans who favor the estate tax do so because they understand that taxpayer investments like those made in the Gates family helped build our society and economy. That the supporters of *an* estate tax are led by Bill Gates Sr., along with billionaires Warren Buffett and George Soros, is an inconvenient fact for Soldano and her backers. They have worked so hard to create the impression that opposition is universal among all but estate tax lawyers and the random socialist or communist, yet here are these rich men saying keep the estate tax.

While Bill Gates himself has not lent his name to the cause, there is no question that he supports his father's work. He made his father president of the Bill and Melinda Gates Foundation (the largest private foundation in the world), which works to improve the chance that children born in poverty will get a shot at a healthy and successful life. And he has his own plans, which he will announce in his own time, that will eventually demonstrate his own awareness that his fortune was not the result just of his negotiating skills and smarts, but of public investments in his family, in education and scientific research and in the precursor to the Internet.

"What makes America great are the things we have done to strengthen equality of opportunity," Bill Gates Sr. and Chuck Collins wrote in their slender book defending the estate tax, *Wealth and Our Commonwealth*.

Gates Sr. had the integrity to acknowledge, on the very first page, that "it could be argued that a society based on opportunity for all could still flourish in a nation with great inequalities of wealth." He does not believe that, but he affirms that the other side has an idea worthy of debate. His principled conduct contrasts with the estate tax opponents who have vilified him and mocked him. Journalists asked him on one national television program if he wasn't a fool for favoring the government taking part of his grandchildren's inheritance. He said his grandchildren would have more than enough, that his worry was about all the poor children who would never get a chance like he did and like his son did if concentrations of hereditary wealth passed down untaxed forever.

Gates Sr., Buffett, Soros, Paul Volcker (the former Federal Reserve chairman), and thousands of other rich Americans who favor retaining and reforming the estate tax all stepped onto their soapboxes in broad daylight. They have willingly suffered the slings and arrows of the enemies of *any* estate tax, who hide in the shadows, as Soldano did for years when she hired well-paid political mercenaries to do the public debating.

Buffett believes that America has been a huge economic success because open political debate has helped to get the rules by which society functions right enough for both freedom and wealth to flourish. Without an estate tax, these rich men believe, America will have a growing concentration of power, not in the hands of the industrious or even the merely lucky, but in the hands of people whose only smart economic decisions were picking their parents and staying in their good graces.

Repealing the estate tax, Buffet said, is "the equivalent in economic terms of choosing our Olympic team by picking the eldest sons of the gold-medal winners in the 2000 Olympics. We would regard that as absolute folly in terms of athletic competition. We have come closer to a true meritocracy than anywhere else around the world. You have mobility so people with talents can be put to the best use. Without the estate tax, you in effect will have an aristocracy of wealth, which means you pass down the ability to command the resources of the nation based on heredity rather than merit."

Buffett said that he favors even higher estate tax rates so that the

majority of each giant fortune flows to government c⟨
ple dies to make America's dream available to the ⟨.
the same time he would raise the threshold for paying
was $1 million in 2003, so that it is focused on giant fortu⟨
own, not on the moderately rich.

Better to defer a tax until one is gone, Buffett said, than pay it dน̆
ing his lifetime. This is an important consideration, overlooked in the
"death tax" debate, because repeal of the estate tax means a heavier re-
liance on taxes paid during life such as income taxes. Simply repealing
the estate tax is yet another tactic by some of the richest Americans to
shift the burden of sustaining our society onto those with less. Yet this
issue is hardly mentioned in the debate and most news coverage has
contained only the unstated assumption that the estate tax is suspect,
without consideration of the moral issue of shifting burdens from the
richest Americans to those with less.

The idea that the estate tax promotes a society based on merit
rather than inheritance may not be valid. Does taxing large fortunes at
death encourage a meritocracy, as Gates Sr. and Buffett contend? Likewise, should we ponder whether the estate tax could be a way to require those who benefited the most economically from everyone's tax
dollars to give back?

Should we also debate whether, from a tax standpoint, it makes
sense to look at wealthy Americans the way they look at their stock
portfolios? There will always be investments that lag or go sour, just as
there will always be people who, because of illness, accident, crime or
their own shortcomings, will become *taxeaters,* burdening all of society. An investment portfolio makes up for losing investments by har-
vesting the winning investments so that, overall, there is a net gain.
One tax strategy would be to harvest from the gains of those who have
a large surplus to make up for the drag on the economy from the un-
fortunate who cannot be productive.

The debate about the estate tax largely ignores these questions.
There is no room for such thoughtfulness in a debate driven by slogans
such as "It's your money."

There is also room for mischief when politicians use Frank Luntz
slogans to win votes without having to present any detail of their plan.
Throughout the 2000 election George W. Bush would not give out

ıny details of his tax plan. But days after he took office a bill to repeal the estate tax was introduced for the White House. Buried in it was a massive giveaway to the super rich, one that voters had been given no hint of during the election.

The giveaway was in two provisions in the bill and how they interacted. Of all the journalists who wrote about the bill's introduction, few read it. Only by reading the bill and thinking about it could a huge new loophole be observed.

One provision retained the existing estate tax law rule that let inheritors of stock and other assets sell them without incurring any tax. It was known as "step-up in basis." It meant that whatever the original buyer paid for the stock, its purchase price, or basis, for the inheritors was its value on the day the owner died.

The second provision repealed the gift tax. At first blush it would seem that if the estate tax is repealed, there would be no need for a gift tax, which is what prevents someone on his deathbed from just giving his fortune to his heirs to avoid estate taxes. Repeal the estate tax and the need for a gift tax would seem to evaporate.

But the gift tax serves a second purpose. It is also a backstop to the income tax. Repeal the gift tax while retaining the step-up rule and a huge new loophole would be created for living Americans.

Imagine that you bought some stock that soared in value. To make the math simple, imagine the stock cost you a dollar and that it is now worth $100 million. If you sell the stock, you owe capital gains taxes, which in 2001 would have been $20 million, leaving you with $80 million. However, if the gift tax is repealed and the step-up rule is retained you could escape the capital gains tax.

Here is how: First, you give the appreciated stock to your favorite elderly aunt in a trust, which dissolves when she dies and the trust assets pass to you. The stock comes back to you under the step-up rules with a cost, or basis, not of the dollar you originally paid, but the $100 million it was worth when your aunt died. Now you can sell the stock and no capital gains tax would be owed.

Achieving this requires passing through some technical hoops, but the other person who immediately spotted the loophole was none other than Jonathan Blattmachr. Other tax lawyers looked at this idea and agreed that it would work if the Bush bill became law.

Blattmachr, who calls himself "a card-carrying Republican," said that the effect of simply repealing the gift and estate tax ignores the fact that the various federal levies interact like the pile in a game of pick-up sticks where removing one stick can change everything. With repeal of both taxes, he concluded, the already rich could live lavishly without putting another cent into the public till. "This will shift the tax burden from the wealthy to everyone else," he said, because the wealthy will no longer have to pay taxes.

That a gift tax is needed to ensure the integrity of the income tax should not have come as a surprise to the tax experts in Washington who were involved in drafting the tax cut legislation. The gift tax was adopted in 1924, sponsored by Representative William Green, the Iowa Republican who chaired the House Ways and Means Committee.

A gift tax "is needed on account of the income tax," he said on the House floor. Green said that wealthy men, all of whom, as Charles Dickens noted, have more than their fair share of poor relations, had been renting out the tax status of those relatives to escape income taxes at great cost to the government.

Representative Edward Denison, Republican of Illinois, dismissed such concerns. "While many attempts are made to beat the law in all probability . . . there are many gifts that are made in good faith."

Representative Green, in his reply, went straight to the principle of fairness at issue: "Whether they be in good faith or for the purpose of defrauding the government, the effect is the same . . . the government loses revenue that ought to be paid. I do not see why we should tax the man who has labored hard day by day and who accumulates small savings, sometimes a nickel or sometimes a dollar at a time . . . and then not tax a gift of $40,000 or $50,000. I cannot imagine."

Nearly 80 years later Douglas Freeman of Freeman, Freeman & Smiley, one of the biggest estate tax law firms in California, said the loophole Blattmachr found showed that the drafters of the original Bush tax cut bill either had planned the loophole or had not been very thoughtful. He said that without a gift tax, many other ways would be found to escape income taxes at huge cost to everyone who could not avail themselves of these techniques, which meant anyone not already seriously rich.

But the concern for such fairness that dominated Congress and the

White House in 1924 was gone by 2001. Senator Zell Miller, a Georgia Democrat who was one of the sponsors of the Bush tax cut bill, dismissed Blattmachr and Freeman as "propeller heads" whom no one should pay any heed. Ari Fleischer, the presidential press secretary, promised that the possibility of a loophole would be looked into. He went on to give a broader observation about the administration's attitude about loopholes and fairness in taxation. He characterized repeal of the estate tax as a moral issue, but did not apply the same standard to tax-free living for those who were already rich. That some wealthy Americans might exploit new loopholes to escape income taxes, Fleischer said, should not prevent "the many being relieved of the unfair burden of a tax that should not exist."

A cynic might also say that Blattmachr and Freeman were just trying to protect their lucrative work as estate tax lawyers. The problem with that argument is that repeal of the gift and estate tax would mean even more work for them in the short run and probably through the end of their careers. Even without the estate or gift levies, both men would have no trouble making a living from the myriad complexities of income tax law. Indeed, Soldano herself has said that repeal of the estate tax will not result in any less planning by the rich on how to manage their wealth.

In working to kill the estate tax, Soldano has no closer ally than Frank Blethen, publisher of the family-owned *Seattle Times* and owner of the Web site deathtax.com. He believes that the estate tax encourages the sale of family-owned businesses to publicly traded companies either in anticipation of the founder or majority owner's death or soon after. Such a sale, he said, eliminates any risk that the family may not have enough cash lying around to pay estate taxes.

"If you like corporate culture, and think America needs more of it, then you love the estate tax," he said. "I think this march toward corporatism is not healthy and we lose innovation, jobs and charitable giving."

When the loophole was explained to Blethen a few weeks after the President's bill was introduced, the publisher gasped audibly.

"That's not fair," Blethen blurted out.

It was one thing to repeal estate taxes, he said. But if and when inheritors sell an asset, they should not also be allowed to escape capital gains taxes on the appreciation in value over the years. One or the other, he said, not both.

For a few seconds Blethen, a ruddy-faced man in his midfifties with a short beard gone white, fell silent as he considered the significance of estate, gift and, for assets owned at death, capital gains taxes all being repealed. He wanted desperately to see the estate tax gone, but this unexpected news troubled him. Then he announced that he really disliked the idea because not only was it unfair, more importantly it was bad for family-owned business.

The problem Blethen perceived was in the incentive to heirs when the old man is dead and buried. The new incentive would be to sell the family business the minute he was gone.

Owning a business is for many a route to prosperity and even riches. The *Seattle Times* was founded more than a century ago with $3,000. Frank Blethen has rejected an offer of $750 million for his family's controlling half-ownership stake. But ownership of a family business also comes at a price. Most owners keep nearly all of their wealth in one basket, the family business. Instead of lots of cash and stocks and bonds that can be spent freely, their wealth is tied up in machinery, buildings and office equipment.

With no taxes of any kind due at death, he said, heirs would have a powerful incentive to sell right away. Right then would be their best opportunity to reduce the risk of having all their eggs in one basket (which economists call concentration risk) and to get cash to buy a diversified investment portfolio. The publicly traded companies would just love that, Blethen said, musing about how this could have gotten into the bill.

Didn't anyone think this through? he asked.

What America needs, he said, is to let capital gains taxes be deferred when the business owner dies, but only for so long as the family owns the business. That way families will own more businesses and publicly traded corporations will not be so dominant.

The prospect of having to hand over a fifth of the value of a business like the *Seattle Times* would encourage heirs to learn the family business and run it well, he said. "You want that tax liability there as an incentive to keep the business in the family, but if they sell, then they should have to pay their 20 percent tax right back to dollar one."

Now that the capital gains rate is down to 15 percent for the rich, that incentive to keep the family business has been reduced by a fourth.

Blethen's published remarks played a role in the stealth loophole coming out of the bill. So did two cleverly written requests to the Joint Committee on Taxation staff for its authoritative estimates on the cost of this stealth tax cut for the super rich.

John Buckley, the chief tax lawyer for the House Ways and Means Democrats, suspected that a direct question to the committee about the loophole might result in no answer or one he could not trust. So Buckley had two different requests for analysis sent to the committee staff. One asked how much retaining the step-up rule would cost the government. The other asked how much repealing the gift tax would cost. When the charts in the two estimates that came back were laid side by side, they showed a figure so large that even Blattmachr was surprised. The new loophole would save the richest Americans $250 billion in the first decade alone, an immense giveaway to the rich that almost slipped into law unnoticed.

Only when these figures became public did the White House quietly agree to revise the step-up in basis rule, limiting the benefit to $1.3 million, and to retain the gift tax.

The rest of the bill changed little, except that repeal was delayed until 2010. It was also limited to a single year. That was done because the costs in lost revenue were so huge that President Bush could not get the estate tax repealed and cut income taxes on the super rich by as much as he wanted. Repeal, thus, was clearly about political possibility and expediency, of balancing income tax cuts for those who make the most against estate tax cuts for those with the most wealth. It was not a moral issue after all.

Paul Krugman, the Princeton economist and fiery op-ed page columnist for *The New York Times,* wrote that the estate tax repeal bill was immoral because it created an incentive for murder. It should be called the "throw momma from the train bill," he wrote, because in 2010 some heirs were sure to consider knocking off parents who might live beyond December 31, when their fortunes would again be subject to the estate tax.

In 2003 President Bush was working to make repeal of the estate tax immediate and permanent. Whatever the fate of those efforts, they illustrate the drive by the political donor class to free itself from the burden of taxes and, in this case, to lift a burden from the fortunes of the dead and place it on the backs of the living.

When estate tax exemption takes effect, if it ever does, one of the clear winners will be Patricia Soldano, not just because she will have proved her doubting clients wrong, but because repeal will make her richer. The fees that her firm charges are based on the amount of wealth her clients have. With the estate tax gone, Soldano's clients will have more wealth on which she can levy fees.

While Washington continues efforts to ease the burden of taxes on the super rich, Congress is taking the opposite approach with the millions of Americans who make between $50,000 and $500,000. They make enough to be an attractive source of taxes, but not enough to join the political donor class and buy access to their senators and congresspeople. And what some of them are already finding out is that they are being squeezed to subsidize tax cuts for the rich.

The Stealth Tax

7

Promises of tax cuts are sweet music to Thomas and Cindy Toth, a couple in their thirties with three daughters, the youngest born in 2003. They are both very intelligent people who live within blocks of their parents in suburban Orange County, California. An outgoing, well-spoken guy who exudes warmth, he's from Chicago, where his Serbian grandfather prospered. She's first-generation Mexican American, Southern Californian and all Mom.

Tom is a trainer at the high-tech company that makes the telephone scramblers used by the White House. From his salary and a side training business he makes about $90,000. Only by skillfully buying their way up in the Southern California housing market were the Toths able to acquire their cottage-style home in Orange County with a fenced backyard where the children can play. They first bought a condominium in a rundown neighborhood, the kind they did not want for their children. That purchase let them hold down their housing costs and benefit from a rising market. After a year they were able to swing the mortgage on their 1,600–square-foot home, which cost $350,000, nearly four times their annual income.

The Toths are determined that Cindy will stay home even though, at least for a while, it means coping in suburbia with one car. At the age of 34, Tom focuses not on the struggle to support his family, however, but on his success, saying proudly, "I have the American dream."

The Toths were solid supporters of the Bush campaign in 2000, in

good part because of the promise that families like theirs would pay
less in federal income taxes. "When we first got married, I thought we
were going to die with all the taxes," Cindy said. "I truly believe that
if I worked, we would be hit harder with taxes." And they would, of
course, because they would make more money. Cindy would like to
see a tax break directed at couples with stay-at-home mothers, an idea
common in Europe, but also denounced by some leaders of her party
as a socialist idea to redistribute income.

Tom says that the $600 tax rebate check that the couple received a
year after George W. Bush was elected "wasn't a big deal for us, but it
sent the message that we have a surplus and we want you, the people,
to get your money back," Tom says. "It was basically our money anyway." The rebate came from lowering the tax rate on the first few dollars of taxable income from 15 percent to 10 percent.

While the White House said the rebates were for all taxpayers, one
in four households received nothing. Only 60 percent of households
received checks for the maximum—$300 for singles, $500 for single
parents and $600 for couples. Among the poorest fifth of married cou-
ples the average rebate was just a dollar. Among the 60 percent of Americans making $44,000 or less in 2001 the average rebate was $185. But
the affluent were another story. Among those making $72,000 or
more, a group slightly larger than the top 10 percent of the population,
virtually everyone received the maximum amounts cited by President
Bush. The reason for this disparity is that the rebate could not be more
than actual income taxes paid. Many Americans making $44,000 paid
less in tax than the rebate maximums.

Tom Toth says he is comfortable with the fact that not everyone received a rebate. And he is also comfortable with the aspect of the Bush
tax cuts that drew the most criticism, the fact that 43 percent of the income tax cuts, and more than half of the total tax cuts, go to the top
1 percent. "The top 1 percent is probably paying more than 43 percent
of all the taxes, so they should be getting the cuts," he said.

But Tom is mistaken. The tax burden on the top 1 percent is
nowhere near that high, although so many politicians and antitax advocates have made such false claims so many times that millions of
Americans believe it to be true. The top 1 percent paid 36 percent of

the income taxes in 2001. But when the burden of all federal taxes is added up—corporate profits, estate, gift, Social Security, Medicare and excise taxes—they only paid 25 percent.

When the Bush tax cuts of 2001, 2002 and 2003 are fully in place in 2010, the share of taxes paid by the bottom 95 percent of taxpayers will rise by 3.8 percentage points, while for the top 5 percent it will fall by the same amount. Nearly all of the tax savings will go to the top 1 percent, whose share will decline by 2.7 percentage points.

The official government data show that the burden on the very rich is even lighter. The federal Bureau of Labor Statistics, in its annual consumer expenditure survey, looked at the burden of local and state taxes as well as federal levies. This government survey does not break out the top 1 percent, but it does divide the populace into fifths. For 2001 the government found that all taxes at all levels of government consumed 19 percent of the incomes of the best-off fifth of Americans, those individuals and families whose average income was $116,666 that year. Down at the bottom the poorest fifth, whose average income was $7,946, paid 18 percent.

What this means is that the entire tax system at all levels amounts to a flat tax, one that is crushing the poor and one that does not extract the harsh levies so often cited by politicians who owe their allegiance to the political donor class. This leveling of tax burdens between those most able to pay and those least able to pay reflects the regressive nature of sales taxes on merchandise, excise taxes on various consumer goods and the high rate of property taxes in poor communities. The burdens of these taxes diminish as incomes rise.

To Tom Toth, like many Americans, such figures are mere details that miss the larger political landscape, which he sees as divided between "liberals who want to take my money and spend it" and those allied with President Bush, "who has my best interest as a taxpayer in mind." To the Toths the $600 income tax rebate was just a small start on what they expect will be significant tax relief with Republicans in control of the White House and Congress.

But the Bush tax code contains a nasty surprise for parents like the Toths and just about everybody else who makes $50,000 to $500,000, especially if they are married or have children. The Toths probably will not get their tax cuts in full. And if they have more children, they may not get any tax cuts.

The reason is another levy, one that few Americans have heard about even though it has been a part of the tax code since 1969. It is called the alternative minimum tax. It operates alongside the regular income tax, but in what Congress described in 1986 as a "parallel universe" with its own tax rates and its own stingy rules on what is deductible. The alternative minimum tax is also known as the "stealth tax" because of the way that it sneaks up on people. Most people are unlikely to be aware of the alternative minimum tax because most tax returns are prepared using computer programs, the software silently calculating the stealth tax in the background. The software calculates income and deductions under both the regular system and the alternative system and the taxpayer owes whichever is higher. Unless a paid tax preparer points it out, or one looks at line 43 of the Form 1040, the levy appears to be just wrapped into the overall tax bill.

For people whose income and deductions place them at the edge of each tax system, the alternative minimum tax's first effect is to reduce the value of their exemptions and deductions until they are gone. This causes more and more of their income to be taxable, which is why most people pay more on this tax than on the regular income tax. Officially there are only two rates in the alternative minimum tax, 26 percent and 28 percent, but as people phase out of the regular income tax and onto the alternative tax, their marginal tax rates can go as high as 35 percent.

In 1995 about 414,000 taxpayers paid this tax. By the year 2000 about 1.3 million taxpayers, roughly 1 percent, paid it and the Department of the Treasury estimated that by 2010 about 17.9 million families would pay it. That was before the Bush tax cuts began. The design of the Bush tax cuts doubled that number to 35.6 million households.

Between 2003 and 2012 the Bush tax cuts will force an increase of $560 billion in taxes to be paid under the alternative minimum tax, virtually all of it from the pockets of people like the Toths. This huge sum represents a subsidy by those who pay the alternative tax to those who get their tax cuts without being hit by the stealth tax. It is a subsidy of the super rich paid for by the middle class and the upper middle class.

Many More Will Pay the AMT

By 2010, the alternative minimum tax
will replace the regular income tax for
most upper-middle-class taxpayers and
many families, taking away part or all
of their Bush tax cuts.

Income Category (in thousands)	Year 2003	Year 2010	Average AMT in 2010 for Each Taxpayer
All taxpayers	2.6%	30.4%	$ 3,751
$30–$50	0.1%	6.9%	$ 809
$50–$75	0.5%	36.6%	$ 1,301
$75–$100	1.1%	72.9%	$ 2,023
$100–$200	9.3%	92.0%	$ 3,661
$200–$500	55.3%	96.2%	$ 12,206
$500–$1,000	28.9%	49.3%	$ 20,496
$1,000 or more	19.3%	24.3%	$ 117,302

Filing Status

Family of 4; $75,000 to $100,000	1.0%	97.2%	$ 2,855
Married Filing Joint	3.7%	53.5%	$ 3,946
Single Parent	0.8%	9.2%	$ 1,643
Singles	0.5%	2.4%	$ 4,749

Source: Tax Policy Center

What makes this upside-down subsidy truly astonishing is that the alternative minimum tax was enacted and refined over the years, with solid support by Democrats, to address the very rich who found ways to enjoy big incomes while paying little or no income tax. It was originally adopted to apply only to the richest taxpayers, those making the equivalent of more than $1 million in 2003. The periodic debates in Congress show that it was never supposed to apply to people like the Toths. But over the years, mostly when the Democrats controlled Congress, the law was tweaked again and again in ways that made a growing slice of people with middle-class and upper-middle-class incomes subject to the stealth tax. The Bush tax cuts magnified these effects.

News coverage of the Bush tax cuts focused on the $1.3 trillion total and on how the cuts were skewed toward the richest 1 percent.

Hardly any attention was paid to how the tax cuts only appeared to give tax breaks to the majority of the upper middle class and a large segment of the middle class. Most of the extra 17.6 million taxpayers who will lose part or all of their Bush tax cuts to the alternative tax are, like the Toths, parents raising children. The Democrats who denounced the Bush plan as a giveaway to the rich barely raised the issue of what was, by the Bush administration's own standards, a tax increase on these millions of Americans. To press the issue would have required pressing for the interests of families making six-figure incomes, which many Capitol Hill Democrats believe is at odds with showing their support for the three fourths of Americans making less than $60,000 a year. In not raising the issue, they in effect declared that prosperous families in the upper middle class are not part of their constituency now or in the future. With minimum debate in Congress there isn't much news to cover, so the public learns little about issues like the stealth tax.

The alternative minimum tax is also a nasty surprise for people who are victims of age, sex, religious or racial discrimination and prove their case in court. Nancy Hukkanen-Campbell worked in Missouri as a clerk and secretary for Local 101 of the International Union of Operating Engineers for six years until 1984. She quit after the repeated lewd advances and touching by her boss, Sam F. Long, the local's chief executive, escalated to what a judge called a "gun-enforced threat of rape." A judge awarded her more than $266,000 in damages, including lost wages. In 1993 she settled for $150,000, nearly half of which went to her lawyers. The IRS then audited Mrs. Hukkanen-Campbell and said she owed taxes on the full amount because, under the alternative minimum tax, she was not entitled to deduct the fees paid to her lawyers. The IRS acted because Congress had passed a law denying deductions for legal fees in cases unless there was physical injury. Had her boss used the gun, then the legal fees would have been deductible under the alternative tax.

Mrs. Hukkanen-Campbell sued the IRS over the $17,000 in additional taxes, but lost in Tax Court. On appeal to the Tenth Circuit Court of Appeals she also lost. Judge Monroe G. McKay, writing for a unanimous three-judge panel, expressed sympathy with her plight, however. "Congress, not this court, must correct any shortcomings in the AMT's application," Judge McKay wrote. The Bush administration

filed a brief opposing a hearing before the Supreme Court, which refused to hear her appeal.

Mrs. Hukkanen-Campbell says she is angry at Congress. "It was a
very long hard fight just to get this case to court, and the judge found
for me," she said. "I settled for less than what the judge gave me, and
now the government is leaving me with almost none of my lost wages
and pension benefits. It's just not fair."

Victoria L. Herring, an employment discrimination lawyer in Des
Moines, had a client who was awarded $1 in actual damages and $15,000
in punitive damages in a job discrimination case. A judge also awarded
him $170,000 in legal fees, most of it because of what the judge found
were extraordinary tactics by the other side to thwart the litigation. The
IRS notified the man that he could not deduct the money paid to his
lawyer. That meant he pocketed $15,001 and was required to pay
$67,791 in alternative taxes. "My client won, but he is far worse off for
having brought this case," Ms. Herring said. "It is simply not fair."

The alternative tax is also morphing into an unexpected tax on
family businesses. Six members of the Charles Allen family of Seaford,
Delaware, whose Allen Family Foods is one of the largest chicken growing and processing operations in Delaware, were told after an IRS audit
that they owed $255,000 more for 1994 and 1995 because of the al-
ternative tax. They sued in Tax Court and in 2002 Judge David Laro
issued a decision against them that challenged the long-held notion
that the regular income tax and the alternative tax operated in parallel,
but separate universes.

Judge Laro held that the two tax systems interact when it comes to
certain tax breaks, like a tax credit that the Allen family took for providing jobs to people who had been chronically unemployed. The judge disallowed this tax credit, as had the IRS, because of the alternative tax. As
a result of Judge Laro's ruling, the alternative tax "may also have unfore-
seen implications in other investment situations where business tax credits get involved, such as the low-income housing credit," Burgess J. W.
Raby, an Arizona tax lawyer, and William L. Raby, an accountant, wrote
in the journal *Tax Notes*. They said business owners and their lawyers must
now evaluate interactions between the regular and alternative tax systems,
some of which may not occur until years after a deal is made. That
would add both complexity and uncertainty to investment decisions.

What happened to the job discrimination victims and the Allen family is certainly not what Congress intended when it imposed the tax. What will happen to the Toths is not what the law originally intended, either. But over the years Congress tweaked the law in small ways that cost people like the Toths, Nancy Hukkanen-Campbell and the Allens. The design of the Bush cuts, however, marked an explicit wholesale shift in the burden of the alternative tax, giving relief to the super rich and making it the fastest growing tax on middle-class and upper-middle-class families like the Toths.

In the first decade of this century the stealth tax is expected to grow at a compound annual rate of 31 percent. It cost everyone $9.6 billion in 2000. Those making $1 million or more paid 28 percent of that amount. By 2010 it will cost $141 billion, but just 5 percent will come from those making more than $1 million a year, the only people it was supposed to apply to when it was originally adopted. And for the super rich, the 130,000 richest families, the alternative minimum tax will disappear.

The future growth in the alternative minimum tax falls mostly on those who are not rich. For each dollar of alternative minimum tax paid in 2000, in the year 2010 those making $1 million plus will pay $2.60, while those making less than $1 million will pay $19.40.

This massive increase in the alternative tax, and the shift in burden, is a stealth tax increase in 2010 alone of $131 billion for those making less than $1 million annually. People in the Toth's income group on average will be denied 42 percent of their Bush tax cuts in 2010 because of the alternative tax, and sooner if the Bush tax cuts are accelerated. Families in high-tax states like California will lose more than the average. So will families with more than three children. Many large families in high-tax states who make from $50,000 to $100,000 will never see a dollar of the Bush tax cuts.

The Brookings–Urban Institute studied the issue and concluded that in 2010 about 97 percent of families with two children whose income is between $75,000 and $100,000 would be forced off the regular income tax system and onto the alternative minimum tax. "This is a cop married to a nurse," said William G. Gale, a Brookings Institution economist. It is also a couple with no access to the exotic tax avoidance strategies used by many of the super rich.

The analysis also found that what forces people off the regular income tax and onto the alternative minimum tax is heavily influenced by family status. Leonard E. Burman of the Urban Institute said that "we're talking about a really nasty marriage penalty because you are 25 times to 30 times more likely to be on the alternative minimum tax if you are married rather than single."

If the Toths prosper, either because Tom's salary grows or his side business takes off, or because Cindy goes back to work, things will get worse for them under the Bush tax cut plan before they get better. For families making between $100,000 and $500,000 the alternative tax will take away on average more than 71 cents of each dollar in Bush tax cuts in 2010.

Things begin to change, however, if the Toths become hugely successful. If their annual income grows to more than a half million dollars, then in 2010 they will get to keep most of their Bush tax cuts. Those making a half million to a million dollars will lose on average 18 cents of each dollar of their Bush tax cuts. Those making more than $1 million will lose just eight cents on the dollar. Among those in the million-dollar-and-up income category, most of the alternative tax will be paid by families whose income is either just above the million-dollar threshold or who have profits from a tax-favored form of compensation known as incentive stock options.

As a corporate trainer, Tom Toth has virtually no chance of ever earning a big enough salary to be assured all of his Bush tax cuts. To get his income above $1 million annually, he would have to switch careers or go into business for himself, both risky propositions for a family struggling to pay a big mortgage, and then he would have to experience extraordinary success in business. More likely the Toths, and millions of other Americans in their income category, will just have to live with being cheated out of what they were promised to subsidize the tax cuts for the super rich, who will get all of what the Bush campaign promised.

What is this alternative minimum tax? And what purpose is it supposed to serve? It was born in the final days of the Democratic Johnson administration. Lyndon Baines Johnson had tried to finance wars on two fronts, in Vietnam and against poverty, in the belief that America was such a Great Society that it could afford both guns and butter.

Joseph W. Barr, who was Johnson's Treasury secretary for less than two months, went to Capitol Hill three days before President Johnson's term ended to deliver a routine economic report. He also disclosed that 155 households paid no taxes in 1966 despite adjusted gross incomes of at least $200,000, which would be roughly $1 million in 2003. Many economists within Treasury regarded the number as meaningless or, at best, as an indication of a need to tighten the tax code a bit. But Barr's announcement struck a nerve with the public. People had been hit with surcharges on their income taxes to pay for what was starting to become an unpopular war in Southeast Asia. Americans in 1969 bombarded Congress with more angry letters about those 155 nontaxpaying rich families than about the war in Vietnam, according to Professor Michael Graetz, a Yale Law School tax professor and a tax policy adviser to the first President Bush.

Congress and President Nixon responded to this popular outcry by adopting its first version of a minimum tax, which limited the use of a laundry list of tax breaks. Anyone could use the tax breaks on this list up to $30,000 (the equivalent of about $150,000 in 2003). But above that there was a tax of 10 percent applied to each dollar deducted. The law was designed to make sure that people with large incomes could not take advantage of so many deductions and tax breaks that they paid nothing. It failed. The design of the original alternative tax was so flawed that by 1974 the number of high-income families that paid no tax had grown to 244.

Over the years Congress changed the minimum tax rules repeatedly, but the number of people who had big incomes and paid no tax continued to creep upwards. In 1982, Congress tried a new approach, one close to the current alternative minimum tax. In an effort to make sure that everyone with a high income paid some tax, Congress labeled some deductions and exemptions "tax preferences" and limited how many could be used in any one year. The preferences were all items that applied mostly to very high income people, such as the lower rates at which capital gains are taxed and the oil depletion allowance, which lets people with black gold in the ground count as income only 87.5 percent of their oil royalties. Still a few hundred people each year found a way to enjoy big incomes and pay no tax.

The alternative tax could have been eliminated in 1986, when the income tax system was overhauled and most tax shelters were killed.

There was serious talk at the Department of the Treasury and on Capitol Hill about doing just that. But keeping it solved a little problem in the 1986 Tax Reform Act, one with important implications for understanding what the administration did in 2001.

Back in 1980 Ronald Reagan had been elected president on a platform that promised tax cuts. The top income tax rate back then was 70 percent, and avoiding such a high rate created a vast market for tax evasion tricks. In Reagan's first year the Congress lowered the top tax rate to 50 percent. It was a key part of supply-side economics, which was supposed to unleash extraordinary economic growth that would benefit everyone by cutting taxes on the rich so that they would invest more.

Five years later the supply-siders were pushing to lower the top tax rate down to 28 percent, a rate paid by the upper middle class as well as the super rich. To achieve this the 1986 Tax Reform Act broadened the definition of income that was taxed and it killed most tax shelters. That added enough money to what was immediately taxable that the top rate could be slashed to 28 percent. This reform came, however, in an era of huge budget deficits and fears that they would continue for years to come. To win enough votes in Congress to become law, the 1986 tax overhaul also had to be revenue neutral. That meant the same amount of money had to come in under the revised tax laws as would have been raised by the existing rules. And therein lay a billion-dollar problem, a fiscal seed from which a mighty thicket would grow to ensnare people like the Toths.

Eugene Steuerle, an economist who worked at the Department of the Treasury in the 1980s and who has been one of the most thoughtful observers of tax policy in the past two decades, noticed in 1986 that the computer models the government used to estimate the effects of tax changes showed a problem in 1986. The overhaul would, the computer models showed, raise about $1 billion less than if the system were left alone. In Washington $1 billion is not much, about $4 for each American. But that last billion had to come from somewhere because revenue neutrality was the price of passage, the lynchpin holding together the bipartisan coalition for tax reform.

The Reagan White House was adamant that *this* billion dollars was not going to come from the pockets of the rich. Any suggestion of taking back some tax favor that affected only the very rich was beyond discussion. So was any thought of a tax rate higher than 28 percent, a number that took on almost magical qualities, as if the figure 29 percent would doom the nation to economic ruin.

To plug that last billion-dollar hole, the list of tax preferences that would trigger the alternative minimum tax was lengthened. Added to the list were the exemptions that taxpayers get for themselves and for their children plus deductions for some medical bills and even the standard deduction. Congress, with Democrats controlling the House and Republicans the Senate, and the Reagan administration decided to treat as tax shelters you, your spouse, your children and that most passive of all deductions, the standard deduction for people who do not itemize.

Steuerle, whose name in German means "little tax," warned at the time that tacking "normal, routine deductions and exemptions that everyone takes" onto the list of preferences would eventually turn the alternative minimum tax into a levy on a group it was never intended to apply to: the middle class.

The White House and key members of Congress never thanked Steuerle for his observation and they ignored his wise counsel. After all, they reasoned, even Steuerle was talking about a problem that would arise "eventually," meaning after the incumbent was out of office. Resolution of the problem could be left to some future administration. By 2003 the cost of interest on this debt, which was growing again, was devouring almost a fourth of all federal income taxes. And falling interest rates did not help much because the government had lots of high-interest 30-year bonds in the market. This rising debt means passing a heavy burden to future presidents and future generations of Americans so that some can pay less in tax to pay for current spending.

In 1987 just 140,000 income tax returns showed any alternative tax was due. The tax paid was $1.7 billion, well above the official estimate. Those who paid owed on average $12,000. It was that year a tax was imposed on those with very high incomes who took excessive deductions, just as Congress had intended when the levy was first drafted. But the policy of making sure that at least every person with an adjusted gross income of $200,000 paid some tax still failed. That year 472 of these high-income Americans paid no income tax, more than triple the number in 1966, and 364 of them paid no income tax anywhere in the world. And it appears these taxpayers were not using tricky tax shelters, but just had unusual combinations of circumstances that let them fall into a no-tax zone.

In the 1981 Reagan tax cuts Congress had made one very significant decision, which hardly anyone noticed at the time, about inflation in the parallel universes of the regular income tax and the alternative minimum tax. Under the regular income tax the tax brackets, along with personal exemptions and many deductions, would be automatically adjusted for inflation each year. Not so the alternative. The reason? It held down the cost of the Reagan tax cuts in years ahead. The result was that the regular income tax was largely insulated from inflation, while the alternative tax began a steady shift downward, affecting fewer and fewer of the rich, but an increasing number of people farther down the economic ladder.

By 2000 those making more than $1 million were paying just 28.3 percent of the alternative minimum tax even though they were the only group who should have paid anything under the original plan. Those making $100,000 to $500,000 paid more than half of the alternative tax. And that year 12,000 people making less than $30,000, some of them single mothers, were forced to pay the alternative tax.

In 2000, in the back pages of a routine report that the IRS filed with Congress without seeking any news coverage, it revealed that a family with five children who made $70,000 and took the standard deduction would lose some of that standard deduction to the alternative tax. Just two years later Philip Schwindt, a tax analyst with CCH, a major publisher of tax information for accountants and tax lawyers, calculated that by the year 2006 one-child families with $71,000 of income would get hit by the alternative tax. And families at that income with two or more children would see their tax credits for child care and college education expenses either reduced or wiped out.

In the year 2000 about one in every 100 taxpayers was affected by the alternative minimum tax. For the income group that includes the Toths, those making $75,000 to $100,000, one in 40 taxpayers was affected. The average cost for the nearly 9 million households in this group was $28 per taxpayer, a trifle. The stealth tax is sneaking up fast, however. By 2010 it will affect 8 of every 10 taxpayers in the Toths' income group and deny them on average 42 percent of their Bush tax cuts.

One of the first families to feel the sting of this stealth tax were the Klaassens of Marquette, a Kansas farming town of 500 people about 80 miles north of Wichita. David and Margaret Klaassen and their 13 children constitute almost 3 percent of the local population.

Dave Klaassen is a lawyer who works out of the family home. Margaret is his secretary. Like the Toths, they are salt-of-the-earth people, the kind anyone would want as their next-door neighbors. In 1997 the Klaassens made $89,751, a modest sum considering the size of their family. One way the couple pinches pennies is by doing their tax return themselves the old-fashioned way, with pencil to paper on forms they get for free from the government. The taxes-owed line came to $5,989, almost seven cents of each dollar of income.

The IRS computers flagged their tax return and sent the Klaassens a notice demanding $3,671 more. Dave Klaassen immediately grew irritated because he had been meticulous in filling out the forms, especially since his family was on such a tight budget that he had to take care to avoid unexpected expenses. Most of the extra money the IRS demanded was the alternative minimum tax. But it also included a few dollars of interest and a penalty for not having paid the stealth levy. That this tax would apply never even occurred to Dave Klaassen until the IRS demanded more money.

The notice did not explain in any meaningful way the reasons that the Klaassens owed more. Like most IRS notices, it was more chart than letter, long on taxspeak and short on plain English. Dave Klaassen set to work reviewing his income tax returns and soon realized that extra tax was due because of the size of his family and their medical bills. And the IRS said the Klaassens owed more for prior years, too, including $1,085 for 1994.

Doubting the IRS's math, Dave decided to test what would have happened had he filed the same tax return, but had fewer children. He found that if he had seven or fewer children, the alternative tax would not have applied in 1994. But the eighth child set off the alternative tax at a cost of $223. A ninth child raised the bill to $717. And 10 children, the number the Klaassens had in 1994, increased the tax bill by $1,085, the exact amount that the IRS said was due in extra taxes for 1994.

Dave Klaassen could hardly believe what his own work showed him. And it made him angry because he had never cut corners on his taxes. "I've never invested in a tax shelter," he said. "I don't even have municipal bonds. We love this country and we believe in paying taxes. But we cannot believe that Congress ever intended to apply this tax to our family solely because of how many children we choose to have. And I have shown that we are subject to the AMT solely because we have chosen not to limit the size of our family."

What really hurt was the denial of a deduction for about $2,200 of medical bills, money spent on their son Aaron, who soon after his birth in 1982 developed leukemia. Under the alternative tax the amount of medical bills that cannot be deducted is one third larger than it is under the regular income tax. Aaron's childhood cancer had gone into remission, only to return in his teenage years. "What kind of policy taxes you for spending money to save your child's life?" Mr. Klaassen asked. A corollary question would be how could those members of Congress who pose as pro-family advocates have allowed this to happen without their at least making a major issue out of it?

The Klaassens appealed to the IRS. Too bad, the auditors and appeals officers told them. Congress says you owe and we have no discretion, so pay up. Unlike a traffic cop, who can choose whether to write a ticket or only issue a warning after pulling you over, or the prosecutor who can decide whether to charge a suspect or let him go, Congress gives the IRS no discretion when it comes to ordinary citizens whose returns are audited. If an audit shows tax is due, then billing is automatic.

There is one way that ordinary Americans who are not bankrupt can get out of an IRS demand for more taxes following an audit. It is to vigorously apply all of the complex taxpayer rights protections that Congress enacted in several stages in the late 1990s. The hope here is that the IRS will give up. Tax protesters sell books and run seminars teaching people how to gum up the gears of tax law enforcement by playing games with the IRS. The tactics include demanding hearings at every stage of the proceedings, filing lots of frivolous paperwork and even making false accusations against IRS agents so that they will come under investigation, as required by the 1998 law. The theory of such tactics is that, because of their piling on extra and unpleasant work, the IRS worker assigned the case will make a mistake that will end the effort to collect, such as missing a deadline or misplacing a file. The odds that such tactics will work improve as the IRS budget is constrained and the agency drops cases because of the flood of new ones coming in.

Dave and Margaret Klaassen had no interest in playing games with the government. They were confident that a judge would see how unfairly they were being treated and so they took the IRS to Tax Court. The IRS, in defending its demands for more tax, noted that there is no right to any tax deduction or exemption or break. The language granting Congress the power to tax is broad. Article I, Section 8, of the Constitution says simply, "Congress shall have power to lay and collect taxes." Any tax breaks, the IRS noted, are by "legislative grace."

The judge who heard their case, Robert N. Armen Jr., had plenty of sympathy, but said he could do nothing. He said that the way the law was written, it seemed clear that Congress intended to tax large families. The IRS, he held, was just applying the law that Congress had passed and Ronald Reagan had signed into law. Tax Court is not a court of equity, of fairness, with Solomon-like powers, but an administrative court whose duty is to mechanically apply the law as written. An appeals court upheld Judge Armen.

The Klaassens were devastated, not just financially, but emotionally, by the decision. The incident shook their faith in their idea of America. "This law was passed to catch people who use tax shelters to avoid their obligations," Dave Klaassen said. "But instead of catching them, it hits people like me. This is just nuts."

Millions of people like the Toths who believe fervently in the idea of lowering taxes, and who supported the Bush campaign because of its tax cut promises, are going to find themselves in the same predicament as the Klaassens in the years ahead. And, like the Klaassens, most of them have little or no idea that they will not get what they were promised or that the Bush tax cut plan was profoundly unfair to many families making $75,000 to $500,000. This ignorance did not come about by any fault of taxpayers. Their elected leaders tricked them. Jane Bryant Quinn, the influential personal finance columnist for *Newsweek* magazine, described the Bush 2001 tax cuts as "a contemptible piece of consumer fraud." *Time* headlined an article on the bill "Stupid Tax Tricks."

During the 2000 campaign the Bush camp refused to discuss the details of its tax plan and specifically would not go into details about how it would interact with the alternative tax. The Bush campaign Web site prominently displayed an interactive feature that allowed people to plug in their income and family status to learn how much they would save under the Bush plan. The numbers were generous. That was because the alternative minimum tax was not taken into account in the Web site calculations. Also, the Web site worked only for incomes of $100,000 or less, obscuring the way the plan was crafted to favor the highest incomes.

The exclusion from the Bush campaign Web site of the effect that the alternative minimum tax would have was not for lack of knowledge. Among economists it was well known that the alternative minimum tax was a growing problem for upper-middle-class taxpayers. The chief architect of the Bush tax cuts was Lawrence B. Lindsey, President Bush's chief economic adviser during the campaign and later director of the National Economic Council at the White House. Lindsey said that he worked on the Bush tax cut plan for two years. Interviewed after the election, he said that he was fully aware of the alternative minimum tax.

Once he was in office, President Bush had to lay out the details of his tax cut plan in the form of a bill. That gave him an opportunity to address the alternative minimum tax so that everyone would get the full tax cuts he promised on the campaign trail. President Bush let the opportunity pass. His bill ignored the issue, but what he signed into law did raise slightly, and temporarily, the amount of deductions and exemptions that taxpayers could take before the alternative minimum tax cut in. For couples the threshold was lifted to $49,000 from $45,000. But even the higher threshold was less than a third of the original 1969 level adjusted for inflation. The $49,000 threshold is not nearly enough for families like the Klaassens and, in the years ahead, the Toths. So they will lose some or all their exemptions for themselves and their children, as well as their deductions for state and local income and property taxes.

When the 1997 tax cut law was passed, marketed by politicians as middle-class tax relief, its centerpiece was a child credit. The sponsors, House Republican leaders, had it start out at $400 and grow over time to $1,000 per child, although because of inflation it would be worth only about $861 when the full credit was in place. The fine print showed that the credit was available only to a narrow band of families—those that made less than $110,000 and those that paid in income taxes at least as much as the credit. There was no debate at the time about how the credit was not available to couples making more than $110,000. However, some Democrats complained that the credit was unfairly being denied to those who paid little or no tax and they proposed to make the credit available even if the government had to write a check, the way it does with the earned income tax credit. They lost.

What the sponsors knew, but did not mention, was that the alternative minimum tax would take away the child credit for millions of families. One member of Congress, a former high school economics teacher from Massachusetts named Richard Neal, saved the credit from the alternative tax.

Neal, a vociferous critic of laws that shower tax favors on the rich, seized the issue and made it prominent enough that in 1998 Congress agreed, temporarily, to exempt the child credit from the alternative tax. As soon as Neal raised the issue during the debate over the 2001 Bush tax cut proposals, it was agreed to make this exemption permanent. But even with the child credit safe, so many taxpayers will still lose their exemptions for themselves and their children to the alternative tax that the number of people paying it will double between 2001 and 2010. And most of those who get hit will be families like the Toths, who, if their income goes up much more, will also lose the child credit because the Republican sponsors of the bill believe that they would then make too much to deserve it.

Just as it would not discuss the alternative tax in detail during the campaign, the Bush White House tried hard to avoid addressing the issue after the election. Four months after President Bush was sworn in, Mark A. Weinberger, the Treasury assistant secretary for tax policy, finally made the new administration's first substantive comment on the alternative minimum tax and how it was sneaking up on millions of Americans. In an interview with this author, he acknowledged that the tax cuts that President Bush was asking Congress to make would never materialize for millions of families, but he said the tax cut plan would not be revised to prevent this.

"President Bush was elected on a promise to cut taxes, not to reform the alternative minimum tax," Weinberger said. He vowed that once the Bush tax cuts were enacted, the administration would turn its attention to the alternative tax. President Bush signed the tax cuts into law on June 7, 2001, less than five months after he took office. Despite Weinberger's assurances that the alternative minimum tax would be dealt with once the tax cuts became law, the administration did nothing.

In the fall of 2002, 15 months after the tax cuts were passed, the president proposed another round of tax cuts, again designed to over-whelmingly benefit the highest-income Americans, the thin and rich slice at the top of the top 1 percent. The centerpiece of this plan was to make dividends tax-free, at least for people who did not own them in their 401(k) and other retirement plans, as most of the middle class and the upper middle class do.

And what of the promised action on the alternative tax so that the middle class and upper middle class would get their Bush tax cuts? It did not make it into the second round of Bush tax cut proposals. Pamela Olson, who succeeded Weinberger as the top tax policy official at Treasury, said in late 2002 that the Bush administration had not forgotten about the problem or its promise to address the issue. She said that a study of how to address the alternative minimum tax would be made beginning in 2005. By then President Bush will either be in his second term or be out of office.

The design of the Bush tax cuts made sure that the very rich, those making $1 million or more per year, got nearly the full measure of the cuts that candidate Bush promised. Not so those making less. To hold the cost of the tax cuts to $1.3 trillion over the first 10 years, someone had to lose out. The administration could have decided to cut the top tax rate of 39.6 percent to 36 percent instead of 35, for example. It could have revised the alternative minimum tax to make it fall more heavily on the very rich so that those making less than $1 million or $500,000 could be exempted. Instead, the administration relied on the stealth approach of letting the alternative tax silently take back from those making less than $500,000 a year some or all what they were told to expect. This design meant that the upper middle class, families mak-ing $75,000 to $500,000, would subsidize the tax cuts for those in the million-dollar-and-up income class.

The Bush tax cuts will start sweeping large numbers of middle-class and upper-middle-class families into the alternative minimum tax in 2005, according to a study by Jerry Tempalski, a career staff economist with Treasury's Office of Tax Analysis. Tempalski issued periodic reports on the alternative minimum tax for years. His last public report was issued during a speech in 2001 to the annual conference of the National Tax Association, where the audience was stunned by his presentation showing that that most people making $75,000 to $500,000 will never get their full Bush tax cuts.

Based on data from the Department of the Treasury's own computer model, Tempalski revealed that:

- In 2004 about 64 percent of taxpayers who make $200,000 to $500,000 will be subject to the stealth tax because of the Bush tax cuts, instead of the 36 percent who would have been affected without the Bush cuts.
- In 2004 about 5.6 million families will pay the alternative tax. The next year the number affected will more than double to 13.4 million families.
- By 2010 there will be 17.2 million additional taxpayers forced onto the alternative minimum tax because of the Bush tax cuts.
- About 10 million of these will be households making $100,000 to $200,000.
- In that income category about 85 percent of all households will be forced onto the alternative minimum tax.
- By 2010 about 8.6 million households will be denied their entire Bush tax cuts because of the alternative minimum tax.
- Alternative tax payments will triple from $32.4 billion in 2001 to $96 billion in 2010, making it ever more costly to fix.

Those figures cover only the effect of the alternative minimum tax through 2010. Beyond then the trend is also clear: more and more middle-class and upper-middle-class Americans will be moved off of the regular income tax and onto the alternative tax. At the same time fewer and fewer of the top tenth of 1 percent will pay the alternative tax. Together that means a growing burden on the middle class and upper middle class to subsidize tax cuts for those who make much more.

These figures were so devastating in revealing the true nature of the Bush tax cut plan that Tempalski's name has not appeared on any published Department of the Treasury studies since his talk. As Martin A. Sullivan, a former Department of the Treasury economist, wrote in the journal *Tax Notes* after Tempalski's speech, "It is unlikely Treasury economists will be allowed to embarrass the Bush administration with any update of their excellent work."

Others, however, picked up on Tempalski's work. The most thorough analysis was made by the Tax Policy Center, a joint project of the Brookings Institution and the Urban Institute. Using its own computer model, one that in many details comes to conclusions similar to those of Treasury's own, it showed that Tempalski's analysis had understated the problem.

For starters, the Bush tax cuts meant that some of the working class will be forced onto the alternative tax to make sure that the million-dollar-plus–income taxpayers can have their marginal tax rate cut to 35 percent. Among people making under $30,000, less than one in 2,000 was affected by the alternative minimum tax in 2002. This will grow to one in 500 by 2010, a fourfold increase to about 130,000 families. Single mothers head many of these families. These women, some widows and others divorced, already have to cope with a modest income, rearing children and a property tax bill on the family home if they are lucky enough to own one. Now they will lose some or all of their tax cuts to make sure that people making $1 million or more can pay less tax.

The Tax Policy Center analysis also found that between 2000 and 2010 the alternative minimum tax will reach far down the income ladder:

- Among those making $30,000 to $50,000, a fifth of taxpayers, the number affected by the alternative tax will rise sharply, from one in 500 families to one in 11.
- For those making $50,000 to $75,000, the increase will be even greater, from one in 100 to nearly one in two.
- In the high-tax states, which are mostly the states with the highest incomes, the alternative tax will take away the vast majority of the Bush tax cuts and for many families all of the promised cuts. Families in California, Connecticut, Georgia, Massachusetts, Oregon, New Jersey, and New York and other states that generate much of the country's economic bounty will be hit hardest.

- For those making $75,000 to $500,000, the alternative minimum tax will become by 2010 the de facto tax system with only a tiny minority remaining in the regular income tax.

In essence, the Bush administration knowingly chose to squeeze the middle class and the upper middle class to give unhindered tax relief to the people with the very highest incomes, the political donor class.

"What was a class tax is becoming a mass tax," said Len Burman, the Urban Institute economist who worked in the administrations of Presidents Reagan and Clinton. By 2010 about 85 percent of all taxpayers with two or more children will be forced off the regular income tax and onto the alternative minimum tax. This fact alone reveals the hollowness in all the years of talk on the campaign trail by Democrats and Republicans running for Congress and the White House about giving tax relief to families. The fact is that while constantly promising tax relief to middle-class families, politicians in both parties adopted a profoundly antifamily tax policy, especially for those families whose annual income is $50,000 to $500,000, roughly the seventy-fifth to ninety-ninth rungs on the income ladder.

The burden of the alternative minimum tax will shift from the richest Americans to the middle class, which the authors defined as including people making up to $100,000.

In the first decade of this century taxpayers earning $50,000 to $100,000 will see their share of the alternative tax explode from about 3 cents out of each dollar of alternative tax to 21 cents.

Families in the $100,000 to $200,000 income class will be hit so hard that they will pay a much larger share of all income taxes. They paid 22 cents of each dollar the government collected in 2002, but by 2010 they will be paying more than 27 cents. At the same time those making more than $1 million will see their share go down by three pennies, to less than 19 cents.

In 2000 the alternative tax raised only $9.6 billion, about 1 percent of all federal individual income tax revenues. But by 2010 it will bring in $141.4 billion or about a tenth of federal income tax receipts. And $127 million of that increase, 96 percent of it, will be paid by people like the Toths.

The most troubling finding by the Tax Policy Center, especially in light of the third round of Bush tax cuts, is that the cost of fixing the

Middle Class Pays so the Rich Can Pay Less

The burden of the alternative minimum
tax, originally intended to go after
aggressive and rich tax avoiders, shifts
under the Bush tax cuts to people making
less than $200,000 who take deductions
for their children and state and local taxes.

Income Category	Share of Alternative Minimum Tax	
(In thousands)	2003	2010
$30–$50	0.2%	1.1%
$50–$75	1.2%	7.2%
$75–$100	2.1%	14.0%
$100–$200	15.9%	36.3%
$200–$500	43.0%	30.7%
$500–$1,000	13.8%	4.2%
$1,000 or more	22.5%	6.0%

Source: Tax Policy Center

system is growing beyond the country's ability to ever repair it. Congress put in temporary fixes that help a few people in the 2001 and 2003 tax cuts, but the fundamental problem was not addressed.

Burman and Gale, two of the Tax Policy center's economists, calculate that by 2008 the government will have become so dependent on the alternative minimum tax that it would cost more to repeal it than to repeal the regular income tax. They estimate the cost of repealing the alternative tax in 2003 at $950 billion, assuming that all of the tax cuts enacted in 2001 are implemented in the years ahead and are made permanent. And that nearly trillion-dollar cost estimate does not take into account the further tax cuts that President Bush was working through Congress in 2003, which raise the cost of repeal even higher.

Having granted huge tax cuts in 2001 and with more cuts in 2003, and with the huge budget surpluses predicted during the Internet bubble having turned into federal budget deficits expected far into the future, where would the trillion dollars or so be found to reform the minimum tax?

After the problems of the Klaassens and others were reported in *The New York Times,* many members of Congress began denouncing the alternative tax and its effect on middle-class and upper-middle-class families. Senator William Roth of Delaware, who was behind the 1997 and 1998 hearings on the IRS, said in 1999 that what happened to the Klaassens "simply isn't fair" and "is not what Congress intended." But then he went on to propose only a partial reform, as have so many other lawmakers who rail against the alternative tax, but never vote to fix the problems.

The largest organization of tax preparers, the National Association of Enrolled Agents, says the alternative minimum tax is the "biggest

The Stealth Tax Will Grow

The alternative minimum tax was scheduled to grow before President Bush championed his tax cut plans. If the Bush tax cuts are made permanent, this stealth tax will cost taxpayers an extra two-thirds of a billion dollars over 10 years.

Year	ATM Growth Without Bush Tax Cuts	AMT Growth Under Bush Tax Cuts if Made Permanent	Extra AMT Because of Bush Tax Cuts
(Figures are in billions of 2003 dollars)			
2003	$14.5	$15.9	$1.4
2004	$16.3	$18.0	$1.7
2005	$18.7	$46.4	$27.7
2006	$21.2	$58.1	$36.9
2007	$24.8	$69.9	$45.1
2008	$29.2	$88.1	$58.9
2009	$33.7	$103.1	$69.4
2010	$39.7	$126.5	$86.8
2011	$47.1	$145.6	$98.5
2012	$55.2	$167.8	$112.6
2013	$64.6	$191.5	$126.9
TOTAL	$365.0	$1,030.9	$665.9

Source: Tax Policy Center

headache for practitioners and their clients." W. Val Oveson, the former IRS taxpayer advocate, describes the alternative tax as "absolutely, asininely stupid."

Antitax Republicans in Congress say the solution is to just repeal the alternative tax. Representative Max Collins of Georgia, a member of the Ways and Means Committee, has sponsored a bill to do just that, but not until 2010, when the cost of repeal would be well north of $1 trillion and the middle class and upper middle class would already have paid half that much in stealth taxes. Collins argued that the alternative tax "has long outlived its purpose . . . is punitive in nature, overly cumbersome, and affects taxpayers who were never intended to fall into this trap."

Just repealing the alternative tax would create its own new problems. Because the tax system is interconnected, repealing one part of it can shift the rest of the system in unanticipated ways, just as removing one stick in a game of pick-up sticks can shift the dynamics of the whole pile.

Jonathan Blattmachr, the New York lawyer who is a master of tax avoidance for clients such as the Rockefeller family, believes that repeal would be tantamount to a full employment act for tax lawyers. "There are lots of things you would not even think about because of the alternative minimum tax," Blattmachr said. "But if you repeal it, then there are all sorts of things to start thinking about." His first thought was of municipal bond interest, some of which can become taxable under the alternative tax. And Blattmachr is just one of thousands of lawyers and tax engineers who, with the alternative tax repealed, would put their minds to work helping the rich escape taxes entirely.

The way that President's Bush tax cuts interact with the alternative minimum tax is bad news for families like the Klaassens and the Toths, who will lose some or all of their tax cuts. The money they do not save, however, made it possible to design the tax package so that the rich could save even more. The way that the alternative minimum tax takes away tax savings and thus benefits the rich is not unique to the Bush tax cuts. For two decades the vast majority of Americans have been forced to pay extra taxes to finance tax cuts for the super rich. This subsidy for the rich is all the more notable because the Democrats sponsored it.

How Social Security Taxes
Subsidize the Rich

Each fall newspapers and business magazines publish year-end tax saving tips. Accelerate deductions into December, delay income until January, and you can defer part of your tax bill until April 15 of the following year. The articles explain the mechanics of the tax rules that must be followed, but rarely is the underlying principle articulated: a tax paid tomorrow costs you less than one paid today.

Tax lawyers like Jonathan Blattmachr and compensation experts like Bud Crystal have developed exotic techniques to help the super rich delay millions of dollars of taxes for many tomorrows. Chief executives use tax-deductible dollars from their corporate treasuries to pay the Blattmachrs and Crystals to develop and refine techniques that enable executives to delay paying their taxes—not from December to January, but for years, even decades.

Invest those deferred taxes year after year and soon an economic snowball starts rolling, with one's wealth growing faster and faster (thanks to the magic of compound interest) until a great fortune is built, like the billion dollars of untaxed wealth amassed by the Coca-Cola chief executive, Roberto Goizueta.

Deferral, the tax lawyers say, is 90 percent of tax planning. Delay a tax for 30 years and its cost in today's money is almost nothing. Inflation and investing the unpaid tax should cover the whole bill.

Delaying a tax for three decades is just what William Esrey, the chief executive of Sprint, tried to do in 2000 when he bought a tax shelter from Arthur Andersen, the big accounting firm. The shelter was designed to let him defer until the year 2030 about $80 million of taxes on $200 million of profits from exercising Sprint options, a once-in-a-lifetime windfall. But this particular shelter also illustrated one of the hazards of deferral for both the deferrer and the government. The taxes will never be paid because the shelter required Esrey to hold on to his Sprint shares instead of selling them. Sprint shares plunged in value. Worse, the IRS audited Esrey's tax return and rejected the shelter. So instead of having $120 million or so after tax, Esrey was left with Sprint shares worth far less than the taxes he owed. And the scandal over his buying a tax shelter from the accounting firm that was supposed to independently examine Sprint's books cost him his job.

Esrey's misfortune is not the norm for those who delay taxes, only a cautionary tale about what can go wrong for taxpayer and government alike when taxes are paid at a time other than when they normally would come due. Paying at any other time introduces risk and sometimes disaster follows.

If a tax delayed is a tax reduced, then the opposite also must be true. A tax paid today that could have been paid years or even decades from now costs more, a lot more. People who pay any tax sooner rather than later have less of their money today to either spend or save. Because their after-tax income is reduced, either they have less to support their immediate lifestyle or they have less to save, which means a less prosperous future.

For two decades working Americans have been paying far more of one particular tax than they needed to at the time. That means they either spent or saved less. For those living on a thin margin between their income and expenses, this extra tax pushed them over the line, forcing them to borrow. And debt, like wealth, can snowball as interest compounds around principle into a crushing obligation.

The tax being paid in advance is Social Security.

From 1984 to 2002 the government collected $1.7 trillion more in Social Security taxes than the agency paid out in benefits to retirees, widows and orphans and in disability benefits.

That is enough to double the value of all the 401(k) retirement plans in the country.

That is enough to pay off all the consumer debt in the country at the end of 2001, a burden that has almost tripled in real terms since 1983.

It is an average of $16,000 that each family did not have to spend on improving their lifestyle or on investing for the future.

From 1983, when the overtaxing began, through 2002 Social Security benefits rose by half in real dollars while Social Security taxes almost doubled. As a result, three out of four households now pay more in Social Security taxes than in income taxes.

Social Security does not apply to all income so not everyone was affected in the same way by the tax increases. The government takes 6.2 cents out of each dollar of salary, but only up to a ceiling that was $87,000 in 2003. People whose salary is higher than this get a tax break on every additional dollar they earn. For chief executives the Social Security tax is often a tiny fraction of 1 percent of their total compensation.

In 2003 President Bush sought to eliminate taxes on dividends paid to shareholders, saying that it was wrong to tax a dollar twice. Since companies pay dividends out of their after-tax profits, and shareholders must then report these dividends as income, the president argued that the same dollar was being taxed twice and that this was fundamentally unfair. "It's a matter of principle," he said.

Social Security also represents a double tax. The Social Security tax applies to wages that have already been subject to the personal income tax. If double taxation is fundamentally unfair, a stronger case can be made for the unfairness of Social Security as a double tax than for the tax on dividends. Among other things, many dollars of corporate profit are not taxed, despite the seeming requirements of the law, and so in a system in which people can collect dividends tax-free they may earn income that is completely untaxed, escaping both the corporate income tax and the personal income tax.

The amount that is withheld from paychecks for Social Security taxes represents only half of the total levy. The tax is double the amount withheld from paychecks because it is paid half by workers and half by their employers. Economists of all stripes agree that the Social Security tax paid by the employer is really paid by the workers, that it is simply an invisible part of their compensation. Thus a married couple who together earned $87,000 paid $10,788 in Social Security taxes, the same amount paid by someone who earned $1 million or even $100 million. For the married couple working two jobs, this tax cost them every eighth dollar earned while for the executive with the million-dollar salary the tax cost every ninety-third dollar earned.

The cap on wages subject to Social Security taxes means that the moment people's salary passes this level, they get a tax break. Their take-home pay increases by 6.2 cents on each additional dollar of income and their employer saves the same amount, which boosts high-end wages even more. The tax savings means those who earn more than the maximum for the Social Security tax can spend, or save, more.

For those in the top half of 1 percent income class, the extra Social Security taxes are so minor as to be lost in the rounding.

To understand how the politicians switched Social Security from a pay-as-you-go system to a system of imposing a tax today for a benefit due by and by requires going back to consider the issues and the era.

Ronald Reagan was elected president in 1980 on two big promises. One was to stand up to aggressors, especially the Soviets. In just nine years the unimaginable goal of crushing Russian communism was achieved without war between the superpowers. The second promise was to cut taxes, especially the high rates paid by the richest Americans, on the theory that it would promote economic growth. The highest income tax rate then was 70 percent and many in the middle class paid 40 cents on their last dollars of income, a higher rate than the rich paid even after the 1993 Clinton tax hikes.

The Democrats, sensing Reagan's popularity with much of their traditional constituency like blue-collar workers, and lacking any cogent theory on taxes, tried to out-Reagan Reagan by proposing even bigger tax cuts.

All of this tax-cutting frenzy took place when the government had not balanced its books since the sixties and was nearly $1 trillion in debt. In 1981 Washington borrowed $125 billion, better than one of every 10 dollars the government spent that year, by selling bonds and government IOUs in the securities markets.

The champions of supply-side economics surrounding Reagan promised that lower tax rates would mean more investment and that, in turn, should always result in more economic growth, which in turn means growing tax revenues. Congress passed the biggest tax cut in history, but things didn't work out as promised, at least not in the short run.

The 1982 federal budget deficit was more than double that of the year before. The next year it grew again, to $343 billion, approaching triple the level when Reagan took office. Washington was borrowing almost one of every three dollars it spent. Unemployment hit 10 percent, an issue the Democrats seized on to attack Reagan's economic policies.

The federal government's red-ink spending was so out of control, and so damaging to the rest of the economy, that one year after Reagan signed into law the biggest tax cut in history he had to accept a host of tax increases. Reagan would not openly acknowledge that these were tax increases and when he was finally forced to refer to them, when he signed them into law, he referred to them as "revenue enhancements." They could also have been called tax hikes on Joe Lunchpail to benefit the rich. The 1982 tax law did not raise income tax rates. Rather, there were increases in excise taxes, including a nickel-a-gallon increase on gasoline. Two decades later the Heritage Foundation, a major promoter of the Reagan tax cuts in 1981, issued a report saying that excise taxes hit the poor hardest and ought to be scaled back.

In 1983, though, public attention was diverted from the immediate fiscal crisis by reports out of Washington that Social Security was in trouble, deep trouble. The idea that upon their retirement, Social Security might not be around anymore worried many people. Letters and calls flooded the offices of politicians and the issue was in the news day after day.

For the Reagan White House fears about Social Security's solvency diverted attention from the government's immediate solvency. It also turned attention away from Reagan's attitude toward the millions of people without jobs, summarized in his denigrating criticism of news reports on the subject: "Is it news that some fellow out in South Succotash someplace has just been laid off, that he should be interviewed nationwide?"

The year before, Social Security had run a modest deficit, taking in about a nickel less than each dollar it spent, largely because 10 million people were out of work. A commission, chaired by Alan Greenspan,

who would later head the Federal Reserve and have his finger on interest rates, said disaster was looming. If nothing was done, Greenspan
said, Social Security would start running in the red, forcing the government to borrow money to pay benefits. The problem, he said,
would start in about 31 years.

Critics said this was a mirage, that economic growth and perhaps
trimming back on the generous inflation adjustments each year in benefit checks would keep the system solvent. But with great waves of red
ink washing over Washington's ledgers, the distinctions between government spending policies were not well appreciated by many voters.
The Democrats, who controlled both House and Senate, decided it was
time to "bail out" Social Security.

Former Representative Andy Jacobs, Democrat of Indiana, recalled the political algebra of shared pain that went into the bailout.
"We said everybody is going to have to give a little; workers are going
to pay a little more, recipients are going to have to get a little less, and
we said, 'While we're at it, let's even tax a little bit more than that and
build up a surplus to meet the baby boomers when they retire.'"

Senator Daniel Patrick Moynihan, a New York Democrat and a
scholar with a long history of studying social policy issues, said the Social Security scare was a phantom. He said raising more from Social Security taxes simply masked the drop in tax revenues caused by the
Reagan tax cuts. Moynihan called the Social Security tax hike "thievery." The beneficiaries of the stolen goods, he said, were the rich who
would get to keep their Reagan income tax cuts while everyone below
them paid more in taxes.

Whether it was a mirage or a real problem, the decision to tax
people immediately for a benefit due half a lifetime off meant that
people were paying even more in real terms than if taxes were just
raised three decades into the future.

In the beginning the overtaxing was modest. Social Security taxes
in 1983 were just $4.5 billion greater than benefits, an extra 2.7 cents
on each dollar of tax needed to maintain the plan on a pay-as-you-go
basis. But each year since, the extra tax has increased. By 1990 the extra tax had grown to $1.20 for every dollar needed immediately to pay
benefits.

In 1999 through 2002, Americans paid almost $640 billion more in

Social Security taxes than were paid out in Social Security benefits, an extra $5,100 of tax per household. Had Social Security taxes equaled what was needed to pay benefits, then each household would have averaged an extra $100 each month to save or pay bills.

The rise in the maximum Social Security tax has been sharp. In 1970 the maximum tax was $327. Three decades later the maximum tax was $4,724 or more than 14 times as much. In 2003 it was almost $5,400, an amount matched by the employer. For a married couple both earning the $87,000 maximum subject to the total tax, it comes to $21,576 or more than $400 paid to the government each week.

Once the Democrats made the decision to tax their constituents decades in advance of when they would receive their retirement benefits, they also had to assure people that that money would be there when they filed for their retirement benefits. Again and again Americans were told that the money would go into a trust fund and that it would earn interest.

But the money was not used in the way most people think. It was not put into the commercial market and invested or loaned.

The extra Social Security taxes were spent on the day-to-day operations of the federal government. Instead of buying municipal bonds or shares of IBM, the extra Social Security taxes were spent on cruise missiles and salaries of FBI agents and running the Environmental Protection Agency. That is, Social Security taxes were used to pay the ordinary bills of the government, making up for the taxes that were no longer being paid by the rich because of the 1981 income tax cuts.

In only two years since the 1981 tax cuts has the federal government kept spending in line with its revenues other than Social Security, and in one of those two years the surplus was a only by a hair's breadth. The one clear surplus year was 2000, when the Internet bubble popped.

In the two decades beginning in 1983 the government has spent almost $5.4 trillion more than it took in from income, estate, gift and excise taxes. The reason that government debt grew by only $3.6 trillion was because of those excess Social Security taxes that were used to finance income tax cuts for the rich.

Using Social Security taxes to subsidize tax cuts for the rich has taken a terrible toll on the finances of those who make up to the maximum wage subject to that levy. The 90 percent of Americans who make less than the maximum wage taxed for Social Security had $1.7 trillion in extra taxes taken out of their paychecks just to help the rich. That is a vast reservoir of money that people could have decided to spend or save, stimulating the economy either through their purchases of goods and services or by investing for the future.

Of course, had the extra Social Security taxes not been collected, the government would have had to do something else about the size of the deficits. It might have cut spending. It might have allowed inflation to run wild, eroding the value of the debt. When Washington finally did do something, in 1991 under the first President Bush and again in 1993 under President Clinton, it raised taxes on the upper middle class and the rich.

What the government actually did with the excess Social Security taxes was use them to allow the rich to enjoy big tax cuts. It used the excess Social Security taxes to make up for part of the taxes from which the rich were excused in 1981. In effect the government took dollars from Joe Lunchpail so that the rich could stuff even more into their silk pockets.

That is, the money was used in a socialist scheme to redistribute income. Only instead of taking from those with big incomes to dole out money to the poor, this money was used to redistribute income up.

Much of the political rhetoric in America for the past three decades has been about redistributing income. Politicians in both parties have sought votes by fostering the idea that hard workers in the middle class and the highest income earners are being squeezed to subsidize the indolent poor. If that were true, it would be an important story. But the flow of Social Security taxes does not substantiate this deeply ingrained societal myth.

Instead, what happened was that the working poor and the middle class, indeed everyone making up to the maximum wage taxed for Social Security, paid more taxes than were needed to allow generous tax cuts for the rich. That meant that the rich could save more and everyone else had to save less. Keep in mind that, after adjusting for inflation, the richest 13,400 households had more than five dollars in the year 2000 for every dollar they had in 1970 while the remaining 99 percent of households had only eight cents more per dollar.

Keep in mind that a tax not paid means more wealth over time, while a tax paid before it is necessary means less wealth and, for some, growing debt, over time.

Social Security itself is a redistribution scheme. It started out with a minimum benefit, which provided a minimal income to those with very little official work history, notably women who worked in jobs like housecleaning, where they were paid in cash. The affluent who employed these maids saved money because wages paid under the table are usually discounted for the taxes not paid. In the early days of the Reagan administration, the Democrats killed this minimum benefit. They did so after warnings that Social Security was facing problems decades into the future when it might not take in enough money to pay benefits. The end of the minimum benefit drew hardly any mention in the news at the time, like many cuts that primarily affect the poor.

Critics who say that Social Security is an income redistribution program are correct. Those with the smallest incomes get a benefit larger than they have earned and those who pay the maximum tax get less. It is the middle class and the upper middle class who pay the price for this inequity. The rich get nearly a free ride because of the cap on wages subject to Social Security taxes.

But the modest socialism that remains in the Social Security bene-fit formula pales compared to the redistributive effect of raising taxes on Social Security wages to help finance tax cuts for the rich. That is a massive redistribution program right out of George Orwell's *Animal Farm,* where the ruling pigs declared that some animals were more equal than others. That teachers and cops and truck drivers and clerks pay extra Social Security taxes so that the rich can pay less income tax is an economy Orwell would have understood.

All governments affect the distribution of incomes by how they tax and spend. A decision to cut taxes on any group is also a decision to help them prosper either now or later. A decision to raise taxes on any group is a decision to leave them with less to get by on now and less to save for the future. On the spending side, a decision to cut spending for, say, higher education is a decision to deny a better future to those too poor to afford any tuition, even those with bright minds and good grades. Decisions to cut spending on public health or roads or air traf-fic control are decisions that some people will get sick or hurt or die.

A decision to tax a group today for a benefit they cannot collect for

decades to come is extremely costly to them because of what economists call the time value of money. A dollar today is worth much more
than a dollar in the future. And just as deferring a tax for three decades,
as Sprint chief executive Esrey and his top lieutenants tried to do, can
make taxes vanish, speeding up a tax can make a burden far more harsh.

Such a tax policy also introduces an element of unfairness since
many of those who pay today will not be around if, and when, the dire
predictions that Social Security will be unable to operate on a pay-as-
you-go basis come true.

Having less to save, or going into debt, because of a tax paid sooner
rather than later is not the end of the story. When a tax is paid at a time
other than when it would normally be due there is also, as Esrey discovered, an element of risk.

Fear that the excess Social Security taxes would be used to finance
the tax cuts on which George W. Bush campaigned in 2000 prompted
him to promise again and again on the campaign trail he would not
touch that money. "In my economic plan, more than $2 trillion of the
federal surplus is locked away for Social Security," Bush said. "For
years, politicians in both parties have dipped into the Trust Fund to pay
for more spending. And I will stop it." Two months after he was sworn
in, Bush said that "another priority is retirement systems of Americans. And so the budget I set up says that payroll taxes are only going
to be spent on one thing, and that's Social Security. But the Congress
won't be using the payroll taxes for other programs. *Lockbox,* I think, is
the terminology they like to use up here."

By then *The Wall Street Journal* had already concluded that Bush intended to pick the lock on the Social Security box. Bush's economic
plan, the *Journal* reported, uses "all the Social Security surpluses . . . to
fund the government for the next two years, and to spend well over
$100 billion of Social Security funds in each of the following three
years."

What George W. Bush said about protecting Social Security was
just another politician's promise, worth just what it cost: nothing. Soon
after the better newspapers reported that Bush's tax plan depended on
raiding the Social Security lockbox, the White House itself began quietly backing away from its lockbox pledge to safeguard the Social Security surplus. Unlike the promises, there were no presidential speeches

saying, in effect, we didn't mean what we said. As with all politicians, as with the presidents who came before and no doubt those who will come after, the backing away was done by those unnamed senior administration sources whose nuanced remarks tend to run deep inside the newspaper and rarely make the broadcast news on which so many Americans rely.

On June 7, 2001, President Bush signed his tax cut package that lowered rates on the rich, eliminated the estate tax for one year and gave more than half of the estimated $1.3 trillion tax cut to the richest 1 percent. It was a tax cut that also promised years of budget deficits, meaning more borrowing to pay the government's bills, more raiding of Social Security so that the middle class could subsidize the rich.

Just 12 days after Bush signed his tax cut bill, Treasury Secretary Paul H. O'Neill gave a speech at the top of the World Trade Center. He spoke to the Coalition for American Financial Security, an organization of investment managers who want to replace part of Social Security with private investment accounts, from which they would collect fees costing many times the current costs of administering Social Security.

"I come to you as managing trustee of Social Security," O'Neill said. "Today we have no assets in the trust fund. We have promises of the good faith and credit of the United States government that benefits will flow."

All Americans had, he said again and again, was "someone else's promise" that the pieces of paper held by the Social Security Administration would be paid off with hard dollars by the United States government. And the implication was that the unsecured debt might not be repaid.

His remarks were astonishing because O'Neill was doing something rare for Washington. O'Neill was telling the truth.

The only way that the taxes that Americans have paid in advance for their Social Security benefits can be turned into retirement checks is by a new round of taxes to redeem the IOUs. The Social Security taxes people paid in advance are gone.

O'Neill, in his own way, was admitting that the extra Social Security taxes were used to make up for the income taxes not paid by the rich. In this the rich discovered the other 10 percent of tax avoidance, the part that was not covered by the schemes of tax lawyers and accountants to make taxes shrink by deferring them into the distant future. The other 10 percent was the part where taxes did not have to be paid at all. Only instead of having to pay counselors to dream up risky and complex schemes, all this took was for Democrats and Republicans alike to make taxes disappear through lower rates and various favors. And to those with such good fortune it meant more money to buy stocks and jewels and Renoirs at Sotheby's.

Even more surprising than O'Neill's telling the truth was the moral component of his speech. Less than two decades earlier Senator Moynihan had described the advance payment of Social Security taxes as thievery. O'Neill said not one word about the money being stolen, about the Social Security taxpayers being cheated. Not one word about how people had lost not just what they paid, but the opportunity to have invested that money for themselves.

Instead, the Treasury secretary encouraged his audience to promote the Bush administration plan to require people to keep paying these excess taxes and, if they wanted, to divert part of them into individual investment accounts, on which members of his audience and their highly paid peers could charge fees.

Working Americans who were forced into paying an unnecessary tax that was diverted to make the rich richer were not alone in feeling painful economic blows. Their government, beholden to the political donor class, was attentive to the needs and desires of the rich first and foremost. The access to politicians that the rich bought gave them ample opportunity to make their concerns known, crowding out much of the time that might have gone into considering the needs of those unable to buy access to their elected leaders. Those with no hope of access, the industrious among the poor, were also learning how callous their government could be.

Preying on the Working Poor

Maritza Reyes, suspected tax cheat, took the witness stand in the brightly lit Los Angeles courtroom to tell her story. Ms. Reyes, a woman of poise and dignity, is a domestic. She mops the floors and scrubs the toilets of others, hard work that earns her $7,000 a year, which is just about the sum that the Internal Revenue Service said she had stolen from the government. The IRS did not have much evidence to support its claim. Indeed, all it had was a half digit on her address, the fraction that distinguished her tiny cottage on the back end of a lot in impoverished East Los Angeles from the address of the house that fronted the street.

Ms. Reyes is one of about 19 million Americans who each year apply for a tax break for the working poor called the earned income tax credit. About five million of these families are lifted above the official poverty line because of the credit, which is designed to encourage the poor to take tough, low-paying jobs, many of which net less than welfare.

The costs of holding a job, like commuting, combined with losing welfare benefits and paying taxes can make staying on welfare rolls seem safer than taking a low-wage job. Together costs, benefit losses and tax rates can easily come to more than 100 percent on the dollar, meaning work is sometimes a losing proposition. Yet without work, there is no hope of acquiring skills and experience that earn a living wage and turn people from tax*eaters* into tax*payers*. Arthur Laffer, the supply-side economist, famously showed with a curve drawn on the

back of a napkin that at tax rates of 100 percent the government collects no taxes, because no one works just to pay taxes.

That the Maritza Reyes case was worth the time and money for
lawyers and auditors and the judge and his staff illustrates how President Clinton and Congress had focused the shrinking resources of the
IRS on the crumbs falling off the golden cake of the American economy. This focus also emboldened cheating among those who were
served the biggest slices because their chances of being caught fell away
to next to nothing. The IRS audited 397,000 of the working poor
who applied for the credit in 2001, eight times as many audits as it
conducted of people making $100,000 or more. That works out to
one of every 47 returns seeking the credit, compared to about one in
every 366 taxpayers who did not apply for it. Small businesses with $5
million of assets were about as likely to be audited as the working poor
despite the far greater potential for tax cheating by the business owners. The businessmen and women could charge off parts of their living
expenses to their business and they controlled what reports flowed to
the IRS computers about their incomes. What Clinton did in stepping
up audits of the working poor was the equivalent of a mayor pulling
detectives off the homicide squad to write parking tickets.

Congress in 1975 enacted the earned income tax credit to create
incentives to work. It is in effect a tax-based welfare program, heavily
focused on families, the first of what in the nineties became a host of
aid programs run through the tax system because the cost shows up not
as spending, but as reduced government revenue. Those who are eligible for the credit can get back the income taxes withheld from their
paychecks and collect a check from the government, making it a form
of negative income tax.

The amount of the credit rises to encourage those who make almost nothing to work more, then falls back until it is phased out entirely. The maximum negative income tax payment in 2002 was $4,140,
an amount that for a family with two children was available to those
making between $11,550 and $13,350. Above or below those income
levels the credit was phased out. At the maximum income, to get the
maximum credit a family of four would have earnings and a tax credit
totaling $17,390, barely escaping the official poverty threshold, which

was $16,500. Without the credit, the number of officially poor Americans would rise by five million and half of those would be children.

Because it only goes to those who work, President Reagan called it "the best anti-poverty, the best pro-family, the best job creation to come out of the Congress." The first President Bush persuaded Congress to expand the program. So did President Clinton, who arranged to make the credit available to poor individuals without children, although their maximum credit, or negative income tax, is less than a dollar a day.

After Reagan left office, however, others in his party began to attack the credit as a socialist plan to redistribute income. They also asserted that it was rife with fraud and errors. In its early years the credit was ripe for cheating because of the way that Congress designed the credit. Parents were not required to produce a Social Security number for each child and, just as with regular tax returns, far more children were listed than existed. The IRS was not given access to Social Security records so cheats had virtually no risk of being caught. Many times it was not calculated cheating, but the claiming of children by both parents following a divorce. The most vociferous critics of the credit were those in the forefront of the campaign to cut taxes on the rich, notably House Speaker Newt Gingrich and Senators William V. Roth Jr. of Delaware and Don Nickles of Oklahoma. Nickles in 1995 denounced the credit as "the Federal Government's fastest growing and most fraud-prone welfare program and we need to call it that. That is what it is . . . it is a welfare program. It is an income redistribution program."

Nickles's remarks came as House Republicans, in the majority for the first time in four decades, pressed either for major cuts in the earned income tax credit or to end it entirely. They sought this cut for the working poor at the same time that they were pushing a $500 annual credit for each child, a proposal promoted by the Christian Coalition. Under this plan the poor like Maritza Reyes and her son would get nothing. Middle-class families earning just into six figures, however, would qualify.

That reflected the middle-class and more prosperous nature of that Christian Coalition membership, whose tax proposals seemed blind to Christ's teachings, such as that the rich should "sell all that thou hast, and distribute unto the poor, and thou shalt have treasure in heaven." Nickles and other politicians who share his views said that it was fair to deny the credit to the poor because they were not taxpayers—by which he meant *income* taxpayers. Besides, he considered the earned income tax credit welfare, an income redistribution scheme that moved money down the income ladder, when his voting record showed support for schemes to redistribute income upward.

President Clinton, fearing that the new Republican majority had the votes to savage the program, proposed a diversion. How would Congress feel, Clinton asked, about giving the IRS more than $100 million a year just to audit applicants for the credit to make sure that only the deserving working poor benefited? Congress went for the deal.

In 1999, for the first time, the poor were more likely than the rich to have their tax returns audited. The overall rate for people making less than $25,000 was 1.36 percent, compared with 1.15 percent of returns filed by those making $100,000 or more, the top income tier broken out by the IRS in its reports on auditing. Over the previous 11 years audit rates for the poor increased by a third, while falling 90 percent for the top tier of Americans.

One of those the IRS audited was Ms. Reyes. Her tax return was scrutinized not because the numbers did not add up or because she had unreported income or because of suspiciously large and undocumented deductions. Maritza Reyes took the standard deduction. She was audited because of her address, which differed by a half digit from that of the man with whom she had lived and who had fathered her two children. Her case illustrates how the rules were written with suburban middle-class assumptions about how people conduct their lives. The earned income tax credit is available to low-income married couples with children. It is also available to couples who divorce and split up the children, each of whom then qualifies as a head of household for their own credit. When single parents with children who are poor despite work marry, they have their benefits cut because they get only one credit, not two. In these ways it is the worst kind of marriage penalty, one of several aspects of marriage penalties in the tax code that, as we shall see, the self-proclaimed family advocates in Congress manage to ignore.

When the Reyes couple split, Maritza took their little boy and moved into a cottage at the back of the property, the only place she could afford, while Mr. Reyes stayed with their teen-age boy in the house on the front of the lot. Under the rules set by Congress, Ms. Reyes was entitled to the tax credit if she was a head of household, a single parent. If she lived under the same roof with her husband, she was not. The IRS, on the basis of nothing more than her address, decided that she was not a bona fide head of household and demanded that she return several years of credits.

The IRS notice put Ms. Reyes into a panic because she knew that she could never pay it back, that the interest would grow and grow, ruining any hope she might have to ever get ahead despite her lack of education. Unlike the many people who ignore IRS notices, figuring it is bad news and hoping that it will just go away if they do not acknowledge it, Ms. Reyes took action. She went to the local IRS office, trying each time to explain her situation. Relying on informal translations by whoever was around, IRS people wrote down notes of what they understood to be her story.

Finally, Ms. Reyes turned to Chapman University Law School in Orange, about 30 miles away. The college runs a tax clinic for low-income people caught in disputes with the IRS, one of several dozen programs around the country that rely on students to investigate such cases. Pallavi Shah, an accountant who was studying for her law degree, took on the Reyes case and quickly discerned that the IRS considered Ms. Reyes untrustworthy. Each IRS official had, Rashomon-like, written down a different version of what Ms. Reyes had said. The IRS had concluded that Ms. Reyes was dissembling.

Tax Court judges visit cities around the country and, when one of them came to Los Angeles in March 2000, Ms. Reyes told her story under oath, through a trained interpreter. Shah guided her through her story of how the couple had separated and that only because of the little place out back was she not forced into even more dire circumstances.

On cross-examination the IRS lawyer peppered Ms. Reyes with questions aimed at showing her claim was a fraud. How often do you go into the other house? Where do you go to make telephone calls? Where do you watch television? The answers all made it clear that the Reyeses were no longer a couple. The IRS had no witnesses, no documents, to show that the living arrangement was a sham. All the government had was suspicion born of that half digit. To Pallavi Shah the case was a troubling introduction into how the government treats the poor and inarticulate, as well as how it wastes money pursuing minor matters. Shah concluded that the case would not have gone to trial, indeed that she would have never even heard of Ms. Reyes, had anyone at the IRS cared about the facts. "If just one person had taken the time to listen to her they would have seen what the judge did, that she was a bona fide head of household," Shah said.

To Frank J. Doti, the Chapman law school professor who runs the clinic, the Reyes case is typical of those he has seen over the years, typical of the way the government comes down hard on the poor. They make easy targets because so few fight back and those that do must rely on their own wits or on law school students. Despite his sympathy for the poor, Professor Doti believes that the cheating that does occur necessitates the audits. "There have been some people who have played the system and gotten credits they are not entitled to so the IRS people distrust everyone who claims the earned income tax credit," he said.

The extra money that Congress gave the IRS beginning in 1995 to audit the working poor came as it was reducing the ability of the IRS to audit corporations and the affluent. By 2002 the number of auditors had been slashed by a fourth, to fewer than 12,000, and many of the most experienced auditors had resigned or retired. That year the IRS audited five of the working poor for every affluent American it audited.

The year before, the disparity was even greater. In 2001, the IRS audited 397,000 of the nearly 20 million returns filed by the working poor who applied for the earned income tax credit. The IRS audited about 50,000 of the more than 7 million returns filed by people making $100,000 or more. That means that while there were close to three times as many working poor as affluent, the number of their tax returns chosen for audit was nearly eight times as many. Indeed, of all the 744,000 individual tax returns that the IRS audited in 2002, more than half were filed by the working poor, who account for less than one in 6 taxpayers.

Looked at another way, one in 47 of the working poor had their returns audited, compared to one in 145 of the affluent and one in 400 returns filed by partnerships, which are used mostly by the wealthy. Many of the affluent rely on wages for most of their incomes, so they have few chances to cheat, which helps explain their low audit rate. But how, then, to explain the fact that among businesses with assets of $1 million to $5 million the audit rate was just one in 49, almost exactly the same as that of the working poor despite abundant opportunities for these business owners to cheat?

Like those African Americans who get stopped on the highway for DWB—driving while black—the working poor are scrutinized closely by the tax police because that is what the elected political leaders ordered. It is a major reason that a fifth of those who are eligible do not even apply for the credit.

When reports came out in 2002 showing that the poor were being audited more than the rich, some advocates of lowering taxes on the rich said that seemed perfectly reasonable.

The Heritage Foundation, the most influential marketing organization in Washington working to lower taxes on the rich, was a leader in urging close policing of the working poor. The foundation says that while it is often portrayed in the news media as an ally of its rich donors, it believes it is an advocate of policies that would most benefit the working poor. Daniel J. Mitchell, a Heritage tax expert, wrote that no one should think much of the fact that the poor are audited more than the rich. "With fraud rates as high as 25 percent, what choice does the agency have?" Mitchell wrote. The slippery phrase in Mitchell's article is "as high as." It allows him to leave the impression with readers that the credit is rife with fraud when it is really rife with errors and problems caused by the confusing rules Congress established for the credit.

During the six years, (from 1995 through 2000) that he was chair of the House Ways and Means Committee, Representative Bill Archer of Texas regularly railed about what he said was a 20 percent or 22 percent or 25 percent fraud-and-error rate in the earned income tax credit. His stern voice always emphasized "fraud" rather than "error." Archer often went on to talk about protecting the government's revenue from thieves. And he opposed any expansion of the credit as a way to encourage more of the poor to seek work. "There's absolutely no reason why the EITC should be expanded until this terribly costly problem is fixed," Archer said in 2000.

Representative Anne M. Northup, a Kentucky Republican, said that lawmakers should not feel "embarrassed or ashamed" about auditing the poor intensely. Northup also wrote to her hometown newspaper, the *Louisville Courier-Journal,* to criticize an April 2002 column about how it made no economic sense to audit the working poor at a higher rate than the rich. Northup's letter asserted that columnist David Hawpe did not know what he was writing about. "The IRS's most recent statistics report that EITC claimants are audited at less than half the rate of those who make over $100,000 annually," Northup wrote. Northup's office was repeatedly asked for a source to support this claim, which is not supported by the official IRS statistics. Her spokesman, after listening to the question, said she would look into it. She did not return follow-up calls.

For those who apply for the credit and are audited, the system can be as uncaring about the facts as Representative Northup. A lack of language skills may be used against the taxpayer, as Maritza Reyes discovered. Congress lets the IRS deny the credit for two years if it concludes there was a significant error on a return claiming the credit. The denial can last a decade if the IRS asserts an "intentional disregard" for the rules. The career civil servants at the IRS got the message: across the country complaints about unreasonable IRS denials of the credit have poured into tax clinics, into agencies that help the poor and into some newsrooms. Parents who produce report cards and letters from neighbors have been told that that does not prove their children live with them. So have parents who produce medical bills, letters and other documents not just once but two or three or five times.

Audits of the credit extract a high price for honest taxpayers. The average delay in getting the credit once an audit is ordered is 265 days, about nine months. And in the end two thirds of those audited get a refund, the average check totaling $1,420, IRS Taxpayer Advocate Nina Olson told Congress in her annual report in 2003.

That two thirds of audited returns filed by the working poor still result in a refund stands in sharp contrast to the audit statistics, which show that two thirds of audits result in more tax being owed. Even though most audits of the working poor are simple and can be done by highly trained clerks, the level of audit resources used to police the working poor is out of all proportion to the risk to the government. This is especially so when compared to the opportunities to cheat, and the much larger dollars at issue, with businesses and partnerships.

Before she became the taxpayers' advocate within the IRS, Olson ran a low-income tax clinic in Richmond, Virginia, where she observed another problem. Olson said that unregulated tax preparers "who turn a blind eye and do not protect the tax system when confronted with taxpayers who play fast and loose with the system" caused much of the fraud. Her suggestion that all tax preparers be regulated—as accountants, lawyers and those tax preparers known as enrolled agents are—were ignored despite the potential to reduce fraud of all kinds.

Based on the stories told by people who came to her clinic and others, Olson estimated that a fourth of what the IRS called improper payments were made to people who properly claimed the credit, but failed to respond quickly to IRS audit notices. Many of these people are functionally illiterate and may not understand the IRS notices or may ignore them. Others are too poor to have a telephone or work in jobs where they are not allowed any time off, even without pay, to satisfy IRS demands for documentation. And not a few lack the skills to obtain documentation such as marriage licenses and birth certificates from the various bureaucracies that the IRS demands.

The IRS also seemed to pay little attention to people who claimed the credit but who were hardly among the working poor. At least one earned income tax credit check in the mid-1990s was written to a resident of Olympic Towers on Fifth Avenue in Manhattan, a luxury apartment building that is home to members of several billionaire families from other countries. The taxpayer secrecy laws protected the individual's identity, but Treasury officials said the claimant was the beneficiary of a gigantic offshore trust, one that by law could give her income free of tax. By working briefly in a job—whether it was acting, modeling, selling jewelry or flipping burgers could not be determined—she made enough to qualify for the credit.

Gregory Mueller, a tax preparer, observed a more prosaic form of manipulation in St. Louis. One of his clients owned his own business and reported $11,000 of wages from it, an amount that qualified for the maximum credit. The client also reported $80,000 of dividends from his real estate business, offset by a paper loss of the same amount, which he was entitled to as a full-time real estate professional. This person's real income was $91,000, but under the earned income tax credit rules his family qualified for the maximum credit. Mueller said this device also meant that the client's teenage child qualified for college financial aid.

No member of Congress, not Representatives Northup or Archer, has made any moves to change the rules so that children of foreign billionaires and wealthy real estate investors could not qualify for the credit.

Those in Congress like Northup who favor a crackdown on the working poor say that a high level of audits is necessary because cheating among the poor is rampant. That is not what reports by the IRS, the General Accounting Office and others show. These reports cite errors, not fraud, as the major problem. By far the biggest problem arises when a couple separates and both parents list the children in claiming the credit. Congress also applies unique definitions of *family* and *head of household* to those that seek the credit, further vexing the working poor. Then there's the special rule on who makes the most. Had Maritza Reyes moved into the home of her mother, and if her mother made $1 more per year than Maritza, then the grandmother would have been eligible for the credit, not Maritza. Another problem is the government's practice of issuing the credit as an annual lump sum. This encourages a windfall mentality among recipients. The law allows for the credit to be paid out over the year, increasing weekly pay by as much as $80, but employers have no incentives to adopt the practice and hardly anyone takes advantage of this. This is clearly one area in which the people who get the benefit could improve their lot by exercising their responsibility to take the credit as they earn their pay and in which government could fashion rules to reduce fraud and abuse.

The rules for this credit also illustrate how harshly Congress treats the working poor compared to the well off. As Ms. Reyes found, this tax credit can be denied based on nothing more substantial than suspicion born of a half digit difference in an address. Congress also lets the IRS deny the credit for 2 years or even 10 years. The rich are treated gently. Penalties for errors are rare and those for cheating are often waived when the IRS deals with the highest income Americans and the biggest companies. In 2002 the IRS assessed just 22 negligence penalties against 2.5 million corporations, a decline of more than 99 percent from 1993 when nearly 2,400 penalties were imposed. Even when it catches corporations cheating, the IRS is not so harsh with them as with the working poor. Beginning in 2002 the IRS offered to settle cases with companies that had cheated on their taxes under terms that excused them from any penalties. In some cases it let the companies keep a fifth of their ill-gotten tax savings.

Taxpayers are not the only ones who make errors. Congress makes mistakes every time it passes a tax bill, the result of tax laws being drafted in secret and often passed without anyone having time to read the actual language. A solution has been instituted to deal with this. Congress regularly passes what it calls technical corrections laws, as if to say, "Oops, ignore that law over there because we didn't mean what we enacted."

Just such an error turned up in the 1997 tax cut law. This mistake helped only beneficiaries of the 400 or so estates that each year are worth $17 million or more. The error was worth $200,000 in tax savings to each such estate, a total of $880 million over a decade. As soon as the text of the law became available, tax lawyers and congressional staffers spotted the error and notified the Department of the Treasury, which recommended a technical correction. The Senate moved to fix the problem before anyone got the unintended tax break. But Representative Archer, the vehement foe of the earned income tax credit who complained at every opportunity about how much it was costing the government, stopped the corrective process. Archer explained his action in a letter to the National Federation of Independent Businesses, an ally in Archer's efforts to eliminate the estate tax. "While some might argue that the proposed change is a mere correction of a drafting error made last year, I view it as an increase in federal death tax rates," Archer wrote. "Accordingly, I cannot support any change in law that would go in the opposite direction by increasing death tax rates."

Archer's spokesman, Ari Fleischer, who later would become the White House press secretary, explained Archer's stance in political terms which spoke to partisanship and political advantage, rather than any concept of principled conduct. "When the Democrats controlled Congress and drafting errors worked against the taxpayers, the Democrats let them stay in the law," Fleischer said. "Now, when one works against the Government and for the taxpayers, we're in no rush to correct it."

Democrats disputed Fleischer's two-wrongs-make-a-right statement. "Every time a technical error has been found, either way, we corrected it," said John Buckley, the chief tax lawyer for the Ways and Means Committee Democrats.

Six years later this error by Congress remained uncorrected at a cost to taxpayers, and a benefit to heirs of the super rich, of more than a half billion dollars and growing.

The one high-level person in Washington who grasped that the problem with the earned income tax credit was errors, not fraud, and that the intense auditing was a waste of time was Paul H. O'Neill, George W. Bush's first Treasury secretary and the former chief executive of Alcoa. O'Neill thought it was poor practice to focus auditing on people who at most could take the government for $4,140. O'Neill ordered an IRS committee to come up with a way to reduce errors and fraud so that auditing could be cut back.

Part of O'Neill's plan was to come up with a uniform definition of the word *child*. The tax code has five definitions of *child*. Depending on which credit or exemption a taxpayer is seeking—personal exemption, child credit, child care tax credit, adoption credit or earned income tax credit—a child is defined as someone under the age of 13, 17, 18, 19 or 24. A child must be 12 or under for the child care credit, but 17 or under for the child credit and 18 or under to be claimed as an exemption, unless the child is a full-time student, in which case the limit is through age 23. Foster children who live in a home for 11 months cannot be counted as exemptions. O'Neill noted that more than 52 million taxpayers in 2003 have children. "The child credit, the child care credit, the earned income tax credit and other provisions are there to help these taxpayers by reducing their tax burden. Why should we make it so difficult for taxpayers with children to receive these benefits that clearly the Congress intended?" he asked.

In the spring of 2003 the IRS came up with its solution to stop the intense auditing of the working poor. Rube Goldberg would have been proud. The plan was to require as many as five million claimants—more than 12 times as many as were audited in the peak year—to prove in advance that they qualify. People would have to submit records of marriages and births and residency. Under the plan a landlord could certify residency, but a building superintendent could not, an indication of how much social class bias undercuts the constitutional premise of equality for all. It was also dubious on practical grounds. Landlords may live miles, even oceans, away from their property, while superintendents are typically there every day and are better qualified to judge who actually lives in the buildings they maintain.

The proposed rules also required that people produce these records within 60 days or be barred from getting the credit. That poses a bit of a problem for people wed in California, where the state is so strapped for funds that requests for copies of marriage licenses are being delayed more than two years. The rules also ignored state laws that make many records private. For example, in New York birth certificates are not public records, which would make it difficult for someone who took in a dead relative's child to get the document.

In crafting the rules the IRS also reinvented a wheel, ignoring practices long in place at the Department of Agriculture for food stamps, which have a much lower fraud-and-error rate than the tax credit. That the IRS would devise such a complex and cumbersome procedure illustrates the need for Congress to pay serious attention to the boring work of how government agencies actually administer the law instead of having show hearings and making uninformed and false pronouncements. The rules also maintain the history of treating the poor differently than everyone else, of treating their conduct as more suspicious than that of people of means. Neither Americans who earn more than poverty-level wages nor corporations nor investment vehicles like partnerships are required to prove in advance that they are qualified for a tax break.

There is one other aspect of the earned income tax credit that is significant in understanding how the tax system is being tilted to make money flow toward the rich. It is the role of business in profiting off the credit.

Tax preparers and lenders take in about $1.75 billion in fees each year from the roughly $30 billion in earned income tax credits. That is nearly six cents of every dollar of aid that goes to these poor families.

The biggest tax preparation firms, H&R Block and Jackson Hewitt, which is owned by the Cendant conglomerate, skillfully target the working poor and the economically illiterate to profit from their misery. They earn substantial fees preparing the tax returns of the working poor, even though for most a one-page tax return and an application for the tax credit are all that is required. Block and Jackson Hewitt also have deals with Household International and Pacific Capital Bancorp to profit even more by lending the amount of the tax credit until it arrives. These loans, known as RALs or refund anticipation loans, come at astronomical interest rates that help these companies to pick the pockets of the poor in ways that are perfectly legal.

Jackson Hewitt, by focusing on preparing returns for the working poor and arranging loans for them, grew from 15 offices in 1986 to 3,800 offices in 2002. Michael Lister, the president of Jackson Hewitt, said we "concentrate our efforts on people who make less than $30,000, or $50,000."

These loans are possible because the IRS has agreed to advise the lenders with an electronic signal whether a refund is likely to be issued. The loan is made to the taxpayer once the IRS signal indicates a tax refund check will be cut. Customers then get their loans after a delay of one or two days. Meanwhile the IRS takes from two to 17 days to issue the tax credit, which is sent electronically not to the customer, but to a special bank account created by Block or Jackson Hewitt to collect the government check and use it to pay off the loan.

The working poor typically pay flat fees to borrow the amount of their earned income tax credit for the few days until the IRS issues the refund. The typical charge in 2003 was $78 or $88. These fees equate to annual interest rates far beyond what is charged on credit card debt. One study found the lowest rate was 97 percent annually, a rate of 222 percent was typical and in some cases the rate was greater than 2,000 percent, surely figures that would make a mob loan shark envious. Sometimes the interest rate cannot be calculated because the IRS issues the credit, which automatically pays off the loan, before the loan check clears Block's or Jackson Hewitt's account.

Many of the working poor pay such onerous amounts because they are in dire straits. Block agents say it is routine for people to say they need their check to avoid eviction, recover a car that has been repossessed or turn the utilities back on. The tax system is not the best way to address the anxiety and other problems of poverty. But Congress has so far agreed to use a tax credit to help the poor rather than undertake serious policy changes aimed at raising low-end wages and easing the many economic risks that the working poor are shielded from by governments in most other industrialized nations.

The Consumer Federation of America and the National Consumer Law Center uncovered great discrepancies in how these services are sold. They found that the highest rates were charged in the neighborhoods that have the most tax preparation and loan offices, meaning competition did not drive down prices. In the South, two thirds of the people who claim the credit take out a loan. In San Francisco, by contrast, just one in nine families does. In New York City a fifth of people claiming the credit take out a loan, a rate no doubt held down by the fact that the city has twice gone to court to fight what it viewed as deceptive advertising of the loans.

As pressure to stop such high-interest lending has grown, the tax preparation industry has come up with a new device—fast cash—to profit even more.

Once customers of Block get their high-priced loan, they just step across the carpet at their Block office and put the check into a kind of automated teller machine. These fast cash services to the working poor for the earned income tax credit funds generated $357 million in profit in 1999, more than double the profit in 1998, one study estimated.

At many of its offices Block installed self-service check-cashing machines owned by Ace Cash Express of Irving, Texas. When Block tax preparation customers cash their loan or refund check, Block gets a cut of the fee charged by Ace. In 2001, Ace cashed 102,000 checks at such machines (including those not in Block offices), charging an average fee of $17.65, or 2.2 percent of the check amount. The machines placed in Block offices charge more—from 2.9 percent to 3.4 percent of the check amount. The higher rate is curious since it suggests a greater risk that a check will not be honored despite the fact that Block issued the loan checks after making sure the customer would probably get his or her refund from the IRS. And the higher rate is especially curious when a refund check from the IRS is being cashed.

On a $3,000 loan, Ace would collect $87 to $105 just to cash the

Block customer's loan check, plus a $3 fee for first-time users of its machines. This is in addition to the refund anticipation loan fee, which is typically $78, and income tax preparation fees. Block did negotiate one money-saving feature for its biggest customers. Regardless of the size of the loan check, Ace's fee is capped at $120. Add up all these charges and for the typical earned income tax credit of $1,600 or so, that means 11 percent is being used to pay fees to corporations, surely an inefficient way to provide benefits.

Simplifying the tax credit could not only reduce fraud and errors but it could also make sure that more earned income tax credit dollars remain with the working poor rather than flow to big corporations like Block, Cendant, Household International and other banks that have acted as lenders over the years. But this issue is not on the front burner in Congress, whose members rely for campaign contributions on the kind of people who own companies, not on the people who pay loan-shark rates to borrow.

Congress has in recent years shown a deep interest in tax policy and, especially, the IRS. But that interest has not been directed at fundamental reform to make the tax system fit with the changing economic order. And it certainly has not been directed at funding the IRS so it can accomplish all the tasks set for it, from collecting taxes to enforcing the law against cheats to providing it with the technology needed to make the system work smoothly for taxpayers. Instead, the IRS has served as a powerful tool to whip voters into a froth.

Handcuffing the Tax Police
10

Senator William Roth of Delaware, an old lawyer with long jowls and a strong tendency to listen to yes-men, produced Senate Finance Committee hearings on the IRS in 1997 and 1998. It was the first time in decades that the Senate had conducted any broad oversight of the IRS and the hearings were a year in preproduction.

When the doors opened for the first session, Roth displayed a previously unknown flair for the dramatic. For starters he staged the hearings in a Senate committee room specially designed for intelligence briefings. Its walls were thought to block electronic eavesdropping, while its only public door stood at the end of a long corridor with guards at the far end, lest someone walking by overhear state secrets. Guards searched everyone before they could enter.

Roth said he wanted to "address three fundamental questions. First, does the IRS have too much power? Second, if Congress were to limit that power, what expectations do we have that the new limits will be more effective than the old? And third, how do we go about changing the culture of the IRS?"

On the second day the audience arrived to find its view partially blocked by a black curtain. Behind the curtain sat six IRS employees, identified only by numbers. All had their voices electronically distorted, the way turncoat mobsters who feared their godfathers would have them whacked were allowed to testify. At a time when some members of Congress were describing government law enforcement agents as "jack-booted thugs," the impression that the IRS was a government Mafia that could have you killed for breaking its code of silence was unmistakable.

It was great drama, just what Roth wanted. Over six days in the fall and spring the television networks and newspapers gave mostly breathless accounts of a rogue agency ruining lives with abandon until Roth came to the rescue. The tens of thousands of words of testimony were reduced to sound bytes, devoid of nuance. The story: unnamed IRS agents falsely making unnamed people pay taxes they did not owe; dozens of criminal investigation agents, brandishing guns, entering peaceful offices and homes as if they expected armed drug dealers; agents issuing subpoenas for no purpose except to embarrass people. There was even testimony that an IRS agent held a gun on a girl, caught in a raid on her parent's home, and forced her to change her clothes while he watched.

There was one problem. Most of it wasn't true. But that would not come out for months and when an official inquiry that Roth ordered from the investigative arm of Congress, the General Accounting Office, found little to support what had been presented at the hearings, the senator did his best to make sure the public would never see the full report.

The hearings did produce important insights, but they were not so much about a rogue agency out of control as about Congress creating IRS problems. Six IRS employees and several outside experts, whose testimony was largely ignored by the news media, told about the internal workings of the agency. There was far too much work and not enough workers or equipment. Bosses pressed people to work the easiest cases to generate numbers for statistical reports because that was what Congress demanded. The poor and vulnerable were pursued because their cases were more easily brought to a close, which generated lots of numbers for statistical performance reports, while those with money to fight back sometimes were allowed to slip away without paying. That, too, reflected the demands by Congress both to generate statistics and to not roil the friends of the elected. Procedures were not always followed, sometimes because of corner cutting to meet productivity demands, more often due to lack of training, which was continually cut because Congress did not pay for it. There were complaints that high-level managers took care of friends and made life difficult for those they disliked, an issue that Roth did not pursue. And there were complaints of petty abuses, like arranging a stop at an outlying office to squeeze some extra time at the start or end of a vacation, that hardly seem worthy of a congressional inquiry.

The news reports gave at best passing mention to these important insights into how the IRS operated and what vexed it. It was that curtain and the distorted voices that made headlines and the evening news. Like a Hollywood blockbuster about a historical event, the news coverage was long on powerful images and short on just what made the event important.

The following spring Roth held a second round of hearings, which generated a lot more breathless coverage, although a few journalists this time paid closer attention and saw more comedy than drama in the hyperbole.

Senators Trent Lott of Mississippi, the majority leader, and Frank Murkowski of Alaska accused the IRS of "Gestapo-like tactics."

Senator Don Nickles of Oklahoma, the majority whip, charged that "the IRS is out of control!"

Committee Democrats took a more cautious approach, saying that it appeared that the IRS was being asked to do too much work with too little money and so corner cutting and excessive work schedules should be expected. But they joined in criticizing IRS raids on several businesses when just subpoenaing the documents might have been enough.

Senator Bob Kerrey of Nebraska said popular discontent arose because of "a breathtaking gap between what the IRS can do and what the private sectors do. . . . Taxpayers don't compare the IRS with the tax collection agency in Australia or the Federal Republic of Germany. They compare it to what they can get with their ATM card. And there is a tremendous difference between what the IRS can do and what the private sector could do."

There was also a moment during the hearings, just one, when a senator reached out to a witness and made it clear that he stood side by side with him. It was Senator Phil Gramm of Texas, who described how he tried to dissuade the testimony of the only member of the political donor class who appeared before the committee, oilman William

A. "Tex" Moncrief. Gramm referred to him as "an old and dear friend of mine" and said he feared that his testimony would not be accepted by all at face value.

Moncrief, then 78 years old, testified that "on the morning of September 1, 1994, the IRS raided the Fort Worth office of my family-run oil company. Making sure my employees saw their guns, they stormed the offices like an army landing on an enemy beachfront. My employees heard the agents shout, 'IRS. This business is under criminal investigation. Remove your hands from the keyboards and back away from the computers. And remember, we are armed.' They rummaged through every inch of our building, breaking into offices, barking orders like 'Open the doors or we'll knock them down.' One special agent told my son that he could blow the hinges off his safe if he wouldn't open it. Agents even removed sheet rock from the walls, as if they were looking for illegal drugs. They herded my employees down to a first-floor dining room, treating them like criminals. No food, no phone calls and, for some, no chairs. My entire staff at the time consisted of less than 35 people, mostly women. That's a ratio of nearly two armed agents per employee. One employee commented, 'For the first time in my life I feel bad to be an American.' I was humiliated and branded a criminal before anyone in the IRS bothered to consider that I hadn't done anything wrong."

It was, Moncrief testified, the beginning of a 16-month ordeal that cost him $5.5 million in legal and accounting fees before the Department of Justice would drop its criminal case.

As Moncrief began his testimony, it was so troubling that even Senator Daniel Patrick Moynihan of New York, the scholar in the Senate, joined in the denunciations of the IRS from the dais, decrying the "paramilitary performance of the Internal Revenue Service . . . it's government violence directed against citizenry."

By law the IRS was not allowed to respond to any of the charges made against it. Doing so would have violated the confidentiality of the taxpayers and others who testified, the legacy of a law passed when President Nixon had tried to use the IRS to go after his enemies. What was intended to be a shield for taxpayers had been turned into a sword that Senator Roth gave witnesses, including the six anonymous IRS agents, to wield against the agency.

Despite the secrecy law, much of the story of Moncrief's case found its way into the public record because of several related lawsuits. One of them involved his top finance executive, who sued the IRS when it would not pay him any reward and who Moncrief was pursuing in court.

It turned out that Moncrief's top financial executive had gone to the IRS with documents suggesting a long-running tax fraud. The IRS was so persuaded by the documents that it signed a contract with the informant promising to pay him a reward of up to $25 million if the government ultimately collected the full amount of tax that the documents indicated were due—$300 million.

Part of this huge tax bill was owed for a gift supposedly made by Moncrief's elderly mother, who had won $40 million in a legal settlement over some gas wells and passed the money to Tex and his sons without paying gift taxes. The oil company's records also indicated that just before Moncrief's mother died, she sold $190 million worth of oil and gas wells to her seven grandchildren for about $12.5 million, cheating the government out of either gift or estate taxes.

Then there was the time that one of Tex's sons got into financial trouble and the rest of the family bailed him out by paying $40 million for property worth a fifth as much, another apparent gift tax dodge.

Finally there were records showing personal expenses being charged to the business, like when Tex would take his jet out west to his retreats in Palm Springs and Colorado. Then there were the salaries for his personal chauffeur and other servants, as well as bills from his 15,000–acre Texas ranch with its stock of zebras and other zoo animals, that showed up as business expenses.

Even without this information, which came out months later, Moncrief's story became too much for Senator Moynihan once the oilman testified that the entire affair was a "figment" of his finance executive's imagination, that the IRS never presented him with a tax bill and that it "extorted" $23 million from him.

Moynihan ridiculed the idea that Moncrief would pay such a large sum if the IRS investigation was baseless. "Take this $23 million—I want to get back to my golf," Mr. Moynihan said, chortling. "I don't believe him. I simply don't believe him."

The senator suspected that the armed raid was a blessing in disguise. Since the IRS had computerized copies of the business records, the massive display of force was overkill, a cowboy move by some IRS official who had been helping federal narcotics agents for too long. Moynihan figured that the family's lawyer, Robert Bennett, who also represented President Clinton, negotiated a 93 percent discount on Moncrief's tax bill in return for not suing the IRS.

After the second round of hearings the Senate voted 97 to 0 to pass the IRS Reform and Restructuring Act of 1998. The House followed and Clinton signed it into law.

The law created an advisory oversight board for the IRS, set the term for a commissioner at five years and moved the internal affairs squad out of the IRS and into the Department of the Treasury. It made the chief IRS lawyer independent of the commissioner. It also required the IRS to grant relief to innocent spouses, those who could show that they had nothing to do with tax cheating by their former, or current, spouse. And it banned the use of anything that might even smell like a quota to measure the performance of IRS employees.

The provision of the law that had the greatest effect was what came to be known as the Ten Deadly Sins. The law mandated the firing, following an administrative inquiry, of employees found to have committed any of 10 acts, among them violating a taxpayer's constitutional or civil rights, threatening an audit for personal gain, making a false statement under oath or falsifying or destroying documents to conceal mistakes. Only the commissioner can reduce the mandatory discharge to a lesser penalty.

In effect, the law handcuffed the tax police.

The law quickly became a boon for tax cheats of all kinds. Promoters began holding seminars on how to use the law to get out of paying taxes or to tie the IRS up in so many procedural knots that it would never be able to collect the money. Irwin Schiff—who, despite twice serving time for tax crimes, still runs a business out of Las Vegas teaching people how to not pay taxes—said business took off after the hearings and the passage of the new law. Soon his ratty old car and worn wardrobe were replaced and he was back to being a natty dresser driving new wheels.

IRS tax collectors came under intense pressure from Congress to be nicer to taxpayers. Some complained that they received threats of being reported for committing one of the Ten Deadly Sins if they did not back off. Even if an accusation lacked merit, just the filing of a complaint could mean a grueling round of inquiries by the Department of the Treasury's inspector general for tax administration.

The inspector general's office relentlessly pursued suspected misbehavior by IRS employees. One clerical worker in Manhattan was put under surveillance for several weeks because of a complaint that she was a drug dealer. She was videotaped every day when she went to a bench outside the government offices to eat her brown-bag lunch. When no evidence turned up that she did anything but work, go to church several times a week and care for grandchildren who lived in her home, she was rousted from bed before dawn and hauled downtown for a grilling. It turned out the complaint had been made by a real drug dealer, albeit a small-timer, whom she had banished from her house when she came home and found him trying to make time with her grown daughter.

The inspector general, David Williams, went so far as to develop his own quota system. His office sent an e-mail setting a goal of 440 cases each for his agency's Atlanta, Dallas and New York offices and smaller goals for seven other offices. The e-mail said that "to reach your divisional goal is the responsibility of the special agent in charge" and those managing agents "will need to use the resources effectively to obtain the goal."

When the quotas were disclosed in *The New York Times,* Williams hesitated for a day, then gave an interview to *The Washington Post,* which reported that he had rescinded the quotas. But a careful reading of his remarks showed he had only created an appearance of withdrawing the quotas without actually doing so. Pressed by *The Times* on whether he was going to actually rescind the quotas, Williams fell silent for 42 long seconds and then said that the quotas were no longer operative. The quotas were then dead.

The effect of all of this on IRS staffers, whose job was to collect taxes that were due, but had not yet been paid, was immediate. Property seizures plummeted 98 percent to just over 200 in 1999 for the entire country. Levies of bank accounts and garnishments of paychecks fell by three fourths, to 458,000 from 1.8 million two years earlier. Liens, which ensure that taxes are paid when real estate or other property is sold, fell by two thirds to 98,000 from 272,000.

The effect was especially significant in changing the behavior of the low-level IRS managers. They are in effect the sergeants of the Tax Police Department and, just as with regular police sergeants, their attitudes and decisions determine how the laws are actually administered. Many of these managers concluded that to keep their jobs and advance up the ranks, they were expected to wilt before the rich and powerful, especially those who can get a politician on the telephone.

"Don't aggravate taxpayers—that's what our managers are telling us," said a longtime revenue agent in New York, one of scores interviewed about the changes in the agency after the new law was passed. As he spoke, six colleagues nodded in agreement and offered similar comments made by their bosses. A revenue agent in Florida said his manager told him, "Don't probe deeply. Just find three or four obvious items and close the case."

In Nashville, a revenue agent said anyone there could get a tax case resolved favorably if the taxpayer had enough influence to get a senator or congressperson to complain to the IRS. "We just collapse," the 14-year veteran said.

"Please don't call us tax collectors in the newspaper," one longtime revenue officer in New York said. "We don't collect taxes anymore. We aren't allowed to."

Even more amazing than these comments was the response of the chief of IRS operations after he was advised of those and other remarks from interviews with IRS workers in California, Connecticut, Florida, Georgia, Illinois, Michigan, New York, Tennessee, Texas and Washington, nearly all of whom spoke on condition that they not be identified.

"None of these comments shock me," John Dalrymple said. "I also am hearing things that have the same general tone."

Dalrymple said he would characterize their comments this way: "Hey, what is the service's policy going to be around compliance and enforcement? And how are we going to balance the need for good customer service on an individual basis with our responsibility to make sure that people are paying their fair share?"

"Frankly, it is a discussion that we have been having at the highest levels of the organization," he said. Dalrymple said he and other agency executives had traveled the country telling IRS workers that enforcement was important and that all taxpayers were to be treated alike, without regard to their economic or social standing. However, that message was not getting through, and efforts to stamp out the mistaken belief that official policy favored the wealthy were failing, he said.

Dalrymple said the belief, growing out of the Senate hearings, that the rich and connected were to be treated with gloves so velvety soft that if they put up a fight they had to be allowed to slip away was not limited just to IRS workers, either. It was also gaining currency among some taxpayers. "Managers and employees are looking for some definitive statements" from the top, Dalrymple said, "about what to do in certain circumstances that are fairly egregious in terms of not complying with the law."

Donald Alexander, the Nixon administration tax commissioner, was astonished at what his party, the party of law and order, had done to breed disrespect for tax law enforcement. Alexander, who had gone on to become a prominent Washington tax lawyer, said he would have none of the fashionable Republican view that law enforcement was good, audits were bad. And he believed that weakening the IRS was an unprincipled way to restrain the growth of government because the benefits went to the sharpers at the expense of the honest.

"It's a dumb law," Alexander said of the reform act and its Ten Deadly Sins. "When someone can fail to meet his or her tax obligations without a worry about having enforcement actions taken, then other creditors are going to come in first and get paid, and the deadbeat taxpayer wins."

The Roth hearings that led to the law were not just a result of the senator's eagerness to bring the IRS in check. They were part of a strategy by a segment of Washington Republicans to win votes by going after the IRS and the tax system. It was a strategy urged by a young pollster named Frank Luntz, who had provided the party with important insights into how voters felt about taxes, including a segment of young people who he believed could be persuaded to vote Republican if the party understood their concerns. Attacking the IRS, Luntz told his patrons, was the single best way to win those votes.

Luntz had gotten into politics in 1992, advising Patrick J. Buchanan, the CNN commentator who described Adolph Hitler as "an individual of great courage, a soldier's soldier in the Great War, a leader steeped in the history of Europe." Luntz said he taught Buchanan and then Ross Perot, the populist billionaire, how to attract votes from people in their twenties and thirties who were not getting ahead economically and who hated being talked down to by politicians. He moved on to work for Rudolph Giuliani's campaign for mayor of New York and then found his way into the good graces of Newt Gingrich, the Georgia congressman who led the Republicans to control of the House in the 1994 elections.

Saying something the right way could have a major impact on whether you appealed to voters, Luntz taught these politicians. To express this idea, Luntz picked up some tips from Trent Lott and worked up a new lexicon for taxes. It goes something like this:

"You wake up in the morning and have your first cup of coffee, you pay a sales tax. You go to your garage; you start your car; you pay an automobile tax. You drive to work; you pay a gas tax. You go to work; you pay an income tax. You turn on the lights; you pay an electricity tax. You flush the toilet; you pay a water tax. You fly somewhere; you pay an airport tax. You stay overnight; you pay a hotel occupancy tax. You call home; you pay a telephone tax. You finally get home; you pay a property tax. You turn on the TV; you pay a cable tax. Even when you die, you pay a death tax. You are taxed from the moment you wake up in the morning until the moment you go to bed at night. You're taxed from your cradle to your grave, and hardworking American taxpayers deserve a break."

Luntz said that "usually when I do this, everyone stands up and applauds. You do that really fast, really loud, and get in their face and these guys really get it." Using that technique in a commercial for Representative Mike Rogers of Michigan increased his winning margin from 100 votes in the election before to 1,000 votes after it was aired.

Luntz's favorite survey question of all time is about the IRS. He asked people, "Which would you prefer: having your wallet or purse stolen or being audited by the IRS?" and learned that "45 percent said wallet or purse, 45 percent said IRS, and 10 percent said no difference."

He taught his clients that promising to reform the IRS wins votes because people fear the IRS, even if they have never been audited. "Most people have never been audited, but most people know someone who has been, and it is a grueling awful procedure. Since we like to share our pain with others, people don't hide the fact that they've been audited anymore. It's almost a badge of honor. So we all know somebody who's been through it and we think, 'There but for the grace of God go I.' We don't want to be afraid of our government. And we don't want to be afraid that one little mistake somewhere at sometime could come back to haunt us. We're scared. The IRS is a frightening concept."

Yet while Luntz acknowledges that fear of the IRS is probably badly out of proportion with the reality, he says that in terms of winning votes that does not matter. "Perception is reality. People are afraid, whether they should be or not. As a child you are afraid of monsters in the closet. To my knowledge there has never been a monster found in the closet of a five-year-old, but how many five-year-olds are afraid of monsters? Same thing here. The rich are afraid that they'll get busted, the upper middle class are afraid that they'll get fined, the middle class are afraid of the time commitments and the lower middle class are afraid they'll get thrown in jail. So the fears are a little different. But it's fear nevertheless."

At the end of the hearings that were inspired by Luntz's research into the political advantage of going after the IRS, Roth ordered up two investigations. He had to, under Luntz's theory, because he had to show he was willing to take action. Roth assigned the investigative arm of Congress, the General Accounting Office, to look into the abuses alleged at his hearings. The other inquiry, into those gun-toting criminal investigators, was assigned to William Webster, the former FBI director and one of Jonathan Blattmachr's law partners.

The Webster report, issued a year later, did not support the rhetoric of Senators Roth, Lott, Murkowski and Nickles about an out-of-control Gestapo.

"No evidence was found of systematic abuses by agents," Judge Webster reported, although his investigators did find "isolated and individual" examples of misconduct. Judge Webster concluded that there was "no evidence in the use-of-force incidents to suggest that . . .

agents are overly aggressive, use force unnecessarily, or are improperly trained."

Roth tried to keep the other report, by the General Accounting Office, locked up. When the journal *Tax Notes* pried it loose through the Freedom of Information Act, the reason Roth hoped it would never get out became apparent.

"Generally, we found no corroborating evidence that the criminal investigations described at the hearing were retaliatory against the specific taxpayer," the report said. "In addition, we could not independently substantiate that IRS employees had vendettas against these taxpayers. . . . Our investigation did find that decisions to initiate the investigations were reasonably based on the information available to IRS at the time and were documented in agency files when they were made. Further, we found no evidence that IRS employees had acted improperly in obtaining and executing the search warrants."

Investigations by *The New York Times, Tax Notes* and *The Wall Street Journal* also showed that the most explosive charges at the hearings simply did not withstand scrutiny. (Later court proceedings brought forth even more to discredit the hearings.) When the General Accounting Office report made the light of day, Marie Cocco, a columnist for the Long Island newspaper *Newsday,* wrote that the Senate Finance Committee inquiry "turns out to be the biggest tax fraud of the decade."

Fraud or not, the damage to the tax system had been done. Tax cheating was on the rise as the tax cops struggled against their handcuffs. But even a hobbled law enforcement agency has work to do. A new tax commissioner, the first who was not a tax lawyer, made it his mission to remake the agency. He didn't know much about law enforcement, but he did know a lot about customer satisfaction.

Mr. Rossotti's Customers

11

If we can't make sure that everyone pays their fair share,
then honest taxpayers get stuck making up the difference.

—Treasury Secretary Paul H. O'Neill

The first time that Charles O. Rossotti had his income tax return thoroughly audited was in 1997. For years the wealthy businessman and his wife Barbara, a corporate lawyer, just dropped their 1040 in the mail, where it joined millions of others on its way to one of the IRS processing centers. The centers are spartan, low buildings that sit behind high fences topped with barbed wire. Inside is the tax pipeline.

To visit one of these centers is to travel back in time to when cars lacked air conditioning, prime time was black-and-white and merchants posted accounts by hand. It is here that tax cheats gain two advantages. Some of them get lost in the volume of information. Others exploit how the IRS sifts through the data on tax returns.

Returns filed electronically now move over distant data lines to air-conditioned rooms where banks of computers organize the data for the agency's master files. But in Austin, Atlanta and eight other regional centers, the IRS pipeline processes paper tax returns. Each spring postal service 18-wheelers line up at the loading docks around the clock. The clang of metal, like prison doors slamming shut, jars the air as steel carts roll off the mail trucks to be parked in bare concrete hallways until the envelopes are fed into a machine that sands them open.

Trays of opened envelopes then roll into a windowless room where clerks sit silently at desks of laminated blond wood, like the kind used in school desks. A superstructure of thin wooden shelves has been added to each desk. These are the Tingle tables, named after the IRS official who decades ago figured out how to sort millions upon millions of tax returns efficiently. The clerks extract the returns and checks, discarding staples, paperclips and the occasional dead mouse. From large manila envelopes, it is said, slender snakes sometimes slither.

In the next room, acres in size, more clerks check for minor or obvious errors before sending each sheet of paper sideways to a conveyor belt and through a machine that stamps it with a number in the unlikely event that it must be retrieved later from storage. Across the way banks of clerks sit at computer terminals, nearly all of them women who work for the IRS only during tax season. As fast as their fingers will move, they transcribe data on the tax returns. More than a few errors creep in because speed is critical to keep the pipeline from clogging up with unprocessed paper.

Only about 40 percent of the information that taxpayers enter on their returns is transcribed, with some of the specific lines changing each year. The cost of transcribing any given line on a tax return is measured and charged to the budget of the IRS unit that wants the information. The IRS knows how much it costs to transcribe any line from a paper tax return into the computer. It does not know how much ignoring a line costs in lost tax revenue, though there is evidence that penny pinching on transcription allows many billions of dollars to go untaxed, especially from tax forms used primarily by the richest Americans.

For years now these transcription operations have been make-work projects because the vast majority of tax returns are prepared on computers, then printed onto paper only to be restored to digital form by the IRS. Congress could have required electronic forms years ago, lowering costs and allowing thorough analysis of tax returns, but instead it approved meager funds for a series of failed technology projects, like an optical scanner that kept going blind.

In all the IRS spent $4 billion on computers, scanners and the like that did not work. Experts who knew the inner workings of the projects noted that instead of hiring companies that designed systems for big banks and financial houses, Congress made the IRS give the jobs to big military contractors, who were hurting for government business after the West won the cold war. The connection between warfare technology and tax administration technology escaped everyone except the members of Congress who relied on the Daddy Warbucks segment of the political donor class. Congress also would not approve the kinds of competitive salaries needed to hire first-rate technology talent. Citibank and American Express bought computer systems so powerful that a couple from Ohio on vacation in Budapest can find out within minutes of leaving their table whether the restaurant charged them the correct amount for lunch. Congress neither properly financed nor exercised oversight to make sure the IRS had what was needed to build comprehensive systems like that.

Lacking modern technology, the front-line task of finding improper or suspect entries on tax returns falls to the seasonally employed transcription clerks working the pipeline. They are supposed to spot things like zeroes on the lines for income and for tax due. Suspect returns are to be dropped into a "funny box" at each clerk's feet. But the clerks are under such intense pressure to type quickly to hold down costs and keep the paper flowing through the pipeline that many funny returns slip by and, along with them, refund checks. About $30 million was refunded in 2000 and 2001, for example, to people claiming a bogus slavery reparations credit before the IRS caught on. Then the clerks were told to funny-box returns with the words "slavery" or "reparations" or seeking $43,209, the supposed value of 40 acres and a mule adjusted for inflation from the end of the Civil War. It was through this penny-pinching hole that Nick Jesson, a California businessman who does not pay taxes, got a refund of all of the taxes he withheld from his workers' paychecks.

The 40 percent of the data that are transcribed from paper returns are used to select audit targets. The rest of the details on the tax return stays on paper. Once the paper reaches the end of the pipeline, it is boxed up and sent to a warehouse, where it will molder for six years and then be ground into pulp.

Months after tax-filing season ends and the flow of paper through the pipeline slows, IRS computers in Martinsburg, West Virginia, analyze the data extracted from each return. This takes a long time in part because all the data are stored on reels of magnetic tape, a technology abandoned elsewhere years ago. The data are processed on computers designed when Eisenhower was in the White House and installed when Kennedy was president. In the twenty-first century, some still bear the nameplate of Sperry Univac, communicating in a computer language so ancient that, but for the IRS, it would be deader than Latin. It will be years before these computers are replaced.

The aging computers make simple comparisons using a crude statistical technique known as the *discriminant function* or *dif.* Each return is compared to other returns of similar income to look for deductions that appear to be too large based on detailed studies of how people cheated in the past. The last of these studies was made in the eighties, rendering the data of little value and requiring the IRS to apply a variety of fudge factors and estimates. Finally, every single tax return is given a "dif score" and rank ordered as a candidate for an audit from no. 1 down to the return least likely to have any cheating, chiseling or error. The dif score system is so out of date that in recent years a third of audits resulted in either no change or a refund to the taxpayer, a huge waste of the agency's shrinking complement of tax detectives.

In the eighties the IRS had enough money to audit about one of every nine tax returns filed by high-income Americans, those making more than $100,000 annually. Charles and Barbara Rossotti were deep into that class. As time passed, their odds of being audited grew ever slimmer as Congress steadily eroded resources to enforce the tax laws. By 1997, when the Rossottis' tax returns were finally audited, their odds of being picked were just one in 66, or less than once in an adult's lifetime.

There was a good reason to reduce audits of one group of high-income taxpayers: those who relied on salaries for most or all of their income. Because employers reported what they made to the IRS, banks reported how much they earned in interest and paid on mortgages, and companies reported how much they received in dividends, most wage earners had little chance to cheat. They could overstate charitable deductions or property taxes and, if they had capital gains, understate their investment profits. But since those making less than $1 million a year counted on wages for three fourths of their income, the opportunities were mostly to chisel, not cheat, on income taxes. The big opportunities to cheat were to be found among those who controlled what was reported to the IRS about their income: business owners, landlords, stock market investors and people who invest in partnerships.

As it happened, however, the Rossottis had their tax returns audited not because of a high dif score or a lot of business income, but because passing an audit was a job requirement. Charles O. Rossotti was about to become the commissioner of internal revenue. Like everyone who worked for the IRS, right down to the Tingle table clerks, he had to show he was an honest taxpayer to get hired and to keep his job.

Charles and Barbara Rossotti were exactly the kinds of people that the tax system had been designed to levy. He was the son of an Italian immigrant who owned a printing business in Manhattan. Rossotti learned the attention to detail necessary for a printing business, where ordered thinking and advance planning go together with ink-stained hands. He graduated magna cum laude from Georgetown University and in 1964 earned a masters degree at the Harvard Business School. He went to work at the Pentagon, one of McNamara's whiz kids, and for five years was assistant secretary of defense for systems analysis. He also came under the wing of another defense secretary, David Packard.

Then, like many who come to Washington to do good, Rossotti set out to do well. With a friend he founded American Management Systems, which contracted with government agencies to integrate technology and management. By 1997, American Management Systems had become one of the thousand largest publicly traded companies in America. Rossotti was its chairman, with a small fortune of about $40 million and an annual household income from the company and from his wife Barbara's legal practice of more than $1 million a year. He was also, at age 57, bored.

Rossotti had already begun to withdraw from his firm, awarding titles and delegating responsibilities to subordinates, when an executive recruiter called. The man asked if Rossotti knew anyone who might be interested in running the IRS, someone who understood technology and how large organizations function. What the headhunter really wanted to know was whether Rossotti was interested in the job. It was a thankless post at best and one that until then had always been held by a tax lawyer. Rossotti soon found himself daydreaming about how he could fix the IRS and help relieve millions of Americans of the torment of dealing with a dysfunctional agency. After all, he understood how computer technology and organizational culture could frustrate people. And his best friend had already left the company to finish out his career with a high-level federal post. Running the IRS, reforming the IRS, would be a way both to show what could be done with smart management and to give back to the country. When Rossotti told his wife what was on his mind, she told him that he was crazy.

Rossotti devoured internal reports and studies on the IRS and sat through hours of briefings, all before he had the job. He soon developed an idea about how to fix the IRS, one that appealed both to key members of Congress and to the Clinton administration. Both were tired of hearing complaints about how no one answered the telephones at the IRS and how hard it was to get the smallest problem resolved. Rossotti thought of people like himself not as taxpayers, but as customers of the IRS.

"People don't like paying taxes, but they understand the need to," Rossotti said. "Ninety-eight percent want to comply, and our job is to help them—it's that simple." Sheldon Cohen, who had been the Johnson administration tax commissioner, told Rossotti that much as service needed to be improved, that was not the key issue. To think that the IRS was anything but the tax police was foolish, Cohen counseled. Many people paid not out of a noble sense of commitment to country, but only to avoid having the tax cops at their door. The IRS was needed to patrol the financial throughways, looking for people who try to speed by without paying their toll and keeping the rest of the economic traffic flowing smoothly. Rossotti saw things differently.

Before he was sworn in, the Rossottis took a suite at the Ritz-Carlton in Naples, Florida, the kind of luxury hotel that a couple of their substance could easily afford. It was supposed to be a vacation before starting on a tough new job, but Rossotti brought along his laptop. He wrote a 68-page plan for remaking the IRS. He called it "Modernizing America's Tax Agency" and he sent signed copies of the booklet to important players in the tax world. He knew his plan was risky and that it would take a long time, perhaps a decade, to remake the IRS. "I'm no fool," he said. "There's no guarantee that this will be successful. We could crash and burn in any number of ways, but I think it's worth it, and I think I can do it."

He reasoned that since enforcement brought in relatively few dollars, just that last 2 percent or so by his reckoning, the best way to increase government revenues was to focus on the 98 cents of each tax dollar that came in the door easily. One mistake of the past, he concluded, was to focus too much on raising more money through audits, collections of past due taxes and criminal investigations, work that together consumed 40 percent of the agency's budget. "Enforcement revenue is not a good measure of success in achieving the strategic goal of service to all taxpayers," Rossotti wrote.

He also jettisoned the agency's old mission statement—"to collect the proper amount of tax." In its place he wrote a nuanced mission statement. From now on, the job of the IRS would be to "provide America's taxpayers top-quality service by helping them understand and meet their tax responsibilities and by applying the tax law with integrity and fairness to all."

Missing from the new mission statement was a key concept. The new mission statement said nothing about actually collecting taxes.

Rossotti also made two important observations, one of which he kept pretty much to himself at the time. Privately, he concluded that outdated as the IRS technology was—agents in the field did not even have the Windows operating system on their laptops, but used the old MS-DOS system from the early eighties—the biggest problem lay elsewhere. What the IRS needed was a new culture, one that acknowledged problems and did not punish those who brought them forward. Institutional paranoia was eating away at the agency, he believed, and his prescription was for lots of sunshine, but not any rest.

Publicly, Rossotti said that the IRS was in crisis because too much was in flux, in good part because of annual major changes in the tax laws. "There is so much change going on that it appears bewildering to our people, and they don't understand why we are doing what we are doing," he said.

Rather than slow down the pace of change, Rossotti did the opposite. He hired Booz Allen & Hamilton, the management consultants, paying them $400 million over several years to help completely reorganize the IRS. A system built on geographic areas that served all taxpayers was turned into four separate divisions that served taxpayers by type. Larger businesses were in one division, small businesses and

the self-employed were in another, tax-exempt and government entities were in a third and salaried taxpayers in a fourth.

During the upheaval his reorganization caused, with endless meetings for managers and training sessions for everyone, Rossotti also had
to fulfill his promise to himself and to Congress to serve customers
better. For starters, he had the telephones staffed around the clock. The
only way to accomplish this was to pull resources from somewhere
else. So Rossotti ordered auditors and tax collectors to answer telephones. From inane inquires about whether April 15 was the deadline
to file tax returns, to complex questions about how to reduce an unusual
economic event to a line on a tax form, the auditors and tax collectors
took the calls. Most of the revenue agents and revenue officers answering these calls were ill prepared for the task. Instead of being tax gen-
eralists, most were highly trained specialists who earned about $70,000
annually. Many had advanced degrees in accounting or law and knew
in fine detail the economics of a handful of industries and the sections
of the tax code relevant to that industry. But many knew so little of
general tax issues that they had professionals prepare their own tax returns. To Rossotti, having highly paid law enforcers do the work of
clerks worth less than half as much was just a transition cost from the
old IRS to the new: a temporary, if costly, necessity.

Congress loved the new approach because complaints about busy
or unanswered telephones dropped.

Since there is no free lunch, the cost of the telephone answering
brigade had to be paid and it was—by a sharp drop in tax law enforcement that, in turn, allowed many billions of dollars of tax to go unpaid. Except for one category, audits fell off sharply for every kind of
taxpayer. The audit rate for people making more than $100,000 plum-
meted further from the low rate when Rossotti's own returns were examined in 1997. By 2000, it was down to one in 145.

Audits of the largest corporations, which pay about 85 percent of
the corporate income tax, fell too. In the late 1980s, two out of three
large companies were audited. By the time Rossotti was hired, only
half of the big companies were being audited. That rapidly fell to one
in three.

Many of the audits that were done lacked the depth and quality of previous examinations. Interviews with revenue agents across the country revealed that many audits were narrowly focused, their recommendations to pursue promising avenues of tax avoidance sometimes thwarted by their immediate supervisors or the bosses one rank further up. Some revenue agents even coined a term for the new superficial style of examinations: *audit lite.*

The reason these audits fell was entirely the change in the way IRS resources were used. But the effect was also sure to reduce complaints by those in the political donor class about IRS agents harassing them.

For those seeking a free ride on the economic highway, it was as if the cops were either dallying at the doughnut shop or napping on the side of the road. Companies are supposed to pay 35 percent of their profits in taxes. Companies with less than $250 million of assets, that is all but the 10,000 or so largest companies, did pay that much on average. But the top tier of companies saw their real tax rate fall to an average of 20 percent.

Cheating became even more prevalent among wealthy individuals making gifts to heirs. Among gifts of $1 million or more, IRS auditors recommended more taxes on four out of five returns that they audited beginning in 1997. The average return understated the true value of the gift by $303,000, a sum that suggests not chiseling or minor differences over an asset's range of values, but calculated cheating.

Since 1997 the number of gift tax returns has been rising much faster than the number of estate tax returns. The reason is a provision in the 1997 Tax Relief Act, which its sponsors said was to help middle-class families with children, but whose other provisions helped the very rich dramatically lower their taxes. One provision required the IRS to audit gift tax returns in three years or accept them as filed. Under the old law, gift tax returns often were not audited until the donor died and his estate tax return was filed, sometimes decades later.

The IRS has just 78 lawyers to work on gift tax returns, many of which run to dozens of pages with appraisals. Of those returns examined, the average audit lasted just 31 minutes. The widespread knowledge among tax professionals that the IRS cannot audit all gift tax returns, and must give a cursory review to those it does examine, created an incentive for taxpayers to aggressively undervalue assets. Adding the three-year limit on challenges to gift values made playing the audit lottery much more attractive and partly explained why the number of million-dollar-plus gift tax returns jumped 21 percent after the law changed.

In Manhattan, the nation's wealthiest tax district, a frustrated IRS lawyer looked at tall stacks of gift tax returns on his desk. "There is all this added work and no staff," said the lawyer, who insisted on not being identified. "I know that there are millions and millions and millions of dollars being passed untaxed right over my desk and there is nothing I can do about it."

To Donald Alexander, who was the Nixon administration tax commissioner, the decline in tax rates paid by the largest companies and the increased willingness of rich Americans to hide income and to undervalue gifts were the predictable results of slashing the number of auditors and then handcuffing those that remained. It was, he said, as predictable as drivers hitting the accelerator after they pass a gaggle of highway patrol cars at the side of the road. "The fewer traffic policemen you have, the more chances people are going to take," he said. "And as people find that their neighbors are not paying their fair share, they are encouraged to not pay their share, either." JJ MacNab, a Maryland insurance analyst who tracks tax frauds as a hobby, took a similar view of how the level of law enforcement affects human behavior: "It used to be everyone knew someone who was being audited and it kept people honest," she said. "Now hardly anyone is getting audited."

The exception to the general rule of reduced audits, as revealed in Chapter 9, applied to the working poor who applied for the earned income tax credit. Their odds of being audited began rising in 1995 until by 2000 one in every 47 of the working poor had their tax returns challenged, making them about three times more likely to be audited than the affluent and rich. They were even slightly more likely to be audited than businesses with assets of $1 million to $5 million, whose audit rate was one in 49. To own a business of this size is to be presented with a world of special tax breaks allowed by law, as well as many do-it-yourself tax breaks—from not reporting all revenue to charging living expenses to the business. The working poor could collect a maximum of $4,140 in EITC in 2002, a pittance next to the tax avoidance opportunities available to business owners. But the business owners had an important advantage in Washington: they made campaign contributions, they could get their congressman on the telephone and they had lobbies to keep up a steady din of complaints about how the IRS oppressed them.

The IRS also cut back sharply on audits of the types of business entities favored by the rich. One is the subchapter S corporation, which is favored by many doctors, lawyers and other professionals because it does not pay taxes directly, but instead passes tax liabilities to their owners. Their audit odds fell to one in 233. Sole proprietorships, businesses that file a schedule C on an individual tax return, saw their audit odds plummet to one in 83 if they had $100,000 or more of revenue, but those with revenue of less than $25,000 had a much greater chance of being audited, one in 37. The IRS explanation for why tiny businesses were audited more closely than big ones related back to the working poor: the IRS suspected that some of these tiny firms inflated their income so that the owners could qualify for the maximum earned income tax credit.

Soon after he took office Rossotti was asked if he thought the system for enforcing the tax laws through auditing was fair, especially since the trend toward more audits of the poor and fewer of the rich was clear by then. Rossotti was sensitive to the issue as a practical and political matter as well as a moral one. Rossotti conceded that the IRS was able to more accurately tax people with wage income, because of reports by their employers, than business owners, professionals, landlords and investors. But Rossotti at that time characterized this as a perception problem. There is an appearance that enforcement may be unfair, he said, but he did not accept that the audit rates showed any actual unfairness. In saying that, he was in accord with the Clinton White House, which in 1998 said that the falling level of audits affecting higher income taxpayers may "unintentionally make it easier for noncompliant taxpayers to avoid paying their fair share of taxes."

This natural human tendency to ignore the law when the cops are either absent or not looking closely for wrongdoing showed up particularly in the area of partnerships. Like the subchapter S corporations used by many doctors, partnerships themselves are not taxed, but the partners are. There are many ways to organize partnerships, including mixing together as investment partners individuals or corporations on one side and tax-exempt entities such as Indian tribes, pension funds, university endowments and sometimes foreign banks on the other. By taking advantage of the tax-exempt status of these entities, an individual or corporation can defer taxes for years or even make them vanish. Layering one partnership on another, sometimes with one or more of the partnerships located offshore, can make fortunes invisible to all but the most determined auditors with lots of time to probe.

Partnerships are primarily a vehicle for the rich. Three fourths of reported partnership income goes to the richest 2 percent of taxpayers, those making more than $200,000 annually in 2000. But that's just the reported income. Finding the unreported income was the job of one man. His name is Jerry Curnutt.

For Want of a Keystroke
12

A pair of CD-ROMs in Jerry Curnutt's little Dallas office held the financial details reported by every partnership in America, all 2 million of them. Not every detail was there, just those that the IRS had decided were valuable enough to lift from the tax returns and keypunch into its computers. Curnutt was the IRS partnership specialist, the only person in America authorized to look at every partnership tax return. Together with three subordinates, who were scattered in IRS offices across the country, Curnutt's job was to figure out how to mine and refine the data on the discs, to separate from the minutia the facts that would identify likely tax cheats.

On this morning in 1998, however, Curnutt—a tall, thin man with an angular beard gone gray—found himself in an East Coast IRS office reading over a single tax return filed on paper. An auditor in the field had asked Curnutt to examine it, wondering if was a clue to an important shift in tax evasion tactics. As Curnutt pored over the paper tax return, his mind kept bringing him back to one line of detail. It reported an investment of 10 bucks.

Curnutt thought that this was probably the best-invested $10 in history, at least if one believed what the partnership had reported on its tax return. The partnership had been around for just three years and yet the $1,000 of capital invested in it had earned almost a half billion dollars of profits. The partner who had put up the 10 bucks received 1 percent of these profits, while the other 99 percent went to another partner, who put up $990. There was one other salient difference between the partners. The one that put up the $10 was a business that by law must pay taxes on its profits. The other partner, the one receiving 99 percent of the profits, was tax-exempt.

Curnutt was certain that all of the profits would eventually make their way back to the taxable business, despite its having only a 1 percent interest. And he was certain that the scheme was to make the money flow in a way that would not appear on a tax return as profit, which would be taxable.

When the tax-exempt turned the profits over to the partner who had put up the $10, the money would be reported not as profit, but as a return of capital. Taking savings out of the bank to spend is not a taxable event, just as moving a dollar from your left pocket to your right is not taxable. Neither is a return of capital by a partnership to an investor. The way this deal was structured, lining up a series of income tax and accounting rules to be used in a way that was never intended when each law and rule was adopted, that $10 of capital would magically turn into a half billion dollars of capital. The only taxes paid would be on 1 percent of the gain, the tiny sliver of profit originally assigned to the partner who invested $10.

So this tax dodge involved two steps. The first trick was to report the profits, but assign them to a tax-exempt partner, avoiding about $160 million of federal income taxes. That was easy since its $990 investment bought the tax-exempt partner 99 percent of the profits. The second trick, the more difficult one, was characterizing this profit as capital that was due to the other partner so that no tax would be paid. This second step carried with it the ability to double the tax savings. The complex inner workings of the deal resulted in the return of capital in the form of property that could be depreciated. By writing off a portion of the value of the half-billion-dollar asset each year, the investor could reduce its taxes on other profits it earned.

As Curnutt thought about the investment results, he chuckled to himself. This was so much better than Warren Buffett's biggest success that it probably outdid the Oracle of Omaha's wildest dream. For $10, the investing company would get out of paying more than $330 million of taxes over a few years. Buffett, the most successful investor of all time and the second richest man in America, had a return on investment after nearly four decades of about 2,200 to one. The tax return in Curnutt's hand indicated a return of 33 million to one in tax savings alone. And if the IRS simply accepted the partnership tax returns as filed, if it never audited the partnership's tax returns, then it was all perfectly legal.

Even though this scheme was designed to cheat the government out of a third of a billion dollars, there was virtually no chance that anyone would go to jail. Department of Justice policies allow indictments only of tax cases so solid that convictions are a virtual certainty, which makes the kind of sophisticated tax cheating that Curnutt worked to uncover beyond consideration for criminal charges. The year he obtained the return, only 1,445 federal indictments were handed up for tax evasion, a figure that had been falling for years and that by 2002 would be down to 954 indictments nationwide. Most of those indicted were small fry who had failed to report income on their tax returns. The partnership's minority owner was a big, respected business, and the partnership had reported the income, however misleadingly.

Furthermore, most big tax sheltering deals include a lengthy letter from a tax lawyer expressing his professional opinion that the deal complied in excruciating exactitude with the tax code. With a 50-page letter in the files, the chances of a criminal prosecution are zero since jurors know little about tax laws and no matter how smarmy the deal might be, just one juror giving the benefit of the doubt would prevent a conviction. That the opinion letter may make dubious claims and that the lawyer who wrote it may have charged a fee of $1 million was, as a practical matter, beside the point. The letter was insulation from civil penalties. In the unlikely event that a tax shelter was discovered, as this one was, and that the IRS denied the tax breaks, the attempt to cheat would be a free ride. The foiled cheats would just pay the taxes they would have owed anyway plus interest. All they would be out would be the cost of the deal itself, including whatever was paid for the opinion letter. Escaping penalties, however, made such letters a form of insurance well worth the cost.

As for the tax savings, they were nearly certain to come through, because for this scheme to fail, four distinct elements would have to all fall into place.

First, the partnership would have to be audited. This one had been, but that was indeed rare since only one partnership in 400 was audited.

In comparison, an individual earning $100,000 was about three times more likely to be audited and a poor family claiming the earned income tax credit was about eight times more likely to be audited.

Unlike the strict scrutiny that Congress ordered of tax returns filed by the working poor, no such scrutiny was legislated for partnerships. But the relative amounts of money involved in this one partnership and in the entire earned income tax credit program illustrated how Congress sent the IRS after small fry, many of them hapless small fry, while not giving it the tools to go after the most cunning big fish. Finding just 24 more deals the size of this one would protect as much money as the highest estimate of all the possible errors and fraud in the earned income tax credit. Since there were two million partnerships in America, the likelihood was that the tax losses from these deals were far greater than from what were mostly errors committed by the working poor.

Since Congress did not demand, or fund, partnership audits, the IRS had little interest in them, however. Partnerships do not pay taxes; they just pass on their profits and losses to the partners themselves, who then owe taxes on any profits and get tax breaks on any losses. That means a partnership audit by itself does not generate any additional taxes, which makes IRS performance statistics look bad.

The nonprofit was in this deal because it was paid a fee that was found money. Basically the business partner rented the other partner's tax-exempt status. Curnutt reasoned that the fee was small because there were lots of nonprofits willing to make such deals, driving down the price in the market for tax-evasion partners.

To the nonprofit, the fee for servicing its partner's scheme carried little downside risk. Legitimate charities would never touch such a deal. But there are more than 25 other types of tax-exempt, nonprofit organizations in the tax code, from Indian tribes and tax-exempt insurance companies to pension plans, many of which do not depend on donations so they have little or no concern about public image.

The more significant reason that partnerships are not policed as closely as the earned income tax credit is that, unlike the working poor, partnership investors are drawn heavily from the political donor class, whose campaign contributions buy them access to senators and congressmen. Unlike the working poor, these taxpayers can get their legislator on the phone, or even into their living room, to complain about being harassed by the IRS. And in this case the campaign donor could buttress his complaint by noting that he took such care to comply with the law that he had paid a lawyer to make sure that every detail of the investment complied with the law.

Second, for the scheme to fail, an auditor would have to be sharp enough to figure out just how the deal worked. This particular partnership's tax evasion was pretty blatant. Most such deals are not, relying on complex and difficult-to-follow transactions done through layers of partnerships and other business entities that kept the evasive activity well insulated from the evaders themselves. An audit of the wrong layer of one of these partnership arrangements would find nothing. An audit of the right layer in the wrong year might find nothing. Many partnerships also used offshore banks and businesses to evade tax, relying on the strict secrecy laws in many tax havens to shield their cheating, an issue whose significance Curnutt understood well.

Third, an auditor would have to persuade his supervisors to press the case by demanding payment of the taxes. Even with $330 million at stake, there were plenty of reasons that the IRS might look the other way. The IRS has so few resources to pursue cases that if the partnership owners made it clear they would fight any adverse audit to the death, then a decision would have to be made on the costs of litigation and the likelihood of success. That would raise serious career concerns for IRS bureaucrats because pursuing a single contentious fight would tie up auditing and litigation resources for years, yet in statistical reports it would count as just one case. Better to go after many taxpayers, even if the dollars were smaller, because in the statistical reports it would show lots of activity. By severely limiting IRS funding, Congress ensured that the agency would bring the full force of the law upon those least able to fight back—and those from whom they could extract very little unpaid money.

Fourth was the issue of influence within the IRS, where by law disputes over taxes remain secret unless a lawsuit is filed by the taxpayer. Inside this veil of secrecy, many former IRS executives make a good living representing taxpayers. They work quietly to make favorable deals for their clients. They challenge what auditors find. They wheedle and cajole. They delay producing documents until the time

period set for the audit is nearly done or the time to challenge a tax return is about to run out. They may come up with the most minimal
documentation to support a deduction or they may drown an auditor
in paperwork. And if all else fails, they can get in the door of senior
IRS officials, knowing which ones plan to join them in leaving for lucrative private practice and need good references.

Even when an audit uncovers massive fraud, the scam may continue if the IRS backs down. That is just what happened with Enron.

An IRS audit discovered that in 1993 and 1994 Enron had made
false reports to shareholders and to the Securities and Exchange Commission, inflating its profits significantly. Congress does not allow the
IRS to report such discoveries to the SEC or to prosecutors, just as it
cannot tell authorities when a tax return shows that an individual is a
marijuana farmer or pimp. But if the IRS demands more taxes after an
audit and sticks by its position, and if the taxpayer is unwilling to pay
the extra taxes, then the case will eventually enter the public record
through a lawsuit in tax court, a federal district court or the federal
court of claims.

IRS auditors denied Enron various tax breaks, so the Houston energy trading company took the matter to an IRS appeals officer, still
safely inside the veil of secrecy imposed by Congress, the Senate Finance Committee revealed in 2003 in the back pages of a massive report on Enron. The appeals officer, Bradley Herbert, wrote memos and
letters to superiors arguing that the audit should be upheld because
that would force Enron to take the issue to court, where its fraudulent
reports to shareholders would have been exposed. "Should the IRS
condone this?" Herbert asked in one memo.

IRS higher-ups gave Enron its way and closed the audit in October 1999, effectively covering up crimes for the company. Just how it
did that was never explained in the congressional report. But the IRS
decision let Enron continue its scam for more than two years, enrich-
ing chief executive Kenneth Lay and other executives, causing electrical
shortages and huge costs in California and other states and eventually
costing investors tens of billions of dollars in losses. And the IRS never
collected the taxes that the government was owed, either.

Enron, like nearly all big businesses and many wealthy individuals,
employed former IRS officials as its tax representatives. These people

know how to work the system (which by law operates in near total secrecy to protect the rights of taxpayers) both formally and through informal channels. Since enactment of the 1998 IRS Reform and Restructuring Act, the ability of these former insiders to intimidate IRS auditors and their first-level supervisors has grown enormously. Under Section 1203 of that law, a mere accusation of harassing a taxpayer initiates a grueling investigation of the auditor, who, if found to be in the wrong, must be fired unless the IRS commissioner personally intervenes. "I'm going to 1203 you," is not a hollow threat to an auditor, especially one with any other complaints in his personnel file, an interest in future promotions or an eye on qualifying for retirement.

As Curnutt looked at the partnership return with the amazingly lucrative $10 investment, what troubled him was that this tax return had not turned up in any of the searches he and his staff had made of the data on their CD-ROMs. Here was a smoking gun, except it was invisible to the IRS computers. Only because of serendipity—a rare IRS audit of a partnership, combined with a sharp auditor who knew about Curnutt's work and took the initiative to ask his advice—had the scheme come to the partnership unit's attention.

This tax return was just what Curnutt had been looking for to show his bosses that more data needed to be transcribed into IRS computers from the paper tax returns moving through the pipeline. Curnutt said that tax cheats "have a hard time getting away if we ask the right questions on the tax return—and then we put the answer in the computer. If we don't ask the right question, or we don't put the answer in the computer, then we can't find" the tax cheats.

Curnutt immediately started thinking about how to get a question added to the partnership tax return or what question could be replaced. Just rewording one question, and then lifting the answer off the paper return, and Curnutt was confident that his desktop computer would spit out lists of tax-evading partnerships.

Curnutt had gotten access to the pipeline once before, shortly after he had come back to the IRS after nearly a decade off the job. After 18 years in various IRS jobs, Curnutt had quit in 1982 to care for his son, Kevin, who was playing with a friend on Super Bowl Sunday 1981 when a man with a shotgun opened fire on them. Kevin survived, paralyzed from the neck down at age 13. At first Curnutt tried to continue working, but Kevin needed round-the-clock care so he resigned. By 1990 the Curnutts had run through their savings and needed a steady paycheck again.

Those senior IRS officials who knew that tax fraud was growing among the wealthy, but lacked hard proof or a systematic way to identify such cheats, were thrilled to have Curnutt back. They respected his unusual blend of skills and knowledge. He was steeped in the sections of the tax code dealing with investments and partnerships. He understood databases and computer code and could organize complex projects on his own initiative. And he had the puzzle-solving curiosity of a detective. Curnutt had planned to become an FBI agent and, but for his mild asthma, would have been hired.

When he rejoined the IRS in 1990, Curnutt's first job was to come up with a systematic way to identify taxes owed from real estate partnerships. At the time about 600,000 such partnerships filed tax returns each year, but the IRS was having little luck finding unpaid taxes. Unless human nature had changed, Curnutt figured, the problem was that the IRS either was not collecting the right information or was not analyzing it properly. He wrote computer programs to comb through the real estate partnership tax returns and eventually made a simple but significant discovery: the IRS could pretty much ignore 19 out of every 20 returns. "These partnerships last on average about 20 years," Curnutt said. "What we needed to do was pay very close attention to the final year, when the partnership had used up all the tax benefits in its buildings and was selling them."

For every year but the last one or two, the investors in many real estate partnerships expect to receive reports showing they lost money. Copies of these reports go to the IRS. When partnerships show losses, they haven't really lost money, however. Each year an expense is taken for depreciation to account for the declining value of a building as it ages, often creating a loss on paper. Of course most buildings actually gain in value over time, but the depreciation rule is well established in both accounting rules and tax law. When the building is sold, the partnership reports the sales price, subtracting from it the value of the building. The difference is profit. Since the value of the building has been reduced by the annual depreciation, however, most or all of the sales price is supposed to be reported as taxable profit.

Curnutt found that a small but lucrative minority of real estate partnerships simply did not report the profit. Many more, he found, reported the profit as a capital gain, which is taxed at about half the rate of wages for most partnership investors, instead of as ordinary income. Other returns ignored a rule imposing a special tax rate of 25 percent, more than the capital gains rate but less than the tax rate on salaries for most partnership investors. All together perhaps one in a dozen partnerships used one of these techniques to cheat.

"Out of a universe of 600,000 or so partnership returns, we showed that only 30,000 or so needed to be looked at closely in any year," Curnutt said. "By refining the data from those partnerships we got down to 3,000 to 5,000 returns that were solid audit candidates. In at least half of those the profits either just were not reported or were reported improperly."

While partnerships do not pay taxes, they file annual tax returns on Form 1065 that detail revenue, expenses and earnings. The partnership sends partners reports called K-1s that detail how much money each of them made or lost as well as identifying whether this money should be taxed at rates for ordinary income or at the lower rates for capital gains.

The IRS receives copies of both the partnership and the K-1 income data, just as it gets salary information from both employers and individual workers. But the IRS does not treat K-1 income the same way that it does reports of people's wages filed on W-2 forms or the reports of income from dividends, interest, royalties and contract jobs reported on Form 1099. IRS computers match every wage, dividend, interest, royalty and contract job report to what is listed on individual tax returns to make sure that every dollar earned in these ways is taxed. Not so partnership and K-1 reports.

There was no matching of partnership reports to individual or corporate income tax returns. Congress did not require such matching. Perhaps that's because the members whose job is to oversee the IRS pay little attention to such administrative matters, which carry with them little opportunity to raise money from donors. Perhaps it's because they do not want the tax police looking too closely into the activities of those who finance their campaigns. Whatever the reason, Congress did not give the IRS special money to match partnership reports and K-1 income to tax returns of individuals and corporations, as it did with the extra funding it voted starting in 1995 to police the tax returns of the working poor. But even if Congress had, the matching would not have done much to find tax cheats. That was because of the way that the IRS had designed its various tax forms. The IRS carefully crafted the W-2 and 1099 reports so that the income they reported flowed to specific lines on the tax returns filed by individuals. Mismatches were spotted by IRS computers, which automatically sent out notices in minor cases and prepared lists of audit candidates that were sent to revenue agents. But the IRS neglected to coordinate the partnership tax returns and K-1 reports of income and losses with specific lines on individual and corporate tax returns.

The lack of matching, together with the failure to coordinate partnership data to tax return forms, created opportunities for two kinds of cheating. One was to not report profits, especially from real estate partnerships in the year that the properties were sold. With no matching, the IRS computers would not detect anything amiss and would not generate notices the way they do automatically for people who forget to include interest from a bank savings account in a town that they moved away from years earlier. The other way to cheat was by reporting real estate profits in the wrong category so that they would be taxed at the lower capital gains rate.

For investors with a million-dollar cash-out from a real estate partnership, the savings in 1998 could be as much as $396,000 by not reporting and $196,000 by reporting ordinary income as capital gains. These savings would be in addition to nearly two decades of paper losses for depreciation that reduced their income tax bills each year. Curiously, while the IRS failed to match income from partnerships to individual partners, it almost always accepted without challenge the partnership losses reported on individual and corporate income tax returns.

Just like the partnership with the $10 investment, in real estate a carefully planned tax dodge could cheat the government twice. In the case of real estate, the order was simply reversed. Depreciation came first, untaxed profits second. On a deal that earned a legitimate profit of $1 million when the partnership was closing down, an investor could pick up about $800,000 more through tax evasion with the only risk of being caught coming in the year the partnership was closing up.

Since partnerships are highly leveraged, using a lot of borrowed money on which interest payments are tax deductible, it might take only a few tens of thousands of dollars in the original investment to turn a $1.8 million profit, of which close to half was from tax evasion.

By May 1996 Curnutt had been promoted to the specialist in charge of all partnerships, more than doubling the universe of tax returns to which he had complete access. His focus was on finding the same kinds of reporting flaws that had revealed cheating in some real estate partnerships so that audits would focus on those and ignore honest deals. The work was not going as well as Curnutt had hoped, however, until the day that he was shown the paper partnership return with the $10 investment.

The information needed to detect this tax dodge, using a computer search of the IRS business master file data, was not on either of the two discs of partnership tax return data in his office. The key, Curnutt knew, was identifying partnerships in which one of the partners was tax-exempt. The partnership tax return form asked a question that touched on this: "Does this partnership have any foreign partners?" The problem was that the tax return did not ask whether a domestic tax-exempt organization was involved. The proof that the question needed to be refined was on the tax return Curnutt was holding in his bony hands. Here was the single most useful piece of information to find cheating partnerships and the crucial question was not even being asked.

Nonetheless, Curnutt smiled. He had his smoking gun. All he had to do now was make presentations to ever-higher layers of management within the IRS. Once he progressed far enough toward the top, his superiors would surely tap the pipeline for this and other valuable information. It was, after all, an incredible investment. For a few million keystrokes, the yield in taxes would run into the billions of dollars.

Curnutt had persuaded his bosses once before to capture more data from partnership returns flowing through the pipeline. In that case he wanted to know which partnerships had checked a box indicating they had an offshore partner. Foreign banks, especially Dutch banks with offices in the West Indies, often rent their tax-exempt status to various American investments that are designed not so much to earn profits as to escape taxes, a practice encouraged both by laws Congress has passed and tax treaties that the Senate has ratified. To get even that one detail keypunched, however, the cost had to be covered by the budget of some unit within the IRS. Curnutt had no budget for data collection, just for analysis of what was given to him. The cost for collecting this bit of information, for transcribing it into the IRS computers, came to $15,000. The office in charge of all industry specialization units in the IRS said it would pay. The cost would be recovered many times over as Curnutt and his team identified suspect returns beginning in 1997.

Within weeks of learning about the lucrative $10 investment, Curnutt was in Washington making a presentation to senior IRS officials. As with earlier presentations, he won plaudits for making such a terrific discovery. Curnutt's personnel file was already thick with letters of commendation for his innovation and his success in identifying tax cheats that had eluded everyone else, and soon more were added. In his presentation Curnutt showed how a small investment in capturing more data would pay off in billions of dollars in taxes.

Curnutt also emphasized that not asking the right question and then capturing this data were already having a corrosive effect on the tax system. The profit earned on the $10 investment was so outrageously beyond reason that the only conclusion to be drawn was that the partnership never expected anyone to look at the paper tax return. Clearly, years of the agency's failure to examine many partnership returns, and of not matching partnership profits to individual and corporate tax returns, were emboldening those with less than rigorous ethical standards. No doubt, Curnutt thought to himself, former IRS officials who knew about the lack of scrutiny of partnership income were making lucrative fees advising wealthy people and corporations on how to earn untaxed, or partially taxed, profits through partnerships.

Months passed as Curnutt waited for an answer on whether he would get the funding to siphon a little more data from the pipeline. As he waited, changes began to occur around him. Commissioner Rossotti's plan to reorganize the IRS, eliminating the district offices that served geographic areas and replacing them with four divisions serving different groupings of taxpayers, was beginning to take shape in 1998. Under Rossotti's plan, partnerships with lots of assets would be the responsibility of the Large and Mid-Sized Business division known as LMSB, which had the most sophisticated auditors. Partnerships with few assets would be assigned to the Small Business and Self-Employed division (SBSE).

"The division was arbitrary and not good for tax enforcement, at least for partnerships," Curnutt said. "It appears from the 1065 that the assets are very small, when in reality they are at their highest value."

If the IRS were to count both assets and depreciation, then the big partnerships would be subject to examination by the more sophisticated auditors in the large and midsized business division of the IRS. But that idea went nowhere. The decision to effectively assign many partnerships to a division not well trained for the complex issues involved disturbed Curnutt less than the reorganization itself. He is one of many inside the IRS who worry that organizing the agency to focus on types of taxpayers, rather than geographic areas, is sowing seeds of corruption. He believes the new structure makes it easier for well-connected tax advisers, many of them former IRS officials, to wield influence on behalf of clients to get unfair tax breaks.

In 2000, Commissioner Rossotti, who had seen some of Curnutt's incriminating evidence although they had never met, began to publicly hint at a problem with unreported K-1 income from partnerships and similar tax-exempt entities. Rossotti's statements became more forceful until in 2001 he reported to the Senate Finance Committee that perhaps one in every five dollars of K-1 income was not showing up on income tax returns. The cost in lost tax revenue was perhaps $30 billion each year. What Rossotti's reports revealed was the utter misallocation of law enforcement resources. At the behest of Congress, the IRS was auditing the working poor at eight times the rate of partnerships and yet the losses from partnerships were at least four times as large.

To the IRS the issue was not how it used its resources, but rather how society was embracing cheating.

One of Rossotti's deputies, Dale Hart, sought to deflect attention from how Congress allocated money and how the IRS used it. Yes, cheating was on the rise, she said, but not because of any failure by the IRS to police partnership tax returns. The problem was that the public had changed. Historically, she said, accountants kept the system honest and investors were people who feared trouble with the IRS because their reputations could be ruined. "We believe we have seen a change in the population," she said.

The estimated losses from partnerships and similar entities were so large that they caused Rossotti to reconsider his focus on customer service and give more thought to the policing side of his job. When those with partnership and other income do not get careful scrutiny, Rossotti warned, "the effect may be perceived as, and will in fact be, unfair because higher-income taxpayers will not have their returns verified to the same degree as middle-income taxpayers." Rossotti finally concluded that the tax system was being undermined because it depended on honesty from the majority of people calculating the taxes they owed. And it was clear that honesty was no longer something the IRS could count on.

But while several senators said they were appalled to learn that cheating was rampant among partnership investors, there were no hearings on national television to expose the cheats and no extra funding was allotted to hire and train auditors to hunt for these cheats. There was an effort to match K-1 reports to individual tax returns, but it was shut down after a few months in 2002 because it did not work. They couldn't find a way to match up partnership income to lines on tax returns the way wage income could be matched up. This meant that the IRS computers churned out notices galore to people who owed no tax, while missing many who did.

Meanwhile, as part of Rossotti's vision of the IRS as a customer service organization, each unit within the IRS was told to identify its customers and get to know their needs. This created a problem for Curnutt. "If you are working with automobile manufacturers or petroleum companies there are industry groups" representing carmakers and oil companies, Curnutt said. They are the obvious "customers" representing an interest group. Curnutt thought cozying up to such groups was an invitation to disaster because the interests of these groups were less in the efficient administration of the tax laws than in getting the IRS to be their friend. Curnutt's problem was that there was no partnership industry, no natural constituency for him to get cozy with even if he wanted to do so. Partnerships were in the realm of entrepreneurs who had few common interests and few trade associations. But the order from IRS management was clear: identify your customers and build alliances with them. Curnutt said he "thought about it for quite awhile and then decided that my interest group was the state tax agencies, since they collect taxes on income from partnerships."

Curnutt began meeting with state tax officials to tell them about how the data analysis he had done, together with that extra detail from the pipeline about real estate partnerships with offshore partners, could help identify untaxed dollars. But at the second of these meetings, in Sacramento, a California tax official whose job was to analyze computer data pulled him into a hallway during a break. "Where is this data you are talking about?" the data man asked. "The IRS isn't sending us anything like that."

Curnutt was dumbstruck. Of course the IRS was sending it, he thought at first. The states and the IRS had signed contracts that required the IRS to provide this information. But then Curnutt realized that despite agreements requiring the IRS to share with the states, the work he had done had not gotten through to the people who prepare the data for sharing. He went back to Dallas and began trying to funnel the data to the states. He succeeded and quickly. But he also received word that the IRS was not going to revise any of the questions on the partnership tax return to identify domestic tax-exempt partners and then transcribe that detail into its computers. Even though it was costing the government billions and billions of dollars, no one had room in their budget to pay for the keystrokes to capture the data.

In 2000, long after he had become eligible for retirement, Curnutt left. He then went into business trying to show the states how they could fill their budget gaps by pursuing partnership cheating. Citing Rossotti's IRS report that perhaps one in five dollars of partnership income was not being reported, he did an analysis of what that would mean to 29 states and then wrote to their tax commissioners. He told those in New York, New Jersey, Massachusetts, Wisconsin and nine other states that their own tax forms contained the data that would identify tax cheats. For New York he estimated that $2 billion of state tax was unpaid for the years 1996 through 2000, and for the other dozen states another billion and a half in all.

The tax commissioner in New York, Arthur J. Roth, responded that it was more important to hunt for people who failed to file partnership returns than for partnerships that did file, but cheated. He boasted that the state's efforts had recovered $34 million in 2001. But that was less than a dime on the dollar that Curnutt estimated the state should be collecting that year through proper audits of partnerships and partners. What Roth did not say was obvious to Curnutt: auditing partnership returns carried a political risk; there was a very good chance such audits would turn up the names of important campaign contributors and others with influence. Curnutt's views were not idle speculation. Curnutt was told by one Kentucky official that the state did not want his services precisely because of fear that it would rile influential citizens, the kind who donate to political campaigns.

Curnutt thought his proposal would be especially appealing to Wisconsin, a state in such dire straits that it pulled state tax auditors away from examining returns to open envelopes and process the checks enclosed with state tax returns. The state revenue secretary, Richard G. Chandler, was putting in a half day each week in spring processing income tax payments to show some solidarity with his auditors, who were angry at having to do clerical work and not chasing after tax cheats. Chandler looked into Curnutt's proposal, but decided not to hire him. "We agree with his concept," Chandler said. "But my people are not convinced that what he proposes will work as well as he thinks it will."

That these officials did not want to hire Curnutt is in some ways not surprising. There are a host of tax experts out pitching their ideas. And the states were, like Congress and the IRS, slashing money for tax law enforcement, leaving little for outside consultants. Wisconsin announced that it planned to lay off nine auditors who examine corporate tax returns until one of them, Art Foeste, took his vacation to travel around the state protesting to every legislator, civic group, newspaper editor and radio talk show host who would listen. In South Carolina in 2002, the state legislature slashed 200 of the 500 jobs at the state tax agency, a cut so deep that the tax agency estimated the real cost at many times larger in lost revenue than what was saved in salaries. And most of that lost revenue came from corporations and the rich, the sources of the biggest campaign contributions. But even for states strapped for funds, Curnutt's offer came with little risk. He asked only for airfare, a motel room and meals while he worked and, in the event he found tax money, a modest consulting fee. Even if he found every dollar he was sure was out there, his proposal would not make him rich. But it would prove he was right.

In 2003 one state, Pennsylvania, finally decided to invite Curnutt to test his ideas. It was not his first choice, because of features peculiar to Pennsylvania tax law, but Curnutt flew out to Harrisburg to sift data and train auditors. "The results so far are promising, but not conclusive," Curnutt said. Time will tell if he can find tax cheats and get paid for his work.

Meanwhile, at the federal level, and in the other states, little has changed. The IRS abandoned the effort to match K-1 income to individual and corporate tax returns. Congress did not propose any spending to revise the tax forms so that partnership cheats could be identified. In one of his last reports as IRS commissioner, Rossotti told Congress that the agency needed money both for matching and to examine more partnership returns. Partnerships and similar entities that pass tax obligations on to their owners, Rossotti wrote, "filed 7.4 million returns, reported $5 trillion of gross revenues and $680 billion of income. However, the IRS audited only 29,057 of them."

Partnerships are not the only way to use tax-exempt organizations to dodge taxes. Another technique takes advantage of one of the least known provisions in the tax code, one that allowed some insurance companies to operate tax-free. One of the very few people who knew about this law was a Wall Street billionaire by the name of Peter R. Kellogg.

Mr. Kellogg's Favorite Loophole
13

Few names loom larger on Wall Street than Peter R. Kellogg. For decades his family's firm, Spear, Leeds & Kellogg, has dominated the specialized task of making markets in shares traded at the stock exchanges, ensuring someone will always buy shares of firms or has shares to sell. The firm trades about one in every 20 shares of stock that change hands each day on the New York and American stock exchanges. It is such lucrative work that in 2000 Kellogg sold his firm to the Goldman Sachs investment house for $6.5 billion. After that *Forbes* magazine estimated Kellogg's personal fortune at $1.9 billion, but surely that is a conservative number since in addition to the firm he sold, Kellogg has vast worldwide investments. In recent years he has been the largest shareholder in the stock brokerage Advest, in MFC Merchant Bank in Switzerland and in McM Corporation, an insurance holding company, to name only a few of his assets.

Kellogg's fortune grew even more beginning in the midnineties thanks to a tax law so obscure that the IRS has pretty much ignored it. Perhaps the only piece of the tax code widely known by its number is Section 501(c)(3), which authorizes people and companies to deduct gifts made to charities. It is just one of 21 subsections authorizing tax-free operations by organizations ranging from scientific societies to the National Football League. Kellogg fixed upon subsection 15, which authorizes tax-exempt insurance companies.

That section of the tax code has been around since the early Eisenhower years. It was enacted to help farmers and rural merchants who had trouble getting property and casualty insurance, like fire insurance on their barns, either because they lived too far out of the way for big insurers to be interested or because of some condition peculiar to a community.

Congress intended these companies to be tiny. In recent years companies qualified to operate tax-free only if the insurance premiums they collected were under $350,000 annually. If premiums passed that ceiling, but were under $1.2 million, then under another law taxes were due only on investment profits. Companies that collect more than $1.2 million in premiums are fully taxable on both investment income and earnings from the premiums themselves.

For more than three decades there was little reason to pay any attention to these tax-exempt insurance companies. There were only a few hundred of these tiny enterprises in existence, many of which had only a few tens of thousands of dollars in assets. Furthermore, they were not run to make profits, but rather to spread risks within small communities and keep insurance costs low. By law these tax-exempt insurance companies had to be mutual insurance companies, owned by the people and companies that paid the premiums, rather than stock-held companies owned by investors.

Then in 1986, when the big tax reform act was passed, a change was made that drew virtually no notice. The requirement that these tax-exempt insurers be mutual companies owned by those who bought policies was stricken; investors could now own the tax-exempt insurance companies. In the flurry of news coverage about the Tax Reform Act, this change was one of hundreds of little provisions that never made the mainstream news.

What caught Kellogg's interest was another part of the law, the part that was not there. While Congress had placed a cap on how much these tax-exempt insurers could collect in premiums, no such limit applied to how much capital could be put into one of these companies to invest in the market. And therein was a loophole.

All insurance companies have assets to pay claims. The amount of this capital determines how much insurance the company can underwrite, or sell, and the likelihood that it will be able to pay claims. Most for-profit insurers try to keep the smallest amount they can in reserves dedicated to paying claims because the smaller the reserve, the more

capital they have to invest and earn profits from stocks, bonds and real
estate.

Kellogg (and others) saw an opportunity to stand this idea on its
head and reap huge tax-free profits and, unlike the farmers the law was
meant to benefit, do so without getting his manicured hands dirty. All
he had to do was create a tax-exempt insurer and stuff it with capital
far beyond any possible losses the insurance company might have to
pay on insurance claims.

Kellogg put so much capital into the larger of his two tax-exempt
insurance companies, IAT Reinsurance, that he earned $539 million
of profits free of tax between 1996 and 2001. Had he paid federal corporate income taxes, he would have owed $188 million. His second
company, SLK Reinsurance (as in Spear, Leeds & Kellogg) made $3.7
million of tax-free profits in just 2000 and 2001, saving him $1.3 mil-
lion in federal corporate income taxes.

While his tax-exempt insurance companies held far more capital
than what any group of farmers insuring against fires would need to
make sure all claims could be paid, he did not make much of an effort
to collect premiums. Though the law allowed each of his companies to
collect $350,000 of premiums each year, Kellogg's companies typically
collected less than $8,000 per year in premiums. In 1999, for example,
IAT Reinsurance held $330 million in assets, earned $179 million in
profits and collected premiums of just $3,330. And the amount it paid
out in claims on losses? Zero, just as it did not lose any money to claims
in the three prior years.

IAT did, however, incur some expenses, including a $680,984
consulting fee in 1999 paid to someone who was not identified, a
$129,770 management fee that year and a write-off of $8,315 on a
company car. Some years IAT reported spending more than $1,000
a month on telephone calls. Because each of these expenses amounts
to more than the insurance premiums the company collected annually,
they raise questions about whether the company is principally in the
insurance business or is mainly a mechanism for avoiding taxes. Unlike
Maritza Reyes, the East Los Angeles cleaning woman who was pursued for $7,000 only because of her address, the IRS as of mid-2003 had
done nothing about the $190 million of taxes that Kellogg escaped.

Kellogg was not alone in exploiting this law. Starting in 1996 the number of applications for IRS approvals of tax-exempt insurance companies began to rise, from a handful each year to as many as a dozen in one week, as tax shelter promoters began selling the idea of profiting from owning tax-free insurance companies. By 2000 there were more than 1,400 of these companies. And hundreds of them were organized not in rural counties where farm animals outnumber people, but in places like New York City, Phoenix and Orange County, California. Several hundred of these companies had as their official headquarters Caribbean islands like St. Nevis–Kitts, the Cayman Islands and Bermuda, where the regulation of insurance companies is minimal.

Automobile dealers and owners of appliance and electronic stores owned more than 100 of these tax-exempt companies. The insurance they sold was to extend warranties on cars and television sets. The premiums would be deposited into their offshore insurance companies, which had taken the curious step of choosing to be subject to American tax law. Of course, since these firms were organized as tax-exempts, like Kellogg's two Bermuda insurers, there was good reason to want to combine tax-free status under American tax law with minimal regulatory oversight by the Caribbean countries. In addition, having an insurance company with its nominal headquarters in the Caribbean meant travel there could be tax-deductible.

The major accounting firms, notably KPMG and Pricewaterhouse-Coopers, and some small law firms created brochures and PowerPoint presentations to persuade auto dealers and appliance store owners that setting up a tax-exempt insurance company was a good way to build wealth for their retirement.

Meanwhile, some already big insurance companies found a way to come under the law so that their investment profits would be exempt from tax. The trick was to temporarily stop writing new insurance, or to collect only modest amounts of premiums, so that they could earn dividends, interest and capital gains free of tax. For a stand-alone insurance company this would be a major problem since customers would move on to competitors, but if a company was part of a larger group of insurance companies, then the premiums could simply be directed toward another company in the group. That is what the Alfa Corporation, an insurance group whose stock trades on the NASDAQ, did. Alfa Mutual Fire Insurance in Montgomery, Alabama, saved $58 million on federal corporate income taxes over three years. In 1999 alone Alfa earned $45 million in tax-free profits while collecting just $301,870 in premiums, down sharply from the millions in premiums collected in earlier years. In 2000, having built up $530 million of assets, Alfa dropped its tax-exempt status when its premiums exceeded the $350,000 maximum. The capital that it built up tax-free gives it an advantage over competitors who were fully taxed on their investment gains.

In the Philadelphia suburb of Exton, the Mutual Fire, Marine and Inland Insurance Company avoided $12.5 million of taxes on its gains in the three years 1997 through 1999. The Bank of New York even got in on the deal when it created BONY Trade Insurance, earning $12.1 million tax-free in its first two years of operation, 2000 and 2001. And a consortium of 85 hospitals in New York State escaped $27.5 million in taxes over five years using the same technique. When questioned about these practices, these companies and Alfa asserted they complied fully with the law.

Despite the huge profits earned by Kellogg, Alfa Insurance and others, these tax-exempt firms drew little attention from the IRS. The IRS official in charge of auditing nonprofit organizations acknowledged in 2003 that it had never audited any of the more than 1,400 insurance companies that are allowed to operate free of tax. Another IRS official said that the agency did not even know how to audit these companies. What questions should be asked? What records should be requested? What were the issues that needed examination? To answer these questions, the IRS planned a study of how to audit these tax-exempt insurers.

One thing that the IRS did not do was simply read the annual reports these insurance companies filed. Tax-exempt organizations must file an annual report, known as a Form 990, with the IRS that details their income and expenses and their assets and liabilities and identifies key officials and their compensation. Unlike individual and corporate tax returns, which are confidential, not only are 990s public record, but Congress requires that tax-exempts make their Form 990s available on demand to anyone.

The IRS has plenty of grounds in its regulations to go after Kellogg, Alfa Insurance and the others to make them pay their taxes. Why? Be-

cause the law allowing tiny tax-exempt insurance companies also requires that they be primarily engaged in the business of shifting and
sharing risks. It also specifies that they must be primarily property and
casualty, rather than life, insurance companies.

While Mr. Kellogg would not talk, critics of the tax-exempt insurance company law were more than willing.

Jay Adkisson, a lawyer in Laguna Niguel, California, who tracks
tax frauds and who has helped clients create what he says are legitimate
tax-exempt insurance companies, said many of these companies abuse
the tax exemption. "This law was meant to let small insurance companies start up and grow up to become tax-paying companies," he said.
"That sounds well and good except for the people at the large accounting firms and the tax shelter promoters who are abusing this."

Adkisson said the IRS, if it wanted to, could easily identify sham
insurance companies that were just tax dodges for investors. "To qualify for this you are supposed to be a real insurance company with
actuarial studies and a reasonable relationship between income and reserves to pay claims. . . . Having $1,000 of premiums and $100 million
of reserves is so out of proportion that no actuary on earth would say
that is reasonable," he said.

Adkisson and JJ MacNab, who tracks tax cons as a hobby, both said
that they had told the IRS about promoters who marketed abusive
schemes using the tax-exempt insurance provision. Both said that the
IRS never asked them for more information and that they could find
no evidence that the IRS acted against these promoters. The IRS has
never listed an insurance company in its periodic reports of organizations that lose their tax exemption for misconduct. And a search of court
records revealed no enforcement action against this kind of company.

Giving special tax breaks to one industry, like insurance, can create
vast new tax loopholes for other industries. Consider how a 1997 law
signed by Governor George Pataki of New York makes it possible for
many corporations in that state to operate tax-free by creating a subsidiary insurance company. The technique also eliminates New York
City taxes for companies headquartered there.

In the first step, the corporation creates an insurance company that
it controls, known as a captive insurer, as the 1997 law allows. Then the
company transfers to its captive insurer corporate IOUs, which require

the parent to pay interest to the captive insurer. Under both state and city law, the corporation can deduct interest paid to the captive insurer while the interest is earned tax-free by the insurer itself. Other state and city laws require that the insurance company be excluded from the parent company's income tax return. By simply paying enough interest to wipe out any corporate profits, the 7.5 percent state corporate income tax and the 8.85 percent city tax can be eliminated. The deal is not entirely tax-free, however. The captive insurer must pay taxes on its premiums, although the rate is a bargain. It is a fraction of 1 percent, just $40,000 on $10 million of premiums.

This plan, sold to companies that signed confidentiality agreements by the accounting firm KPMG, does not save federal income taxes. However, KPMG told clients that the plan could be used in some other states to eliminate state income taxes.

Having a tax-exempt insurance company has another value, too, at least for car dealers and appliance store owners. The tax returns for many of them show the premiums collected and the investment profits earned tax-free but not a dollar paid in claims, sometimes for many years. How could that be? Did not one person with an extended warranty need repairs for his automobile or stereo? The likely answer is that the dealer simply performed the repair work and wrote it off against the profits of his car dealership or store. Doing this costs the government tax revenues. It also enhances the value of the tax-exempt insurance company because, if it pays little or nothing in claims, then it has more capital to invest and grow tax-free.

Collecting insurance premiums and then charging repair work to one's business instead of the insurance company is small potatoes, however. Were all of the tax-exempt insurers selling extended warranties made to pay the taxes on their insurance company profits and the taxes they escaped by billing repairs to the businesses, it would not come close to what Peter R. Kellogg escaped in taxes or what Alfa Insurance escaped, either.

Yet when the IRS started its study, it said its focus would be on the warranty insurance deals, which the tax agency calls "producer owned" insurance companies. That is, just as it focuses on the Maritza Reyeses of the world on orders from Congress, the IRS has also gotten the larger message about who is fair game for investigation and who is not.

And while most car dealers are wealthy by definition, they are not in the league of the Peter R. Kelloggs of America when it comes to wealth and exemption from scrutiny by the IRS.

Suppose that you have an asset that has soared in value, making your wealth highly concentrated in this one investment and, therefore, at risk from a lack of diversification of your investments. To make the numbers simple, imagine that your gain in this investment is $100 million and that it is in a stock. Selling the stock would cause a capital gains tax that was $28 million in 1996, $20 million in 2002 and $15 million in 2003. After this tax, and ignoring state taxes, you would have between $72 million and $85 million, depending on the year.

But you could escape this tax entirely by contributing your stock to your very own tax-exempt insurance company. The insurance company could then sell the stock without triggering any tax and use the entire $100 million to buy a diversified portfolio of stocks, bonds and other assets. The dividends, interest, capital gains and other income would then build up inside your insurance company free of tax. After a decade or so, these investment returns could make your fortune grow to $250 million, at which point you decide to close your insurance company and take the money back. Technically you would then owe taxes on the entire $250 million, but the IRS would not have any records of the initial $100 million that you contributed, so as a practical matter you could file a tax return just paying taxes on the $150 million. Even that is unlikely, however. JJ MacNab laughed at the thought that anyone doing this would pay a cent in taxes, noting that the IRS has never audited any of the tax-exempt insurance companies.

So what if you decided to just keep the whole $250 million and not pay any taxes? That is, to cheat? Said MacNab, "The IRS would never notice."

Mass Market Tax Evasion

14

Dressed in a shiny emerald suit with a shirt and tie in clashing shades of green, Nick Jesson tools down the beachfront boulevards in the warm Southern California sunshine, heavy gold rings on each tanned hand, a cigarette affixed to one like an ashen-tipped sixth digit. Thin and in his fifties, Jesson is a character right out of Horatio Alger. In his teens he fled home for the military. Later he ran his own youth program with no help from government or the United Way. Then in Huntington Beach he prospered as the founder of No Time Delay Electronics, a worldwide supplier of electronic components to clients like Fujitsu, IBM, Motorola and Texas Instruments. Jesson's company belongs to the U.S. Chamber of Commerce, as well as the local Huntington Beach Chamber, and the Better Business Bureau. When he is not running his business or coaching a youth soccer team, Jesson often takes one of his exotic sports cars down to the waterfront where he keeps his 50-foot yacht, *Dream Lover*. It cost a half million dollars.

Nick Jesson appears to be a prosperous entrepreneur in need only of a tasteful haberdasher. But there is one other important thing about him. He is a tax cheat.

"I do not pay federal or state income taxes, my company doesn't pay and we give our workers 100 percent of their wages," Jesson says to anyone who will listen. He is partial to what is known as the 861 position, after a section of the tax code whose adherents claim that salaries paid by American-owned companies are not taxable, but he also holds broader views about the power of the government to tax him. Despite all evidence to the contrary, he says he believes that "there is no law that requires Americans to pay taxes, but the government and the media have tricked people into thinking they have to pay."

America has always had tax protesters, even ones like Jesson who insist that they are not protesting at all, but are only obeying the law as they read it. But Jesson is part of a new trend, a trend as disturbing as the government's reaction to it.

In the midnineties tax protesting morphed from two groups, the super rich who could quietly hide their money and mostly low-income holders of fringe political views who had little to tax, into a phenomenon that cut across all income lines. The rich who protested did so quietly using techniques that seldom came into public view to minimize the risk that their considerable assets would be siezed. Now Jesson and others with economic substance have been able, since Senator Roth's hearings, to openly thumb their noses at the tax police, often with the help of former IRS employees who actively promote tax evasion to their clients.

A few certified public accountants, like Joe Banister of San Jose, a former IRS criminal investigator, now work with people who believe that the tax laws do not really require the payment of taxes. Judges in Las Vegas, Honolulu and other jurisdictions have fined or threatened to fine lawyers who argued the 861 position and other theories that have been uniformly rejected by courts as baseless, yet they have spread rapidly. Congress raised the maximum fine for making frivolous arguments like the 861 position in court fivefold to $25,000, but that does not appear to have had any deterrent effect. There is at least one certified financial planner who publicly declares that taxes need not be paid.

Former police officers, manufacturing company owners and at least one major movie star have all filed tax returns using the 861 position to get out of paying or to try to. Wesley Snipes, who has often portrayed federal law enforcement agents in his action films, filed an amended tax return seeking return of $7 million he paid in taxes on the $19.3 million he earned in 1997. He also filed amended tax returns for two other years and tried to pay nothing on his 2000 tax return using the 861 position. Snipes went so far as to sign a subtly altered jurat—the fine print whereby each taxpayer certifies that his or her return is signed "under penalties of perjury." An especially flint-eyed government employee noticed that Snipes's tax returns added two very smoothly inserted letters so that he signed "under no penalties of perjury."

Just as important as the spread of such behavior is how the government responded to these new methods of tax evasion and to their rapid spread. Imagine reading on the front page of the Sunday morning newspaper the names of drug dealers who say that they openly sell marijuana, cocaine and heroin because the drug laws are invalid, an elaborate deception by the government. These drug dealers are not only named, but the locations where they do business are listed. Some of the dealers are quoted as daring the police to come after them. Is there any doubt that even as you were reading those words, the police would be out in force, arresting those selling drugs and rousting the rest of them, lest the police became laughing stocks and the city council fire the police chief?

Just such an article appeared on the front page of *The New York Times* on Sunday November 19, 2000, only it was about Jesson and other business owners who don't pay taxes, boasting about it and taunting the IRS. One of the businessmen, Dick Celata of Gloucester, Massachusetts, said that since opening his Kristi Tool Co. in 1979 he had never filed a tax return and in all that time no IRS or state official ever contacted him. Jesson noted that he filed for a refund for all the taxes he had withheld from paychecks and turned over to the government in 1997 through 1999. The IRS sent him a check for $217,000, which included interest on the money. (The IRS said any refund was a mistake, but it never filed suit to get the money back.) Another businessman, Dave Bosset of Clearwater, Florida, received almost $22,000 in refunds.

Instead of moving right away to stop this new kind of tax cheating, the IRS did nothing. Months passed. Then a year. The IRS took no visible actions against the businesspeople who had quit paying taxes. Dale Hart, an IRS deputy commissioner, chuckled as she told National Public Radio that "the worst mistake that a small businessman could make is to choose to sign onto a scheme like this. They are putting their business and their livelihood at risk."

Jesson said Hart's comments were just so much meaningless blather because the government, in his view, has no authority to make any business owner withhold taxes.

The IRS did take one action. Hart had the IRS sweep its computer files for the names of people who had been paid wages in prior years by the businesses listed in the newspaper. Each worker was then sent a letter warning that they were required to pay their taxes whether their employer withheld them or not. Those who failed to pay would be hit with penalties and interest. The letter showed that the IRS had gotten the message at the Senate Finance Committee hearings when Tex Moncrief, the man who paid $23 million to settle his tax bills, was so warmly embraced. The message was that they had to be very careful going after people of economic substance, especially those who could get access to their representatives in Congress, and to focus instead on going after those Leona Helmsley famously called "the little people."

There is a second advantage to this approach: although it may never collect the taxes, going after the employees instead of the employers means vastly larger numbers for IRS statistical reports to Congress.

The inaction by the IRS is not entirely its fault, however. During the nineties the IRS budget per tax return was cut by 10 percent. The new rules passed after the Senate Finance hearings, along with other taxpayer rights legislation passed by Congress, imposed complex new rules that determined tax evaders can use to tie up the IRS in procedural games.

The price of inaction, whatever its reasons, is high. "The system simply cannot work if they get away with this," Michael Graetz, the Yale law professor who was a tax policy adviser in the first Bush administration and is an influential thinker on how the tax system can and should work. He said the IRS was making a major mistake by ignoring people like Jesson. He predicted that inaction would embolden more business owners to quietly quit the tax system without announcing themselves as Jesson and his confreres had. "They have to act or this will get out of hand very, very quickly," Graetz warned.

As time passed Jesson and the others cited the lack of IRS action against them as proof that they were right, that no law required anyone to pay taxes and that Americans had been tricked into paying taxes when they were really voluntary. "If what I am doing is illegal then why haven't I been arrested?" Jesson asked.

These business owners and others bought a series of full-page ads in *USA Today,* the nation's largest circulation newspaper, featuring photographs of Jesson, Banister and others. The ads touted their views and challenged the government to come after them. They also denounced *The New York Times* for yellow journalism, saying it refused to print that taxes are voluntary. The group also bought ads in *The Washington Times.*

More than two years later no IRS agents had shown up, with or without guns, at Jesson's firm. None of those named in the ads had their bank accounts seized. None had their businesses padlocked. Not one of the horrors that Senator Roth had worked so hard to alert the nation to, and that Frank Luntz accurately predicted would bring in a rich harvest of donations and votes, was visited upon people who were in effect thumbing their nose at tax law enforcement. And despite IRS Deputy Commissioner Hart's remarks on the radio, Jesson still had his yacht.

While the IRS lets well-known tax cheats get away without paying, the State of California took action. State tax agents, who read *The Times* article months after it ran, raided Jesson's business and home looking for payroll and other business records. Jesson challenged the search warrant in court, saying the judge who signed it had no authority. Two years later the case languished in a procedural knot and Jesson had not paid a cent.

The state also sought the records of the other California business owner named in the article, Al Thompson, the owner of Cencal Aviation Products in Lake Shasta. He had written to the IRS that this company was quitting the tax system in July 2000 and then he hired Banister, the former IRS criminal investigator, as an adviser. What happened next is indicative of how not all tax law enforcement has been intimidated by powerful lawmakers who publicly support law and order but whose conduct demonstrates hostility to tax law enforcement. Thompson refused to let California state tax agents see his business records. Judge Richard McEachen of California Superior Court had Thompson arrested and brought to his courtroom. Thompson then promised to turn over the records and the judge let him go home.

A few days later Thompson told Maline Hazle, a reporter for the *Redding Record Searchlight,* that the judge had no authority and that only because he was under duress had he promised to turn over the records, which he had no intention of doing. Four days later, Thompson, dressed in a flowery polo shirt, sat in court waiting for a scheduled hearing on whether he had kept his promise.

"Has he turned over the documents?" Judge McEachen asked a state prosecutor even before he had settled into his seat on the bench.

"No, your honor," said Amy Wynn, a California deputy attorney general.

"You are remanded to custody, Mr. Thompson," the judge said, rising and walking out just seconds after he entered the courtroom.

As Thompson was taken away in handcuffs, he muttered "Good grief, this is not right."

Thompson finally made the records available to the state and was let go after three nights in jail.

After this, and in the face of continuing news accounts about the lack of action against people like Jesson and Thompson, Department of Justice lawyers filed civil lawsuits against a handful of promoters and advocates of the 861 position. But Jesson was not pursued. Jesson and Thompson both ran for office in 2002 promoting their view that the government has no authority to tax their incomes or their businesses. Jesson won 1 percent of the votes in the California Republican primary. Thompson received 9 percent of the votes for Congress in his district's Republican primary.

Jesson had a simple explanation for why he was not prosecuted. "They are afraid," Jesson said, "afraid to let a jury hear the truth because a jury would acquit me and they know it." Having a jury acquit him, Jesson said quite perceptively, would be like spreading gasoline on a fire, sending the message that you really can stop paying your taxes and nothing bad will happen to you.

When Jesson, Thompson and the others first made the news, the IRS sought to downplay the issue. Fewer than two dozen businesses were named, the IRS said, and the report was out of proportion to the problem. The problem, the IRS insisted publicly, was tiny, a view that time would prove wrong. Any refunds were mistakes, the IRS said, though it never filed suit against Jesson to get the money back.

Frank Keith, the senior IRS spokesman, explained that "with limited resources the I.R.S. must often choose which cases to pursue" and that the businessmen were just not that important. Four former IRS commissioners, though, took a different view. They warned that the tax system relied on withholding from paychecks for the vast majority of income and Social Security tax revenue and that a breakdown in that system could have serious consequences. "This is tremendously significant because we have never before had responsible parties—employers—refuse to withhold," said one of the former commissioners, Sheldon Cohen. "The system simply cannot work if they get away with this."

A different story emerged two years later from a document filed by the Department of Justice in the federal courthouse in Tampa. The IRS had identified 1,500 businesses that had dropped out of the tax system after alerting the agency that they were adopting the 861 position and similar schemes. Rae Ann Thurell, an IRS manager, signed an affidavit stating that dealing with frivolous tax returns, especially those promoting the 861 position, "places a severe administrative burden on the I.R.S." Just reading such returns and sending a notice that they are being disregarded takes an average of 2.5 hours each. For 152,000 frivolous returns, that would be 1.4 percent of all the hours of work the IRS has to audit 200 million individual, corporate and other tax returns. Actual audits take much more time, much more than Congress funds.

The day after the Tampa filing, a report by the General Accounting Office put the number of companies known to not withhold taxes at 7,500. Since there are promoters who teach people how to drop out of the income tax system with little risk of being detected by IRS computers, there are no doubt many more businesses that operate tax-free, undetected by the IRS.

The IRS does not know when new businesses are formed or when they simply change their names slightly to evade detection. The state of Connecticut, in contrast, gets lists of every business entity formed in the state and compares them to its tax records. The state tax commissioner, Gene Gavin, said such diligence is a major reason that none of the big tax protests and tax scams have taken root in his state. "If you do business in Connecticut we know who you are and if you don't file a tax return we know it and we take action," he said.

Irwin Schiff, a convicted tax felon and author of *The Federal Mafia,* sells another tax scam that grew because of IRS inaction.

Schiff, who has been sent to prison twice for tax crimes, was on hard times in 1995. He was driving a borrowed car and he talked incessantly about the need to find clients willing to pay for his unorthodox tax advice to cover his bills, a patter that continued in conversations over the next two years. But soon after the first round of Senate finance hearings his business picked up and by 2000 Schiff had become prosperous. He was again wearing finely tailored silk sport coats, tastefully coordinated shirts and Hermes ties, and he had a fancy new set of wheels to drive. He added employees to his bookstore, Freedom Books, just off the Strip in Las Vegas, and moved into a bigger building with a better sign. "I tell you, things are really changing for me," he said soon after Senator Roth's hearings. Schiff is the largest seller of Senator Roth's book about the IRS, *The Power to Destroy,* with thousands of copies available at his shop.

Before the hearings, Schiff's clientele had been mostly down-and-out blue-collar workers and people who for one reason or another had come to loathe American society. "Now for the first time I am getting business people to my seminars."

Schiff teaches people to file returns with "zero" in each tax return box asking about income. From 1999 to 2001 at least 3,100 people filed zero returns and evaded $56 million of taxes. But those numbers are clearly understatements because in court papers the IRS admitted that until 2000 it did not even try to identify people who filed "zero" returns. The IRS also admitted that many people who file such returns simply stop filing after a few years of filling out "zero" returns.

Another long-running tax dodge is Anderson's Ark & Associates, whose sales agents told clients as far back as 1978 that it had a legal way to make them immune from income taxes using trusts and offshore accounts. From 1997 to 1999 alone at least 2,000 people put $50 million into Anderson's Ark. Few if any of the people who put their money with Anderson's Ark in the belief that it was a legal opportunity for Christians to stop rendering onto Caesar were aware of the past of its leader, Keith Anderson. He served two years in a North Carolina prison under the name Phillip Barrett, after being convicted of real estate fraud in 1990, and he has been a fugitive from a state criminal charge in California since the seventies.

Anderson insisted that he was running a legitimate "free enterprise organization." After he was arrested in Costa Rica, following an 87-count indictment charging tax evasion, he called the United States government both a criminal organization and an agent of Satan and said the government was persecuting him for showing Christians that the tax laws are a fraud. Supporters organized prayer circles for him, though prayers for the safe return of their money would seem more in order.

The 861 position and the zero tax return are just two of many techniques being marketed by promoters whose basic pitch is that they have found a perfectly legal technique to escape taxes. Others sell "pure trusts" and "constitutional trusts" and "complex business organizations." There are offshore banks and offshore businesses and a host of other schemes. What all of them share in common is that they are criminal violations of the law, no matter how much the promoters dress them up.

By 2002, when the IRS had wakened to how its years of not enforcing the law had encouraged tax evasion, the problem was significant. At least 152,000 Americans filed bogus tax returns stating they owed no taxes or even seeking money back from the government under a variety of tax evasions marketed by promoters, an IRS report admitted. That was better than one in every 900 tax returns. Since the IRS audits fewer than one in 200 returns overall, that means most of the bogus returns get sent off to the warehouse with no inquiry. Those tax evaders get away with it. So did the countless others who filed no return or who filed tax returns that cleverly disguised their criminal conduct.

The IRS, in court papers in several cases, has said it believes many people who file such bogus returns simply stop filing after a few years. People who follow the advice of promoters on how to make themselves invisible to IRS computers can simply vanish from the government's files and go on with little fear of being detected.

In Washington there is even what the *The New Republic* character-ized as a lobby for tax cheats, the Center for Freedom and Prosperity. It seeks to end policies that hinder efforts by Americans to hide in-come from the IRS and policies that keep foreigners from hiding money from their governments in the United States, which it presents as matters of financial privacy. The center, which has ties to officials of the Heritage Foundation, says that it is seeking to prevent government intrusions that violate people's financial privacy. There is no right of fi-nancial privacy in tax matters, however. The IRS has the authority to summons financial records from taxpayers and from third parties, like banks, vendors and employers. And courts routinely issue subpoenas for financial records sought by tax authorities. The center has been in the forefront of opposing efforts by the Organization for Economic Cooperation and Development, which represents more than 30 ad-vanced countries, to crack down on global tax frauds. The second Bush administration refused to support the organization's initiative, promising it would come up with its own alternatives. The administra-tion also said it was worried about financial privacy, although that con-cern largely evaporated after 9/11 and it became clear that the bank secrecy laws of tax havens had helped Al Qaeda and other terrorists in their plots to kill Americans.

While many mass-marketed tax evasion schemes appeal to people who hate the government, some scams focus on persuading gullible people that there is a perfectly legal way to quit paying taxes if you just know some secrets. Investors in Anderson's Ark and in many other schemes often seem nonpolitical, more lambs being led to the financial slaughter than foes of organized society. Their willingness to buy into schemes that evade taxes, while professing their belief that they are law abiding, indicates an important rip in the social fabric that holds the nation together. It is a tear caused partly by cynicism over the many special-interest favors in the tax code that make the system corrupt in the eyes of many. It is also a response to stagnant wages that have made many desperate to find any way to improve their financial circum-stances. And it is an important sign of falling support for the idea of the commonwealth, without which democracy cannot survive. This tear has been ripped further by leading politicians who have seized on

the advice of Frank Luntz, the pollster who was so influential in showing Republicans that attacking the IRS was their best way to get more
votes.

At least one seller of tax evasion has a good friend in Congress.
Representative Ron Paul, a Texas Republican, was the keynote speaker
when Joe Sweet and his Joy Foundation held a seminar in Cancun in
2001. The Joy Foundation charges as much as $8,235 for a "degree" in
tax avoidance and has taken in at least $6.5 million from clients in re-
cent years.

Dr. Paul said he knew nothing of the Joy Foundation's tax schemes
and that if he had, he probably would not have attended. To be that
unaware, he must not have read any of the organization's literature,
which promotes tax fraud on every page. The doctor-congressman
said that, much as he disapproves of the tax laws, they are valid. But he
went on to volunteer comments that show why he is regarded as a hero
in tax protest circles. Dr. Paul said that he shared the Joy Foundation's
belief that requiring businesses to withhold taxes and keep records
"is involuntary servitude" in violation of the Thirteenth Amendment,
which outlawed slavery. The involuntary servitude claim is widely used
by white racist organizations to justify not paying taxes. The problem
of such claims is serious enough that Congress allows a 20 percent
penalty for those who cite the Thirteenth Amendment as a rationale
for not paying their taxes.

Dropping out of the tax system without getting caught is relatively
easy because of the way that the IRS uses its resources. JJ MacNab,
the Maryland insurance analyst whose hobby is monitoring tax scams,
describes the focus of IRS enforcement efforts as a hunt for "detail
cheating." IRS computers analyze tax returns for deductions that seem
too large and income that is reported by third parties, like employers,
that does not show up on individual tax returns.

Hardly any resources are devoted to looking for those who simply
do not file. When the IRS tried to find such cheaters in the early
nineties, it turned up hundreds of thousands of them without much
effort—and five years later most of those it found had dropped back
out of the system again, no longer filing tax returns. Those who do
drop out can become invisible to the IRS if they follow the advice sold

by promoters. They teach which major banks issue noninterest-bearing accounts to people who refuse to use Social Security cards and how to arrange payments from vendors in ways that are not reportable to the IRS.

"In the past 10 years," MacNab said, "tax evasion has grown from being a secret of the very wealthy to a mass-marketed industry. As the promoters of these plans become more aggressive and their target market widens, this lost tax revenue will only increase. The IRS no longer acts as an effective deterrent to those who cheat, and where most taxpayers in the past begrudged their taxes, they paid them nonetheless, because it was the right and honorable thing to do. Today, many of those same people have decided that the system is corrupt and that only fools pay their taxes."

The IRS has not undertaken a serious study of tax evasion for years. But if the figures from the last study are simply adjusted for the increased size of the economy, then tax evaders cheat the government out of more than $300 billion each year. The problem has grown more than the economy, as Treasury Secretary Paul O'Neill told Congress in 2001. He predicted that evasion by high-income taxpayers using offshore accounts would continue to grow, too.

Evasion has spread in part because a small but increasing number of Americans reject our government, openly denouncing it as a criminal organization. Many of these tax protesters are people who have been crushed economically by government policies that encouraged the movement offshore of manufacturing and other jobs that paid well for people with limited education. It has also spread because technology makes it easier to move money across borders. It has grown because con artists and scamsters always flourish when law enforcement is lax. And those who appeal to people's religious values, like Keith Anderson, and who deceive people into thinking that there are legal ways to stop paying taxes can always find gullible clients. Not all of the evasions are by mass marketers. At the high end, the breakdown in ethical standards in the accounting and legal professions has encouraged some of the richest people in America to cheat. But at whatever level this cheating is taking place, it imposes a severe cost on honest taxpayers. If the government could collect that conservative estimate of $300 billion lost to evasion, then Congress could exempt from taxes the half of Americans who earn less than $532 a week and give tax cuts averaging $4,000 to the rest of the taxpayers.

In June 2003 the Department of Justice finally secured its first indictment against one of the business owners who boasted about not paying taxes. Richard M. Simkanin, the owner of Arrow Custom Plastics in Bedford, Texas, near Dallas, was charged with 27 felony counts. He was accused of not withholding taxes from the paychecks of his four dozen employees and for seeking refunds of taxes he had turned over before he quit the tax system in January 2000. Simkanin's indictment and arrest did not seem to trouble Jesson or any of the other business owners who had quit paying taxes. Most of them still had not received so much as a telephone call from the IRS. Jesson had tied up his civil state tax case for two years with claims that the judge who issued the search warrant for his business lacked authority. An appeals court finally tossed the claim out and in September 2003 Jesson and his wife were arrested by the California Franchise Tax Board for failing to pay taxes on about $1 million per year for three years. Neither the IRS nor Justice has taken any action against Jesson. Two prosecutions out of at least 1,500 businesses are not very intimidating. Since tax law enforcement is based on general deterrence and Congress tightly restricts funding to enforce the law, the likelihood is that at the end of the day only a dozen or so of these business owners will be prosecuted. Those less publicly boastful than Simkanin and Jesson almost certainly will get away with their crimes.

While the IRS has lacked both the will and the resources to pursue businesspeople like Jesson, surely it has pursued others aggressively. If the IRS was handed bank records that detailed tax crimes by people who had secret, and thus illegal, offshore accounts, it would pursue them all, right? And surely it would get the promoter.

Not exactly. In fact, it might just let the promoter go.

Getting off the Hook
15

FBI agents across the country raided warehouses and offices, shutting down a cable piracy ring and seizing thousands of descrambler boxes that let people watch cable television for free, including 3,500 that had mysteriously disappeared from a Los Angeles Police Department evidence locker. They also arrested 14 people including a patrician-looking banker in his late sixties named John Mathewson. What happened next was a complete surprise.

Mathewson was living in San Antonio, but he owned a Cayman Islands bank that had been used to launder tens of millions of dollars from the cable piracy ring going back to 1989. Mathewson offered to turn over the banking records of his 2,000 clients, on two computer discs, and to cooperate in prosecuting them, in return for a get-out-of-jail-free card. The government went for the deal.

The Cayman Islands are three specks in the blue-green waters of the Caribbean with no resources beyond the sun and warm water. Yet these islands are the fifth largest banking center in the world. At the time of Mathewson's arrest in 1996, there were 27,000 businesses and banks on the islands, roughly one for each inhabitant, including branches of nearly all of the world's biggest commercial banks. Individual Americans had about $100 billion deposited there, with corporations using the Cayman Islands for perhaps five times that much. The vaults of Cayman Islands banks were not very large, however. Many of the banks and businesses existed as little more than file folders in the drawers of island lawyers.

The Caymans depend on tax fraud, Mathewson told the Senate permanent investigations subcommittee five years after his arrest:

> The cost of opening a corporate account was $8,000 U.S. There was an annual management fee of $3,000 U.S. or more. If an individual wanted to have an aged corporation, this could cost between $12,000–$16,000 U.S. Additionally, the cost of flying to the Cayman Islands, staying in one of the expensive hotels such as the Hyatt, and eating on the island all involved considerable expense. Without the knowledge that they would be able to evade taxes and hide or shelter funds from the inquisitive, there would be absolutely no point in establishing an offshore account; since almost all of the services offered by offshore banks could be obtained from domestic U.S. banks for no charge. . . . Why would any U.S. citizen wish to go through the time and expense required to establish an offshore account unless it was for the evasion of taxes or the hiding of funds?

Few if any people in law enforcement knew about Mathewson, a Marine in World War II who went on to make a fortune as an Illinois homebuilder, until 1994, two years before his arrest. Jack Blum, a former Senate investigator and sometime consultant to the IRS, caught him on a hidden camera. For years Blum has complained that the United States not only fails to go after tax cheats who use offshore havens, it actually helps them with its laws, treaties and policies. The video Blum made of Mathewson was not for law enforcement, but for the PBS program *Frontline*. The program showed how despite claims of crackdowns on paper companies set up to launder funds, the British Virgin Islands alone increased the number of such shell companies in a decade to 120,000 from just 5,000.

Mathewson got into Cayman Islands banking in 1985 when two men he knew said they could all get rich taking deposits from Europeans. Ironically, Mathewson had to undergo background checks by the FBI and Scotland Yard before he was allowed to invest in the bank. He passed muster, but Guardian Bank failed to attract much European money. Mathewson bought out his partners and started putting ads in airline magazines, the ones passengers find in the seat pocket in front of them, and holding seminars on offshore banking at hotels. "The truth is that without the U.S. client, there would be no banking industry in the Cayman Islands," Mathewson said when he was sentenced.

Mathewson had helped the cable piracy ring, which was headquartered in Omaha, create sham corporations and phony invoices so that money from the cable piracy operation in the United States could be sent to his Guardian Bank and Trust in the Cayman Islands disguised as business expenses. Then the money came back to the United States, invested in accounts at the stock brokerages owned by Prudential Insurance and Charles Schwab.

But the real genius idea was the credit cards. They solved a major problem for people who place money offshore to hide it from the government—how to get your hands on the money to spend it. Wire transfers and checks leave detailed paper trails, records from American banks that prosecutors can obtain with search warrants. These records have names, dates and amounts. Over the years many drug dealers have gone off to prison after prosecutors showed juries the paper trail of their tax evasions.

Mathewson told clients that their Visa gold cards, with spending limits as high as $1 million, meant their tax dodges could not be traced. After all, there were no names on the credit card charge records that flowed through the Visa computer network, just the account number. To get at the name, Mathewson told clients, they had to get at the records in his bank. Under the Confidential Relationships Act in the Cayman Islands and similar laws in other tax havens, the names of account owners were secret.

How well the IRS pursued the Mathewson cases would be an important test for the IRS. After all, it had been handed more than 1,500 slam-dunk tax cases. All it had to do was compare the 18 months of Cayman Islands bank records that he turned over to the tax returns of those customers. Customers who had not checked the box declaring that they had an offshore account had committed a crime and made themselves liable for serious civil penalties as well as prison time. And the bank records would be an easy-to-read road map of big-time tax cheats, showing undeclared income or suggesting faked deductions.

Mathewson's biggest customer, after the cable pirates, was Mark A. Vicini, a New Jersey computer company owner who funneled $6 million in undeclared income to Guardian Bank. Vicini, with help from

Mathewson, bought a $720,000 Florida home through a dummy corporation and then arranged to pay rent that he deducted as a business expense even though the money was circling back to his own account offshore. Mathewson even prepared a lease to make it appear that Vicini was only renting the property, when he was really paying rent to himself, prosecutors said. Vicini pleaded guilty in 1997 to evading $2.2 million in federal income taxes and got a light sentence, just five months in custody.

For months Mathewson sat with IRS criminal investigators, pulling from his extraordinary memory detail after detail. Prosecutors across the country wrote letters asking a federal judge to go soft on Mathewson, whom they described as the most valuable and cooperative witness in the history of tax prosecutions. They wrote letters to the judge saying he had delivered information allowing them to prosecute more than 1,500 tax cheats. Prosecutors said they recovered $50 million with a potential to collect six times that much in taxes and penalties. The judge understood. Mathewson did not spend a single night behind bars.

Once Mathewson was off the hook, however, things did not quite work out as the prosecutors suggested. The IRS only prosecuted 69 cases, charging fewer than one in 20 of Mathewson's customers. And how did it do at collecting the taxes? The IRS will not say. Nor will it say how many of the 1,500 clients were simply made to pay the taxes they had evaded. But there is evidence to suggest that most of them got away with their crimes, quite literally laughing all the way to the bank. Lawyers who represented several of the clients say that they received retainers and prepared to defend their clients, but the IRS never made so much as a telephone call.

Mathewson walked IRS criminal investigators through many cases that were never pursued. John Morrell, a retired IRS special agent, said after that Mathewson spent several days detailing tax fraud by one client, he was sure a prosecution would follow. The individual not only had huge unreported income, he had schemes to fabricate business expenses that were really just circular movements of money, taking a tax deduction on his American tax return for money paid to an offshore company he secretly owned.

Morrell could accept that his superiors decided not to prosecute on this particular set of facts. What angered him was that the tax cheat was not made the subject of an audit so that the case would be pursued civilly and the taxes collected along with penalties. Even if the evidence from Mathewson was ignored, Morrell said, the man himself was a perfect choice for an audit of his latest tax return. There was no reason to think that after years of cheating on his taxes, he had suddenly become a model citizen, Morrell figured. Serious tax cheats are like leopards: they do not lose their spots. But as best Morrell could find out, nothing was done.

Mathewson was a tax cheat. He shorted the government $9 million in the early seventies, Tax Court records show, and he did not file returns for at least three years in the seventies and eighties. Just for the years up through 1985, Mathewson owed the government more than $11 million in taxes, interest and penalties, but when he was living in the Cayman Islands, he ignored the IRS letters demanding payment. When the government took him to court in 1993, Mathewson, who had made a $100,000 deposit, tried to get the deposit back. A judge said no. No one but Mathewson and the IRS knows if he ever paid anything other than the deposit.

Mathewson's case did get the IRS to start investigating the use of credit cards to tap offshore accounts. It went to court for the records of MasterCards and American Express cards that were issued to addresses in tax havens like the Cayman Islands and the Bahamas, but were used to make purchases in the United States. The two companies initially resisted the John Doe summonses and said that, besides, there was nothing useful in their records. The two card companies said that all they had were account numbers, the offshore addresses where bills were sent and the amount and place where each charge was made. Names, they said, they did not have. Just numbered charge accounts.

Joe West, a veteran IRS criminal investigator, had a plan. He knew that if he could get the charge records in electronic form, he could look for patterns of spending and then he could go to restaurants, hotels and other businesses where repeat purchases were made to get reservation and registration records that would yield names. It would be a lot of work and perhaps only a few cases could be pursued, but it would send a signal to tax cheats using offshore accounts that the IRS was onto them and that the credit card gambit was no longer a safe way to spend untaxed dollars.

When the companies finally complied with the summonses, the IRS was stunned. There were 230,000 MasterCards, which suggested that, together with the much larger Visa operation, between 1 million and 2 million offshore credit cards had been issued to Americans. Just 117,000 Americans disclosed on their income tax returns having any kind of offshore account, so even if only a half million cards had been issued by offshore banks, the IRS had a major problem.

The bank records also vindicated Jack Blum, the investigator of money laundering who first brought Mathewson to the attention of American authorities. Blum had for years been saying that the United States was losing $70 billion a year to offshore tax fraud and now his estimate no longer seemed beyond imagining. And that estimate meant that seven cents of each dollar Americans paid in federal income taxes were just making up for the offshore tax cheating.

Investigator West and his team soon began to identify some of the tax cheats from their purchase records. But while the IRS continued through 2003 to study the credit card records, the offshore tax cheat business changed, as others noticed, even if the IRS did not.

In Manhattan the district attorney, Robert Morgenthau, who felt that the IRS was always behind the curve on tax cheating, noticed that some of the offshore banks had stopped advertising MasterCards and Visa cards. Instead they were promoting debit cards, the kind people use to draw cash from automated teller machines. Morgenthau fought in court to get access to records of withdrawals made using debit cards issued by tax-haven banks. One banker told him he was wasting his time. Unlike the credit card spending that Joe West and his team at the IRS could tie to individuals with a lot of work, the banker said that debit cards were good for untraceable cash. Morgenthau's gumshoes proved the banker wrong.

Using the debit card withdrawal records they established that one of many cards linked to Leadenhall Bank and Trust in the Bahamas, another tax haven, was used to withdraw $500,000 from Manhattan teller machines in eight months. Morgenthau was certain that if he could identify the card user, he could prove he was a criminal tax cheat.

But the bank records were not the kind of perfect road map that checks and wire transfers provide or even as useful as the charge records that West and his crew were digging into to identify tax cheats. The debit card records did not accurately record the time of withdrawals or even which particular automated teller machines were used. Teller machines have video recorders, but they are not keyed to each transaction. And a fiscal crisis had cut Morgenthau's staff of lawyers and investigators by close to a fifth.

Still, he did not give up. His detectives got lucky when one Leadenhall customer, who had withdrawn about $134,000 of cash in eight months, made a foolish mistake. One day, apparently when his credit card was rejected, he used his debit card to pay for a rental car. "We got him," Morgenthau exulted, sounding like a kid instead of the spry octogenarian he is, after the man pleaded guilty to a tax-related charge.

What Morgenthau found, that the smart tax evaders had shifted from credit cards to debit cards, was borne out by the disclosures the IRS made in court papers about what Joe West and his team found. There were few charges at fine restaurants and luxury hotels. Instead the charge records showed stays at Holiday Inns and travel on Southwest Airlines. That is, once Mathewson spilled the beans, the only people still using the credit card gambit were the middle-class tax cheats, not the seriously rich. This tendency of the IRS to identify a fraud problem and then refine its focus on that fraud even while the scamsters just moved on to a new fraud had been identified in a lengthy report to the IRS by Malcolm Sparrow, a Harvard expert on frauds against government agencies. But Sparrow's report was filed away, its recommendations largely ignored.

Sticking to the credit card cases did assure one thing: there was little risk of running into tax cheats among the political donor class. That means there was also little risk of encountering pressure, from outside or in, to go easy on those with connections, as one IRS executive did until he was shut down.

Peter Coons had a stellar career with the IRS. He won award after award and, once the government started paying cash bonuses to high-performing executives, won the maximum amount every single year. In late 1995 Coons was promoted to chief tax collector for all of Northern California, a job he relished.

Coons had more than 400 people reporting to him and he told them they were going to go after anyone who owed taxes regardless of their social rank or political ties. Just a few months into his job, he pressed to collect $60 million in taxes owed by Golden ADA, a suspected front for Russian mobsters who wanted to get diamonds and gold out of that country and into the United States for sale. Some prominent San Franciscans had been customers of the firm. But the case also had international implications that Coons was unaware of until pressure to back off started to come from the Department of State, from the Russian consulate in San Francisco, from federal prosecutors and finally from the IRS itself. Coons was never sure if there really was some subtle issue of foreign diplomacy that he had blundered into unawares or if this was just raw political help for some of the rich and well connected who had become involved with Golden ADA. He did notice that once he was shut down, the tax bill was settled for $20 million, two thirds off the regular tax bill.

If there was a deeper message here for Coons about picking whom to pursue for back taxes and whom to let go, he did not get it. Soon he was sending his revenue officers out to collect taxes owed by two prominent and very well connected Bay Area families. One was that of Al Davis, owner of the Oakland Raiders football team. The other was the Aliotos, the enormously powerful and rich extended family of Joseph Alioto, a former San Francisco mayor. Both the Davis and Alioto families would later say that in their tax disputes with the IRS they never sought favors. Coons never said they did—he said his bosses wanted him to go easy, apparently to curry favor with the tax professionals representing the two families.

Coons said he was told again and again in 1997 and 1998 that he was pressing these cases too hard, that it would cause problems for the IRS because right then Senator Roth's investigators were looking for angry taxpayers to testify on Capitol Hill about the big bad IRS. "It will look bad" if these cases against prominent people are pressed, he was told.

That infuriated Coons. He recalled firing back that going after some rich tax scofflaws would make the average Joe think he was getting a fair shake from the government. Coons believed that guys with lunch pails should be treated the same as people who dined at the Pacific Union Club atop Nob Hill.

"While influential taxpayers were getting a break, myself and many division managers were being pressured to establish quotas and collect more revenues from the average person," Coons told the *San Jose Mercury*.

Coons had such a stellar record that none of the bosses who wanted to go soft on the rich and powerful could touch him. That changed after he got his first computer.

Like many government executives, Coons had never touched a computer. But one day a technician installed one on his desk, turned it on, opened an Internet browser and told Coons to play with it, just "type in things and see what you find." Coons went Web surfing. Soon he was checking his stock portfolio and he helped one of his staff plan a vacation. There were no formal IRS rules on the use of the computer and all Coons knew about using it came from the technician. One day a woman on his staff came into his office and saw a naked woman on the computer screen. She was so horrified, she testified later, that she could never work around Coons again.

The powers that be in the IRS San Francisco office moved swiftly. They assigned Coons to a new office. No title. No staff. No windows. No phone. No duties. He was a $101,000-a-year clerk, paid to sit at his desk until the clock hit five o'clock. Then they had him questioned. Coons tried to deny the naked pictures, but the hard drive on his computer showed cookies from five pornographic Web sites. He had, he said later, made some stupid uses of the computer. After a few months he was demoted, his pay was cut $15,000 and he was put to work on the annual charity fund-raising drive among federal employees.

Coons hired a lawyer and, to protect his job, went to the Merit Systems Protection Board seeking certification as a whistle-blower. While favoritism in government agencies is usually a matter of a lot of smoke and not much fire, Coons had some specific cases to point to. He was not the only one who saw the IRS as riddled with favoritism to the rich, who hired the right accounting and legal advisers, those from firms that had positions to offer high-level managers ready to retire from their government careers.

Senator Roth's investigators reported that a fifth of the IRS managers they interviewed reported observing "situations where taxpayers with political clout were given preferential treatment." And that wasn't once in a career, but once a year. Had Roth's staff dug deeper, they would have found that such treatment was routine. They would have found dozens of IRS agents in New York, Long Island and Los Angeles with tales of being pressured to go soft on people who were politically connected or who had hired former IRS executives to represent them.

Roth's investigators were also told that those who spoke up, as Coons did, about favoritism or other misconduct came to regret not looking the other way. "We've been inundated with letters from IRS managers and employees who are alleging retaliation within the current culture," William Nixon, Roth's top aide, said. "There is a hang together, circle-the-wagons mentality in the agency. We're going to break this culture."

At his whistle-blower hearing before the Merit Systems Protection Board, Coons encountered a decidedly hostile judge named Phillip Reed. Mary Dryovage, Coons's lawyer, was not allowed to call the IRS executive in charge of discipline for the region. He would have testified that any punishment greater than a two-week suspension was unwarranted, especially in light of Coons's track record as one of the most highly regarded executives in the IRS. Steven Jensen, the IRS executive overseeing the region for the IRS, testified that he regarded him as a whistle-blower. But Jensen said the misuse of the computer, and Coons's initial denials, were so serious that he had no choice but to demote Coons.

Judge Reed, in an opinion long on subjective judgment, denied Coons whistle-blower status because he had given an interview to two newspaper reporters. The message was clear to anyone in the IRS who had not already gotten it: blow the whistle anywhere but to the very bosses you say are showing favoritism and you will be out.

The IRS fired Coons.

Profiting off Taxes

16

For traders in oil company stocks it was a routine September day on Wall Street, a Friday afternoon. The traders in Amsterdam had already finished dinner and perhaps even gone to bed. In New York the minute hand was rising toward four o'clock, when the closing bell would signal that the floor of the New York Stock Exchange would shut down until Monday morning. Suddenly, in brokerages around the world, alarms popped up on the oil traders' computers. A huge block of Royal Dutch Shell, as many shares as usually change hands in an entire day, had just been traded. Then, in the blink of an eye, it was traded again for $1.92 less per share.

Stocks trade on new information, on anything that may signal that shares are worth more or less than the last trading price. An oil tanker fire, an explosion at a big refinery, a coup d'état, the discovery of a new oil field, any of these could lead to a sudden change in the price of an oil stock. All by itself the movement of such a huge block could be important news, a signal that somebody was dumping his holdings because of an important event he knew about—and the traders did not. Even tiny changes in price can be important. The difference in price between the two rapid-fire trades was more than 2 percent of the stock's value. Finding out what was happening, and finding out fast, could mean the difference between these traders making or losing tens of millions of dollars for their clients and whether they got bonuses for the year.

Within seconds after the transaction moved through cyberspace, on what brokers still referred to as the ticker tape, the oil stocks traders hit the speed dials on their telephones to reach Frank Delaney.

What's happening, Frank?

What are the terms of the trade?

Who's buying?

Who's selling?

Delaney is a stock exchange traffic cop, paid to monitor the buying and selling of shares of oil companies to make sure the rules are followed. It is also his job to step in and buy or sell to keep the flow of trades smooth when more shares are being offered for sale than buyers want or when buyers want more shares than are being offered. Delaney told his callers that he had no idea who the parties were and didn't much care so long as they followed the rules.

The rules required what the exchange calls an "open outcry," in which a floor trader says loudly enough to be heard, but not so as to distract anyone, the price at which a specific number of shares is being offered for sale. Other floor traders gathered around to watch, but no one intervened in the fixed trades.

Delaney was inundated with calls from the anxious brokers as more rapid-fire trades took place. In all there would be 46 trades in the few minutes before the closing bell rang. Each trade was the same. A half million shares of Royal Dutch Shell, worth about $40 million, was sold and then bought back a few seconds later, although one time it took the better part of a minute to fill out the trading tickets and enter the information into the computer. When the trades were done, 10 million shares had been sold and every single one of them had been bought back seconds later for $1.92 less than it had been worth an instant earlier.

Despite this enormous volume of shares, the equivalent of all the trades normally made in a month, none of these trades affected the price of Shell stock because the trades were all rigged with the buy and sell prices prearranged. The brokers relaxed. At four o'clock they turned off their computers and went home to their families. No new information had been learned that would influence the price of Royal Dutch Shell stock because what had just taken place, they realized, was not a normal exchange of stock, but a tax dodge.

The guy who developed this particular tax dodge was Robert N.

Gordon, a brilliant and charming fellow with a deep love of Australia. Despite having just a high school diploma plus a taste of college, Gordon teaches at the graduate school of business at New York University. His well-attended class is on arbitrage theory, that is, in taking advantage of inefficiencies in markets. Gordon also owns Twenty-First Securities, a stock brokerage whose specialty is putting that theory into practice.

Understanding what Gordon does, and what was really going on in these trades, is easy once the principles of the transactions become clear. Gordon's deals—and he has invented many of them over the past two decades—are just one small part of a much larger world of tax engineering. At every Wall Street investment house, at the Big Four accounting firms and some of the smaller ones, too, and at many large law firms, whole regiments of incredibly bright people apply their brainpower to inventing transactions that make taxes disappear for their clients, all of whom are rich and few of whom the IRS ever audits.

Many of these deals are arranged so that no hint of them appears on the tax return of the individual or corporation whose tax bill is being slashed. Confidentiality contracts that bar the purchasers from ever talking about the deals are de rigueur. Many times clients will be told that just to hear a sales pitch for a tax dodge they must pay a fee, often $100,000 and sometimes as much as $1 million.

Often participants enter these deals with only the slightest inquiry into just how they work. Executives have testified they put their companies into such deals with no more than a back-of-the-envelope analysis. And people with titles like assistant treasurer of companies have testified that they did not need to seek approvals from top executives because the deals involved such minimal risk that they were within their purview.

In the world of tax dodges the usual sales tools—videos, Power-Point presentations, booklets and brochures—are almost unknown. Ernst & Young sold six different "tax solutions" that it said made taxes evaporate using a single sheet of photocopied paper and the skimpiest outline, written in acronyms without meaning to anyone who did not hear a presentation. One of the firm's spokesmen said it did not print brochures because the profit margins were too slim—this for deals in which the minimum fee was $1 million. Of course, a lack of printed brochures also just happens to avoid a paper trail that might later show the IRS how the deal worked and how it was promoted to customers. Such a paper trail would be great evidence for the government in trying to persuade a court that the deal was solely a tax dodge.

Knowing how this secretive world operates is crucial to understanding how large corporations have been shifting the burden of taxes off themselves and onto you in ways that Congress never intended, that the IRS is ill equipped to deal with and that some judges have found to be perfectly legal.

While the high priests of tax try to make tax shelters sound like unfathomable mysteries on a par with the Holy Trinity, the principles are quite simple.

Calvin H. Johnson, University of Texas professor of law, has a simple definition that goes right to the core of the issue. Usually there are two ways to measure investment profits. The larger is pretax profit. The smaller, what's left after government gets its bite, is after-tax profit.

So how does Professor Johnson define a tax shelter?

"A tax shelter is an investment that is worth more after-tax than before-tax."

That it is possible to have more after paying taxes, not less, was precisely what those curious late-afternoon trades on the floor of the Big Board illustrated.

The Royal Dutch Shell shares were worth about $890 million. They were sold, and then bought back, by Arthur J. Gallagher & Co. insurance broker in Chicago, itself a publicly traded company. It did not own any of the shares. Rather, it had sold short, meaning it borrowed the shares from other owners, sold them, bought them back and then returned them to their owners.

Usually selling short is a way to profit from a falling stock price. You borrow shares from their owner, paying him a fee, and sell the shares. Later, when the stock price is lower, you buy shares and use those shares to replace the ones you borrowed. In essence you sold high and bought low. The difference between what you sold for and what you bought back for is your profit. Sell for $100 and buy back for $60 and you make a profit of $40.

The trouble with short selling is that it is risky. If the price of the stock goes up, you lose money. If you sold borrowed shares at $100 and the price rises to $140, you lose $40. Since there is no limit on how high the price can go, there is no limit to your risk.

Gallagher insurance was not trying to profit from short selling, however. It was simply a straw man, a trader of convenience, in the prearranged deal. The fee showed that these trades in Shell stock on the floor of the New York Stock Exchange were not the usual highly risky transactions, but were virtually free of risk. That the deal was risk-free is shown in the amount of the fee that Gallagher was paid, a fee that did not cover any risk of loss. For selling short $890 million worth of Shell stock Bob Gordon's company paid the Gallagher insurance brokerage a mere $1,000 per roundtrip trade, $23,000 in all.

The real party of interest, if there was one, was on the other side of the deal. The buyer owned each of the 10 million shares for only a few seconds and sold them all at the exact same loss. The buyer was Compaq Computer Corporation. By owning the shares even for an instant on that particular day, Compaq became entitled to Shell's next quarterly dividend of $2.25 per share. It also became liable for a Dutch tax on that dividend that came to a little more than 33 cents per share. Subtract that Dutch tax and the dividend was worth $1.92, exactly the amount that Compaq lost on each share when it sold.

Compaq would later say it was in the trades to make money, to collect that dividend. That was a curious position for the company to take since it sold each share for $1.92 less than it paid for it a moment earlier. If Compaq wanted to profit from the dividend, why did it give up $1.92 per share in each trade to get a $1.92 per share net dividend?

In a word: taxes.

The Dutch government taxes dividends, just as the United States does. Under a treaty with the United States, the Dutch government withholds 15 percent of dividends paid by Dutch companies to Americans (33 cents in this case). Congress lets companies, and individuals, count foreign taxes as if they were paid to our government. With 10 million shares involved, Compaq had more than $3.3 million of tax credits from Holland that it could use to reduce its American taxes. And the rest of the dividend, the $1.92, was precisely accounted for in the difference between each trade.

So what Compaq bought for its momentary ownership was not a pretax dividend or even an after-tax dividend, but a tax credit, called the "foreign tax credit." That credit was valuable because it could be used, dollar-for-dollar, to reduce the taxes that Compaq paid to the United States.

But who would sell such a tax credit? And why?

The answer to the first question is any American pension plan or charitable endowment that owned Shell shares. The second answer lies in a difference between Dutch and American tax law. Pension plans and charities are exempt from American taxes, but not from Dutch taxes on dividends paid by Dutch companies like Shell. To American pension plans and charities with Shell stock, the $2.25 dividend was worth $1.92 in cash. The 33-cent foreign tax credit was worthless to them because they did not pay American taxes.

Enter Bob Gordon. He realized that a company like Compaq might be willing to buy these otherwise useless foreign tax credits. On 10 million shares the credits would be worth more than $3 million, enough to wipe out the federal corporate income taxes on more than $8.5 million of profit.

To make the deal work, however, one had to deal with the fact that while Compaq would collect an after-tax cash dividend of $1.92 per share, it also had a capital loss of $1.92 per share because it sold the shares for less than it paid for them. Because Congress only allows capital losses as an offset to capital gains and not ordinary income like dividends, not just any company could make dividend income and capital loss zero each other out. Compaq could, however, because it had turned a capital gain profit on its investment in the preferred stock of another company, Conner Peripherals.

So what happened to each party in this quick and lucrative game of tax dodge?

- Gallagher insurance made a $19.2 million profit on the trades because it bought the shares back for less than it sold them. But this profit had to be turned over to the pensions and endowment funds in lieu of the after-tax dividends they were entitled to on the stock they had lent to Gallagher. For Gallagher, then, the deal was a wash except for the $23,000 fee.

- The pension and endowment funds received $19.2 million from Gallagher, the exact amount they would have collected, after Dutch taxes on their Shell dividends, plus a tiny fee they were paid to loan their shares out for a few minutes.

- The Dutch government got the same 33 cents per share tax it would have collected if nothing had happened.

- Compaq lost $19.2 million by selling the Shell shares for less than it paid, but it also collected $19.2 million in net dividends, which made it even on the stock trades. Compaq also received foreign tax credits worth more than $3 million that it could apply to reduce its U.S. taxes. Even after paying transaction fees of more than $1 million, Compaq ended up with about $2 million more in its accounts, a fabulous return for almost no effort.

- Gordon's Twenty-First Securities collected fees of more than $1 million. It has never had to disclose how much of that was profit.

- The U.S. government was the only loser, shorted more than $3 million that went, instead, to Compaq and Twenty-First Securities.

- *You* had to shoulder the burden that Compaq escaped.

When the IRS heard about this deal, it audited Compaq and denied it the tax savings. It said there was no business purpose to the transactions, that their sole purpose was to escape taxes. Deals done solely to make taxes vanish have never been allowed by the courts. If they were then trying to tax income, it would be pointless because transactions that make no sense except for tax savings would be executed until all tax bills disappeared. The Department of Justice later described the series of trades that afternoon and the tax benefits that Compaq obtained as "an economic sham serving no purpose other than the manipulation of the foreign tax credit provisions" of the tax code.

Compaq insisted that it was in it for the profit, that what it really wanted was to make money off the Shell dividends. Denied its tax savings, Compaq sued the IRS in United States Tax Court. In September 1998, six years after the trades took place, the case came to trial before Judge Mary Ann Cohen.

Duane Webber, a litigator from Baker & McKenzie, the leading American law firm in promoting corporate tax avoidance using international tax deals, asked James J. Tempesta, who was Compaq's assistant treasurer back then, why the Shell shares were traded.

"Well, again, my function was invest the company's cash, make money. I saw this as a way to make money and enhance the yield on the portfolio."

"So did Compaq enter into the transaction to make a profit?"

"Yes, that's exactly what I wanted to do."

"Did Compaq enter into this transaction to reduce its tax liability, Mr. Tempesta?"

"No."

"Did Compaq enter into the transaction to obtain a tax savings?"

"No."

Judge Cohen did not buy it. She ruled in 1999 that Compaq was not entitled to use the foreign tax credit it had bought to reduce its American taxes because the Shell stock trades had no business purpose, they were done solely to save taxes. She was especially troubled by the lack of a professional analysis ahead of the transactions, which Tempesta testified were approved based on his back-of-the-envelope analysis. She also rejected Compaq's testimony that the deal was risky, that something could go wrong and that these risks, together with Tempesta's stated desire to turn a profit, made the transactions legitimate.

Every aspect of the deal, Judge Cohen ruled, "was deliberately predetermined and designed . . . to yield a specific result and to eliminate all economic risks and influences from outside market forces."

The ruling was significant because Judge Cohen had a well-established reputation as a real softie for the corporate tax dodgers who appeared before her. She found this deal so outrageous that she imposed negligence penalties. For the big corporations that had grown accustomed to an easy ride in Tax Court, the decision drew full attention.

Lee Sheppard, who reviews tax dodges for the weekly journal *Tax Notes,* just the way that film critics review the latest movie for the morning newspaper, declared herself astounded.

"Who'da thunk it? The corporate tax shelter problem has gotten so bad that even Tax Court Chief Judge Mary Ann Cohen . . . has found a case that satisfies her admittedly high threshold of what constitutes tax abuse. Chief Judge Cohen imposed negligence penalties in her recent decision in Compaq Computer Corp. . . . which involved a relatively common dividend dumping transaction designed to capture a foreign tax credit. . . . .There are two firsts here: a tax shelter that Chief Judge Cohen doesn't like, and negligence penalties for guys who wear suits and ties to work . . . It's nice to see some of these problems being resolved by courts while Rome burns and the Republican Congress fiddles."

The decision did not stand. It was overturned by the Fifth Circuit Court of Appeals at the end of 2001, the same week that the IRS reported that corporations turning themselves in so as to avoid being hit with negligence penalties acknowledged saving at least $14.7 billion in 2000 through the use of tax shelters, many of them illegal.

Those voluntary admissions were just the tip of an iceberg that was probably four times that large, according to a study by Harvard economist Mihir A. Desai. After reading articles on tax shelters in *The New York Times* that he suspected grossly overstated the tax-shelter problem, Desai examined the differences between what corporations reported to shareholders in profits and what they paid in taxes. The *Times* articles suggested that tax shelters were costing the government much more than the $10 billion a year estimate used by Treasury Secretary Lawrence Summers, a figure drawn from research by Professor Joseph Bankman of Stanford University. After analyzing corporate and government data, however, Desai changed his view. He concluded, along with respected tax expert James M. Poterba of the Massachusetts Institute of Technology, that the tax shelter problem was indeed huge. Their study strongly suggested that corporate tax sheltering cost the government $54 billion in 1998. Such sheltering is the equivalent of shifting about $500 onto the tax burdens of each household in America.

The appellate court decision that overturned Judge Cohen was welcome news to corporations that want to use prearranged stock trades and other strategies with no business purpose except tax avoidance to shift the burden of government onto others.

The decision was written by Judge Edith H. Jones of the Fifth Circuit Court of Appeals, who is best known for ruling that a defendant received a fair trial and could be executed even though his lawyer slept through parts of the murder trial. Her 14-page opinion acknowledged that the prearranged $1.92 difference in prices on the Shell shares eliminated any significant risk that a real change in the stock price would upset the tax deal. She called that smart planning. "The absence of risk that can legitimately be eliminated does not make a transaction a sham," she wrote. Judges Jerry E. Smith and Harold R. DeMoss Jr. joined in the decision.

The lawyer who argued the case for Compaq on appeal, Mark A. Oates of Baker & McKenzie in Chicago, drew the point more narrowly. "The fact that you can diversify most risk away, or hedge it, does not mean that you had a risk-free transaction," he said.

Other lawyers said that the decision opened up new vistas of tax avoidance, especially in the kind of prearranged trades that the Department of Justice had called a sham. David P. Hariton, a corporate tax lawyer at Sullivan & Cromwell with deep experience in tax shelters, said that the decision "suggests that there are at least some financial transactions that are permissible even though they are designed solely to obtain tax benefits. The interesting question is, which ones?"

Professor David A. Weisbach of the University of Chicago has argued that Congress must prevent corporations from using a patina of legitimacy to justify tax shelters or else kiss the corporate income tax goodbye. He was aghast at the ruling and the signal it sent to corporations and their tax advisers, saying "This is disastrous" for the integrity of the tax system.

Lee Sheppard, the tax critic, said the ruling rewarded legal manipulations that breed disrespect for the rule of law. "The doctrine of statutory interpretation says that the taxpayer is not entitled to the benefit of the statute that it seeks to abuse, even if it has a technical argument for the result," she wrote. The tax system, Sheppard wrote, has to include the concept of economic substance—that is, real business transactions—to justify tax deductions or else lawyers will just move symbols around on pieces of paper and say, "Voilà, no tax!"

"There are, of course, some courts that can't handle the economic substance doctrine," Sheppard wrote. "Judge Edith Jones, who wrote the opinion, is just plain wrong in her application of the economic substance doctrine." Compaq, Sheppard wrote, had no purpose except escaping taxes in a deal in which it had no real risk, and should have been soundly rejected.

The decision by Judge Jones is significant for another reason. She is a leading candidate to be appointed to the Supreme Court. She has inveighed against what she sees as the evils afflicting American society, saying that the legal system has become morally corrupt. America needs, she said in 2003, "a recovery of moral principle, the sine qua non of an orderly society." Yet she sees nothing morally suspect about tax games like the one Bob Gordon devised for Compaq, with rigged stock trades, so long as a technical rule can be applied.

Judge Jones is far from alone among high officials in our government who pose as moralists, but turn a blind eye to techniques by which the rich and powerful shove the obligations of government onto others. Tax shelters are to democracy what pollution is to the environment. When companies spew toxic wastes into the air and water, they are saving money by not running cleaner operations and by making everyone else bear that cost through acid rain, fouled water and diseases like cancer. When they use tax dodges like the rigged Shell stock trades, they are saving money by not paying the price of maintaining the civilization that has made their success possible.

Tax shelters also encourage more tax shelters. The chief executives and chief financial officers of companies pay close attention to the portion of their profits paid in taxes compared to competitors. There are even services that rate the relative tax efficiency of companies, giving bad marks to those that pay more than the average, and praising those that come in below the average. While such measures may encourage companies to plan carefully to pay as little tax as is legally allowed, they also encourage companies to look for any way possible to eliminate taxes. And with audits dwindling, and with pressure to do them superficially, only two types of executives—fools and people with character—would pass up the most odious tax shelter.

Congress, in the Compaq case, sided with Sheppard's view that the rigged trades were unconscionable. It passed a rule that killed this particular shelter. Henceforth a stock had to be held for 15 days, not 15 seconds, for the buyer to make use of a foreign tax credit. Bob Gordon, the guy who dreamed up the Compaq deal, said that rule ended that specific technique for a simple reason: risk. Trading a stock back and forth virtually simultaneously with prearranged trade prices incurred such a small risk that the Gallagher insurance brokerage would do it for $1,000 fee. But market price effects would preclude Gordon's prearranged-trade-pair strategy if the buy and sell transactions have to be 15 days apart.

What Congress did not address were deeper problems in tax sheltering. One problem is how tax engineers can separate the legal ownership and the economic ownership of a share of stock or other capital asset to make money off taxes. If courts allow that, as Judge Jones did for Compaq, there may be little or no limit to the magic clever people like Bob Gordon can work for wealthy clients to make taxes vanish.

There are many other ways to make profits and escape taxes, some of them requiring extreme steps like renouncing America. To the people who grow rich from tax shelters, both selling them and buying them, ideas like national interest and even patriotism take a back seat to what is most dear to their hearts: profits. It starts with renting a mailbox in a beautiful resort city named Hamilton.

Profits Trump Patriotism

17

It was the last day of November 2001; the Internet bubble had burst on Wall Street, deflating the rest of the market. Gloom spread among executives who counted on rising share prices to make their stock options valuable. But a ray of hope, an antidote to the bear market, was being offered by the big accounting firm of Ernst & Young. It was pitching a get-rich-again scheme that worked *only* because the stock market was down.

Kate Barton, a partner in Ernst & Young's Boston office, smiled nervously as the Internet camera focused on her for a webcast pitch. Millions of dollars in extra fees were riding on Barton's success at persuading clients to act on the next big thing in corporate tax avoidance. So many Ernst & Young clients already were in the process of adopting the plan that Barton called it "a megatrend."

The plan was to have companies move the address of the corporate headquarters to Bermuda or another tax haven, such as the Cayman Islands or Panama. That way profits could be earned tax-free in the United States. Under a treaty with Barbados, U.S. profits could be converted into tax-deductible expenses that would become profits only when the money was accounted for offshore. The company's real headquarters would stay in the United States. The Bermuda headquarters would be nothing more than a mail drop.

This arrangement was all benefit and no cost to companies that bought the deal. The U.S. military would still be obligated to protect the company's physical assets in the United States. American courts would still enforce the contracts on which commerce depends. Companies making the move would continue to have complete access to the rich marketplace of the United States. And all of the other benefits of doing business in the United States—a well-educated workforce, research facilities, the FBI—would be available gratis, the costs shifted onto everyone else, who would have to make up the lost revenue.

On top of this came an extra benefit unique to the executives. They could make millions upon millions of extra dollars just by abandoning the United States, at least for tax purposes.

In taxspeak, Barton was proposing a *corporate inversion*. The move to a tax haven required turning inside out the usual structure of an American company with multinational operations. The parent company in the United States would first create a subsidiary in an offshore location, usually Bermuda. Then, in the inversion, the subsidiary was transformed into the corporate parent, making the American company a subsidiary of the new, offshore parent.

Under this new structure, what would otherwise be profits in the United States could be siphoned out of the country as tax-deductible payments to the corporate parent. The Bermuda parent, for example, could borrow capital and lend it to the American subsidiary. There were rules that prevented every dollar of what would otherwise be profit from being turned into interest payments. But there were other ways to turn profits in tax deductions. The Bermuda parent could impose a charge for management services. And it could collect royalties from the American corporate child for such things as use of the company's name and its logo.

With anxiety mangling her syntax, Barton explained to her viewers across cyberspace that "there is a lot of companies we are working with right now that are trying to migrate this through their board. It is a very positive technique. There are many companies that have inverted historically, including Tyco, Global Crossing and Ingersoll-Rand, just a whole bunch, and there is a lot of companies that we are working with, companies right now, that they are trying to migrate this through their board."

One of Barton's partners, Joe Knott, cheerily noted that companies that had already moved their headquarters offshore for tax purposes had received "very positive press" because their after-tax earnings improved. Barton added, "You can get financing and other aspects . . . so it's a real competitive advantage."

When the show's host broke in to observe that "It is hard to say that there'll be a downside to living in Bermuda," Knott corrected him: "The good part is this is substantially a paper transaction. You are not going to relocate bodies."

The host also posed an important question to the two partners of the Big Four accounting firm—"All this sounds positive; what is the downside?"

Barton said, "There are a lot of big issues that need to be worked through and that's why it is usually a long process that companies will go through analysis on. Some of the issues right now is patriotism. Is it the right time to be migrating a corporation's headquarters to an off-shore location? That said, we are working through a lot of companies right now that it is—that the improvement on earnings is powerful enough that maybe the patriotism issue needs to take a back seat."

As Barton spoke of profits trumping patriotism, fires were still burning at Ground Zero, where 2,800 Americans had died in the September 11 Al Qaeda attacks that brought down the World Trade Center towers.

Kate Barton's firm, Ernst & Young, was not alone in recommending a Bermuda address. The law firm Baker & McKenzie was the first to discover this trick. The law firm Skadden Arps Slate Meagher & Flom and the investment houses Goldman Sachs and Lehman Brothers also tried to sell the idea to clients. Ingersoll-Rand's top tax officer, Gerald Swimmer, said all of the major investment houses and accounting firms had presented the idea to his company.

Barton's words were intended for a specific audience, the senior executives of large corporations. But 11 weeks after she spoke, her comments appeared on the front page of *The New York Times.* That set in motion a series of events that would focus attention on the issues of who benefits, and who pays, for maintaining America, on how far executives will go to escape taxes. These events also revealed how duplicitous politicians can be when constituents send a clear message that the politicians do not want to hear.

Barton's words also would lead to a break between the Republican rank and file in the House and their leadership in a floor vote, the only such split since Newt Gingrich and his Contract with America had brought the Republicans to control of the House in the 1994 elections.

The tax savings from ostensibly moving a corporation's headquarters offshore are immense. Tyco estimated that it saved an average of $450 million each year after 1997, when it arranged to make Bermuda its tax headquarters while keeping its executive offices in the United States.

Bermuda charged Ingersoll-Rand just $27,653 a year to use it as a tax headquarters of convenience, a move that allowed the company to save $40 million in taxes to the United States the first year, an expected $60 million the second year and even larger sums in the future. Bermuda gave the same deal to Cooper Industries, a Houston industrial equipment maker that is a major Ingersoll-Rand competitor. Five Houston companies that drill wells and service the big oil companies—Global Santa Fe, Nabors Industries, Noble Drilling, TransOcean and Weatherford International—moved their tax address to Bermuda or the Cayman Islands in 2001 and 2002 and will pay little or no American corporate income tax in the future.

These companies were not required to have any offices in the tax haven country they now legally call their home. The laws of Bermuda explicitly prohibit these companies from doing any business there, lest they interfere with the profits earned by locals on their own enterprises or encourage more immigration to already packed little paradises. (Tyco did maintain a small office in Hamilton, Bermuda, because its inversion involved a historically Bermudian company.) David W. Devonshire, the chief financial officer of Ingersoll-Rand, explained that the New Jersey company's only presence in Bermuda is a mail drop. "We just pay a service organization" to accept mail, he said.

Most of the companies that call a Bermuda mailbox home for tax purposes also declare the company to be a legal resident of Barbados. Doing that lets them take advantage of a little known tax treaty with that Caribbean island country.

To qualify as corporate residents of Barbados, the companies merely need to have someone accept mail and answer the telephone there and to have the board of directors jet down once a year and meet on the resort island. Unlike in Bermuda, income is not tax-free in Barbados. It charges the corporations tax on a sliding scale at which the high point is 2.5 percent. The effective tax rate, the real tax big companies pay for making themselves Bermuda or Cayman Islands companies legally resident in Barbados, is 1 percent, as opposed to the U.S. rate of 35 percent.

Congress was not without experience about the use of what is known in taxspeak as *expatriation* to escape taxes. Frederick Krieble, a director of the sealants maker Loctite Corporation, Ernest Olde, owner of the Olde Discount securities brokerage, John Dorrance III, scion of the family that owns Campbell Soup, and Ken Dart, president of the foam cup maker Dart Container, had renounced their citizenship to escape taxes on the fortunes they made or inherited in the United States. Dart, who owed his fortune to American laws that let his firm patent every design detail of every foam cup the company ever made and then pursue competitors who made anything similar in the seemingly generic business of foam drinking cups, made Belize his country of convenience. He tried to move back to Sarasota, Florida, by becoming that country's consul there, but the Clinton administration rebuffed him.

These moves were defended by many of the same members of Congress who found nothing objectionable about the corporate moves to Bermuda. When legislation was proposed to require those renouncing their citizenship to pay up any taxes they owed before leaving, it was denounced by critics as an exit tax not unlike what the Soviet Union did when it stripped Jews leaving for Israel of their money.

Congress did pass a law, however, in 1996, that made people with wealth subject to American taxes for a decade after they renounced their citizenship. The law also limited the time they could spend in the United States to a few months.

What Congress did not do was approve any money to enforce that law. The results were predictable. In 2003 the staff of the congressional Joint Committee on Taxation reported that the IRS "generally has ceased all compliance" efforts to make sure those who renounced America paid the income, gift and estate taxes they owed. These tax dodgers also entered the United States whenever they wanted, staying for as long as they wanted. Not one expatriate covered by the law was turned away by the government at America's borders.

Congress was not the only place where no one paid attention to expatriation. H&R Block, the big income tax preparation firm, is the one company in America that cannot afford any tax scandal, but in

1999 it almost found itself in one. Block wanted to expand into the financial services business, selling stocks and investing the refund checks its clients get. To do this quickly it agreed to buy Olde Discount, which, like Block, had a mostly working-class clientele.

Even though Block sent Mark Ernst, its new president, down to meet with Olde at his home in the Cayman Islands, neither Ernst nor any of the lawyers and investment bankers working on the deal discovered that Olde had renounced his American citizenship. It would not have been hard to find out. The 1996 law requires the names of those who renounce their citizenship be published in the Federal Register, the official report of government actions. Block was saved from embarrassment only because Olde told the company at the last minute on the advice of his lawyer, who presumably worried that not disclosing could potentially expose Olde to some future legal action by Block.

No one knows if Olde paid the $137 million in capital gains taxes he owed when the $850 million deal closed. His spokesman, however, said Olde would pay any taxes required and had no objection to the capital gains taxes. Ernst said he got the strongest written pledge he could that Olde would pay. Yet even if Olde paid every dollar he owed, he still got a huge tax break. Under the 1996 law, if he lived for a decade after renouncing his American citizenship, he would not owe any estate taxes, although the Congressional report made clear that no one was enforcing the tax on people who died sooner.

When news of the corporate moves to Bermuda broke, the companies that were part of Barton's megatrend blamed the tax code for their actions. They whined about an injustice created by Congress taxing the worldwide income of corporations. Congress also taxes individual Americans on their worldwide incomes.

Many of these companies managed to get reporters and columnists and television newscasters to report that their overseas profits were being taxed twice, once by the foreign government and then again in the United States. There was just one small problem with that claim: it was false.

Congress gives companies and individuals a dollar-for-dollar credit for taxes paid to foreign jurisdictions. When Ingersoll-Rand was an American company and it paid a dollar of tax to the Czech government, it lowered by a dollar the taxes owed to the United States. Corporations complain that because of complex rules they cannot use every single dollar of credit each year. That is also true, but misleading. Each year more than 90 percent of available credits are used by corporations. Unused credits can be carried forward to use in future years. Many large companies also have lobbyists making sure that the policy of taxing worldwide income is kept, not abandoned, for reasons that will be explored in the next chapter.

In Congress a few members in both parties denounced the Bermuda moves as unpatriotic or characterized them as using a loophole that should be closed. A larger number asserted that the Bermuda moves showed that the United States should only tax profits earned in the United States or that the tax code was unfair to companies.

One of the most powerful members of Congress, Representative Dick Armey of Texas, went so far as to say that closing the Bermuda loophole would be wrong. "This is akin to punishing a taxpayer for choosing to itemize instead of taking the standard deduction," he said. Of course, itemizing generally does not reduce taxes to zero and it does not require people to adopt the fiction that they have moved to another country. And while itemizing deductions by individuals is explicitly allowed in the tax code, the Bermuda move was not approved in any statute. It worked by abusing the little known tax treaty between the United States and Barbados. When that treaty was being considered in the mideighties, at least six senators and representatives warned that it could be abused to pay zero taxes on corporate profits, but the Reagan administration dismissed this as so unlikely as not to be worth delaying approval of the agreement.

The Washington Times, the newspaper owned by the Reverend Sun Myung Moon, endorsed the Bermuda moves. In addition, it also published a column by Daniel Mitchell of the Heritage Foundation, who also worked with the tax cheats lobby, the Center for Freedom and Prosperity. Mitchell argued that keeping companies from acquiring a Bermuda mail drop to escape taxes would be similar to the Supreme Court's 1857 Dred Scott decision, which held that slaves did not gain their freedom by fleeing to nonslave states. That was too much for Senator Chuck Grassley, the Iowa Republican who led his party on the

Senate Finance Committee. "Requiring a company to pay its fair share of taxes is not enslavement," replied Grassley, who is otherwise no fan of the current tax system, which he calls "immoral."

Grassley was a tax cutter, but was not in the thrall of lobbyists who favored special tax treatment for their corporate clients. He was the only working farmer in the Congress, and his years of raising pigs kept him in touch with the idea that businesses should get to deduct real expenses, not ones manufactured by tricks like paying interest to a Bermuda address of convenience.

As for the Bermuda move, Grassley said that "there is no business reason for doing this, other than to escape U.S. taxation."

The real reason? "This is corporate greed."

Grassley held a Senate Finance Committee hearing to chastise Stanley Works, the Connecticut tool maker whose shareholders were being asked to approve a Bermuda move, and other companies. Holding up a saw with the bright yellow Stanley handle, Grassley denounced it and the others for "evading U.S. taxes and making profits off the taxes of middle-class Americans who are paying their taxes honestly."

The White House, quick to chastise individual Americans for remarks it felt lacked patriotism after the September 11 attacks, said nothing about the Bermuda moves and their effect on tax burdens. The White House had good reason not to criticize the Bermuda moves. When President Bush was a director of Harken Energy, a Texas oil drilling company, in 1989 it created an offshore subsidiary that would have allowed it to escape American taxes. During the five years that Vice President Dick Cheney was chief executive of Halliburton, the Dallas oil services and engineering company, it created at least 20 subsidiaries in the Cayman Islands.

When the administration finally did take a stand, it came from Mark Weinberger, chief of tax policy in the Department of the Treasury. Siding with the corporate tax cheats, he blamed the tax code.

Weinberger, who before and after his government service made his living helping big companies to cut their taxes, said the moves to Bermuda and other tax havens showed that the American tax system was pushing companies to Bermuda. "We may need to rethink some of our international tax rules that were written 30 years ago when our economy was very different and that now may be impeding the ability of U.S. companies to compete internationally," he said. Weinberger said nothing critical of the companies.

There are many tax havens, but Bermuda was the haven of choice for several reasons, none of them related to its proximity to the United States or the American naval base there.

Under Bermuda law, shareholders have few rights to protect their property from executives and directors who divert company funds to themselves or use sweetheart contracts to enrich their friends. Conflicts of interest are tolerated far more under Bermuda law than in America.

Then there were two practical benefits of choosing Bermuda as a tax headquarters. Bermuda does not have law books that neatly organize and arrange the decisions of its court. Lawyers who want to know Bermudian case law must either ask their peers or go through the court decisions in the court clerk's office one case at a time. Even better from the point of view of managements who want to run companies as they see fit without interference from shareholders, there are no Bermuda law firms that specialize in representing plaintiffs against corporations. Bermuda is a country with a one-sided bar.

Of the companies seeking to join what Barton called the mega-trend of acquiring a Bermuda mail drop, only one, Stanley Works, was a household name. Its sturdy saws, planes and hammers with bright yellow handles could be found in most American homes and tool shops. Most of the companies that made the Bermuda move had little contact with consumers because they sold to other businesses. They had much less to worry about in terms of adverse public reaction than a firm like Stanley, whose profits depended not just on the quality of its tools, but on the positive attitude consumers had toward the company. If a company that was a household name could make the move, however, it meant—as Grassley said—Katie, bar the door.

Stanley was based in the Connecticut town of New Britain, a short drive from Hartford down a freeway whose route, locals say, was picked in part to pave over land that would otherwise have become Superfund sites, the soil contaminated with a century of industrial processing wastes.

New Britain used to greet visitors with a sign declaring itself Hardware Capital of the World, a place where huddled masses of immigrants yearning to be free came to the foundries and factories to do the dirty and dangerous work of forging, cutting and bending metal into tools. At many major corporations today, in high positions, the sons and daughters of New Britain can be found, some eager, and some not, to talk about their modest roots.

After World War II, the hardware companies in New Britain closed, one after another. The jobs moved first to states where people could be paid less and then, encouraged by tax rules set by Congress, overseas where workers could be hired for a few dollars a day. When only one big company was left, Stanley Works, the hardware capital sign came down.

Few companies can match the long-term success of Stanley Works. So prized are its tools that it has paid a dividend every 90 days since 1899. In July 1999 the company's new chief executive, John M. Trani, was invited to ring the opening bell at the New York Stock Exchange to mark a century of unbroken quarterly payments to investors. Four hours later Trani laid off 4,500 workers.

Trani had come from General Electric, where he ran its very profitable medical imaging division, and learned his business philosophy from chairman Jack Welch, whose way was to squeeze the pay and numbers of the rank and file and then richly reward executives. "Lean and mean," the critics called it. Trani saw in Stanley Works a fat and kindly company rich with opportunities.

Trani laid off thousands of machinists in Connecticut who made $14 an hour in cash and replaced them with workers in China who he said earned 25 to 30 cents an hour. Even with the cost of shipping metal parts in a UPS cargo jet now and then when production in China and inventory in America were not in perfect alignment, the cost of making products fell as much as 85 percent. Soon after his bell ringing, machinery in New Britain was being packed in grease and loaded onto ships bound for Shanghai so that less costly hands would work the levers.

"There are so many costs to be squeezed out of this company that it will take me years," Trani observed in an interview.

One day in 2001 Trani picked up his *BusinessWeek* magazine and read that Tyco International had cuts its taxes by $500 million by making Bermuda its nominal headquarters. The article explained in part how profits could be stripped out of the United States as tax-deductible expenses. Trani told his chief financial officer to look into it. What he heard back was that there was no single step he could take to cut costs that would have anywhere near the financial gain of acquiring a Bermuda mailbox.

Stanley Works was almost ready to complete its Bermuda move when Barton's talk of patriotism taking a back seat to profits became news. All that was left was for shareholders to vote in favor of the plan. That posed a problem.

While institutions owned most Stanley shares, the men and women who worked at Stanley Works, or who had worked there, owned the margin of shares needed to approve the Bermuda move, which required a two-thirds majority of shares outstanding.

Workers who had loved the previous chief executive, who drove his pickup to union picnics, said Trani would not deign to speak with them. When he showed up at one event with a driver, the workers thought the man was a bodyguard and took offense.

Mayor Lucian J. Pawlak said the movement of jobs overseas, especially good-paying jobs for people with little education, was not Trani's fault, but part of a Faustian bargain that Congress had made in return for cheap imported goods. "We will be a much poorer city and America a much poorer country as companies move out jobs and machinery, pay less in taxes and take away the jobs that hard-working people without much education used to get their kids into college," the mayor said. But he said the workers did not see the distinction between policies set by the government and a company that was simply doing what made sense in light of those policies. Trani, he said, did nothing but fuel the anger of these workers and everyone else in town.

Trani was not unique in separating himself from the people who made his company profitable, in focusing on financial and production reports and not employees. He was part of a new era of corporate managers, many of them Welch acolytes, who never shook hands with anyone who got grease on theirs, even if they had wiped them clean when their one big chance came to meet the boss. They neither mingled with the people who made their companies' products nor did they appear to think much about their lives. The mayor said his city was left with the economic pollution of jobs going overseas, with people who had put their life into Stanley and had nothing left. "All

those guys walking around with missing fingers and hunchbacks made
Stanley, but Trani doesn't want to hear that."

Hardly anybody in New Britain wanted to do anything to help
John Trani, especially after what he had done at the company's annual
meeting in 2001, the first held outside New Britain.

Trani held the meeting in Columbus, Ohio. Union members and
retirees hired buses and rode for 12 hours just to attend so they could
complain about jobs going overseas. What transpired was an important
lesson in how some chief executives regard the people who own the
companies they run.

"Where is your American pride?" Nancy Mischaud asked.

"I look at it every day in the mirror. I'm proud to be an American.
We just have a different view of the world."

Trani asked shareholders to trust him. "We're on a journey to becoming one of the world's best brands. It's a long journey, not a short
trip," he said as he identified some of the 90 new products the company was making, most of them overseas. "The minute we deliver substantial growth in sales . . . we will see the stock price bump almost
vertically for a little while. There's no doubt in my mind that we are on
the right track."

Workers and retirees walked out grumbling about how they had to
endure the lousy bus ride and that, after all that, Trani had cut them
off, not even giving them respect as company owners. They said all he
cared about was making money for himself. The residue of resentment
Trani created at the Columbus meeting posed a problem for him a year
later, when he was lobbying investment fund managers and others to
vote approval for the Bermuda plan. The problem was that Trani could
not win the vote without a big majority of shares held in the company
401(k) plan.

In a letter to employees and retirees, the company said that unvoted
shares in the 401(k) plan would count as votes against the Bermuda
plan. Many workers said that was just what they wanted so they tossed
their proxy cards in the trash.

Then on the Saturday just five days before the vote, a second, un-
dated letter began showing up in mailboxes. This letter stated that any
unvoted shares would be voted by the 401(k) plan's trustee "in accor-

dance with the trust agreement and applicable law." Many union members figured it was just more lawyer talk and ignored the letter. Even Donald D'Amato, president of the machinists union local, dismissed the letter as insignificant. At least at first.

On the day before the election, the union leaders suspected that something was up. A member said he had gotten a letter in the mail from the company that said something about the vote, though he didn't understand what it meant about how his shares in the 401(k) plan would be voted if he did not vote them himself. At the union office the officers and a secretary dug through their files for a copy of the 401(k) plan to see just what the plan said about voting rights. No one could remember ever seeing the plan document itself and D'Amato was not at all sure that, even if they did, he would be able to understand the legalese. When the scouring of files was done, it was clear that the union did not have the document. D'Amato slouched back in a stiff metal frame chair, looking overwhelmed, outwitted by men who he volunteered were smarter and better educated than he.

By the next morning, when time for the annual meeting came, the unionists were certain that whatever the document said, the company was somehow going to vote their shares for the Bermuda move. D'Amato figured many workers would take the usual two hours off to attend the annual meeting and could vote their 401(k) shares right then against the Bermuda move. But that morning, when some of the men started to shut down their machines, the foremen came around and told them that if they left, they were gone for the rest of the day—and with no pay. A few men glowered at the foremen and walked. Most, though, expecting that they would be laid off soon and needing to earn every dollar they could until then, quietly stayed at their stamping machines and lathes.

At the meeting in the company's auditorium, in a gracefully designed new building set in a picturesque hollow green with the leaves of manicured trees, portable metal detectors had been erected at the doors. Armed police were everywhere. For the first time in the history of the 159-year-old company, reporters were barred from its annual meeting. Executives escorted some men and women, the ones dressed in suits, around the security devices and into the auditorium. Everyone in the cheap clothes of the working class was made to empty their pockets and purses and, if the metal detectors went off when they passed through, they were pulled aside and fully scanned with wands.

When the meeting started, those still in line waiting to get through security complained, but to no avail. Trani told of the glories of the company and how its future would be even better. When he took a few questions, one of those who got to speak was D'Amato, but he lacked Trani's way with words and his point was lost. To a shareholder who complained that this was the only chance for the owners to question their hired managers, Trani said an hour-long meeting, at which he spoke for more than 30 minutes, was all the time shareholders needed.

Then Trani announced that shareholders had approved the Bermuda move with 85 percent in favor. "Our shareholders have strongly affirmed the benefits of reincorporation. The global playing field has been leveled and our company is now better able to compete," Trani announced. He said the Bermuda move would be finished by 4 P.M. the next day.

The Bermuda vote, it turned out, had not passed with 85 percent; that was just the margin of the shares that were voted. All of the 401(k) shares were voted, most of them by the trustee. Even so, the Bermuda plan, which needed a two-thirds majority, carried by the thinnest of margins, 67.2 percent of all shares.

D'Amato knew in his heart how Trani had gotten the winning votes. He walked outside where some reporters stood and said loudly, "They stole the election."

Some of the reporters had no idea who the heavyset middle-aged man in the warm-up jacket was or what he was talking about. They did not care to find out, either. They walked over to listen to Denise L. Nappier, Connecticut's state treasurer, who said she was appalled at Trani's arrogance in cutting shareholders off. "It was quite rude. I don't think that's the way to talk to the owners of the company."

There were about 7 million shares in the 401(k) plan and it turned out that the trustee cast unvoted shares in proportion to how all other votes were cast. That meant that had the unionists all voted their shares, then the Bermuda proposal would have lost by millions of shares.

At the White House, Ari Fleischer was asked if the president had any reaction. "Well, I can't comment on any—on one individual corporate action. But the president does feel very strongly that one of the reasons that we need to have trade laws enacted is so Americans will have incentives to create jobs here at home and to create trade opportunities for Americans here at home."

"That is a tax haven there, Ari," a reporter said in followup.

"Sonya," Fleischer said, moving on to another question.

Trani, however, was in a talkative mood, full of smiles and brimming with confidence. "Tomorrow. It will take effect tomorrow," the son of a Brooklyn longshoreman said with glee.

What about the charge that he had rigged the election, that he had tricked the unionists with the April 4 letter? He said the company had corrected that "little mistake" as soon as it was discovered. And what about the second letter's oblique phrasing? Did Trani think that machinists with at best a high school education understood the meaning of the words "in accordance with the trust agreement and applicable law"?

"They can read," Trani said, adding that no one but a few unhappy union members cared because there was nothing wrong with the election. Trani was wrong about that.

Among those who cared about the integrity of the election were Richard Blumenthal, the Connecticut attorney general, and Treasurer Nappier. Blumenthal's staff spent the afternoon drafting a lawsuit.

The next day Blumenthal's litigators filed a lawsuit accusing the company of using "misleading and deceptive information" to win the Bermuda vote. Then they invited Trani over to the New Britain courthouse for a private chat. Trani sent lieutenants, who listened for more than an hour as Blumenthal's prosecutors laid out their theory of how the election was rigged, of what they said had to have been a deliberate plan to trick the unionists. It was a legal strategy pregnant with implications because, were the Securities and Exchange Commission ever to conclude that the election had been rigged, then it could permanently bar anyone involved from being an executive of a company with publicly traded stock or debt. The prosecutors said that every aspect of how those letters to the 401(k) plan members were drafted would be examined. Every e-mail and note would be read, every telephone log reviewed and every executive and secretary questioned under oath.

Trani's lieutenants got the message. They phoned the boss with the bad news, telling him that, if he did not disavow the vote, it was clear that a judge would issue an order stopping the Bermuda move anyway.

Soon Blumenthal was on the steps of the modern New Britain courthouse. Behind him passed some young men with no jobs or prospects who had found themselves in trouble with the law and were coming to the courthouse to get their due process. Blumenthal announced that Stanley Works would not be going to Bermuda that day.

"What we've done today is used the level of the law to stop an illegal act by Stanley Works," Blumenthal said, holding high a mahogany bubble level that a different chief executive had given him 10 years earlier for helping the company defeat a hostile takeover by the plastic container maker Newell Rubbermaid. "Stanley broke corporate governance laws that assure fairness, and there is evidence that Stanley Works broke federal securities laws. Stanley Works made a hammer with two heads. One was slipshod, and the other was dishonest. This victory is a major win for shareholder rights, but the debacle has decimated the company's credibility."

And what if the company sought a new vote? "We will critically scrutinize it to stop management's misleading statements about the move overseas," Blumenthal said. "Even before any revote, Congress should close the federal tax loophole that is motivating Stanley Works to abandon America and Connecticut."

Trani stayed in his office. The company issued a statement saying all was well with the vote but that "even the appearance of impropriety is unacceptable," and so there would be a second vote.

A month later, in June, a hearing on the Bermuda moves was held by a subcommittee of the House Ways and Means Committee at which the members treated Stanley Works as if it were toxic. The company, to the relief of the lawmakers, decided not to show up. Representative Kevin Brady, a Texas Republican who never met a tax he felt was reasonable, said that "no one on this panel is defending" the Bermuda moves.

Representative Scott McInnis of Colorado, a former cop who has also made a name for himself as a tax cutter, said he was appalled that corporations would even consider a move to Bermuda while a war against terrorism was being waged. "Focus for a moment on the young men and women who are fighting the war on terrorism" in Afghanistan, he said. "I would like to think that if these soldiers can shoulder their burden, we can expect our companies to shoulder their own fair share."

McInnis said that Trani had come to his Capitol Hill office to seek support for his company's move to Bermuda. McInnis handed Trani a small card imprinted with the names of American soldiers killed in the war in Afghanistan. "I told him to keep it in his wallet and to take it out and look at those names each time he talks about" using the Bermuda loophole to stop paying taxes.

When Trani was asked what he had done with the card, his spokesman issued a curious statement for a company that had in just a few years thrown thousands of Americans out of work and moved the machinery they used to China: "We believe keeping jobs in the U.S. is patriotic."

Some Republicans spoke more mildly than McInnis about the Bermuda move. But when Representative Mark Foley of Florida, a rising Republican star, referred to "apparently unpatriotic" corporations, he drew a retort from Representative Richard E. Neal, a Massachusetts Democrat and a leading enemy of corporate tax shelters and loopholes. "Mark, do you really think 'apparently' unpatriotic? I think they are unpatriotic."

Stanley Works pressed ahead with the revote and Blumenthal went back to court in July, saying that Stanley Works was misleading shareholders again. This time he tried to up the stakes by asking the SEC to investigate the company because its statement on the vote, called a prospectus, contained "conflicting and confusing statements" on how the rights of shareholders would be affected by a Bermuda move.

Stanley Works, in its prospectus for the revote, said that "despite differences, the corporate legal system, based on English law, is such that your rights as a Stanley Bermuda shareholder will be, in our view, substantially unchanged from your rights as a shareholder in Stanley Connecticut." Yet on another page, deep in the document, it said that "because of differences in Bermuda law and Connecticut law and differences in the governing documents of Stanley Bermuda and Stanley Connecticut, your rights as shareholders may be adversely changed if the reorganization is completed."

Accenture, the big global consulting firm, had earlier been much more blunt in telling shareholders the meaning of its formation under Bermuda law. "There is some doubt as to whether" Bermuda courts "would recognize or enforce judgments of U.S. courts against us or our officers or directors . . . or would hear actions against us."

Rigging an election was no small matter to Blumenthal. "The SEC may be focusing on the headline issues of corporate malfeasance and mismanagement" at WorldCom, Tyco International, Enron, Martha Stewart Living Omnimedia, ImClone Systems, Global Crossing and other companies just when it needed to focus on Stanley Works. "The real nuts and bolts of corporate accountability often depend on ordinary shareholders to enforce accountability on management," he said.

The SEC did nothing. It took the position that only a proposed prospectus on the vote had been filed.

Trani's determination to get a Bermuda mailbox would certainly be good for company shareholders. As it turns out, it would also be good for him.

While Americans like Ken Dart who renounced their citizenship did not have to pay what the critics called an exit tax, companies were required to settle their tax obligations on the way out. There were two ways to do this. One would be to tally up the embedded capital gains on the company's books and have the company pay the bill, which no one did. The other was to foist the obligation onto shareholders, who would owe capital gains taxes on the difference between the price they paid for their shares and their value on the day of the Bermuda move. As Kate Barton explained in her webcast, with the stock market down, it was a good time to make the move because shareholders would owe less.

Stanley Works estimated that shareholders overall would owe just $30 million in capital gains taxes because shares held in 401(k) plans, pension plans and charitable endowments were exempt from this rule and many shareholders in the tax system had owned their shares only a short time. Of course, the people of New Britain who had been buying shares for decades would be the hardest hit by the tax.

One person who would not be hit was Trani.

On the day he had planned to make the Bermuda move, Trani was the biggest individual shareowner, yet he would have owed less than

$50,000 in taxes, which was a smaller sum than his weekly salary and bonus. Trani owned just 16,688 shares outright and therefore subject to tax and he said that to avoid paying any taxes he planned to give those shares to charity, a move that would reduce his federal income taxes by about $300,000.

Most of Trani's shares were either in his retirement accounts or in the form of stock options that he had not yet exercised. None of these shares would be taxable upon the acquisition of a Bermuda address.

Trani would, however, see his fortune rise on the day of the Bermuda move or soon after because he estimated that the move alone would increase the price of Stanley Works shares by 11.5 percent. That would make the shares in his retirement plan and his potential profits on his stock options jump by $17.5 million. Since he had said that the company would save $30 million the first year in taxes by the Bermuda move, it meant that Trani personally stood to gain 58 cents for every dollar of benefit to the company.

Over time Trani stood to make even more money for himself than the American government would lose in corporate income taxes. If after a Bermuda move the company's stock price doubled in eight years, then all shareholders would experience an increase in their wealth of $3.3 billion. The government stood to lose at least $240 million of corporate income taxes during that time.

Such an increase in the price of Stanley shares would mean a bigger salary and bonus for Trani. In addition, it would make it more likely that he would receive all the additional options he was eligible for under the company's stock option plan. If that happened, then he could pocket at least $385 million from exercising those options, or far more than the taxes the company would save. When these figures were published in *The New York Times* from its analysis of company disclosure statements, Trani issued a brief statement saying they were not correct, but he declined to provide more precise figures.

Trani was not alone in positioning himself for huge gains through a Bermuda move, shifting the immediate tax bill to shareholders and then cutting off revenue to the American government. Eugene M. Isenberg of Nabors Industries, H. John Riley Jr. of Cooper Industries, Herbert L. Henkel of Ingersoll-Rand, and Bernard J. Duroc-Danner of Weatherford International are among the chief executives who stood to also make huge gains because their companies had already made the Bermuda move.

At Nabors Industries of Houston, the world's largest operator of land-based oil drilling rigs, Isenberg stood to gain tens of millions of dollars each year because of the Bermuda-via-Barbados move. His stock options alone stood to gain $100 million in value, compensation lawyer Brian Foley calculated after reviewing the company's disclosure reports to shareholders.

Isenberg also stood to gain because of an unusual clause that gives him 6 percent of the company's cash flow, a measure of profits before certain expenses are deducted. With less money going to taxes, Nabors would have more money to pour back into the business, increasing its cash flow. Another unusual clause, Foley said, guaranteed Isenberg a payment of about $180 million if he decided to retire, became disabled or died.

Isenberg was already paid extraordinarily well. Nabors in 2000 had total revenues of $1.3 billion. Isenberg made $127 million, nearly 10 percent of that, mostly through exercising stock options. His compensation almost equaled the company's profits, which were $137 million, a simply astonishing compensation feat.

Meanwhile, the Bermuda issue was stirring in Congress. A spending bill came to the House floor only after Republican leaders stripped out the provision barring government contracts to companies that had a Bermuda tax address. The Democrats saw opportunity and pounced. For five hours, as viewers watched on C-SPAN, the Democrats lambasted the Republicans as "allies of corporate traitors."

Representative Lloyd Doggett, a Texas Democrat who for years has introduced bills to shut down corporate tax shelters, led the attack. "The Republicans' mantra to their corporate buddies is 'Friends don't let friends pay taxes,'" Doggett said.

Then Doggett, a former Texas Supreme Court justice, shifted gears, saying that the Democrats had become the guardians of business interests. "We need to take a pro-business stance and level the playing field so thousands of businesses that stay here and pay their fair share are not at a disadvantage" to those that avoid taxes through a Bermuda address, he said.

Doggett said that as he spoke, lobbyists for Accenture were in the Capitol working to make sure it could continue to get government contracts like the one it had to run the IRS Web site. Companies that renounce America for Bermuda can win such competitively bid contracts, Doggett said, because taxpaying companies have to bid higher to make a profit.

The Republicans insisted that they were as outraged as the Democrats about the Bermuda trick, but that the issue properly belonged before the Ways and Means Committee. "Allowing committees of jurisdiction their proper jurisdiction is the right thing to do," said David Dreier, a Californian.

After that debate President Bush finally spoke up. "I think we ought to look at people who are trying to avoid U.S. taxes as a problem," the president said. "I think American companies ought to pay taxes and be good citizens."

That day news broke that when President Bush was a Harken Energy director, it set up a Cayman Islands subsidiary to escape taxes. Ari Fleischer, the White House spokesman, said no taxes were avoided, which was true only because no oil was found and so no profits were earned.

A few weeks later another bill came up in the House, about whether companies with a Bermuda mailbox could hold contracts with the new Department of Security, the agency entrusted with keeping America safe from terrorists. The House Republican leadership favored giving Bermuda companies such contracts. The rank and file bolted. For the first time since the Republicans became the majority in 1995, the leadership lost control as 110 Republicans split with the leadership and voted to bar such contracts.

That was enough for Trani, who a few days later announced that Stanley Works would stop seeking shareholder approval to acquire a Bermuda address.

Just before the Congressional elections in the fall of 2002, eight months after the Bermuda story broke, the chief economist for the United States Chamber of Commerce, Martin Regalia, told a Senate hearing that Congress should not act in any way against companies that use the Bermuda tactic. The law requires companies to not waste corporate resources and companies may have a legal obligation to acquire a Bermuda mailbox if it means they can stop paying taxes. Companies that do not get a Bermuda mailbox could be sued, he said, although no such suits have been filed.

On the campaign trail the candidates heard a very different reaction from the relatively few voters they encountered. Among the few who actually attended campaign events, many raised the Bermuda issue, angry that corporations were shirking their obligations. But a funny thing happened after the elections, in which the Republicans won control of both the House and Senate. Congress voted to bar contracts to Bermuda mailbox companies—with a loophole that allowed their American subsidiaries to get contracts.

That was not all that the government did to favor Bermuda companies over those that remained loyal taxpayers. The Department of the Interior and other agencies had specifications for their office door—the kind that open automatically—that required the use of systems sold by Ingersoll-Rand, a Bermuda company. Stanley Works, which also made automatic doors and which was still an American company, was shut out of this government business.

The megatrend Kate Barton extolled has stopped, at least for now. But the underlying effort to enjoy the benefits of selling in America without sharing in the costs continues. A company does not need to make a high-profile move of its legal headquarters to escape American taxes. Sometimes just mailing a letter overseas can make American taxes vanish.

Letters to Switzerland

18

When the IRS sent a new team in to audit the big oil company Unocal in 1997, one of its members was Ron McGinley, a lanky grandfather who goes to church almost every day. McGinley thinks often about moral issues. His deep sense of right and wrong saved him from becoming a felon in the eighties, when he was an executive at Northrup. He refused to sign papers authorizing a payment that, after the Koreagate scandal broke, was revealed as a bribe. Later, when McGinley was forced out, the best job he could find was at the IRS as an economist working on corporate audits.

As the IRS team planned its Unocal audit strategy, it agreed to closely examine the company's Science and Technology Division in Brea, California, home to one of the world's largest seismic databases for oil drillers. The company had spent many hundreds of millions of dollars on this Oracle database, filling it with knowledge that accurately pinpoints carbon pools far below the surface of the earth. Unocal used the database for its own drilling in places like Indonesia and it sold access to its database to others.

What the audit team wanted to know was whether Unocal was charging its offshore subsidiaries fees that covered the full costs of the database or was charging less than its real value, which in turn would lower Unocal's profits in the United States.

Normally none of this would ever be known outside of Unocal management and the IRS. Congress makes most taxpayer information confidential, though it was not always this way. The IRS treats corporate audits with such secrecy that McGinley's wife never knew which company he was auditing. If an auditor's car breaks down, he cannot have his spouse or a friend drop him at the company he is auditing; that is a firing offense. Callers reach auditors by dialing their IRS number and leaving a message to be returned later. This blanket of secrecy was broken, inadvertently, by the government in trying to keep McGinley from proving that the Unocal audit was fixed.

Even before they had desks at a Unocal office, the IRS audit team began requesting documents to compare with the company's corporate tax return. The documents flowed slowly, but steadily, except for those about the oil drilling database. Unocal did not want to provide documents or answer questions.

The previous audit team gave the database a pass, McGinley's team was told by Unocal, so it had no business inquiring about it. Unocal's delaying tactics escalated steadily. McGinley said that he found his desk at Unocal rifled, his work papers having been gone through during the night by someone, a not all that rare experience for IRS auditors, who often are not given locks for the borrowed desks they use. Undaunted, McGinley and the others pressed ahead with their requests, only to encounter steadily growing resistance that escalated into stiff words one day between McGinley and the Unocal representative who kept telling him to forget about the database.

Soon the audit team members were getting calls from their superiors, saying that their IRS bosses wanted them to back off. With the Senate Finance investigation, it was not a time to make trouble with a "customer" who was being audited, McGinley was told. But he would not back down despite repeated directives to look the other way.

We know this because later McGinley filed a lawsuit, not against Unocal but against the IRS. He had taken such offense at being told to ignore an issue that could add hundreds of millions of dollars in taxes from Unocal that he complained to the equivalent of the IRS internal affairs squad.

McGinley's complaint should have been investigated by the new treasury inspector general for tax administration, created under Senator Roth's aegis following the Senate Finance hearings. Instead, the investigators handed the case back to the very supervisors whom McGinley had complained about. They would not tell McGinley what they had done in their own investigation, but it was obvious they had done nothing. So McGinley filed suit in federal court to get access to the investigative file and to make himself into a whistle-blower. A document that the government put into the public record identified Unocal.

What the audit team had come across was just one example of one of the biggest and most important ways that big corporations are shedding their tax burden and shifting it onto you. It is a tax dodge available only to companies with international operations, so it hurts purely domestic competitors as well as individuals.

The technique is simple enough in principal: take expenses in the United States and take profits in countries that impose little or no tax.

Congress requires that companies charge their subsidiaries reasonable prices, those within the range that independent parties would negotiate at arm's length. Without this standard, sweetheart deals could be made to load up costs in the United States to reduce taxes and earn profits in places like Indonesia, which has a long history of giving stealth tax breaks to American oil companies. Over a period of even a few years, the stakes were huge, perhaps several hundred million dollars of federal income taxes from just one company.

ChevronTexaco, the world's fourth-largest oil company, evaded $3.25 billion in federal and state taxes from 1970 to 2000 through a complex petroleum pricing scheme involving a project in Indonesia, two accounting professors who studied the company say. Their study grew out of accusations of tax evasion that IRS auditors first raised against Chevron in the early nineties. The company paid $675 million to settle the dispute, far less than the $1 billion it had set aside as a reserve in case it lost the case, which covered the years 1979 through 1987.

As with Unocal, the case involved in good part oil drilling in Indonesia. And like Unocal, Chevron, as it was then known, refused to provide requested documents. In that case the IRS took the company to court, briefly, until the auditors were shut down on orders from the IRS national office. It was this interference from above, and the frequency with which IRS audit managers were retiring from the agency and then showing up on the payrolls of the big oil companies, that made McGinley so determined to press his case. His concerns were

heightened when an IRS manager announced at a national meeting of
IRS petroleum industry auditors that he would retire just as soon as he
decided between competing offers of work from two oil companies,
one of which he was helping at that very moment to audit. No one
objected and no action was taken against the official.

In the Chevron case, a host of documents came into the public
record because of the litigation the IRS briefly brought. James E.
Wheeler, professor emeritus of accounting at the University of Michigan Business School, and Jeffrey Gramlich, a professor at the University of Hawaii, spent years going through the arcane documents before
publishing them and commentary showing that "the evidence is there
that fraud exists." ChevronTexaco said the research paper was nothing
more than a rehash of IRS issues it had settled long ago and were without merit.

Chevron and Texaco, before they merged in October 2001, each
owned 50 percent of a joint venture called Caltex, which pulled crude
oil from the ground in a project with the Indonesian state oil company,
Pertamina. The professors said that Chevron reduced its tax liabilities
in the United States by buying oil from Caltex at inflated prices. One
internal Chevron document set the price it paid Pertamina for oil at
$4.55 a barrel higher than the prevailing market price. Spending more
for the Caltex oil permitted Chevron to overstate deductions for its
costs on its U.S. income tax returns, the authors said. Indonesia appeared to place a 56 percent income tax on this oil, charging far higher
than the United States corporate tax rate. Because the United States
gives companies a dollar-for-dollar credit for taxes paid to foreign governments, every dollar paid to the Indonesian government meant less
money to the United States government.

At first glance that would not seem to benefit Chevron because
what it saved in American taxes it paid in Indonesian taxes. As Professor Wheeler put it, "What sense does it make to move income out of
the U.S. to Indonesia?"

Plenty. The reason was that the Indonesian government compen-
sated Caltex for the overpriced oil and the extra taxes by giving it free
oil. Because Caltex had to pay taxes on that oil, however, the Indonesian government gave it even more oil to cover the taxes. It was the
same technique corporations use when they "gross up" the salary of an

executive to pay his taxes on a fringe benefit. The company has to pay not just the taxes, but the taxes on the taxes. If Indonesia wanted to give Caltex an additional $100 worth of oil after taxes, it had to give it $227 in oil. That amount, taxed at 56 percent, left Caltex with $100. That $100 was never taxed in the United States, the professor said. But that was not the best part of the deal.

Chevron and Texaco got a United States tax credit of $127—the amount of the Indonesian tax—on every $227 of oil that the Indonesian government funneled to their Caltex joint venture. That tax credit reduced the companies' U.S. taxes on a dollar-for-dollar basis.

Professor Gramlich said that with this kind of a deal a company is eager to pay all the taxes it can. "They like paying taxes in Indonesia, because they get their tax money back twice. They pay taxes in Indonesia and get it back in oil, and they get a foreign tax credit from the U.S. government."

A much bigger tax trick involves putting intellectual property—a patent, a drug formula, the ownership of a corporate logo—in an envelope and mailing it to a tax haven. The American drug industry tends to favor Switzerland for this purpose because not only is it politically stable, but it has a side deal with Luxembourg that can result in a tax of less than 10 percent on profits.

The Pritzker family did the same thing with the brand name for its hotel chain, Hyatt. It is perfectly legal to move intellectual property offshore, but the price has to be reasonable. The Pritzkers valued the Hyatt name at just $10,000 per hotel, a figure so low that it does not take a tax expert to know the price was not reasonable.

Putting intellectual property in an envelope and mailing it overseas is "international tax planning 101," according to Richard E. Anderson, an international tax partner at the law firm Arnold & Porter in New York and the editor of a basic reference for international tax lawyers. "You can't pick up a factory and move it to the Cayman Islands," Mr. Anderson said, "so most of the assets that are going to be relocated as part of a global repositioning are intellectual property. In today's economy that is where most of the profit is. When you buy a pair of sneakers for $250, it's the swoosh symbol, not the rubber" you pay for.

From 1983 to 1999 the value of American corporations' assets in Bermuda, the Cayman Islands and 11 other tax havens grew 44 percent more than their assets in Germany, England and other countries with tax rates similar to U.S. rates, Department of Commerce data show. Martin A. Sullivan, a former Department of the Treasury economist, found in a study for the journal *Tax Notes* that the assets moved off-shore were especially lucrative and profits taken in these tax havens grew far faster than anywhere else.

Tax-haven profits rose 735 percent, to $92 billion, during those years, while profits in countries that are not tax havens grew only 130 percent, to $114.2 billion.

Bermuda and the other tax havens accounted for 45 percent of the total offshore profits in 1999, but only a fourth of those assets. A look at the tax rates actually paid shows the reason companies want to move assets to tax havens. The official federal tax rate on corporate profits is 35 percent, while in the tax havens profits were taxed at rates from a fraction of 1 percent to 12.5 percent of profits, the Department of Commerce data show.

In all, the 10,000 biggest American companies reported $758 bil-lion in profits worldwide in 1999 and paid taxes to the United States of $154 billion, or 20 percent, which was well below the statutory rate.

A big part of the $113 billion difference between the statutory tax rate and what the big corporations actually paid is due to tax shelter-ing, including moving intellectual property offshore. What these com-panies are doing is systematically reducing the tax base in the United States, and that costs you money. Over time erosion of the tax base has to mean either sharply higher taxes on you or less government services or more government debt, which means both a burden passed on to future generations and a growing share of current taxes being used to pay interest on money the government spent long ago.

The Bermuda moves, which were both high profile and, to many Americans, offensive, involved far less money. The official estimate by Congress was $6 billion per year, a figure that assumed not many com-panies would renounce America as Stanley Works tried to do and Ingersoll-Rand and some others did. But the subtle moving of assets offshore goes on every day.

The accounting profession has become so creative at these tricks that it has even found a way to fabricate profits, which conveys two ad-vantages. Higher reported profits mean a rising stock price. And if the profits can be engineered in a way that no taxes are due, then a company gets to report both fake profits and low taxes. That is exactly what Enron did and it explains how in five of its last six years before bankruptcy it reported huge profits and paid no federal corporate income taxes.

Enron created 881 subsidiaries abroad, almost all of them in tax havens, including 692 in the Cayman Islands, 119 in the Turks and Caicos, 43 in Mauritius, 8 in Bermuda and 19 others.

After Roth had left office, the Senate Finance Committee ordered a detailed investigation of the collapse of Enron. What the Joint Committee on Taxation staff found surprised even its most veteran members.

Lindy L. Paull, chief of the joint committee staff, told the Finance Committee in 2003 that Enron used tax shelters that allowed it to report $2 billion of profits almost immediately, even as the company was saving $2 billion of federal income taxes over a period of years. The tax savings and the manufactured profits "were mostly from internal machinations where we couldn't find any benefit to the company," Ms. Paull said.

Most of the shelters were put together in the nineties by Wall Street firms, led by Bankers Trust, which later became part of Deutsche Bank. It was paid more than $40 million by Enron for tax shelters. One shelter used a "triad" of Cayman Islands entities to hide money from the IRS, an example of what Ms. Paull said were transactions so complex that the IRS lacked the capacity to deal with them.

She also criticized an 85-page opinion letter by William S. McKee and James D. Bridgeman of McKee, Nelson, Ernst & Young, a tax boutique set up by the Ernst & Young accounting firm. Enron paid more than $1 million for the letter. Ms. Paull said it skirted crucial issues that made the deals improper. One part of the opinion, the report said, "may not be patently false, but it understates" a crucial issue. The shelter, called Project Cochise, involved the transfer of real estate interests subject to accounting and tax rules that do not match. This generated both income and deductions, which were inflated by taking some of them twice, not unlike the deal Jerry Curnutt uncovered in which he calculated that a $10 investment would eventually cost the government a third of a billion in lost taxes.

McKee, the lawyer who wrote the million-dollar letter, said later that "the opinion is fine," and the shelter so carefully conformed to the tax laws that he did not even regard it as aggressive tax avoidance.

Senator John B. Breaux, Democrat of Louisiana, said that "instead of drilling for oil and gas, Enron was drilling the tax code, looking for ways to find more and more tax shelters." Senator Grassley said that "what hit me the most was the moral fiber of the people involved," who he said displayed "unbridled greed and blatant disregard for the law of fairness."

There is a structural reason that abusive tax shelters, the muscling of IRS auditors like McGinley and the widespread use of corporate tax devices that hurt all Americans in the long run have grown so in recent years. This factor has received virtually no mention in the news media, although it is the subject of an extensive and lively debate in law reviews and professional journals. It is the emergence of legal and accounting firms whose names end with the letters LLP, which stands for Limited Liability Partnership.

One law review article described LLPs as "a lamb with mandibles of death."

The problem is that the LLP structure destroys the self-policing mechanism that helps to keep legal and accounting firms from using their enormous power to the detriment of others, especially the third parties like investors who rely on the integrity of audited financial statements to make decisions on buying and selling stocks.

Traditionally, legal and accounting firms operated as professional partnerships. Under this arrangement, each partner was individually liable for misconduct by any other partner. This created a powerful incentive for legal and accounting firms to monitor each partner, to make sure that they not only were honest, but acted reasonably, lest every partner be exposed to lawsuits and damages. All partners had to worry, and watch, to make sure that one bad apple did not destroy everyone else in the firm by such acts as helping a client company cook the books.

Then along came the savings and loan crisis in the early 1980s, when a number of financial institutions turned out to be giant frauds or piggy banks for their executives. Some of the executives went to jail and the taxpayers were stuck with a bailout to protect savers that cost many billions of dollars. Partners at some of the legal and accounting firms paid by these failed thrifts, the evidence showed, shirked their

duties to find obvious fraud. A few partners were even actively involved in the looting. Under partnership law, these failings of professional duty made the rest of the partners in their firm liable. Some
firms went out of business and some partners who had done nothing
wrong—except fail to monitor their partners—mortgaged their homes
to pay their share of the damages.

The problem for the legal and accounting firms was that they had
no way to measure their potential exposure to wrongdoing. One partner who helped executives loot one big bank could wipe out his firm
and his partners' personal fortunes.

Had the market been left alone, it would have solved this problem
by pricing legal and accounting services, and malpractice insurance, in
ways that made sure that legal and accounting firms adequately moni-
tored their partners to stop errant behavior. But the invisible hand of
the market was stayed by political interference. The legal and accounting professions, themselves rich with members of the political donor
class, went to government for special protection.

First, in 1988, they got the IRS to rule that a professional firm
could be organized as an LLP (limited liability partnership). Then in
1991 the legislature in Texas, home to many of the biggest of the savings and loan and bank collapses, passed the first limited liability law.
Soon every other state and the District of Columbia followed and
most professional firms switched to the limited liability structure.

In doing so, they eliminated the incentive for the partnership to
spend much money or effort monitoring the conduct of each partner
because the worst that can happen is that the partnership will be put
out of business. The individual partner was no longer at risk of his
own net worth if one of his partners helped crooks or was himself a
crook. The old rule that required partners to stick their noses into each
other's business was replaced by a new one. It said that so long as you
do not stick your nose in you are not personally liable for any misconduct of your partners.

This new limited liability structure creates what economists call a
moral hazard—rules that encourage and even reward misconduct at
the expense of others. Clearly, when legal and accounting firms sell tax
shelters that do not pass the smell test, yet tell unsophisticated buyers
that the shelters are not just sturdy, but safe, we see evidence not just of

a moral hazard, but of real harm. Would the accounting firms and the law firms be so eager to sell abusive tax shelters if each partner had to put her own assets at risk in each of these deals? The answer is obvious.

Some critics have said that the traditional partnership structure is economically inefficient because it encourages excessive monitoring of conduct and these costs lower productivity. That argument may be valid when the limited liability concept is applied to creating companies that sell products and most services. But to apply it to the legal and accounting professions is to extend a good policy into an area where it can only encourage bad behavior by breaking down the duty of loyalty, also known as fiduciary duty, that is essential to the integrity of the economic and tax systems. Delaware has gone so far that it allows limited liability partnerships to hire out fiduciary—duty of loyalty—functions.

Government regulation cannot be the answer to the moral hazard problem and to the actual amoral and immoral conduct encouraged by the new limited liability rules. Government cannot effectively, efficiently or fairly regulate the activities of the legal and accounting fields because their day-to-day operations are all judgment calls. Government can set minimum standards for admission to these professions. It also can pursue wrongdoers after the fact. But the blunt instrument of a regulatory agency can never be fine enough to police the professions. These day-to-day judgment calls can only be made by those in the firms themselves, who can decide what is acceptable conduct and acceptable risk. The old partnership form accomplished just this with the savings and loan scandals serving as a reminder to behave properly, a reminder that was turned into an exercise in shedding professional responsibility.

So long as the limited liability partnership form is allowed for the professions of law and accounting, no investor's dollar is safe. And so long as the structure is allowed, the government will have to divert resources to demolishing abusive tax shelters or else all taxpayers will suffer from this cheating.

Some of the best evidence of how limited liability partnerships are a bad deal for society, how they drive up costs for everyone else because of the bad behavior that they encourage, can be found in the growing problem the IRS has faced since the midnineties trying to catch tax cheats. While a few like Nick Jesson stand on their cyber-space soapbox and announce themselves, most tax cheats rely on the accounting and legal firms to craft the complex, hard to find and even harder to understand tax shelters that Jerry Curnutt worked so hard to identify by sifting through the inadequate data that the IRS lifted into its computer files from tax returns.

Like guerrilla soldiers, a small army that moves stealthily in dark-ness can disrupt and perhaps even destroy a society that operates in the open. Hunting down hidden tax cheating is a costly, inefficient and messy business, especially with handcuffs on. In 2002, as his five-year tenure as the first businessman to run the IRS came to an end, that is exactly what Charles O. Rossotti came to realize.

Gimme Shelter

19

The large color photograph in New York Life's 2001 annual report shows two men in dark suits wearing looks of warm confidence. The positioning of the photograph and the discreet caption are meant to honor the two men to whom the insurance company owes much. One is Louis P. Kreisberg, owner of a phenomenally successful insurance brokerage in Manhattan called Executive Compensation Group. The other is his friend and rainmaker, Jonathan Blattmachr, the genius tax lawyer from Milbank Tweed Hadley & McCloy.

For most of the past two decades, sales of life insurance have been in decline, the number of new policies off by roughly a third. Blattmachr, however, has opened a whole new book of business for New York Life—and on a fantastic scale. Some idea of that scale is found in the program for one dinner held in honor of top New York Life producers. Kreisberg led the list with premiums of $11 million. The next guy on the list was way down near $1 million. Competitors said Kreisberg's firm collected more than $100 million in premiums from Blattmachr's insurance plans in 2000 and 2001.

All this premium money flowing into New York Life wasn't really for life insurance, at least not in the sense that most people think of it. The purchasers were not making sure that if Mom or Dad died unexpectedly, there would be money to raise the kids or pay off the mortgage. The buyers were all rich, many of them with so many hundreds of millions or billions of dollars that life insurance in its conventional sense would be ridiculous.

These buyers were not shopping for the lowest possible rates, either. Each of them paid the highest possible price. Many paid four or five times the lowest price. At least one paid 12 times that price.

What they were buying from New York Life was a Blattmachr tax dodge.

Since 1913, when the income tax began, life insurance has received special treatment. Generally life insurance proceeds are free of tax. The law began as a protection for widows and their children in an era when death was a common danger for industrial workers, with insurance salesmen going door to door each week collecting dimes, quarters and an occasional dollar of premiums.

Today life insurance is largely a tax avoidance product. Purchasers can buy stocks, bonds and mutual funds, wrap a life insurance policy around their portfolio, and let their investments grow free of tax. Money withdrawn during life is taxed, but money paid to heirs after death is generally tax-free. Barry Kaye, who preaches about the use of insurance as an alternative to direct investing in stocks and bonds, says that he has sold policies for as much as $1 billion. And insurance can be combined with trusts to pass unlimited sums around the gift tax and estate tax.

Blattmachr is a leading authority on creative uses of insurance. He even shows people how to use untaxed dollars to buy life insurance that will pay out vast fortunes of untaxed dollars. It is fact, not boast, when Blattmachr proudly says that he counsels more wealth than anyone else in America.

In Alaska, Blattmachr is the father of a law that created a new kind of trust. For centuries trusts have been allowed to exist for the lifetimes of all those beneficiaries who are living when the trust is created plus 21 years after the last beneficiary dies. The law Blattmachr drafted allows a trust to exist in perpetuity. A small but growing number of states have similar laws, shielding fortunes forever from the only federal taxes on wealth, the gift tax and the estate tax and a special generation-skipping tax on gifts to grandchildren and later generations of heirs. Valuable as a perpetual trust can be, Blattmachr said that, unfortunately, he had persuaded only a few of his clients to put some of their wealth in the Alaska Trust Company, which is owned by his brother, Douglas.

A second Alaska law that the Milbank Tweed partner drafted reduces the tax people pay on their insurance premiums. On premiums above $100,000 the tax is reduced to insignificance. In 1999 such insurance premiums totaled just $1.1 million in Alaska, but the premiums had ballooned to more than $80 million in 2001. These tax records are the only public record of how much insurance was sold based on Blattmachr's tax advice, but since only a few of his clients set up Alaska trusts, it hints at the scale of this insurance sold in other states.

The insurance plan that made Blattmachr so important to New York Life that it pictured him in its glossy annual report was devised with the help of Michael D. Brown, a former chemical engineer who owns Spectrum Consulting in Irvine, California. The way the plan works, a dollar put into a life insurance plan can avoid nine times as much from taxes. Put $10 million into the insurance and escape $90 million of income, gift, estate and generation-skipping taxes.

"I'm not saying this is the best thing since sliced bread, but it's really good for pushing wealth forward tax-free," Blattmachr said.

Buyers were told that the plan was perfectly legal because it was based on a private letter ruling from the IRS. Private letter rulings are a way for people to find out in advance from the IRS whether a tax scheme is acceptable to the government or not. While such rulings technically apply only to the person who received the letter, they are widely used to persuade people that a tax device is valid.

The Blattmachr plan was shown only to clients and their advisers, who signed confidentiality agreements, so its precise details are not known. Each plan was also tailored to suit the client's circumstances. But in general the plan worked this way:

The wealthy client creates a life insurance trust. Premiums paid for insurance in the trust are gifts under the tax laws, but the proceeds from the policy are paid to heirs free of tax.

Next the client reports on a gift tax return only a small part of what was actually paid in premiums. Wouldn't the IRS say that is cheating? No. It's perfectly legal. The reason is that insurance companies offer many different rates for the same policy. And the buyer is allowed to declare on his gift tax return the insurance company's lowest premium for that amount of insurance, even if that person could never qualify for that rate because of his age and health, and even if no one has actually ever been sold a policy at that rate. The smaller the premium reported, the smaller the gift tax, while the larger the actual premium paid, the more wealth that can be passed on to heirs untaxed.

In an example cited by one agent, a customer paid a $550,000 premium for the first year alone, the highest price offered by the insurance company, for a policy that could have been bought for just $50,000, the lowest price. The gift tax on the reported premium was only $25,000—50 percent of the lowest premium—instead of $275,000, which is 50 percent of the highest premium.

But not even that $25,000 tax was paid because Blattmachr came up with a way to make it go away. The trick involved briefly involving one spouse in the trust because gifts of money between husband and wife are never taxable.

One buyer of an insurance plan similar to Blattmachr's paid $32 million in the first year for a policy that will pay $127 million tax-free to the grandchildren without paying any gift tax.

If the policyholder continues to pay huge premiums year after year, he can pass along much or all of his fortune tax-free if he lives long enough. Brown, the California insurance broker, said clients in their fifties and sixties, working with other agents, intended to do that.

Blattmachr, referring to Mr. Brown, said that "In 1995 I was told that this was the stupidest idea ever by a guy who is now collecting millions in commissions from selling."

The plan is a variation of an insurance device, known in taxspeak as reverse split-dollar family life insurance, which Blattmachr had done much to develop and expand. But many lawyers, including Sandy Schlesinger at Kaye Scholer, warned clients to stay away from the plan, fearing that if the IRS ever found out just what was happening, it would deny all the tax benefits Blattmachr described. "My mother taught me that if something seems too good to be true, it isn't true," he said. Other lawyers said they warned clients to stay away because it relied on a disguised gift and that if the IRS understood the plan, it would be disallowed.

When the IRS issued its latest rules for such insurance in 2002, Blattmachr was delighted. He said the new rules strengthened his plan. Then an article appeared in *The New York Times* outlining the plan. The Department of the Treasury responded 18 days later with a new rule that killed the plan, denying tax breaks to those who had bought the overpriced insurance. Pamela Olson, the chief tax policy official at the Department of the Treasury, said that under the new regulations "any scheme to understate the value of benefits for income or gift-tax purposes won't be respected" in audits.

Significantly, the Treasury notice did not describe the insurance device as a tax shelter. If it were held to be a tax shelter, then Blattmachr could have been required to turn lists of clients who used the techniques over to the IRS. The reason for Treasury's description is another loophole in the law. The tax shelter laws apply only to income taxes, not to gift and estate taxes.

Representative Lloyd Doggett, a Texas Democrat who has for years introduced bills to close tax shelters and loopholes, had sent a news clipping to Olson, which prompted her to issue the new rules disallowing the Blattmachr plan. "I am encouraged that this particular tax shelter has been shut down," Doggett said, "but for every narrow loophole that is closed, there are dozens if not hundreds more tax shelter schemes that remain available to be exploited by those who choose not to pay their fair share for necessities like national security."

Blattmachr has already moved on to create new tax dodges and will do so for as long as he practices law, the government catching up with him only now and then. But not all tax avoidance deals are based on creative legal interpretations. Some are written into the law. One of these is the exchange fund, which under government rules is available to only a few thousand Americans.

When most Americans sell stock, they must pay taxes on their profits by the following April 15. But it's perfectly legal to defer the taxes for years if you have $5 million of stocks and bonds—and you promise to keep a secret. The exchange fund is one example of how the tax laws currently grant certain favors only to the very wealthiest.

Exchange funds work like this: executives and investors contribute at least $1 million of their stock in a single company to a pool into which others in the same situation have contributed their own shares. When one wants to withdraw from the pool, the partnership gives them not their original shares or cash but instead shares of a variety of stocks held by the pool. As a result, someone with too much money in one stock can quickly diversify into a more balanced portfolio. But unlike other investors, who have to pay taxes on profits when they sell a stock, no taxes are owed on the profits of the shares contributed to the pool. If investors stay in the pool for seven years, the stocks they receive at withdrawal do not incur capital gains taxes. Those taxes only come due when these stocks are sold.

The Eaton Vance mutual fund company in Boston and Goldman Sachs are by far the biggest operators of investment pools based on this tax avoidance technique, with at least $18 billion of stocks in what are known in the investment business as exchange funds or swap funds. Bessemer Trust, Credit Suisse First Boston, Merrill Lynch and the Salomon Smith Barney brokerage unit of Citigroup have exchange funds, too.

To get in on these tax avoidance deals, investors must sign statements promising never to disclose the terms to anyone except their financial advisers. Eaton Vance's confidential offering showed that stocks of more than 700 corporations are in its pools.

Representative Richard Neal pressed the Department of the Treasury about why the Bush administration would not shut down exchange funds as loopholes since the administration had said it opposed such devices on principle. Mark Weinberger, who at the time was chief of tax policy at Treasury, replied that the Bush administration "is not for or against swap funds, but we are against taxes on capital gains in general and so we will not take any action against the funds."

The Congressional Joint Committee on Taxation, without any supporting data, told Neal that closing exchange funds would not raise any tax revenue because "the class of investors engaging in swap funds" would find other ways to avoid the tax.

They can avoid the tax because the tax shelter business ballooned during the Clinton administration as stock market profits soared and IRS funding was squeezed. The big accounting firms, the Wall Street investment houses and many law firms all had teams working on devising new ways to get clients to pay nothing to the government and large fees to themselves. A second-tier accounting firm, BDO Seidman, used a wolf as the symbol to encourage its partners and managers to sell tax shelters, boasting of the multimillion-dollars fees brought in by

various members of the wolf pack. The strategy worked. BDO Seidman collected $2.6 million in tax shelter fees in 1998 and nearly $102
million in the first half of 2000.

Another technique, one that can trick investors, was pioneered by
Goldman Sachs, but is open only to people with $10 million or more
in a single stock.

Imagine you had started one of the Internet companies, there is an
initial public offering of stock and the price of your company's shares
heads for the moon. Suddenly you have $1 billion on paper in your
company, but no cash in your pocket. And if the stock collapses, you
will end up with nothing. If you sell much of your stock, the market
will take it as a signal that it is time to get out and the price of your
company's shares will nosedive. But what if you could retain the *legal*
ownership of your shares while eliminating your *economic* ownership?
That way, you would not pay any taxes. And if your stock collapsed,
you would be able to walk away rich. And investors would think you
still were betting all of your wealth in the company whose stock they
were buying.

Here is how it works: you deposit your shares in one company
with Goldman Sachs or another investment house and sign a contract.
Typically the contract says that if your shares go up in value, Goldman
gets all of the gain up to a new level, typically a one third increase in
the price, and a portion of any increase above that.

Next, the investment house loans you more than 90 percent of the
value of your shares at a very low rate of interest, as little as 1 percent
annually. You then use this money to buy a diversified portfolio of
stocks and bonds, which you have to hold in your Goldman account.
Now you have eliminated the risk of having all your wealth in one
basket, while investors continue to buy shares believing that your fortune is tied to the company's fortunes. You also have replaced your Internet shares that did not pay a dividend with a mix of stocks and
bonds that pay dividends and interest both to cover Goldman's fees and
to put spending money in your pocket.

Goldman, meanwhile, goes out and shorts the market in your
company's stock, something that by law you cannot do as an executive
of a publicly traded company. That is, Goldman borrows shares and
sells them. Goldman makes money if the price of the company's shares

falls. If the price rises, it gets the first 35 percent or so increase, hedging its position, giving it plenty of room to get out of its short position with no risk.

The government gets nothing. You, however, are enjoying the equivalent of selling your shares without paying taxes, so instead of being left with 80 percent of your wealth after taxes, you have 100 percent of it invested in a diversified portfolio of stocks. All in all, a very sweet deal for those who are in on the deal—and a sour one for those who are not.

Not everyone has their wealth tied up in stocks that Wall Street finds attractive. But there are endless ways to get around taxes for the rich and all of those ways are exceptionally lucrative to those who create tax dodges.

Sheldon Cohen, who had been IRS commissioner in the Johnson administration, said he could not imagine any easier or more dishonorable way to make a fortune than to design tax shelters. "You come up with an idea and spend maybe 10 hours refining it plus a week of research by a law firm associate and you have a product you can sell to a client who will pay you $10 million to get rid of 10 times that much on taxes—and it works so long as the IRS never figures out just what is going on."

The tax shelter business also expanded from the very largest corporations to rich individuals. Ernst & Young sent sales agents to smaller accounting firms, offering to split fees with them in return for introductions to clients who had a large slug of income or a gain from their investments or sale of the business. The accountants at the local firms were told that they had a chance to score a big fee, but to find out about it they had to sign a confidentiality agreement first. Then the Ernst & Young sales agents handed out not brochures, but a single photocopied page outlining four tax shelters and then asked for all of the copies back. At least one photocopy was not recovered, though.

The sheet showed how someone selling a business for a $100 million profit, on which she would have owed $20 million in federal capital gains taxes alone, could pay a $5 million fee to Ernst & Young and nothing to the government.

In another example used by the firm, someone with a $20 million paycheck on which he would owe $7.7 million in federal income taxes would delay the tax for 20 years, effectively reducing the tax to $1.4 million. The fee charged by Ernst & Young would be $1.2 million.

The chief executive of the Sprint Corporation, William T. Esrey, bought a similar tax shelter, only his was designed to delay paying the taxes not for two decades but for three. Esrey had hit the jackpot in the Internet bubble and in a failed merger with MCI WorldCom, which later collapsed from massive accounting fraud. Esrey was allowed to cash in the stock options he got for arranging the failed deal. In 1998, 1999 and 2000, his options generated a profit of $159 million. Had he just paid the $63 million in federal income taxes, he would have been left with $96 million. Instead he kept the shares and watched their value plummet when the stock market bubble burst.

The IRS, which had been alerted to this tax shelter by an article in *The New York Times,* audited Esrey's tax return in early 2003, a time when his Sprint shares had fallen in value to $40 million, well below the taxes he had not paid. When Esrey told his board that he was facing bankruptcy because of the tax dodge, and that other top executives had bought the same tax shelter from the Arthur Andersen accounting firm, he was fired.

Richard, Stewart and Tom Coleman were ready and willing to pay the taxes they owed when they sold their shopping mall in Asheville, North Carolina, for a fat profit. Then William Spitz came calling. Spitz told the Colemans that there was no need to pay the taxes because, for a fee, his firm would make them go away. Spitz was no fly-by-nighter. He worked for one of the biggest accounting firms in the world, KPMG, and he said that the tax shelter would withstand any audit because it "used the IRS's own rules against itself." Several hundred rich Americans had used the strategy without a hitch, Spitz said, including racecar driver Dale Earnhart, who saved $4 million in 1997. The shelter was called Currency Options Bring Rewards, or Cobra.

The Colemans signed up, paying hundreds of thousands of dollars in fees to KPMG and nothing to the IRS.

In Lake Mary, Florida, Joe Jacoboni listened to a similar pitch after he sold his software company for a profit of $28 million. Jacoboni wanted to have his own lawyer look over the deal, but KPMG said the shelter was proprietary and no outside professionals could look over the deal, out of fear that they would steal the concept and sell it themselves.

KPMG prepared a tax return that showed that rather than having a profit of $28 million, Mr. Jacoboni had a loss of $2 million. Jacoboni decided to go ahead, persuaded by KPMG that it was just letting him in on a perfectly legal way to escape taxes that was routinely used by many people who were far wealthier.

The Colemans and Jacoboni are just a few of thousands of wealthy Americans who were solicited to buy tax shelters and did. And while they got caught and are now suing KPMG, sales continue to flourish because the IRS never finds most tax shelters. And many of those it finds are allowed to stand for lack of resources to demolish them.

Only the very rich can buy these tax shelters. Ernst & Young has been known to charge people a fee of $1 million just to look at a tax shelter proposal. But then, compared to paying taxes, tax shelters can be a real bargain. One Ernst & Young shelter cost $5 million to wipe out $20 million in tax obligations, according to its confidential offering. Ernst & Young sold a similar shelter that promised people with salaries of $20 million or more that they could live tax-free. KPMG and BDO Seidman, in particular, fought government efforts to learn about their tax shelters and who used them.

Among those who were pitched the KPMG shelter were William E. Simon Jr., who had defeated Nick Jesson in the primary for governor of California in 2002, but lost the general election after he admitted using a Cayman Islands tax shelter. Court papers also named as potential or actual buyers his late father, former Treasury Secretary William E. Simon Sr.; Gary Winnick of Global Crossing; Earl N. Phillips Jr., the ambassador to Barbados; Henry Nicholas III, chief executive of Broadcom Corp.; Robert K. Shaye, chairman of New Line Cinema; and J. Paul Redder, the founder of Ditech, the mortgage loan company known for its television commercials.

When Jacoboni and others sued KPMG over their failed tax shelters, the accounting firm tried to prevent them from learning all about the deal they had bought. That effort drew a sharp rebuke from a federal magistrate named David Baker, who ordered KPMG to turn over documents to its clients. "The shroud of secrecy that KPMG kept over" its tax shelters "has been lifted," Baker wrote, noting that the firm was being accused of fraud and that the IRS was investigating the shelters. "KPMG should recognize that its role in these transactions will be examined with no presumption of confidentiality," Magistrate Baker wrote in a ruling that was upheld on appeal.

In Manhattan, four Indiana men who sold their computer distribution business for a $70 million gain in 1999 sued Ernst & Young, saying it sold them a tax shelter after the IRS had already declared it improper. To escape $14 million in capital gains taxes, the men paid $1 million to Ernst & Young and $2 million to Jenkens & Gilchrist, the Dallas law firm that had conceived the shelter.

The four also paid $75,000 to Sidley Austin Brown & Wood, a major law firm, for a letter attesting to the propriety of the tax shelter. That lawsuit opened the door on another secretive aspect of the tax shelter business—opinion letters.

Like sellers of treasure maps, promoters of tax shelters promise that for a large fee, one can navigate a secret route through the tax code. What clinches these deals is not the chart itself, though, but a second document that appears to warrant that the map is as good as gold. That document is an opinion letter and it blesses the tax shelter as a perfectly legal way to reduce taxes. Written by tax lawyers using the embossed stationery of their firms, the letters typically cost $50,000, $75,000 or more, and require a signed promise to keep the contents secret, like the treasure map, lest the Internal Revenue Service discover where untaxed fortunes lie. Opinion letters often run to 100 pages. The cover page offers comforting assurances, typically saying that even if the IRS finds out about the shelter, it is "more likely than not" that taxes will never come due. The rest of these letters are economic and legal analysis weighted down with enough caveats to sink a Spanish galleon.

As Esrey, Jacoboni, the Colemans and others discovered, when the IRS manages to find a shelter, the opinion letters they paid so dearly for may not be worth the paper they are written on. The letters can be quite lucrative for law firms, because the same opinion can be sold over and over to buyers of an identical shelter simply by changing the name on the opinion and adjusting a few key facts to fit the circumstances of the buyer.

Even sophisticated tax shelter buyers often fail to appreciate that "it's just an opinion, it's not an insurance policy," said David Hariton of Sullivan & Cromwell in New York, who does not write such letters. He said promoters try to imbue opinion letters with great significance, even implying that there is some standard for grading the quality of the assurances, but this is not true. Bruce Fensterstock, a lawyer for the Indiana clients, said, "Even for people who are sophisticated, it doesn't mean they understand anything about the complexities of tax shelters." Larry A. DiMatteo, a Florida professor who has studied opinion letters, said that even financially smart people "treat opinion letters as if they were binding, when under American law they generally have no legal consequence."

Basically an opinion letter is an expensive document that says that a tax shelter works unless the IRS says that it does not. The real value of opinion letters is as a shield from government penalties for not paying taxes when they were due. Penalties are usually waived when a taxpayer relied on professional advice that the IRS regards as reasonable and given in good faith. And the IRS, like the courts, tends to grant respect to opinion letters even if they encourage misconduct.

When penalties are waived because an opinion letter accompanies a tax dodge, it creates an incentive to cheat because there is no risk of loss and, if the shelter slips by, then the taxpayer saves money. Representative Doggett, a former Texas Supreme Court justice, says that an opinion letter is "essentially a get-out-of-jail-free card because penalties are waived. That makes tax shelters a no-risk strategy because your chances of getting caught in the audit lottery are low."

As Jerry Curnutt, the IRS partnerships expert, found, those small audit odds shrivel even more when layers of partnerships are used to keep a tax dodge several steps away from an individual tax return. At an IRS research conference in June 2003 officials were told about how one tax shelter was found only because someone noticed that the two least significant entities in the deal shared an address. Thus for less than 50 bucks to rent another mailbox, that shelter could have been made invisible to the IRS.

While people who get once-in-a-lifetime windfalls sometimes fall prey to tax shelter schemes, the law specifically allows for tax sheltering of income in pension plans and 401(k) retirement savings plans. These vehicles are supposed to provide those who forgo some of their income today with a retirement income they can count on. But that money is not safe anymore, either.

Only the Rich Deserve a Comfortable Retirement

20

John Patrick Pusloskie Jr. was the first in his family to graduate from college. But soon after earning his degree in finance from Canisius College in Buffalo in 1989 he surprised his family by announcing he was going to work for the Rochester Telephone Company, where his father had worked as a repairman for 22 years. Pusloskie liked the fact that a repairman's pay was dependable enough that his father had provided three children with a middle-class upbringing, that he could work outdoors and that his job would require solving problems. Mostly, though, even as a young man, he was drawn to a traditional defined-benefit pension that rewarded a career with one company and provided a risk-free retirement. Pusloskie figured he would be able to retire in his late fifties with a secure lifetime income, supplemented by whatever he saved in a 401(k) plan, and company-paid health care.

In the next few years Pusloskie married, fathered two children and bought a home in the rural countryside of Avon, a half-hour from downtown Rochester and a few miles from his parents' place. Because of his finance background he was recruited to help his union, Local 1170 of the Communications Workers of America, assess the value of its contract. As a regulated monopoly Rochester Telephone earned steady profits, paid a reliable dividend and provided its workers with a secure income, although the union had to negotiate a new contract every few years. It was good, interesting volunteer work—until the change came.

Ronald L. Bittner, who had started out as a trainee at the company in 1963, had risen over three decades to become chairman, president and chief executive. Bittner immediately set out on an ambitious plan to take Rochester Tel into the big leagues. Early on Bittner grasped the significance of the long strands of glass that were being developed at Corning Glass, another big company in the Finger Lakes region of New York. Fiber optic cables could carry immense volumes of telephone calls and data. Bittner persuaded his board of directors to invest in what would become the first large fiber optic network to carry long-distance calls and computer data. He also had Rochester Tel buy an independent long-distance company in Detroit, whose employees earned less than the union workers at Rochester Telephone and received far less in fringe benefits. Bittner promised to keep the regulated monopoly and the competitive long-distance businesses separate and he renamed the entire company Frontier to signify a new era. "Healthy competition is beneficial to customers and shareholders, and we are determined to prove it," Bittner declared in late 1994.

Because of the ventures into fiber optic and long distance, Frontier's revenues in 1995 exploded to more than $2 billion and Bittner predicted a glorious future. "Frontier will double again in size by the year 2000," Bittner vowed when he announced the results the following spring. This bright future was made possible by Congress, which through several laws including the 1996 Telecommunications Act opened opportunities for Frontier to grow as it wished, unhindered by state utility regulators. "We are uniquely positioned among all industry players to benefit from these expanded opportunities on the state level," Bittner crowed. Shareholders were prepared to believe Bittner because the rising stock price, together with their dividend checks, gave them a phenomenal 46 percent gain for a single year. More than 40 cents out of every dollar paid by customers in 1995 became operating profit and stodgy Rochester Telephone had its best year ever.

Despite these lush profits, Bittner was determined to pay less to Rochester Telephone workers. He wanted their wages to be more in line with what the Detroit staff earned. When its contract expired, the union would not accept his terms so the company imposed them, as federal law allows.

On the last day of 1996, just seven months after Bittner predicted a profitable future, the company froze the pension plan that had drawn

John Pusloskie into the company. Pusloskie had earned just six years toward his pension, far short of the 35 or more years he expected to count when he turned in his spikes. His benefits would be frozen in 1996 dollars, inflation eroding their value for three decades to come.

Frontier told its workers that the stock market was responsible for their situation and also that it would make them rich. The company just could not afford to put money into stodgy pensions anymore in the newly competitive and unregulated world of telephone services, which—unlike the regulated monopoly position of traditional phone services—did not come with profits almost guaranteed. Traditional pensions did not reward performance, the workers were told. They were not told about the risks that go with rewards for performance, especially the risks that all of them could do their jobs well and suffer because of decisions by those at the top, decisions over which they had no influence.

The theory of aligning the interests of rank-and-file workers with shareholders was being similarly pitched across the country at companies that wanted to dump their traditional defined-benefit pensions in favor of what were being promoted as "modern retirement plans."

In these modern plans, also known as defined-contribution plans, the company contributes a specific amount of money to a retirement plan. The worker then assumes all risks of investing that money. If the employee is an investment whiz or just plain lucky, she will end up with a lot of money. But if the money is invested too conservatively or too aggressively, or if the worker is not free to change investments when the market shifts, then there may not be enough money to finance a retirement, forcing her to keep working lest her money runs out before life does.

From the viewpoint of executives these modern plans have many advantages, though few outside the executive suites know about them. By replacing the security of a traditional defined-benefit pension with a risky defined-contribution retirement savings plan, executives improve the financial performance of their companies, or at least make them appear to improve in the short run. The switch means less cost and more profit. And on top of that the taxpayers can be drawn, however unknowingly, into helping enhance executive riches.

While promoters of defined-contribution plans emphasize their potential profits, there is also a deeper idea behind them, one that adds to managerial power. The idea is this: if workers have to rely on stock of the company where they work to finance their retirement, then they will work harder and smarter, and will oppose union work rules that management believes hinder profits. Unsaid is a hope that unions will be voted out because, with the union gone, wages could be held down and workers could be pressed to work longer hours without overtime. This also has a spillover effect because, as the share of the workforce with union wages declines, the overall wage levels needed to retain good workers can be restrained or even lowered.

The companies promoting this line of reasoning in the nineties had a model to point to: Microsoft. No matter that Microsoft's enormous growth in value rested on its monopoly status in controlling the operating system for 9 out of 10 desktop computers. Never mind that Microsoft was being sued for hiring lots of workers on contract so that they did not share in the bounty of its rising stock price. The message at Frontier and other companies was that even clerks could get rich, just like the clerks at Microsoft, if they would stop listening to their unions and trust management.

Getting rich and getting paid with stock, like executives are, were themes Pusloskie heard over and over as the company described the wonders of its new retirement benefits. "They told us we were all going to be millionaires," Pusloskie said. To many members, the lure of a pot of gold from a few slivers of silver each week was bedazzling. And when Frontier shares started going up again, workers started to buy into Bittner's plan. Pusloskie's own father, who owned 3,000 shares of the regulated utility Rochester Telephone, kept all of his retirement savings in Frontier shares.

Among the issues that Frontier management did not preach about were the very different conditions of stock ownership that applied to senior executives like Bittner compared to the rank and file. Nor did the company explain how the so-called modern plans can artificially inflate company finances and enrich executives while leaving workers holding an empty bag if things go wrong.

The executives had much more freedom to sell their stock when their insider knowledge told them that was a profitable move. Those with stock options could sell them for a profit when the market price for their shares was higher than the fixed price they had to pay. These profits were then paid in cash, which the executives could use to buy a diversified portfolio of stocks and bonds from many different companies. The executives, in other words, were encouraged to follow all three rules of investing: diversify, diversify and diversify.

Other companies—notably Eastman Kodak, IBM and the CSX railroad company—required senior executives to retain much of their wealth in the company they worked for. However, the executives were rewarded for the increased risks they incurred because their wealth was concentrated. The reward was enormously outsized compensation, so large that even if the company faltered, they would remain wealthy. Louis V. Gerstner Jr., after just nine years as IBM chief executive, was worth more than $600 million. George Fischer, who became Eastman Kodak chief executive in 1993, was given $100 million of Eastman stock on top of millions of stock options.

The exact opposite happened to Pusloskie and workers at many companies whose risk-free traditional pension was replaced with the concentrated risk of relying on their employer's stock for their old age. Frontier workers could not sell for at least five years. That was better than at some companies that required workers to keep all of their stock in company shares until they turned 55, when a federal law allowed them to begin slowly selling those shares to diversify their portfolios. Of course, at age 55, it is a little late to make up for sharp drops in the value of the shares of a single company. And at many companies workers did not sell, perhaps because the company did not remind them of the opportunity. Or perhaps because the company did not provide them with the kinds of sophisticated financial planning advice routinely doled out to executives.

At many companies, though not Frontier, executives received professional investment advice with the company not just paying for the advice, but paying the taxes on the value of the advice. At many companies such advice for senior executives cost more than most workers made in a year and sometimes ran into six figures.

Rank-and-file workers like Pusloskie, however, most of whom knew next to nothing about either corporate finance or investment theory, received no such advice because Congress prohibited it. If the workers wanted investment advice, they would have to pay for it with their own after-tax dollars. As a result, many of them were not aware that Frontier and many other companies violated every basic tenet of investing by requiring workers to hold most of their retirement funds in the stock of their employer. If the company gets into trouble, both job and retirement fund can evaporate—concentrating risks in a way that no financial planner would advocate.

As part of Bittner's plans, Rochester became the first city in the country with open competition for local telephone service. Instead of being a regulated monopoly, any telephone company was free to offer local telephone service. Pusloskie and his colleagues were told to expect that 30 percent of Rochester Tel's customers would switch to another carrier and that layoffs were likely. Bittner fared better. His pay rose 50 percent. His award of stock options grew more than 10-fold. Moreover, along with a handful of other senior executives, he was exempted from the pension freeze. Frontier said it wanted to make sure that they stayed with the company.

Weeks after the pension was frozen on the last day of 1996, the 800 or so working members of Local 1170 voted on a new contract. In addition to the freeze on pension benefits, it froze their pay for three years and capped the health benefits of retirees at several hundred dollars a month below what those benefits cost. The union voted it down 555 to 44. Randal Simonetti, the company spokesman, gave management's blunt assessment: "The company is very disappointed the vote went down and disappointed in the employees. These folks are not interested in competing in an open market. They are interested in entitlements."

Entitlements was the watchword for management at Frontier and many other companies working to reduce compensation of those down in the bowels of the company, even as dollars flowed ever more generously to management, especially those at the top. Every Frontier manager, down to the lowliest foreman, was given a booklet that labeled the pension and health care benefits negotiated between the company and the union as "entitlements." The union members, Frontier managers were told, were like the lazy bums who collect welfare checks because they are entitled to them, the only difference being the unionists show up for work.

Frontier executives said they needed to align the interests of the workers with the company's shareholders because that was what the stock market demanded. And the way to do that, they said, was to make sure that Rochester Telephone employees counted mostly on a rising price for Frontier shares to fund their retirement. The aligning part came in how the new plan was to be financed. The company would give the workers stock in Frontier equal to one half of 1 percent of their wages. For a lineman making $50,000 annually that would come to $250 each year or about a $1 per day worked. This was less than a fourth of what the company had been putting away for decades in the traditional defined-benefit pension, which carried no risks for workers and, since 1974, had been guaranteed by the federal government.

Frontier did not tell the workers how they would have fared had this plan been adopted years earlier. If the plan had been in effect from 1960 through 1995, a repairman would have retired with a retirement account, payable as a lump sum, of about $17,500 instead of a pension of more than $19,000 per year for life.

There was a second provision in the modern Frontier retirement arrangement, a 401(k) plan in which those workers who saved 3 percent of their pay would get a dollar-for-dollar match from the company. The match would be paid in Frontier shares, which were counted at current market value despite the five-year restriction on their sale. The matching shares meant that a repairman like Pusloskie would get another $1,339 in stock from the company each year. Even with this match the company would be spending far less than in the traditional pension plan.

Had the plan been in effect since 1960 and a worker saved 3 percent of his pay each year, the company would have bought company shares worth another 3 percent plus the half percentage point that everyone got, saver or not. After 35 years of purchases, the company shares would have been worth less than $71,000.

Because Rochester Tel was a regulated utility, it would be fair to ponder what would have happened had the same 3.5 percent of pay been invested by the company in a diversified portfolio of stocks and bonds that grew at a healthy 10 percent per year. That would have created an account worth $122,000, or about what the defined-benefit pension would pay in the first six and a half years.

Frontier never gave workers comparisons like these. Instead the company kept telling everyone about the rich future, and many Frontier workers enthusiastically bought into the modern retirement plan, even as their union continued to demand that their traditional defined-benefit pension be restored. Pusloskie remembered the rallies the company held, the gleeful sales pitches and the unsubtle reminders from bosses that people who were loyal to the company would put their 401(k) savings in Frontier stock. At the time Frontier stock was doing fabulously well and the early talk of an information superhighway was shortening into a one-word description of the future: Internet. With Bittner boasting that Frontier was the best positioned of all telecommunications companies to profit from the Internet, the idea looked attractive to many of the rank and file. If the value of the investments goes up, the workers could get far more than the pension plan, the Frontier managers kept telling the unionists and others under them. No one mentioned what would happen if the investments lost value.

The local head of the Communications Workers union, Robert Flavin, thought that the new retirement plan was a huge take back from workers just because it would cost the company less. Stock prices go up and they go down, he warned members, and if one is buying when prices are high and retires when prices are low, the result is disaster. He reminded them of the Great Depression years and how from 1966 to 1981 the stock market went nowhere. He warned members that Frontier executives knew more than anyone else about where prices were going and could cash out when it was smart to do so. But management was locking the union members into their shares, which could not be sold easily. And with the new plan it was violating the principle that an investment pool should be diversified to reduce risk without giving the workers any additional compensation to make up for that risk, as chief executives like Jack Welch and John Snow demanded and got for having their investments concentrated in the stock of one company.

Besides, Flavin told his members, they had bargained for a defined-benefit pension. If the stock market was entering such a glorious era of growth, then why should Frontier be worried about the future costs of the pension plan, he asked. If Frontier was right, then the rising market should make the pension plan's diversified portfolio of stocks and bonds grow steadily in value. Indeed, if the market was such a certain place for investments, Frontier might not even have to make future contributions to the pension plan because the rising market would more than cover the costs.

While Frontier, like many companies, was putting less into the retirement plan for the rank and file than it had been under the traditional pension, chief executives Goizueta, Welch and even Bittner arranged for themselves just the opposite. Their executive retirement plans were padded and stuffed with many millions of dollars and then stuffed more through tricks to enlarge their retirement.

One device was to simply credit chief executives with years they never worked to boost their pensions. John Snow, the second Treasury secretary in the second Bush presidency, worked for 25 years at the railroad company CSX, where he required every worker to own company stock to keep their jobs. After he became chief executive, his pension plan was credited with 19 phantom years so his pension was based on 44 years of service. Those phantom years meant that for each dollar of pension Snow actually earned, he collected $1.76 in pension benefits.

When Stephen Wolf resigned as chief executive of US Airways Group in 2002, his pension was based on 30 years of service, even though he worked only six years at the airline company. He was also credited with almost twice as much salary and bonus as he actually earned. That inflated his pension, which he took in a lump sum, from less than $2 million to $15 million. The airline's number-two executive, Rakesh Gangwal, pocketed $15 million, too. Gangwal's pension also credited him with five years for each year actually worked and it was based not on his actual salary and bonus, but on his authorized salary and "assumed maximum bonus." (Wolf and Gangwal also took no salary during their last few months at the company because of its cash squeeze.)

Most workers, like telephone repairman Pusloskie, get a pension based only on their base salary, while most executive plans are based on salary plus bonus. Snow was among a growing number of senior executives who got other compensation counted, too. In Snow's case the board spiked his pension by counting the value of 250,000 shares of CSX stock, which with the phantom years boosted his pension to just under $2.5 million annually. Terrence Murray, the chief executive of FleetBoston, had earned a pension worth $2.7 million for his 39 years with the bank when he retired in 2001. But Murray's board decided at the last minute to count the value of his exercised stock options toward his pension, boosting his annual retirement check to $5.8 million.

Another way to plump up executive pensions is applied at IBM. Its pension formula has one rate for workers making five figures and a higher rate for those who make six or seven figures. IBM said this was so to make up for the fact that Social Security benefits did not apply to such high salaries.

Getting credit for years not worked, adjusting upward because of limits on Social Security benefits and having virtually all compensation counted toward pension benefits are what Judith Fischer, managing director of Executive Compensation Advisory Services, calls "the eternal wealth syndrome." Her reasoning is that pensions alone provide senior executives with more than needed in retirement, which means they never have to consume any of the millions of dollars salted away during their working years.

Diverting all this extra money to executive pensions puts a strain on company budgets for personnel. When executive pension costs grow faster than company revenues and profits, then something in the company's compensation budget has to give. Congress, in a series of little-noticed laws over the past three decades, has told companies that they can balance their compensation budgets by stealthily taking away retirement income from workers who lack keys to the executive washroom.

Unbeknownst to millions of workers, their company pensions will be reduced by part of the amount they collect in Social Security benefits. This offset for Social Security benefits primarily hurts two groups of workers: those in low-paying jobs and those who leave a job after qualifying for a pension, but years before they are eligible to collect that pension. In some cases workers will collect less than a fifth of the dollars they expected, getting a check for less than $100 a month when the company plan appears to pay $500. The reason is that Congress, listening to the pleas of companies whose contributions got them access, quietly passed laws that allow companies to apply inflation in two different ways to reduce the benefits of workers who switch jobs long before retirement. The first way is the straightforward effect of freezing benefits in the dollars of the year the worker left his job. The second, and subtle, rule gives full credit to the inflation adjustments that over time boost the size of Social Security checks. By applying the actual size of Social Security benefits paid years later, the pension can be offset even more.

While companies have been padding executive pensions, known as supplemental executive retirement plans (SERPs), this has not been the case with pensions for everyone else. From 1978 to 1998, corporate spending on pension plans fell by 22 percent. Partly that was because stock market gains reduced the need to contribute more funds to those pension plans that soared along with the overall stock market in the eighties and nineties. But mostly it was because of benefit cuts, some explicit and many stealthy. During those two decades the portion of men whose jobs came with traditional pensions fell from above half to below. The percentage of women with pensions fell over those two decades, too, from 43 percent to 39 percent.

All those years of contributing less to pension plans came at a huge price. When the bubble burst on Wall Street the value of pension plan assets fell. In 2003 corporate pension plans had $400 billion less in assets than they owed to workers and retirees, a shortfall of about 20 cents on the dollar. Had the pension plans invested only in fixed income assets like bonds, as pension finance theory says they should have, there would be no shortfall and pensions would be secure. Doing that would have required a steady flow of corporate money into these plans. But Congress, listening to the political donor class, does not enforce the rules requiring that pension plans be run solely and exclusively to benefit workers and retirees. Congress allowed 60 percent of pension assets to be invested in stocks and other equities, a risky strategy. During the stock market bubble very little cash went into pension plans as rising stock prices made these plans appear to be sound. Not spending money on pension obligations also made companies appear more profitable than they really were, propelling stock prices even higher and enriching those who cashed out. Now that the bubble has burst these same companies are seeking, and getting, from Washington special rules that let them defer making up the shortfall they caused. There may be no other option at this point, but there has also been no move in Congress to make sure these plans are properly funded at all times and run solely to benefit workers and retirees as the law says is required.

Some workers who think they have pensions coming will be in for an expensive surprise when they are old. Congress allows companies to exclude 30 percent of workers from pensions. A company can, for example, have a pension plan that covers everyone except inside sales agents or janitors or copy editors. So long as it does not run afoul of discrimination laws—for example, by excluding only secretaries when all of them are women and they are the majority of a company's female workers—companies have wide latitude to say who is in and who is out.

"Most members of Congress think the rule is that whether you are the janitor or the CEO you get a pension based on a percentage of your salary times your years of service," said Mark Iwry, the senior Treasury pension expert in the Clinton administration. "We have nothing like that rule because business has been able to get away with something more discriminatory from the get go. Companies are allowed by Congress to count Social Security benefits as if they were provided by the employer and they have numerous other ways to skew the benefits so that lower paid workers get less and those higher up get more. If everyone received the same percentage of pay, adjusted only for years of service, when they retire that would be, well, that would be too simple for the business community. Industry would fight that to the death."

By switching from a traditional pension that pays a government-guaranteed retirement benefit to a so-called "modern retirement plan," as Frontier did, some companies have slashed their expenses for retirement benefits by much more than the discriminatory practices authorized by Congress. Some companies reduced their costs by 90 percent, although a third is typical, Notre Dame pension economist Teresa Ghilarducci found after examining hundreds of big company pension reports.

Cutting costs is not the only reason that so many companies have switched from traditional defined-benefit pensions to the risky plans promoted as modern.

That so many companies use shares of their own stock to fund modern retirement plans, including matching what workers save in 401(k) plans, is encouraged by accounting and tax rules. Using company stock to fund a retirement plan can bring a company tax-free cash, cut its taxes, make its finances appear stronger than they are and make executive stock options more valuable, at least in the short run.

How? Let's follow the flow of cash.

When John Pusloskie saved 3 percent of his pay in the Frontier 401(k) plan to buy company shares, the company gave him an equal number of shares. To make the numbers simple, assume that the amount he saved was $100 and that each share sold for that price. And let's assume that the company is also due a tax refund from the government that year.

The company pays Pusloskie $100. Pusloskie puts the $100 into the 401(k) plan, which then pays the $100 to the company in exchange for one share of stock, which the company takes off the shelf where it keeps authorized but unissued shares. No tax is due by the company because the $100 is now an addition to its capital, not taxable revenue.

The company also issues a second share of stock for the 401(k) match. It also values this share, which comes from the pile of authorized but unissued shares in its vault, at $100. But no cash changed hands for this share.

The company at this point has zero cash expense. The $100 salary it paid to Pusloskie came back to it tax-free and the second share of stock, the matching share that was plucked from the company vault, was simply declared to be worth $100 because that was how much shares trading on the stock exchanges sold for that day.

The company gets a tax deduction both for the $100 it paid in salary to Pusloskie and for the share of stock it imbued with $100 of value when it put it into the 401(k) plan. At the 35 percent corporate tax rate the company gets $70 added to its refund from the IRS. So far not one dollar has flowed out of the company and $70 has flowed in.

The two shares that the company issued add to the capital structure of the company. They make its balance sheet stronger, under the accounting rules, by $200 even though it sold one share for cash at the market price and issued the second for what it said was the value of Pusloskie's labor.

If a company issues a small number of shares, relative to the number outstanding, and the enterprise is growing, no one will notice the minor dilution of value for the shares already issued. But issuing new shares this way year after year has a corrosive effect, just as inflation erodes the value of the dollar over time. To adjust for this, companies sometimes take the money that workers put into the 401(k) plan and buy stock in the open market. And many companies take some of their cash flow and use it to buy shares, too. If the company buys more shares than it issues, everything else being equal, then the value of each remaining share rises because it represents a larger piece of the company's worth.

Company dollars used to buy back company shares are not dollars invested in improving the business. Those dollars are not being used to build new factories or buy more efficient computers or otherwise grow the business. They may, however, put upward pressure on the company's share price for another reason. If the company steadily buys its own shares through ups and downs, then it creates a steady demand for those shares. Stronger demand for shares means higher prices and that, in turn, means that executives collect more when they exercise their stock options.

In the long run such manipulations will have little effect, if any. But in the short run, which may mean several years, the effect of buying shares with the 401(k) savings of workers like Pusloskie tends to prop up the price of a company's stock. Reduced pension costs also improve profits. Those who cash out in the short run, as when executives turn stock options into cash, walk away with more money. It also means that those who hold on to their shares for the long run, as Pusloskie and many others workers in 401(k) plans are required to do, end up paying inflated prices for their shares and in the end get less.

The shares in John Pusloski's retirement plan have different voting rights than shares investors buy through brokers, another advantage for management. The stock is held in a trust that management controls. In most plans when workers do not vote their shares, and many never do, the trustee votes them in proportion to how everyone else voted. The significance of this, and how it can hurt workers, became apparent in Chapter 17 concerning an attempted tax dodge by the toolmaker Stanley Works.

In March 1999, just three years after Bittner had outlined a glorious future for Frontier, it was sold. The buyer was a new company, Global Crossing, which had itself commenced operations just two years earlier with plans to lay a fiber optic cable under the North Atlantic, the first in a planned network of marine cables girdling the planet. What Global Crossing needed, but did not have, was a domestic telephone company to help fill its strands of glass with chatter and data. Bittner was by then sick with cancer. He died in September 1999, just weeks from the death of Bob Flavin, the Rochester Tel union president who fought him on the pension issue. It would not be long before the name Frontier would also pass into history.

Frontier was purchased with shares of Global Crossing that the market valued at $11.5 billion even though Global Crossing had no operating business and huge losses. Its only revenues came from selling capacity on the marine cable it was still laying across the North Atlantic. That revenue amounted to just $178 million and it was really advance payment for use of the cable, which would incur operating costs once it was started. Basically Global Crossing was pure speculation, a claim of big things to come that the stock market had inflated until, based on the last 100 shares traded, all of them were valued at more than the Ford Motor Company.

Global Crossing was the child of Gary Winnick, a former partner of Michael Milken, the junk bond king of the Roaring Eighties before his manipulations made the billionaire financier an admitted felon. Winnick controlled Global Crossing through his Pacific Capital Group. Global Crossing rented space from it and paid fat fees to use its corporate jet. Winnick also collected a huge salary, one that compensation expert Bud Crystal characterized as egregious even by the outrageous standards of chief executive pay.

When Frontier was sold, the shares that Pusloskie and his coworkers had in Frontier were automatically converted to Global Crossing shares. That is, a reasonably solid investment in a company that relied heavily on the predictable profits from Rochester Tel and 37 other local telephone companies were swapped for stock in a company with no profits. And the workers were not allowed to sell any of their shares.

Winnick and his wife, Karen, could afford risks that working men like Pusloskie could not. They had so much money that they paid $16 million for a new home, the 12,000-square-foot mansion of Henry Salvatori, the late oilman whose financial support had been critical to Ronald Reagan's climb to the presidency. The home, set on four stunningly beautiful acres in the Bel-Air section of Los Angeles near the Reagans' own retirement spread, was a beauty that even the neighbors marveled at, and was considered the finest creation of the architect Paul Williams. The Winnicks bulldozed it. In its place they planned a palace that the neighbors considered a monstrosity, an ostentatious mess of a building with underground parking for 100 cars. But they sold without building.

Winnick could afford this and more because, while he and his highly paid retainers pressed everyone else to buy Global Crossing stock, and forced it on people like John Pusloskie, he was selling his shares. Despite the lack of profits, the more stock analysts like Jack Grubman wrote glowing reports about how rich buyers of shares would become, the higher the price of its shares rose. The chief executive of the company's Rochester telephone company took out the license plate Global 50. When the price of Global Crossing shares doubled, he changed his plate to Global 100. The company held rallies to urge employees to buy all the stock they could. And management and union workers alike who did not buy shares were chided by their bosses for their lack of loyalty to the company.

In the summer of 1999 Global Crossing tried to buy another local telephone company, U S West, which serves the Rocky Mountain states. When U S West backed out of the deal, it was required by contract to buy 10 percent of Global Crossing's shares at an above-market price, which allowed Winnick to sell more than 5 million of his 100 million shares for $350 million cash. Within nine months those shares would be worth only half that much.

Investing, the Wall Street promoters remind us at every opportunity, is about the future. Today's stock price is said to reflect the future earnings of a company. A rising price, all else being equal, is a vote by investors demonstrating their belief that tomorrow's profits will be bigger than today's. But Winnick was voting against Global Crossing every time he sold shares. Even as workers like John Pusloskie were being forced to stuff Global Crossing stock into their retirement plans, Winnick unloaded Global Crossing stock.

In the fall of 2001, another company with a hot stock, Enron, filed for bankruptcy. Many of its workers lost their retirement savings because their only investment was shares of the Houston energy trading company. At Global Crossing shares were losing value, too, and one of its executives was asked about the Global Crossing workers whose retirement was in Global Crossing shares. "This is completely different," Anthony Christie, a senior vice president, said. "We're an asset-based company," he said, differentiating it from Enron, which mostly traded energy.

Despite Christie's soothing words, the company's executives were not at all sanguine. That same month that Christie spoke and that Enron filed for bankruptcy, Global Crossing amended its executive retirement plan. All but 15 of the 80 eligible executives took the opportunity, converting $15 million of unsecured promises to pay into $13 million of cold cash.

In all, Winnick and other insiders unloaded $5.2 billion of stock in the 41 months between the initial public offering of stock by Global Crossing in August 1998 and its bankruptcy filing in January 2002. The company never earned a profit. Winnick says he was a victim of the market. And he says that he should not be criticized because he only sold a sixth of his shares and lost a much larger fortune on those he held onto. That is, had he been able to unload all of his shares at the peak, he would have pocketed more than $6 billion.

During its brief money-losing existence, Winnick had Global Crossing buy insurance, not against the possibility that by selling so much stock he had lost out on an even larger fortune, but as political insurance. From 1999 to 2002 Global Crossing gave $3.5 million to Republican and Democratic politicians. That was more than even Enron, which for all of its political influence only gave $2.9 million. Global Crossing gave $1 million for the Clinton library and $145,000 to California Governor Gray Davis. The presidential campaign of Senator John McCain of Arizona received $31,000 and the Republican Party received checks totaling $210,000. Winnick also hired Clinton's chief fund-raiser, Terry McAuliffe, to advise Global Crossing, paying his $100,000 fee with shares that McAuliffe sold for $18 million. All these gifts meant that Global Crossing was sure to get its telephone calls returned and its policies considered, even advanced, in Congress. That is, Winnick used Global Crossing money to buy the access to politicians that John Pusloskie did not have. That meant that members of Congress heard the rich man's version of events, but not that of the telephone repairman who was forced to become an owner of the company that employed him.

In January 2002, the company moved up its normal payday by a week and then filed for bankruptcy, saying it had $12 billion of debts and, except for the businesses formerly owned by Frontier, just a trickle of revenue.

Later that year the old Rochester Tel was sold to a new owner, Citizens Utilities, a Connecticut company that runs many small telephone companies. Pusloskie and the others thought their ordeal was over. It was not. The sale terms required that the pension plan, the one that Bittner had frozen on the last day of 1996, be turned over to Citizens. But Global Crossing's creditors had another idea. They wanted to seize the half billion dollars in the pension plan for themselves, buy annuities for the Rochester Tel workers and pocket the difference. If that happened, the workers would lose the federal government guarantee on their pensions. If the annuities went sour, they could end up with nothing.

In a strange twist of fate the falling stock market saved their pensions. As the values of stocks overall fell, so did the value of the pension plan and instead of having the $100 million surplus that the creditors wanted to take, it was, by the arcane rules of pension accounting, short about that much. Rather than have to make up that loss, the creditors finally agreed in late 2002 to let the pension plan go to the new owner of the old Rochester Tel.

So how did Pusloskie, the young man who wanted the security of a pension in his old age, fare? His defined-benefit pension is frozen in 1996 dollars. By the time he retires in 2029 or later, he figures it will be worth about $100 a month in today's dollars. "Maybe it will be enough to pay my cable television bill," he said.

And what of that modern pension plan that was supposed to make him a millionaire—the same kind of plan that millions of other workers now must rely on in their old age under rules made by Congress? Pusloskie saved as much as the plan allowed and at its peak he had $100,000 in Global Crossing shares in his 401(k) plan. The last time he could bear to look at his statement, before Global Crossing shares became worthless, his were worth $14.

What happened to John Pusloskie can still happen. That it happened is a sign of how little Congress pays attention to anything other than the concerns of the political donor class. The legal, structural and economic concerns that combined into the perfect demolition of Pusloskie's life savings did not arise suddenly and without warning.

Is Reform Possible?

21

Among our 535 senators and representatives, only one—Amo Houghton—has ever been a chief executive officer. He is also the richest man in Congress, a billionaire heir of the Corning Glass fortune in upstate New York, a man with so much money flowing into his accounts that his financial disclosure statement runs to more than 350 pages of small type. Since 2001 Houghton has been chairman of the IRS Oversight Subcommittee of the House Ways and Means Committee, making him most important member in Congress for making sure that the IRS does its job.

In 2002, a few weeks before the April 15 deadline for filing income tax returns, Houghton was asked why his subcommittee had not held, or scheduled, any hearings on tax cheating, especially by high-income taxpayers and by corporations.

"I'm not aware of any problem in that area," he said, except for offshore credit cards being used in a tax dodge, an issue that his staff had just brought to his attention by showing him an article in *The New York Times*. Item by item, Houghton was asked about tax dodges, the collapse of tax law enforcement, the Nick Jessons who publicly boast of not paying taxes, the widespread selling of tax shelters to rich individuals and the largest corporations. He expressed ignorance, saying that he had never heard of any of it. He added that he did not read *The New York Times*. Of course, these issues had been on the front page of *The Wall Street Journal*, *The Washington Post* and other major newspapers; they had been cover stories in magazines like *Forbes, Fortune,*

Newsweek and *Time* as well as the subject of reports on network television news shows. And on top of all that the IRS had been sending reports to Houghton's subcommittee explaining the problem of tax cheating and the IRS's lack of resources to enforce the law. Yet Houghton claimed to not have a clue, even though he was the point man in Congress for this issue.

Soon after his remarks were published, Houghton told his staff to arrange a hearing on tax cheating and on the ability of the IRS to enforce the law, and to make Charles Rossotti, the businessman who gave up his career to try and remake the IRS, the main witness. Learning that there was official concern about cheating by high-income Americans, Houghton wondered whether "we have enough money going to the I.R.S. to do the job at the same level as in the past."

The tax cheat hearing was set for the following October. It was never held.

Had the hearing been staged, here is what Rossotti would have told Houghton: "The tax system continues to grow in complexity, while the resource base of the IRS is not growing and in real terms is shrinking. Basically, demands and resources are going in the opposite direction. This is systematically undermining one of the most important foundations of the American economy."

Much as Rossotti wanted to speak those words to Congress, he could not. Rossotti was muzzled by the administration—and would have been by any White House because his testimony would have asserted, in effect, that the president has no clothes, that the administration had asked Congress for a budget insufficient to enforce the law. Telling that truth to Congress would have put Rossotti in an untenable position because, as he noted, "I am still a member of this administration."

Rossotti was determined, however, to spread the word about what he had learned in his tenure as the first tax commissioner who was a business executive instead of a lawyer. He succeeded thanks to the law that Senator Roth sponsored after his hearings, the IRS Reform and Restructuring Act of 1998. That law created an oversight board, which had no power except to receive reports and issue recommendations. The board asked Rossotti for a final report, an assessment of his five years, and there was no way the results could be squelched.

Rossotti's final report showed that he had come a long way from when he wrote his 68-page booklet on how to modernize the IRS. Back then he had wanted to focus on helping cooperative taxpayers so much that his new mission statement did not even explicitly mention collecting taxes. But on Rossotti's watch tax evasion spread like an aggressive cancer and Rossotti acknowledged that painful fact.

Not only was cheating rampant and growing, he reported, the vast majority of cheats were being allowed to get away without paying because there was no money to pursue them.

Tax Cheats and Debtors Get Away Without Paying

The IRS has only enough money to make a minority of known tax cheats and debtors pay. The rest get away without paying.

	Cases	Cases Not Pursued	Percent Allowed
Unpaid Taxes	4,506,060	2,689,347	60%
Did Not File Tax Returns	2,490,749	1,865,724	75%
Offshore Tax Evaders	82,100	65,100	79%
Underreported Tax; Income of $100,000 or More	123,006	68,538	56%
Underreported Tax; Income of Less Than $100,000	843,380	546,394	65%
Small Corporations Owing Taxes	39,659	9,938	25%
Middle & Large Corporations Owing Taxes	24,523	6,839	28%
Matching Tax Returns Filed by Partnerships and Similar Entities to Individual Tax Returns	13,300,000	2,926,980	78%

Source: Commissioner Rossotti's final report to IRS Oversight Board, September 2002

The reasons for this were clear. The biggest was funding. Between the time Rossotti started in November 1997 and his departure five years later, the IRS budget was reduced in real terms by 10 percent per tax return. The IRS had about $46 per tax return to process returns, educate the public, advise on complex rules, audit, conduct criminal investigations and collect taxes. In comparison, many vendors of 401(k) plans charge $50 annually just for record keeping and mailing quarterly statements.

Most IRS spending is for routine work like processing tax returns so that an overall 10 percent reduction per tax return meant a 28 percent decline in money for audits, investigations and collections, he told the oversight board. "The IRS is simply outnumbered," Rossotti wrote.

With regard to partnerships the numbers were especially disturbing. The commissioner's final report bore out what Jerry Curnutt, whom he never met, had been saying about how a few dollars to capture one more line of data from partnership tax returns could bring in billions of dollars of taxes. The estimates of what could be collected were all over the map. The high estimate was $64 billion annually. But even the $7 billion estimate in Rossotti's final report showed how just a modest investment in data analysis could pay off both in taxes collected and in treating honest taxpayers fairly.

Rossotti wrote that to close the law enforcement gap the IRS needed $1.9 billion more for the budget year 2003, 51 percent more than was budgeted for tax law enforcement. He said it needed to hire 29,306 more people, on top of the 48,000 it already has in compliance and enforcement. And at a bare minimum, a 2 percent annual budget increase above inflation was needed just to keep pace with growth in the tax system. Otherwise tax cheating would just get worse as more people and companies cheated and got away with it.

News stories about Rossotti's final report infuriated officials in the Office of Management and Budget. They could not shut down his report to the IRS Oversight Board, but they could and did tell him to not say another word until he was out of office. Mitchell B. Daniels Jr., who directed the budget office, noted that while many agencies had their budgets held flat or cut, the IRS received a 4.8 percent increase in its law enforcement budget, to $3.7 billion. "I am confident that these resources," together with tax simplification and other reforms being studied by the Department of the Treasury, "will allow the I.R.S. to effectively attack the serious noncompliance problems Treasury has identified," Daniels wrote to one senator.

Fundamental tax reform will remain elusive so long as occupants of the White House from both parties treat the IRS like an uninvited and unwanted guest in the government. The need for nearly 30,000 more people to enforce the tax laws demonstrates neglect that began many administrations ago, a festering sore that both parties have let worsen to the detriment of honest taxpayers. The Bush administration at least offers a ray of hope, saying that it will begin to study fundamental reform of the tax system. But it has set the date to begin such work as February 2005, when a new occupant might be in the White House.

Many years of malign neglect have left deep problems embedded in our economy, in our tax law and in tax law enforcement.

The IRS made its last serious effort to measure the tax gap, the difference between the taxes that would be paid if everyone obeyed the law and what is actually collected, way back in 1988. The economy has changed significantly since then, with an explosion of executive pay, the widespread adoption of 401(k)-type retirement savings plans in place of traditional pensions, a continuing shift away from manufacturing and toward services and the spread of openly marketed tax evasion schemes. Adjusting the 1988 tax gap estimate just for the growth of the economy shows that in 2003 the tax gap would be approaching $200 billion. Given the growth in the selling of schemes to evade taxes, the figure is higher. Some tax experts have said that $300 billion is a cautious estimate for 2003. That is a significant shortfall since the income tax is expected to bring in a little more than $1 trillion that year.

Historically much of the tax gap has been attributed to the underground economy, to people who work for cash or report only part of the receipts of their businesses. That, too, is changing. Paul H. O'Neill, the Treasury secretary in 2001, acknowledged that tax cheating using offshore accounts is a serious and worsening problem. And that is just one area of cheating in the new era of tax evasion by those with substantial incomes.

The spread of tax cheating is a predictable outcome of the government's failure to direct audit resources where they are most needed, at the types of income most subject to manipulation and to underreporting. Business owners, investors and landlords are largely in control of what is reported to the government, unlike wage earners. That gives them opportunities to report less than their actual income, to charge part of their personal lifestyle to their business and to exaggerate business expenses. But instead of focusing on those with the most opportunities to cheat, the IRS continues to pour resources into the tax returns of wage earners, hunting for so-called detail cheating by people who overstate how much they put in the church collection plate or paid in property taxes.

The sharp drop in the number of revenue agents—who audit tax returns—has also encouraged cheats. The IRS had 16,600 auditors in 1988. By the year 2002 it was down to 11,500 auditors, a 30 percent decline. Over those years the number of individual income tax returns grew by almost half. The result of these two trends is that audit resources per tax return in 2002 were half what they had been in 1988.

The increasing sophistication of tax avoidance schemes requires much better auditors, too, as the tax evasion schemes of Enron revealed. Enron built tax shelters that simultaneously fabricated profits to fool shareholders and faked deductions to fool the IRS.

The tax shelters were intended to allow Enron to book $2 billion of profits almost immediately, even as the company was saving $2 billion of federal income taxes over a period of years, according to an exhaustive three-volume study by the Joint Committee on Taxation. The study showed that of the $3.3 billion in profits that Enron reported to shareholders between 1996 and its collapse at the end of 2001, more than a fifth were faked. The shelters allowed it to report profits to the IRS of just $76 million during those years. At the official 35 percent corporate income tax rate, Enron should have paid more than $1.1 billion in taxes on profits reported to shareholders. Instead it paid just $63 million—and two thirds of that was due to the corporate alternative minimum tax.

Enron's tax department "was converted into an Enron business unit, complete with annual revenue targets," said Lindy L. Paull, chief of the Joint Committee on Taxation staff, when releasing the report. The front page of one tax shelter deal, known as the Steele Project, was titled "Show Me the Money!"

Banks, accountants and lawyers raked in huge fees for schemes to fake profits and eliminate taxes. Bankers Trust, which is now owned by Deutsche Bank, was paid $40.2 million; the accounting firm of Deloitte & Touche was paid $16.3 million; Chase Manhattan Bank was paid $12.7 million. Akin, Gump, Strauss, Hauer & Feld, one of the most influential law firms in Washington, was paid a $1 million fee for an opinion letter that said one of three tax shelters it advised on would work.

"We would question the independence of the advisers" in all of these deals, Ms. Paull said in presenting the report to the Senate Finance Committee in February 2003. "We would say at a minimum that they turned a blind eye to some critical facts."

Significantly, Ms. Paull noted that the tax sheltering techniques of Enron were in many cases difficult to grasp even for the tax experts on her staff.

Any real reform of our tax system must address the virtually unlimited capacity of financial engineers to fabricate profits and losses, to hide them in layers of complex transactions and to withhold documents that would enable auditors to understand these transactions.

Technology could improve tax administration and help spot tax cheats, but there has been little success merging the IRS into a world of modern technology. The IRS has built at least nine major computer systems that do not communicate with each other. Solving the problem of just one taxpayer can require checking as many as 18 different electronic records. And the IRS continues to heavily rely on a crude statistical tool, the dif score, to select tax returns for audits. The tool is so weak, and the data on which it relies so out of date, that a third of audits result in no change to the tax return or a refund.

In 1998 the government gave an $8 billion contract to Computer Sciences Corporation in El Segundo, California, to develop modern technology for the IRS that would replace its Kennedy-era computers. But five years later less than $1 billion had been spent and the General Accounting Office, the investigative arm of Congress, had begun issuing reports that the project faced significant risks. Within the IRS, rumors flew that the new system, still years off, would not allow quick, sophisticated analyses to spot patterns of cheating because of compromises made to hold down costs.

The need not just for auditors, but for sophisticated and highly trained auditors is greater than ever and will continue to grow as the economy becomes more complex. There was a time, until about three decades ago, when IRS auditors were considered the cream of the federal workforce in terms of financial expertise. No more. Pay for auditors has fallen compared to other government jobs requiring similar skills so just hiring more auditors is not enough. The IRS needs to pay market rates and it needs money for training, for research and for investigative tools like databases of businesses and economic data. The same is true for IRS lawyers. Without sufficient brain power and talent, the IRS cannot effectively administer and police an ever more complex tax system in an ever more complex economy.

That complexity would become the friend of the tax cheat is not what voters were led to expect in 1994, when Newt Gingrich led the Republicans to control of the House with his "Contract with America." That election ended four decades of Democratic dominance. Gingrich and those who ran on the contract promised a fairer, simpler and less costly tax system. Early in 1995 Representative Bill Archer of Texas, the House Ways and Means Committee chairman, insisted that his party would deliver on that promise with total reform: "Our challenge is to do no less than pull the current income tax code out by its roots and throw it away so it can never grow back."

Instead, Archer and the rest of Congress started watering and fertilizing the tax code. They made 293 major changes in the next five years that added hundreds of pages to the tax code and required diverting auditors for more training to learn about the charges. Tax bills passed in the late nineties were thick with special interest provisions, favors for individuals and groups. For a spell there was even a rule requiring disclosure of these tax favors. All of the changes, many of which were inserted into bills in the dead of night with no hearing, created countless new opportunities for tax lawyers to fashion loopholes for the very rich.

But the blame does not lie just with the Republicans. They are simply the ones in charge in recent years. The Democrats are the ones who raised the maximum Social Security tax 13-fold and exempted salaries above $84,000 as of 2003. The Democrats enacted the costly idea of excess Social Security taxes today for a benefit by and by and then spent those tax dollars so the rich could have tax cuts. And the

Democrats let the alternative minimum tax morph from a backstop for rich and aggressive tax avoiders into a levy on the middle class. The Republicans have simply picked up on these strategies and expanded them as part of their focused drive to reduce tax revenues.

Comprehensive tax reform would require an immense amount of study to discern how changes would affect the economy and behavior. Several alternatives to our current tax system have been proposed, but none of them would simplify the tax system very much. And all would cause huge economic disruptions.

Consider just one problem in shifting from an income tax, for example, to a national retail sales tax. People would have a huge incentive to stock up on goods, from new cars to groceries, to avoid the new sales tax for as long as possible. The economy would experience a surge in demand for goods as the switchover date approached and then demand would collapse.

A retail sales tax would have to be set at 25 percent or more to equal revenue from the income tax. The tax would discourage people from making large purchases. Because such a tax applies only to what people consume, it would be regressive. That is, it would fall more heavily on people who have less income because they spend most or all of their money on sustaining life. It would also amount to double taxation for retirees who, under the income tax system, had saved money out of their after-tax incomes and would then spend the money under a national sales tax regime.

Those who think that a federal sales tax would eliminate the IRS have not thought carefully about how a sales tax would spawn a black market in goods. Almost inevitably this would lead to requirements to keep sales receipts to prove taxes had been paid on purchases. And there would be the problem of proving that those receipts were bona fide.

The most widely promoted reform has been the Steve Forbes plan for a flat tax, although the tax is far from flat. The flat tax is really a tax on what people consume, on the money they spend on groceries, clothes, vacations and the rest of their lifestyles. With the flat tax the mortgage interest deduction would disappear. So would deductions for charitable gifts. So that the poor would not be unfairly burdened, a base amount of income would be exempt from tax, perhaps $32,000 for a family of four. But because of this base, the actual tax rate would not be at all flat. If the rate was set at 20 percent, for example, someone earning the exempt amount would pay nothing and people earning twice that exempt amount would pay 10 percent of their income.

The Forbes flat tax would apply to wages, but not to income from capital: dividends, interest, rents, most royalties and capital gains. Corporate profits would be taxed, too. But dividends, interest and capital gains would flow untaxed to individuals. Corporations would be allowed to immediately expense all capital expenditures, such as for new factories and equipment, instead of deducting them over a period of years. The same would be true for landlords. If these expenditures were greater than profits, no tax would be due.

Under the Forbes flat tax, a landlord who owns many large buildings would get to deduct their entire value immediately. If his income is less than that value, then the unused deduction would be carried forward—and it would be adjusted for inflation. The result would be that people who have large amounts of real estate when the flat tax goes into effect could live the rest of their lives tax-free, so long as they spent less than the value of their assets on the day the flat tax took effect.

These little-understood features of the Forbes flat tax, as well as its history, go to a fundamental problem with getting off the income tax system: unintended consequences.

The flat tax championed by Forbes had its genesis in Senator George McGovern's failed 1972 campaign for president. McGovern proposed sending a check for $1,000 to every household, a plan that drew hoots of derision from many people, who saw it as a scheme to collect a tax and then return it, less government handling charges. But what he really was proposing was to move America to a consumption tax. That $1,000 was a rebate so that the poor would not be taxed too heavily.

While most Americans were ridiculing the McGovern plan, a young economist named Robert E. Hall was intrigued. Some time later, on a proverbial rainy day, he sat down with a pad of paper and a pen and in a few hours had worked out a way to achieve what McGovern seemed to want, a consumption tax, using income as its base. The idea was to tax wages, except for savings. Wages minus savings equals consumption was the formula. To eliminate the need for the government to write a check so that the poor were not unfairly burdened, Hall decided that a base amount of income would be exempt from tax. Hall reasoned that the plan would encourage savings because income from capital, that is from savings, would flow to individuals without being taxable to them. Hall recognized that even with a flat tax, there would have to be an IRS. He also realized that there would have to be special rules for banks and other financial institutions so that interest payments and charges could not be manipulated to hide taxable income. There would also have to be rules on salaries so that owners and executives could not disguise taxable wages as tax-free dividends, interest or capital gains.

Satisfied with his academic exercise, Hall filed the papers away. Several years later, after he had joined the Hoover Institution at Stanford University, Hall attended a luncheon. He found himself sitting across from Alvin Rabushka, a colleague who was thrilled that California voters had just passed Proposition 13, which slashed property taxes and transferred power from local governments to the state capital. That vote marked the beginning of the tax revolt that is still playing out in American politics today.

Rabushka told Hall he just wished he could find some way to move the country onto a tax based not on what people earned but on what they consumed.

"I've already figured that out," Hall said.

Rabushka became enthused with the prospects. Soon he began developing the ideas Hall had written down, culminating in their 1985 book *The Flat Tax,* the second edition of which became the platform of the Forbes presidential campaigns. It exempted from tax a basic amount of income and taxed only amounts above that which people spent. Every dollar that flowed into savings would go there untaxed and every nickel of interest, dividends and capital gains on that savings would be untaxed, too. A family of four that spent the amount that Forbes would have excluded from tax, about $32,000 in 2000, would pay no tax regardless of whether their income was that amount or $1 million.

In the 1996 presidential campaign, *The New York Times* recalculated the tax returns of President Clinton and Republican challengers

Bob Dole, Phil Gramm and Lamar Alexander using the Hall–Rabushka flat tax and compared the results to what they actually paid in 1994. All four candidates would have paid less, as much as 40 percent less. Forbes declined to make his tax return available, though he said he would if elected. Given his wealth, Forbes's personal tax bill surely would have fallen much more than those of the other candidates. The picture was not so bright for the Smiths, a hypothetical family of four used by the Tax Foundation in its analyses of the various flat-tax plans floating around Washington. The Smiths, who have $50,000 in total income, nearly all from wages, would have seen no change in their individual tax bill if the Hall–Rabushka proposal were put into effect.

While it would slash taxes for those with high incomes, the most significant aspect of a flat tax is that it would reward savers and tax spenders. People who made their old car last or who wore clothes until they wore out would pay little in tax, while those who traded in for a new model every few years and bought the latest fashions would pay taxes. Whatever we tax we will get less of and so a tax on consumption would mean that we would have less consumption. That may be good for the environment, but it surely would not be for those whose jobs depend on consumption.

If large numbers of people did what economic theory says under a Forbes flat tax, then we would have more savings. Over time the country would soon have a much larger store of capital to invest for future economic growth. The rates of return one could earn by putting that capital to work would fall, however, as capital became increasingly abundant. And as Japan has found after years of economic doldrums, a high savings rate does not always mean economic growth.

For Hall, the idea was never for a single tax rate. Rabushka, he said, just talked him into that. Hall, who chairs the committee of economists who decide when recessions have begun and ended, said the idea he has championed could include a progressive tax rate structure— meaning the more people made, the higher the rate of tax on their income. Multiple rates do not add much complexity, Hall said. Even with five rates, the flat tax return could still fit on a postcard.

So a flat tax would neither eliminate the IRS nor simplify the definition of what is income for tax purposes. What the flat tax would certainly do, even with a progressive rate structure, is reward those who are already rich with assets, people who could live the rest of their lives without paying taxes.

As the problems posed by a retail sales tax and a flat tax show, fundamental reform is not simple. And it will remain elusive so long as Congress avoids the serious, and mundane, issues of how tax administration works, puts the willfully uninformed like Representative Houghton in charge of IRS oversight and shrivels the budget for tax law enforcement while handcuffing the tax police.

While reform has yet to be taken seriously in Washington, that can change. Complex, remote and foreboding as our tax system is often made to seem, it is within our power to get a system that is fair and serves the common good. With some effort we can have fundamental reform. We can make our tax system work for us. But we have to demand that reform and we have to focus on the principles that would make a tax system fair, efficient and effective.

Conclusions

In public policy, it matters less who has the best arguments and more who gets heard—and by whom.

—Ralph Reed, former executive director of the Christian Coalition, in a 2000 letter seeking a $380,000 fee to help Enron win profitable favors from Washington

To be successful, to sustain a society and its government, a tax system must flow from the economic order. In an agrarian culture the king could demand part of the harvest, in a pirate society part of the booty.

Our tax system was designed in a bygone era. It worked reasonably well for a national, industrial, wage-based economy. Today, however, we are moving to a global, services, asset economy in which capital flows freely across borders while workers cannot. Our tax system needs more than tinkering; it needs overhaul.

The economic changes remaking our world are affecting all of us from the blue-collar workers whose wages have been falling for the past three decades to the investment bankers whose incomes have soared along with their clients' assets. The response of our elected leaders has been to adjust the tax system to shift tax burdens onto those with good incomes and little political power.

The clear trend in America for the past two decades has been to cut taxes on the rich and to raise taxes on those in the middle class and the upper middle class to make up part of the difference. This was done largely by collecting excess Social Security taxes decades in advance of when benefits would be paid. This trend is growing as the alternative minimum tax hits middle-class families.

Warren Buffett says that on his last dollar of income he pays a lower marginal tax rate that his secretary. He is right. If his last dollar of income is a dividend or capital gain, he pays just 15 cents in income taxes. His secretary pays 15.3 cents in Social Security and Medicare taxes when both the part deducted from her paycheck and the share paid by her employer are counted. And if she is in the 25 percent income tax bracket, then the combination of income, Social Security and Medicare taxes takes from her last dollar of income more than 40 cents.

For three fouths of Americans the Social Security tax is a bigger levy than the income tax. Those excess Social Security taxes rob many of their capacity to save, while tax cuts for the rich expand that group's capacity to save. A tax rate structure that falls too heavily on most Americans and lets the most prosperous save more means that over time the already huge gap in wealth will widen even more.

The income tax is collected only against reported income—and therein lies the real issue about our tax system. The rich have myriad ways to avoid recognizing income for tax purposes, most of them perfectly legal. For those who are daring, the past decade has been a period of lax tax law enforcement in which tax evasion was openly advertised. A few people were caught, but the vast majority of cheats are richer today for their crimes. Congress needs to stop finding ways to let people avoid reporting income and to shift to a system that requires income recognition sooner, not later, and requires that taxes be paid immediatley.

There is much talk these days about our income tax as a socialist redistribution scheme. That is indeed what it has become. But the scheme is not to take from the rich and give to the poor, deserving or not, as the courtesans of wealth in Washington would have us believe when they pontificate on the Sunday morning talk shows.

Rather, as Orwell taught us, ours is like all systems in which some animals are more equal than others—it is the pigs who grow economically fat off the tax system.

We have systematically taken away the ability of most Americans to save by taxing them too heavily, and we have expanded the capacity of those with the most to save even more by lowering their taxes.

The tax system today is not promoting prosperity based on individual enterprise and thriftiness. It is instead working, as all socialist redistribution schemes do, to enrich and benefit those who have access to the levers of power. In America that is the political donor class.

Our tax system is a good part of the reason that the incomes of the richest 1 percent, and especially the top-earning 13,400 American families, have soared while the bottom 80 percent of Americans have seen their incomes stagnate for three decades. That most families now need two incomes shows how our tax system is robbing us and our children so that the already deep pockets of the few may be stuffed even more.

There is a fable of a village in wine country where each fall, after the grapes have been crushed and the vintage bottled, a bacchanal is held. Each vintner climbs a ladder in the town square and pours into a common cask a jug of his wine. One year the last vintner making the climb had fallen on hard times. The weather had not been kind to his grapes and he felt pinched. He decided that no one would notice if he thinned the wine with a jug of water. When he came down from the ladder, everyone applauded and the mayor swung a mallet to knock the cork from the base of the cask, out of which flowed clear water.

The moral is that when one person cheats, no one but the cheat notices. But when everyone cheats, there is no party for anyone.

Our society cannot remain healthy, with a robust middle class that provides economic and politcal stability, if we continue to rob average Americans of time and the opportunity to save so that those with five mansions can own seven, and those with one corporate jet can afford two. In the long run this trend will promote political instability. In time many people will question the value of democratic society if they conclude that its rules do not reward those who work hard and play by those rules.

In the short run those at the very top can benefit from our unfair system, reaping quick rewards and paying little in taxes. But in the long run even they will be losers because their undermining of economic growth and social stability will ultimately reduce the value of their investments.

We need to ask ourselves if adding to the gross national product is the only, or even the primary, measure of our society? If a tax cut would add one more percentage point to economic growth, but come at a cost of a 1 percent increase in the crime rate, would it be worth it? If a tax increase slowed economic growth today, but financed a college education for every student with top grades, would it be worth it?

We live in a society today in which the richest of us enjoy immense benefits from our tax system and the least among us, both the poor and our children, pay a high price.

Since the rich pay most of the income taxes, how can it be said that the tax system benefits them? Are they not the ones who bear a disproportionate share of the burden of taxes? They are, but that is not the only way to look at the issue of tax burdens.

One of the basic principles of economics is known as the marginal utility of money. To someone without enough to eat, an extra dollar can mean life itself, while to someone with a million-dollar income, one dollar more would not even be noticed. It is this concept of marginal utility that explains why even Robert Hall, the co-author of *The Flat Tax,* favors graduated tax rates that fall most heavily on high incomes.

The most important measure of tax burden is how many pennies out of each dollar go to taxes. The top 400 taxpayers in 2000 had an average income of $174 million, yet they paid just 22 cents on the dollar in federal income taxes. That is what a single person making in the low six figures paid. Had the 2003 tax cuts been in effect, the top 400 would have paid just 17.5 cents on the dollar, not much more than the overall national average of 15.3 cents that Americans actually paid that year.

During Clinton's tenure as president, the share of income going to the top 400 more than doubled, from a half of 1 percent to 1.1 percent of all income. But the portion of income going to federal income taxes fell by 16 percent for the top 400, while rising for everyone else by 18 percent. Clearly, favoritism for the rich is bipartisan.

The rich get a fabulous deal from our tax system because it enables them to save and invest on a grand scale, as Warren Buffett's comparison of himself and his secretary shows. While the majority of Americans are having their capacity to save taxed away, the rich are enjoying far lower tax rates on their investment incomes.

When taxes are examined overall—including state and local income, sales and property taxes—America has something close to a flat tax. The top fifth of Americans pays just a penny more out of a dollar in taxes overall than the poorest fifth, 19 cents versus 18 cents.

The unfairness of the poorest Americans facing a tax burden almost equal to that of those who are far better off has begun to sink in with some Americans who have long been in the thrall of the political donor class. As a congressman, Bob Riley of Alabama never met a tax cut for the rich he did not embrace. He actively modeled himself after the great tax cutter Ronald Reagan. But as governor of Alabama in 2003, Riley sought fundamental reform of a system that he said wrongly burdened the poor. Alabamans who earn less than $13,000 pay almost 11 percent of their incomes in state and local taxes, while those making more than $229,000 pay just 4 percent.

The most powerful interests in Alabama soon came out against Governor Riley's plan, which would raise their taxes while lowering those on the poor. He fought back, saying that as a Christian he believes government has an obligation to help the poor, not exploit them. "If the New Testament teaches me anything, it teaches me not only to love thy neighbor but also to help those who are the least among us," Governor Riley said. "Having a regressive tax structure is one thing. But when it starts at $4,600 for a family of four, that's immoral."

That a man with Riley's track record on taxes is leading the charge for reform in Alabama shows that the system has become so unreasonable that there is hope for reform. That the poor wanted to vote down the plan shows how misinformation helps the rich.

So what to do? Edmund Burke, the founder of the modern conservative movement, wrote more than two centuries ago that "the revenue of the state is the state." Do we shrink our government, cutting even more spending on public education, stunting the development of new human capital? Or do we cut spending on research and development, as executives like Jack Welch did to boost short-term gains at the expense of long-term growth?

The fact is that no modern president has left office with a smaller government than when he was sworn in. By nature all presidents are big spenders. "Smaller government" is a nice slogan, but, absent real political will, it is also a fantasy. Yet tax money, if invested in building our society, can pay huge rewards, as the GI Bill showed when we made a college education a paying proposition for millions who otherwise would never have studied beyond high school.

To begin we need to understand the path we are on and where it will take us. Implicit in the 1997 tax cut signed by President Clinton and the 2001 and 2003 Bush tax cuts is a decision to reduce taxes on capital and eventually eliminate them. Repeal of the estate tax is now scheduled for the single year of 2010, but President Bush has said he wants to end it now and forever. Taxes on dividends and most capital gains have been cut to 15 percent, a boon to the top 1 percent, who own half the nation's financial assets.

In effect these changes are moving us toward the underlying idea in the flat tax advocated by Steve Forbes, toward a tax on consumption income and a shift in tax burdens onto wages.

But instead of going at this sideways and by sleight of hand as Congress has done, we should have a serious debate about consumption taxes: Should we stop taxing capital? Should we tax only labor income—wages and salaries? Should we tax corporate profits? And how would changing our tax system affect our society?

In a vacuum it is easy to make the case for not taxing capital. The idea that a dollar out of wages that have been taxed should earn nickels of interest free of tax has an appeal. Surely exempting dividends, interest, rents and royalties from taxes would encourage more saving and investment. But as we have seen, the biggest fortune in America began with a tax-free gift. And the income tax is full of holes through which those who can afford sophisticated advice make fortunes off the tax system. Rather than being a double or triple tax, the estate tax is, for a significant portion of capital, the first and only tax.

Most people do not have capital. But under a system where capital gets favored treatment, savings are sure to rise no matter how hard the income tax falls on labor. Classic economic theory says that as more people save more money, returns to capital must fall. That is, as the supply of capital grows, the demand for it will be relatively less. Likewise, people will spend less on everything from furniture to vacations if we tax consumption. As the Japanese have learned by hard experience, a thrifty society can save far more than it can profitably invest. Who wants to be a capitalist in a world of 1 percent returns?

What is in short supply in America today is not capital, but income—at least for the half of Americans getting by on less than $28,000 per year—and educated minds. But our tax policy is aimed at more capital in the hands of the few, not at higher incomes for most so that they can acquire more assets as a cushion against economic storms, live better lives and spend more time molding their children into productive members of society.

Taxing consumption would have a broad social impact. To most people, money is a stream of income, not a pool of assets. From an allowance in childhood, to a stipend in school, to a paycheck from work, to a pension and Social Security in old age, money flows in a stream throughout the course of a person's life. In a tax system in which streams get taxed and pools do not, the political impact over time is likely to be profound. And either the Forbes plan or the trend now under way in Washington is leading us toward a world in which wages are taxed while individuals with capital incomes will not directly pay taxes.

There is a good chance that continuing down this path will move us toward a government more like those of Germany and Norway, which provide extensive social services. The Norwegians even get winter vacations in sunny climes for those depressed by too many weeks of gray skies. If people look around and see that they are being taxed on their labor while those who started out with capital are not, then they are likely to demand more direct benefits for their taxes. The hidden European roots of the flat tax idea could flower into European-style social policies in America.

If we were to adopt a policy that the earnings from saved dollars are free of tax, then we would need to close all loopholes in the income tax. Right now about half of all dollars of income are not taxed in any given year.

One simple basic reform would be to end all deferrals of income except into accounts like the 401(k) with modest limits. There is no reason for Congress to let executives like Goizueta defer for years paying taxes on their incomes through the artifice of leaving the funds on deposit with their employer. As President Bush said after the Enron scandals, "What's fair on the top floor should be fair on the shop floor." By law only highly paid workers can defer. Such deferrals violate a basic principle of tax administration: matching income to tax payments. Income deferred is less likely to be taxed. Indeed, many promoters are now selling plans that convert executive deferred compensation into life insurance, which means that the deferred income is never taxed.

Executives should be allowed to leave as much money as they want on deposit with their employers, but only after they have paid their taxes on the money just like those on the shop floor must.

A world in which people only paid taxes on their wage income would also require tough rules to make sure that taxable salaries were not paid out in the guise of untaxed capital gains. The 1998 tax return of President Bush is instructive on this point. He reported income of $18.4 million that year, of which $15 million was a gain from his interest in the Texas Rangers baseball team. Based on his investment he was entitled to a $2.2 million gain, but because of his performance as a team executive he was rewarded with an inflated return on his investment. Because his pay for his labor was reported as capital income, it was taxed at the 20 percent rate for capital gains instead of the 39.6 percent rate that year for salaries, saving him nearly $3 million in taxes. A principled consumption tax system would not allow such perfectly legal tricks.

In a consumption tax system, the nickels of interest on saved dollars flow to you free of tax. That raises another question—what happens when you die? Should your son or daughter then get that dollar and continue to receive the income from the dollar you saved without paying taxes? Or in a system where capital is not taxed, should we count that dollar as income to your son or daughter? Do we want an inherited aristocracy of wealth? Or a meritocracy of strivers? Do we want a society where people create new fortunes through their enterprise or a society of people who owe their wealth to what Donald Trump calls the lucky sperm club?

Whatever we decide to tax, there are basic, and very dire, needs for reform of our tax system.

The most overwhelming need is to simplify the tax code. Understandably, our tax code is complex in part because our economy is complex. But complexity also benefits the rich, the well advised and the well connected. Much of the complexity is because of congressional favors for the political donor class, whose access to power benefits them at the expense of those who cannot afford to buy a steady stream of campaign contributions to ensure that their senator or representative takes their calls. These favors add to the tangle of fine details that brilliant minds like Jonathan Blattmachr's weave into legal threads that can be twisted into loopholes for their rich clients.

Congress, in a fairer America, would stop the routine practice of inserting favors into tax bills without public hearing and without accountability. Taxpayers would come out far ahead if every tax bill had to be the subject of open debate with the names of sponsors attached to each change. Transparency is good for taxpayers overall, bad for the favored few.

Most complexity deals with efforts to delay the recognition of income for tax purposes. While this or that industry may benefit from deferral, a cleaner system would simply end all deferrals except for the very limited amounts in retirement savings plans and pension funds.

Congress should stop requiring corporations to keep two sets of books, one for shareholders and the other for the IRS. Whatever a corporation tells its shareholders is its profit should be the figure on which it is taxed; it should be a clear disclosure. When corporations complain of all the complexity in the tax code and pose for pictures with tax returns as tall as the company's chief tax executive, what they do not say is that those piles of paper save them money. So valuable are the tax savings in all that paperwork that in some years the old Chrysler Corporation made more from the work that went into its tax returns than from manufacturing Plymouths.

To those who would argue that shareholder accounting and tax accounting serve different purposes, the question to ask is why.

Does all of the complexity added by letting companies report less to the government than to shareholders really add a benefit to society? And is it worth the enormous cost? If Congress wants to stimulate the economy through a special tax break for corporations, then it should specify it as a line item and require it to be broken out in reports to shareholders. Over the life cycle of a company, if shareholder accounting is a valid measure, then the government will get its proper share of taxes if the company uses the same set of books for shareholders and the IRS.

It is also unfair that some industries, especially manufacturing concerns, pay heavy taxes, and others, like the Silicon Valley industries, pay little. When it comes to collecting taxes, Congress should not care if a firm makes computer chips or potato chips, only how much profit is earned from chip making. Requiring companies to pay taxes on their profits as reported to shareholders and eliminating all of the special-interest favors in the tax code would result in major efficiencies. It would also be fought by those companies and industries the tax law favors, but at least they would be in a position of having to defend special treatment.

Congress should also debate the taxing of multinational companies, which now save huge amounts because of the foreign tax credit system and the ability to park assets like patents overseas. Global companies should not be favored over purely domestic enterprises. And tricks that turn profits into deductions—tricks that favor multinationals over domestics—should not be allowed. Companies that acquire a Bermuda mailbox should be barred from government business and they should be required to pay taxes on the capital gains on the company's books, not on the gains shareholders have in their stock. Treating unexercised executive stock options as taxable, in this one case, would also discourage such moves.

One exception to this rule of requiring that taxes be paid on profits as reported to shareholders could also promote economic growth. Congress should consider allowing each American a one-time opportunity to start a business and pay no taxes on profits for the first two or three years. Few businesses turn a profit immediately so the revenue effect would be small. A one-time rule is needed because many entrepreneurs open a new business for each new venture and then close it, a tactic common to Hollywood producers and to authors, among others. But such a rule might encourage more people to assume the risks of starting their own business, with long-term economic benefits.

The state legislatures and Congress should also eliminate the limited liability partnership form for lawyers and accountants because its very nature breathes misconduct into the system and drives out self-policing. As Mark W. Everson, who became IRS commissioner in 2003, said soon after he assumed his office, "There are clear indications that professional standards have eroded in some comers of the practitioner community. Attorneys and accountants should be pillars of our system of taxation, not the architects of its circumvention."

To those in the corporate professions who will say that the old structure leaves them exposed to unlimited liability, there are three an-swers. First, society functioned well for decades under the old system and some big firms retain it. Second, those who insist on the highest standards of ethical behavior by their partners have nothing to worry about. Third, Congress can cap liability at a reasonable level. With a cap, obtaining insurance for liability would be largely a matter of mar-ket economics, not special interest protection that benefits most those whose conduct is least deserving of protection.

Congress also needs to address the alternative minimum tax. It is outrageous that a family of five making $70,000 should lose part of the standard deduction because of a law that was intended to go after the rich who aggressively use deductions to pay no taxes. The temporary fixes by Congress to address this problem illustrate the need for funda-mental reform, not patchwork repairs. That Congress eliminated this tax for small businesses with revenues of up to $5 million, but not for individuals for whom it is inappropriate, shows the degree to which lawmakers in Washington care about contributors, not constituents. That someone taking only the standard deduction can be hit with this tax shows that fact is stranger than fiction. Fundamentally, that a tax designed to catch aggressive rich tax avoiders is being applied to middle-class families to finance tax cuts for the super rich shows how both parties in Washington have become two wings of the same party. The party of money.

Absent a complete overhaul of the tax code—a white-paper approach—it is crucial that the alternative minimum tax be dealt with through reform, not repeal. As Jonathan Blattmachr has observed, a host of new loopholes would emerge following repeal. Simply remov-ing individuals, dependents and state and local taxes from the list of items in the alternative tax would remove nearly all of the middle class and upper middle class from this levy.

Then there is the IRS itself.

The IRS's focus on cheating by people who file tax returns, look-ing primarily for inflated deductions, is a trivial pursuit when vast sums of untaxed money circulate elsewhere unnoticed. While the IRS could bring the full weight of its powers to bear on Maritza Reyes, the cleaning woman in East Los Angeles who makes $7,000 per year, it never even noticed two billionaires in New York, the art dealer Alec

Wildenstein and his wife Jocelyn, dubbed "tiger woman" for how multiple plastic surgeries changed her appearance. For three decades the couple lived in a Manhattan mansion, enjoyed a 66,000-acre family ranch in Kenya and bought and sold billions of dollars worth of fine art, and yet they never filed a tax return. No criminal charges were filed and Alec insists that he lived primarily from gifts from his father.

Congress should also restore the law that made it public record whether individuals have filed their tax returns and paid the tax that they said they owed. (In the twenties the amount of income and the tax paid were also public record, and when people like Julius Rosenwald of Sears and Roebuck filed their returns, both their incomes and their tax bills were reported in the newspapers.) Paying generous rewards to people who alert the IRS to those who do not file tax returns would be an efficient way to find many cheats. The IRS has been incredibly stingy with rewards, paying only about 11 percent of claims, which may explain why so few bother. To those who call this a tattletale system, there is a simple answer: failing to pay taxes is a crime. The police pay informants all the time.

Likewise, it is an affront to honest taxpayers that one, let alone most, of the clients of John Mathewson's Cayman Islands bank got away without paying. That they did not all become audit targets after the bank closed, to determine if their cheating continued in new ways, is the kind of real issue Congress should have investigated.

Congress needs to unshackle the tax police. It should order them to aggressively pursue people who do not pay any taxes or pay on only a slice of their income. Comparing incomes to zip codes, buying lists of newly formed businesses and otherwise making sure no one can get away without filing a tax return would be both fair and lucrative. The IRS also must be told to immediately pounce on those who promote tax evasion. Only after a steady stream of articles detailing their failure to act, did the IRS and the Department of Justice begin to move against a few of the thousands of businesspeople who for years did not file tax returns and bragged about it in full-page ads in USA Today.

To protect taxpayers from zealous IRS agents, Congress should impose a rule that if a taxpayer is found after audit to owe no taxes or to be due a refund, she would also get a payment from the government, say $100, for her trouble if her tax return was flawless, and a

10 percent bonus on any additional refund. Taxpayers found to have shorted the government as little as $1 would not be eligible.

Finally, we must look to ourselves.

We will always have taxes. Under our Constitution our tax system can be just about whatever we want it to be. We can tax incomes or consumption, the fuel for our cars or the water we drink. We can tax wealth. We can even tax poverty.

We can go on allowing our tax system to further enrich the few and take a heavy toll on the many, undercutting almost everyone's long-term prosperity. To continue this way will discourage merit and perhaps, in the long run, endanger the ideal of self-determination on which our Constitution rests.

Or we could remake our tax system so that it helps us fulfill the premise of our Constitution, to "form a more perfect union, establish justice, insure domestic tranquility, provide for the common defense, promote the general welfare and secure the blessings of liberty to ourselves and our posterity."

Rather than hiding our heads in the sand because taxes are complex and unpleasant, we need to recognize our power and responsibility as a free and democratic people to solve our own problems. We need to exercise our right to vote.

Talk about taxes and our government. Talk to your family, your coworkers, your neighbors. If enough of us start talking seriously about the issue, and listening as well, the hubbub will percolate up through the system and counter some of the access to politicians that the political donor class buys with its contributions.

And don't cheat on your taxes. Don't even chisel. It will hurt. It will also strengthen your resolve to demand change and to get others interested and involved. A great chorus is created from many individuals. So is a great silence.

Time invested in serious examination of our tax system, in a debate that engages you, me and everyone else, can pay us huge rewards. It is by our actions, or inactions, that we create our own future. We can go on with what we have and pay a heavy price in lost opportunity. Or we can speak up one by one until we are heard. Ultimately, we can create a tax system that actually promotes long-term prosperity.

Reform begins with you.

Notes

Page

11   **Add to this reductions:** Author interviews with Edward N. Wolff, New York University economist; see also *Top Heavy: The Increasing Inequality of Wealth in America and What Can Be Done About It,* by Edward N. Wolff (New York: The New Press, 1995).

11   **This does not mean:** Tax Foundation Special Report No. 118, www.taxfoundation.org.

11   **If you tally.** "Doubling Up of Taxation Isn't Limited to Dividends," Daniel Altman, *New York Times,* January 21, 2003, citing Department of Labor Consumer Expenditure Survey.

11   **In the years ahead:** See studies at www.taxpolicycenter.org.

12   **Corporations, for example:** Computed by author from IRS Statistics of Income, www.irs.gov.taxstats.

17   **To pay for World War I:** *The Great Tax Wars* by Steven R. Weisman (New York: Simon & Schuster, 2002), p. 322.

20   **As the experts predicted:** Data on incomes, productivity, housing, television sets, food and clothing are from Statistical Abstract of the United States: 2002; car sales from Mercedes–Benz USA.

21   **In 2000, for each dollar of tax:** Computed by the author from IRS Statistics of Income; see also "The Divine Write-Off," by David Cay Johnston, *New York Times,* January 12, 1996.

23   **This was also an era of rising debt:** Computed by Jarrett Murphy from Federal Reserve Consumer Credit reports at www.federalreserve.gov/releases.

24   **Furthermore, in contrast:** Income data from charts and text in *The State of Working America 2002/2003* by Lawrence Mishel, Jared Bernstein and Heather Boushey (Ithaca, N.Y.: Cornell University Press, 2003).

Page

25   **The growing numbers on paychecks:** From the National
Bureau of Economic Research working paper #8467; updated
charts available from Emmanuel Saez at emlab.berkeley.edu/
users/saez.

29   **It will be several years:** Job loss data from the Bureau of Labor
Statistics Current Employment Statistics Survey at www.bls.gov/
ces.

30   **In 1977, the richest:** Analysis of the Congressional Budget Office data from "The Widening Income Gulf," Center for Budget
and Policy Priorities by Isaac Shapiro and Robert Greenstein,
available at www.cbpp.org/9-4-99tax.htm.

30   **Between 1973 and 2001:** From data at www.census.gov/hhes/
www/income.html.

32   **Thomas Piketty and Emmanuel Saez:** NBER working paper #8467 available at the Saez Web site.

39   **Applying the National Bureau:** Author computations from
Piketty & Saez.

40   **Internal Revenue Service reports show:** Author computations from IRS Statistics of Income; see also "Tax Inquiries Fall
as Cheating Increases," by David Cay Johnston, *New York Times,*
April 14, 2003.

43   **The advantages that:** U.S. Department of Commerce, Bureau
of the Census, Current Population Survey (CPS), November
2000 Voting and Registration Supplement at nces.ed.gov.

45   **In March 1992:** On Goizueta, other executives and their pay
see "Rushing Away from Taxes: Executives Who Earn Now, Pay
Later," by Christopher Drew and David Cay Johnston, *New York
Times,* October 13, 1996; also Coca-Cola Proxy statements 1977
through 1992; "The World's Biggest Brand," by John Huey, *Fortune,* May 31, 1996.

46   **Looked at in the way:** See Piketty and Saez.

55   **As critical as he was:** "Tying Pay Closer to Corporate Performance," by Graef S. Crystal, *Pensions & Investments,* April 27, 1992.

59   **Just as the real value:** "Harvard Editor Faces Revolt over
Welch Story," by James Bandler, *Wall Street Journal,* March 4, 2002,
and subsequent news articles.

Page

60   **Jack Welch left GE** "G.E. Expenses for Ex-Chief Cited in Fil-
      ing," by Geraldine Fabrikant, *New York Times,* September 6,
      2002; details on jet costs from "Cheap Seats on Jet for Executives
      on Vacation," by David Cay Johnston and Geraldine Fabrikant,
      New York Times, September 12, 2002.

62   **Abuses of corporate jets abound:** See "The Imperial Agees,"
      by Richard L. Stern and Reed Abelson, *Forbes,* June 8, 1992; "A
      Celebrity Boss Faces Exile from 2d Corporate Kingdom," by Di-
      ann B. Henriques, *New York Times,* February 10, 1995; "Rush-
      ing" Part 2 by Diann B. Henriques and David Cay Johnston,
      New York Times, October 14, 2002; "The Enron Jet Set,"
      Guardian (London), November 4, 2002; and others.

63   **Robert Packwood:** Congressional Record—Senate, Vol. 131,
      No. 41, April 3, 1985 (debate on February 18, 1985).

71   **"To keep farms in the family . . .":** "Talk of Lost Farms Re-
      flects Muddle of Estate Tax Debate," by David Cay Johnston,
      New York Times, April 8, 2001.

73   **That the White House and the Farm Bureau:** IRS Statistics
      of Income.

74   **A few days after the news hit:** *Wealth and Our Commonwealth*
      by William H. Gates Sr. and Chuck Collins (Boston: Beacon
      Press, 2002), p. 68.

75   **Michael Graetz:** *The Decline (and Fall?) of the Income Tax* by
      Michael J. Graetz, (New York: W. W. Norton, 1997).

76   **The year before all of this:** "Remarks by the President on
      Veto of Death Tax Elimination Act of 2000," White House Press
      Release, August 31, 2000.

76   **A Gallup Poll found:** June 22–25, 2000.

77   **Trying to head off a stampede:** News release from Repre-
      sentative Charles B. Rangel, May 25, 2000, cited in *Tax Notes,*
      May 25, 2000, Document # 2000–14995.

79   **Soldano owns:** Interview with the author February 14, 2001
      and www.cymricfamilyoffice.com.

80   **She also hired Frank Luntz:** Interviewed by Stephanie
      Mencimer, December 6, 2002.

Page

81   **The term *death tax*:** *Today* show, February 5, 2001; *NBC Nightly News,* February 14, 2001; on *The Nightly News* of March 8 and March 29, 2001, Gregory did say "estate or death tax."

82   **Another way to encourage repeal has been to raise dubious claims:** www.center4studytax.com.

82   **Charles Davenport and Jay Soled:** *Tax Notes,* July 26, 1999; see also "Study Contradicts Foes of Estate Tax," by David Cay Johnston, *New York Times,* July 25, 1999.

84   **Gates Sr. had:** CNBC Capitol Report, June 18, 2003. Gates Sr. responded to one question by saying "it's a little strange to suggest that I hate rich people"; another with "that's pure hogwash," said that the real issue is "not the politics of envy; it's the politics of equity."

84   **Repealing the estate tax, Buffett said:** "Dozens of Rich Americans Join in Fight to Retain the Estate Tax," by David Cay Johnston, *New York Times,* February 14, 2001.

86   **Here is how:** Interviews with Blattmachr, January 2001.

88   **In working to kill the estate tax:** Interviewed by the author February 13, 2001, and later.

89   **Owning a business:** "Side Deal Complicates P-I, Times JOA Fight," by Bill Richards, *Seattle Times,* May 28, 2003.

90   **John Buckley:** "JCT Estimates Widespread Evasion with Estate Tax Repeal" by Martin A. Sullivan, *Tax Notes,* March 30, 2001.

92   **Promises of tax cuts are sweet music:** Interviewed by Kate Berry, January 8, 2003.

93   **While the White House said:** "51 Million Taxpayers Won't Get Full Rebates from Tax Bill," Citizens for Tax Justice, June 1, 2001, www.ctj.org/html/rebate01.htm.

94   **When the Bush tax cuts of 2001, 2002 and 2003:** "The AMT Projections and Problems" by Leonard E. Burman, William G. Gale and Jeffrey Rohaly, *Tax Notes,* July 7, 2003.

95   **In 1995 about 414,000 taxpayers:** "EGTRRA Will Subject 'Startling' Number of Taxpayers to AMT by 2010," *Tax Notes,* November 19, 2001, as well as Burman et al. above and other studies at www.taxpolicycenter.org.

Page

97 **The alternative minimum tax is also a nasty surprise:** *Hukkanen-Campbell* v. *Commissioner,* Tax Court Memo 2000–180; Case 00–9030 Tenth Circuit Court of Appeals, 274 F. 3d 1312, filed December 19, 2001.

98 **The alternative tax is also morphing:** *Charles C. Allen III and Barbara N. Allen et al.* v. *Commissoner,* Cases 1287–00 through 1293–00, 118 T.C. 1.

100 **Joseph W. Barr, who was Johnson's:** Graetz's decline (and fall?) tells of the huge volume of mail.

102 **Eugene Steuerle:** Numerous author interviews with Steuerle.

105 **One of the first families to feel the sting:** *David R. and Margaret J. Klaassen* v. *Commissioner,* Tax Court Memo 1998–241; "Funny, They Don't Look Like Fat Cats," by David Cay Johnston, *New York Times,* January 10, 1999.

108 **When the 1997 tax cut law:** "Tax Analysts See Big Gains for Top 1% of Taxpayers," by David Cay Johnston, *New York Times,* May 19, 2001.

117 **Delaying a tax for three decades:** "Tax Shelter Is Worrying Sprint's Chief," by David Cay Johnston and Jonathan D. Glater, *New York Times,* February 6, 2003; the story broke in "Sprint Forced Out Officials Amid Questionable Tax Shelter" by Rebecca Blumenstein, Joann S. Lublin, Shawn Young, Ken Brown and Cassell Bryan-Low, *Wall Street Journal,* February 5, 2003.

118 **From 1984 to 2002 the government collected $1. 7 trillion more:** 2002 Report of the Trustees, Social Security Program, www.ssa.gov.

121 **For the Reagan White House:** "Television News Angers Reagan" by Allen Cromley, *Daily Oklahoman,* March 17, 1982.

122 **Former Representative Andy Jacobs:** PBS *NewsHour,* August 22, 2001.

123 **The extra Social Security taxes:** Computed by Jarrett Murphy from National Income and Product Accounts, Bureau of Economic Analysis, Commerce Department; in 1983 through 1986 taxes other than Social Security and Medicare totaled less than half of federal spending;

Page

126 **Fear that the excess Social Security taxes:** "Governor Bush's Prepared Remarks on Social Security," Political Transcripts by Federal Document Clearinghouse, May 15, 2000.

126 **By then *The Wall Street Journal:*** "Bush Offers $2.13 Trillion Budget, Launching Era of Deficit Spending," by John D. McKinnon and Shailagh Murray, *Wall Street Journal,* February 5, 2002.

127 **Just 12 days after Bush signed his tax cut bill:** "O'Neill Faults 'No Assets' Social Security" by Glenn Kessler, *Washington Post,* June 19, 2001.

131 **After Reagan left office:** Senator Nickles remarks at Senate Governmental Affairs Committee hearing, unofficial transcript in *Tax Notes,* April 5, 1995.

136 **Representative Anne M. Northup:** "Readers' Forum: Rep. North Takes Issue with Hawpe's Column," *Louisville Courier-Journal,* April 28, 2002.

137 **Gregory Mueller:** Letter to the author and follow-up interviews.

138 **The rules for this credit:** Corporate negligence penalties from IRS Databook 2002, Table 26.

139 **Just such an error:** "A Mistake Prevails, as Certainly as Death and Taxes" by David E. Rosenbaum, *New York Times,* June 24, 1998.

140 **Democrats disputed:** Buckley interview with the author.

140 **In the spring of 2003:** "IRS Tightening Rules for Low-Income Tax Credit" by Mary Williams Walsh, *New York Times,* April 25, 2003.

145 **Senator William Roth:** Transcripts of Senate Finance Committee hearings, September 23–25, 1997, and April 28–May 1, 1998, from *Tax Notes;* author interviews and news reports.

151 **The inspector general's:** "I.R.S. Workers Face More Investigations by Treasury Agents" by David Cay Johnston, *New York Times,* November 18, 1999; "IRS Watchdog Says Bark Was Unintended" by Stephen Barr, *Washington Post,* November 19, 1999; "Official Curbs Plan to Investigate Many in IRS" by David Cay Johnston, *New York Times,* November 20, 1999.

Page

154 **Luntz had gotten into politics:** "It's 'Respectable' Buchanan Who Tars Republicans," opinion column by Menachem Z. Rosensaft, *Los Angeles Times,* January 21, 1992, quoting unspecified 1977 writing by Buchanan.

157 **"If we can't make sure":** Treasury Department statement by Secretary Paul H. O'Neill, January 16, 2002, www.ustreas.gov/press/releases/po930.htm. And visits to IRS service center in Covington, Kentucky, interviews with Rossotti.

164 **Since there is no free lunch:** Audits rates from tracfed.syr.edu and trac.syr.edu and IRS Statistics of Income.

174 **An IRS audit discovered:** "Report of Investigation of Enron Corporation and Related Entities, Regarding Federal Tax and Compensation Issues and Policy Recommendations" for Senate Finance Committee by staff of the Joint Committee on Taxation, February 2003, available at www.house.gov/jct.

186 **Few names loom larger:** Form 990s from IRS and Mr. Kellogg.

191 **Giving special tax breaks:** Author interviews with insurance tax lawyers.

195 **Former police officers:** Wesley Snipes tax return filed in *USA v. Rosile,* Case 02-CV-466, Middle District of Florida, March 14, 2002.

198 **These business owners and others bought a series:** *USA Today,* March 11, 2001.

200 **The IRS does not know:** Author interviews with Gene Gavin and Irwin Schiff.

203 **In Washington there is even:** "Saved Havens; The Treasury Coddles Tax Cheats" by Anand Giridharadas, *New Republic,* September 3, 2001.

204 **At least one seller of tax evasion:** *USA v. The Joy Foundation et al.,* Case 02-CV-1069, Central District of Illinois, March 5, 2002; and *USA v. Sweet et al.,* Case 01-CV-331, Middle District of Florida, February 13, 2001.

208 **The Caymans depend on tax fraud:** Testimony of John M. Mathewson, U.S. Senate Permanent Subcommittee on Investigations–Minority Office Committee on Governmental Affairs, Federal Document Clearing House transcript, March 1, 2001.

Page

209 **Mathewson's biggest customer:** "U.S. Unlocks a Treasure of Offshore Bank Scams—Arrested Banker's Records Offer Rare Details of Cash Laundering" by William Kleinknecht and Fredrick Kunkle, Newark (NJ) *Star-Ledger,* August 22, 1999.

210 **Mathewson walked IRS criminal investigators:** Author interview with John Morrell.

212 **In Manhattan the district attorney:** Author interviews with Robert Morgenthau.

213 **Peter Coons had a stellar career:** *Peter W. Coons* v. *Treasury,* Merit Systems Protection Board Docket SF-0752-99-0663-I-1 and related proceedings.

216 **Judge Reed, in an opinion:** "Top Tax Man's tale of Demotion" by Scott Winokur, *San Francisco Examiner,* July 25, 2000.

217 **For traders in oil company stocks:** *Compaq Computer Corporation and subsidiaries* v. *Commissioner,* U.S. Tax Court transcript of trial September 23, 1998.

229 **Kate Barton:** Author transcript from webcast.

233 **Congress was not the only place:** Author interview with Mark Ernst.

235 ***The Washington Times:*** "Bad Tax Policy," by Daniel Mitchell, *Washington Times,* May 8, 2002.

251 **When the IRS sent:** *Ronald L. McGinley* v. *Treasury,* Case 01-CV-9493, Central District of California, filed November 5, 2001.

254 **In the Chevron case:** Documents at www2.hawaii.edu/%7Egramlich/caltex/home.html.

255 **The Pritzker family:** "The Corporate Tax Game: How Blue-Chip Companies Are Paying Less and Less of the Nation's Tax Bill" by Nanette Byrnes and Louis Lavelle with Howard Gleckman, *BusinessWeek,* March 31, 2003.

258 **One law review article:** "They've Created a Lamb with Mandibles of Death" by J. William Callison and Allan W. Vestal, *Indiana Law Journal,* Spring 2001.

271 **Among those who were pitched:** Names from Justice Department release, July 10, 2002.

288 **Frontier was purchased with shares:** Global Crossing filings with Securities and Exchange Commission.

Page

288 **Winnick and his wife:** "In L.A., There's More 'Erase-Atecture' Than Preservation. Are We a Tear-Down Town?" by Christopher Reynolds, *Los Angeles Times,* December 29, 2002; "He Can't Believe It's Really His" by Ruth Ryon, *Los Angeles Times,* April 16, 2000.

290 **In all, Winnick and other insiders unloaded $5.2 billion:** "The Emperor of Greed" by Julie Creswell with Nomi Prins, *Fortune,* June 24, 2002.

305 **In public policy:** "Bush 2000 Adviser Offered to Use Clout to Help Enron" by Joe Stephens, *Washington Post,* February 17, 2002.

Index

Accenture, 245–46, 249
Ace Cash Express, 143–44
Adkisson, Jay, 191
Agee, Mary Cunningham, 62
Agee, William, 62
Airplane use. *See* Private and corporate jets
Alaska Trust Company, 5, 263–64
Alexander, Donald, 153, 166
Alexander, Lamar, 303
Alfa Corporation, 189–90
Alioto, Joseph, 214
Allen, Charles, 98
Allen, Herbert, 56–57
Allen & Co., 57
Alternative minimum tax, 95–116
  Bush cuts and increase in, 95–97,
    99–100, 107–16
  and business owners, 98
  Democratic intention for, 96, 300
  effects on deductions/exemptions, 95
  effects by 2010, 96, 99–100, 104–5,
    110–16
  evolution of, 100–104
  family size/status inequity, 99–100, 105–9
  medical expenses, loss of deduction, 103,
    106
  reform issue, 315
  repeal proposal, 116

  tax on lawsuit awards, 97–98
  and tax preparation, 95
American Management Systems,
  161
Anderson, Keith, 202, 205
Anderson, Richard E., 255
Anderson's Ark & Associates, 201–3
Arbitrage theory, 219
Archer, Bill, 135–36, 139–40, 299
Armen, Robert N., Jr., 107
Armey, Dick, 235
Arnold & Porter, 255
Arthur Andersen, 118, 270
Arthur J. Gallagher & Co., 220–21
Atkin, Gump, Strauss, Hauer & Feld,
  298
Atlanta Journal-Constitution, 54
Audits. *See* Internal Revenue Service
  (IRS) audits
Automobiles. *See* Company-car, record-
  keeping, tax reform

Baker, David, 271
Baker & McKenzie, 223–24, 226, 231
Banister, Joe, 195, 198
Bank of New York, 190
Bankers Trust, 257, 298
Bankman, Joseph, 225

Bankruptcy, rise in (1980–2002), 23–24
Barbados, and corporate inversion scheme, 229, 232–33
Barr, Joseph W., 100–101
Barrett, Phillip, 202
Barton, Kate, 229–31, 246
BDO Seidman, 14, 267–68
Bennett, Robert, 150
Bermuda
    and corporate inversion scheme, 229–50, 256
    as tax haven, 12, 212
Bill and Melinda Gates Foundation, 83
Bittner, Ronald L., 274–82, 287–88
Blattmachr, Jonathan, 86–88, 155, 315
    on alternative minimum tax, 116
    life insurance trusts, 262–65
    tax-avoidance strategies of, 5–15, 117
Blethen, Frank, 88–90
Blum, Jack, 208, 212
Blumenthal, Richard, 243–44
Boggs, Patton, 79
BONY Trade Insurance, 190
Booz Allen & Hamilton, 163
Boschwitz, Rudy, 64
Bosset, Dave, 196
Boston Globe, 53–54
Bracket creep, and inflation, 18
Breaux, John B., 258
Bridgeman, James D., 257
British Virgin Islands, 208
Brown, Michael D., 264–65
Buchanan, Patrick J., 154
Buckley, John, 90, 140
Buffett, Warren
    marginal tax rate, 305–6
    on success in America, 84
    support of estate tax, 83–85
Burke, Edmund, 309
Burman, Leonard E., 100, 113–14
Bush, George W.
    and alternative minimum tax, 95–97, 99–100, 107–16
    estate tax proposal, 71–76, 86–90
    exchange funds, position on, 267
    family farm and estate tax statement, 71–76
    Harken Energy tax-avoidance strategy, 236, 249
    on Social Security system, 126–27
    tax cuts, 17, 95–97, 99–100, 107–16, 309–10
    tax rebate, 93
    tax return (1998) of, 312
    tax savings to rich (by 2010), 94, 95–97, 99–100, 127

Business owners
    and alternative minimum tax, 98
    audit risk, decline of, 166–68
BusinessWeek, 238

California
    Proposition 13, 302
    tax protesters, actions against, 198–99, 206
Caltex, 254–55
Capital gains tax
    decrease in (1987–1998), 40
    savings and investment tax, use of term, 81–82
Cayman Islands, as tax haven, 207–10
Celata, Dick, 196
Center for Budget and Policy Priorities, 30
Center for Freedom and Prosperity, 203, 235
Center for the Study of Taxation, 79–80
Chandler, Richard G., 184
Charitable trusts, operation of, 7–8
Chase Manhattan Bank, 298
Cheney, Dick, 72, 236
ChevronTexaco, 253–54
Child
    IRS definition of, 140
    tax benefits and age of, 140
Child care credit, and age of child, 140
Child credit
    age of child, 140
    alternative minimum tax inequity, 105–9
    tax credit (1997), 108–9
Christian Coalition, tax proposals of, 131–32
Christie, Anthony, 290
Citigroup, 49
Citizens Utilities, 291
Clinton, Bill
    and audits for poor, 130, 132
    and earned income tax credit, 131–32
    on estate tax, 76, 78
    IRS reform law (1998), 150
Clothing, price reduction, 23
Coalition for American Financial Security, 127
Coca-Cola, Goizueta compensation, 45–50
Cocco, Marie, 156
Cohen, Mary Ann, 223–25
Cohen, Sheldon, 162, 200, 269
Coleman, Tom, 270
College financial aid, 138
Collins, Chuck, 83
Collins, Max, 116
Company-car, record-keeping, tax reform, 63, 70

Compaq Computer Corporation, foreign-tax credit deal, 221–28

Confidentiality agreements, 8

Conner Peripherals, 222

Conti, Leo, 54

Coons, Peter, 213–16

Cooper Industries, 232, 247

Corporate inversion scheme, 229–50
    corporations participating in, 232, 247–50
    Stanley Works example, 237–50
    tax-avoidance mechanism, 229–31
    tax savings from, 232

Corporations
    audit risk, decline of, 166–68
    corporate inversion scheme, 229–50
    corporation inversion, 229–50
    downsizing and cuts, 53
    executive compensation, 46–58
    federal revenues from (2002), 41
    global operations schemes, 253–58
    medical/dental plan cuts, 53
    pension plan modifications by, 53, 276–82, 285–86
    -political connections, 41–44
    profits, growth of, 12
    regulation, lack of, 41, 42–44
    See also Executive compensation

Credit cards, from offshore tax havens, 209, 211–12

Crystal, Graef "Bud," 54–55, 69, 117

CSX railroad company, 278, 282

Curnutt, Jerry, 168–85, 257, 273

Curnutt, Kevin, 175–76

Currency Options Bring Rewards (Cobra), 270

Dalrymple, John, 152–53

D'Amato, Donald, 77, 241–42

Daniels, Mitchell B., Jr., 295–96

Dart, Ken, 233, 246

Dart Container, 233

Davenport, Charles, 82

Davis, Al, 214

Deathtax.com, 88

Debit cards, from offshore tax havens, 212–13

Debt, rise in (1975–2002), 23–24

Deferred compensation packages, 46–58
    features of, 47–49
    growth of assets, 48–51, 57–58, 117–18
    hedge funds for, 57–58
    interest on deferred money, 50–51
    reform issues, 311–12
    stock in package, 46, 52
    and tax avoidance, 46–50, 56–58, 117–18

Defined-benefit plans, 276

Defined-contribution plans, 276–82, 285–86

Delaney, Frank, 218

Deloitte & Touche, 298

Democracy
    and taxation, 2–3
    and voting participation, 44

Democrats
    and alternative minimum tax, 96, 300
    on corporate inversion scheme, 245, 248–49
    on estate tax, 76–81
    and Social Security tax increase, 299

DeMoss, Harold R., Jr., 226

Denison, Edward, 87

Desai, Mihir A., 225

DiMatteo, Larry A., 273

Discriminant function (dif), 160

Doggett, Lloyd, 248–49, 266, 273

Dole, Robert, 65–66, 303

Dorrance, John, III, 233

Dot.coms, rise and fall of, 26–28

Doti, Frank J., 134

Downsizing, cuts related to, 53

Drug companies, intellectual property offshore, 255

Dryovage, Mary, 216

Duroc-Danner, Bernard J., 247

Earned income tax credit, 129–44
    audited returns, 129–30, 132–38
    claim by nonpoor, 137–39
    and college financial aid, 138
    development of, 130–31
    fast cash schemes, 143–44
    and fraud accusations, 129–30, 132–36, 138
    lump sum payment problem, 138
    refund anticipation loans (RALs) on, 142–43

Earnhart, Dale, 270

Eastman Kodak, 278

Eaton Vance, 267

861 position, 194–95, 199, 202

Enron
    IRS coverup of scam, 174
    offshore tax havens, 257
    profits, fabrication of, 256–58, 297
    retirement plan devastation, 27–28, 289

Entitlements, 279

Ernst, Mark, 234

Ernst & Young, 14, 219, 229, 257
    corporate inversion scheme, 229–50
    tax shelter design and sale, 219–20, 269–72

Index

Esrey, William, 117–18, 126, 270
Estates
    average assets in (1999), 75
    taxable by size (2000), 76
Estate tax, 71–91
    average tax paid (2000), 76
    death tax debate, 80–81, 85
    family farm analogy, 71–76
    life insurance trust tax shelter, 263–66
    lobby against tax, 79–82, 85, 88–91
    loophole of proposed bill, 88–90
    middle class fear of, 76–77
    opponents of repeal, 77–78, 83–85
    opponents of tax, 76–77, 79, 88
    proposal, Bush (George W.) proposal,
        71–76, 86–90
    relationship to gift tax, 86–90
    Republican versus Democratic views,
        76–81
    step-up basis, 86
    tax-free asset ceilings, 73–74
    wealthy supporters of, 83–85
Everson, Mark W., 314
Exchange funds, 266–67
Executive compensation
    compensation committee bias, 56–57
    deferred compensation packages, 46–58
    disclosures, lack of, 48–50
    employee price for, 52–53
    growth of packages, 46, 47, 54–55, 57
    hedge fund management of, 57–58
    legal reforms, 56
    media reports, 46, 54–55
    supplemental executive retirement plans
        (SERPs), 282–84
    and tax avoidance, 46–50, 56–58
Executive Compensation Group, 262
Exemption, child, age of child, 140
Expatriation, tax laws related to, 233
    See also Corporate inversion scheme

Fabrikant, Geraldine, 60
Fast cash schemes, 143–44
Federal Aviation Administration (FAA),
        executive air travel payment rule,
        66–67, 70
Federal budget deficit
    causes of, 26
    end of, Clinton-era, 26
    and Reagan era, 120–21
Federal Mafia, The (Schiff), 201
Feldstein, Martin S., 32
Fensterstock, Bruce, 273
Fischer, George, 278
Fischer, Judith, 283
Flat-tax proposal, 300–304, 310
Flat Tax, The (Hall and Rabushka), 302, 308

Flavin, Robert, 281, 288
Fleischer, Ari, 88, 139–40, 242–43, 249
Foley, Brian, 248
Foley, Mark, 245
Food, price reduction, 23
Food Lion, 55
Food stamps, 141
Forbes, 46, 54, 186, 292, 303
Forbes, Steven, flat-tax proposal, 300–304,
        310
Foreign-tax credit deal, Compaq, 221–28
Form 990, 190
Fortune, 55
Foster children, 140
401(k) plans. See Retirement accounts
Freeman, Douglas, 87–88
Freeman, Freeman & Smiley, 87
Frieble, Frederick, 233
Frontier, 275–82, 287
Frontline, 208

Gale, William G., 99, 114
Gangwal, Rakesh, 282
Gates, Bill
    charitable foundation of, 83
    support of estate tax, 83–84
    tax-avoidance strategies, 7
Gates, Bill, Sr., 83–85
Gavin, Gene, 200–201
General Electric (GE), 50
General Mills, 55
Gerstner, Louis V., Jr., 278
Ghilarducci, Teresa, 285
GI Bill, 25, 309
Gift tax
    life insurance trust tax shelter, 263–66
    relationship to estate tax, 86–90
    tax returns and audits, 165–66
Gingrich, Newt, 131, 232, 299
Global Crossing
    Frontier purchase by, 287–88
    retirement plan devastation, 27–28,
        289–91
Global operations, 253–58
    American profits overseas, 255–56
    corporate inversion scheme, 229–50
    Enron profit fabrication abuse, 256–58
    expensing in U.S./profit taking overseas,
        251–61
    intellectual property offshore, 12, 255–57
Global Santa Fe, 232
Goizueta, Roberto C., 45–50, 117
Golden ADA, 214
Goldman Sachs, 267, 268
Gordon, Robert N., 218–19, 221–22,
        227–28
Graetz, Michael, 75–76, 101, 197

Gramlich, Jeffrey, 254–55
Gramm, Phil, 147, 303
Grassley, Chuck, 235–36, 258
Green, William, 87
Greenspan, Alan, 121–22
Gregory, David, 81
Guardian Bank and Trust (Cayman Islands), 208–9
Gunlad, R. Elaine, 71

H & R Block
    Olde Discount purchase, 234
    tax preparation for poor, 141–42
Hall, Robert E., 301–2, 308
Halliburton, 236
Hariton, David P., 226, 272–73
Harken Energy, 236, 249
Harl, Neil, 72–73, 78
Hart, Dale, 181, 196–98
Hart, Peter, 80
Harvard Business Review, 59
Hawpe, David, 136
Hazle, Maline, 199
Health care insurance, cuts by corporations, 53
Hedge funds
    for executive compensation, 57–58
    operation of, 57
Helms, Jesse, 64–65
Helmsley, Leona, 197
Henkel, Herbert L., 247
Herbert, Bradley, 174
Heritage Foundation, 135, 203, 235
Herring, Victoria L., 98
Holmes, Oliver Wendell, 82
Home ownership, mortgage deduction, 21
Houghton, Amo, 292–93
Household International, 144
Hukkanen-Campbell, Nancy, 97–98

IAT Reinsurance, 188
IBM, executive pensions, 278, 283
Income, income measures (1970–2000), 32–41
Indonesia, ChevronTexaco petroleum pricing scheme, 253–56
Inflation
    and alternative minimum tax, 104
    and bracket creep, 18
    tax bracket adjustment for, 104
    wage increase, insignificance of (1973–2001), 25
Ingersoll-Rand, 232, 234–35, 247
In Search of Excess (Crystal), 55
Insurance, life insurance trust, 263–66
Insurance companies. *See* Tax-exempt insurance companies

Intellectual property, offshore scheme, 12, 255–57
Internal Revenue Service (IRS)
    computer operations, 158–60, 298
    foreign diplomacy connection, 214–16
    internal inadequacy of, 146–47, 157–58
    and opinion letters, 272–73
    oversight board for, 293, 295
    reform (1998), effects of, 150–56, 175
    Reform and Restructuring Act (1998), 150, 175, 293
    Rossotti as commissioner, 157, 160–64, 167, 180–83
    Rossotti final report, 293–95
    secrecy rule, 148–49, 174, 251–52
    Section 501(c)(3) deductions, 186
    Senate Finance Committee hearings (1997–1998), 145–56
    tax law enforcement, limitations of, 43
    taxpayer rights protections, 106–7
    Ten Deadly Sins, 150–53
    transcription operations, 158
Internal Revenue Service (IRS) audits
    auditors, reduction of, 134, 166, 297
    cases/cases not pursued (2002), 294
    computerized audit selection, 160
    decline for wealthy, 164–66
    lifestyle trigger, 16–17
    paying up, avoidance of, 106–7
    of poor, 130, 132–41, 166
    and wage earners, 14, 160–61
Isenberg, Eugene M., 247–48
Iwry, Mark, 285

Jackson Hewitt, tax preparation for poor, 141–42
Jacoboni, Joe, 270–71
Jacobs, Andy, 122
Jensen, Steven, 216
Jesson, Nick, 159, 194–98, 206, 261
Johnson, Calvin H., 220
Johnson, F. Ross, 62
Johnson, Lyndon Baines, 100
Jones, Edith H., 225–27
Jordan, Michael H., deferred compensation package, 50
Joy Foundation, 204

Kaye, Barry, 263
Kay Scholer, 265
Keith, Frank, 200
Kellogg, Peter R., 185–93
Kerrey, Bob, 147
Klaassen, David and Margaret, 105–7, 115
Knott, Joe, 230–31
Koreagate, 251
Korean War, 18

KPMG, 189, 192
  tax shelter design and sale, 270–71
Kreisberg, Louis P., 262
Krugman, Paul, 90

Laffer, Arthur, 129–30
Laro, David, 98
Laws
  corporate-related, negative effects of,
    42–44
  executive compensation reform, 56
Lawsuits
  alternative minimum tax on awards,
    97–98
  on failed tax shelters, 271–72
Lay, Kenneth, 174
Leadenhall Bank and Trust (Bahamas),
    212
Life insurance
  life insurance trust, 263–66
  reverse split-dollar family life insurance,
    265–66
  tax treatment, 263
Limited liability partnerships (LLPs), 13,
    258–61
  and moral hazard, 259–60
Lindsey, Lawrence B., 108
Lister, Michael, 142
Loans
  refund anticipation loans (RALs),
    142–43
  against stock ownership, 268–69
Local taxation, 40
Loctite Corporation, 233
Lott, Trent, 147
Louisville Courier-Journal, 136
Luntz, Frank, 43, 80–82, 85, 153–55, 204

McAuliff, Terry, 290
McCaffrey, Carlyn S., 5
McEachen, Richard, 198–200
McGinley, Ron, 251–53, 258
McGovern, George, 301
McInnis, Scott, 244–45
McKay, Monroe G., 97–98
McKee, Nelson, Ernst & Young, 257
McKee, William S., 257–58
MacNab, JJ., 166, 191, 193, 204–5
MCI WorldCom, 270
Manufacturing, U.S., decline of, 28
Marriage penalty, alternative minimum tax
    as, 99–100
Martin, James, 80
Mathewson, John, 207–13, 316
Medical expense deductions, and alternative
    minimum tax, 103, 106
Merit Systems Protection Board, 215

Metzenbaum, Howard, 63–66
Microsoft. See also Gates, Bill
Microsoft, contract workers, 277
Milbank, Tweed, Hadley & McCloy, 5, 262
Milken, Michael, 288
Miller, Zell, 88
Mills, Wilbur, 10
Mischaud, Nancy, 240
Mitchell, Daniel J., 135, 235
Moncrief, William A., 147–50, 197
Moral hazard, and limited liability
    partnerships (LLPs), 259–60
Morgenthau, Robert, 212–13
Morrell, John, 210–11
Mortgage deduction, benefit for wealthy,
    21–22
Moynihan, Daniel Patrick, 122, 128,
    148–50
Mueller, Gregory, 137–38
Murkowski, Frank, 14, 147
Murray, Terrence, 283
Mutual Fire, Marine and Inland Insurance
    Company, 190

Nabors Industries, 232, 247–48
Nappier, Denise L., 242, 243
National Bureau of Economic Research,
    32, 39
National Federation of Independent
    Businesses, 139
National Income and Products Accounts, 32
National retail sales tax proposal, 300
Neal, Richard E., 109, 245, 267
Netherlands, Compaq foreign-tax credit
    deal, 221–28
New Republic, The, 203
Newsday, 54
News media
  on executive compensation, 46, 54–55
  tax/legal issues, underreporting of, 43,
    78–79
Newsweek, 107, 293
New York, tax-exempt insurance
    companies, 191–92
New York Life, 262–64
New York Times, 1, 43, 60, 72, 90, 115, 151,
    156, 196, 198, 225, 231, 247, 265,
    270, 292
Nicholas, Henry, III, 271
Nickles, Don, 131, 147
Nixon, Richard M.
  IRS, confidentiality rule, 148–49
  minimum tax, 101
Nixon, William, 216
No Time Delay Electronics, 194
Noble Drilling, 232
Northup, Anne M., 136

Oates, Mark A., 226
Offshore tax havens, 207–14
    American assets in deposits, 207
    corporate inversion scheme, 229–50
    corporate profits in, 255–56
    cost of use, 208
    credit cards from, 209, 211–12
    debit cards from, 212–13
    and global operations, 253–58
    and hedge funds, 57–58
    secrecy rule, 309
    and tax-exempt insurance companies, 189
Oil companies, expensing in U.S./profit
        taking overseas, 251–61
Oil depletion allowance, 101
Oil stocks, prearranged trades, 217–21
Olde, Ernest, 233–34
Olde Discount, 233
Olson, Nina, 136–37
Olson, Pamela, 110, 266
O'Neill, Paul H., 127–28, 140, 157, 205,
        296
Open outcry, 218
Opinion letters, 272–73, 298
Organization for Economic Cooperation
        and Development, 203
Oveson, W. Val, 116

Pacific Capital Group, 288
Packard, David, 161
Packwood, Robert, 63–66, 70
Partnerships, 168–85
    audit risk, decline of, 170–74
    identification of tax evasion, 175–85
    limited liability partnerships (LLPs),
        258–61
    multilayering strategy, 14, 167–68
    nonprofit scheme, 169–72
    partner liability, legal issue, 42, 258–59
    real estate, 176–79
Pataki, George, 191–92
Paul, Ron, 204
Paull, Lindy L., 257, 297–98
Pawlak, Lucian J., 239
Pension plans
    company funding, imbalance of, 42, 53
    and corporate balance sheet accounting,
        42
    defined-benefit plans, 276
    defined-contribution plans, 276–82,
        285–86
    freezing plans, 275–76, 279, 291
    legal exclusion of workers, 285
    matching contributions, 53
    matching contributions in shares, 280–81,
        285–87
    offset by Social Security benefits, 283–84

stock market effects on, 284
supplemental executive retirement plans
        (SERPs), 282–84
worker losses and company bankruptcy,
        27–28, 289–91
    See also Retirement accounts
Perot, Ross, 154
Pertamina, 254
Phillip Morris, 55
Phillips, Earl N., 271
Piketty, Thomas, 32, 35, 41
Political connections
    of corporations, 41–44, 290
    of partnerships, 172–73
Politics, language and marketing ideas to
        public, 81–82
Poor and poverty
    audit risk of poor, 130, 132–41, 166
    average income decline (1977–1999), 30
    costs benefits of employment, 129–30
    earned income tax credit, 129–44
    IRS lack of attention to, 67–68
    and refund anticipation loan (RALs)
        schemes, 142–43
Poterba, James M., 225
Power to Destroy, The (Roth), 201
Prearranged stock trades, 217–28
PricewaterhouseCoopers, 189
Private and corporate jets
    Boeing 737 Business Jet, facts about, 61
    FAA rules on, 66–67, 70
    IRS taxation formula, 66–67
    tax breaks, 22, 63
    tax reform proposals, 63–66
Project Cochise, 257
Property taxes, 40
Proposition 13 (California), 302
Pusloskie, John Patrick, Jr., 274–78,
        286–87

Quinn, Jane Bryant, 107

Rabushka, Alvin, 302
Raby, Burgess J.W., 98
Raby, William L., 98
Rangel, Charles, 77–79
Reagan, Ronald
    and earned income tax credit, 131
    and federal budget deficit, 120–21
    revenue enhancements, 121
    Social Security taxes under, 121–22
    tax cuts, 19, 102
    Tax Reform Act (1986), 102–3
Real estate, ownership and estate tax issue,
        77
Real estate partnerships, tax avoidance by,
        176–79

Recession, layoffs (2002), high-paid
    employees, 28
Redder, J. Paul, 271
Redding Record Searchlight, 199
Reed, Phillip, 216
Reed, Ralph, 305
Refund anticipation loans (RALs), 142–43
Regalia, Martin, 249
Regressive taxes, effects of, 40
Republicans
    on corporate inversion schemes, 235–36,
        244–45, 248–50
    on earned income tax credit, 131
    on estate tax, 71–81
Retirement accounts
    and estate tax issue, 77
    tax treatment, 273
    See also Pension plans
Reverse split-dollar family life insurance,
    265–66
Reyes, Maritza, 129–30, 132–34, 138
Riekena, Harlyn, 72
Riley, Bob, 309
Riley, H. John, Jr., 247
RJR Nabisco, 62
Rochester Telephone Company, 274–75
Rogers, Mike, 154
Rosenwald, Julius, 316
Rossotti, Charles O.
    final report of, 293–95
    as IRS commissioner, 157, 160–64, 167,
        180–83, 261
Roth, Arthur J., 183–84
Roth, William, 115, 131, 145–47, 148, 153,
    201, 216, 293
Royal Dutch Shell
    Compaq foreign-tax credit deal, 221–28
    prearranged-stock trades, 217–18, 220

Saez, Emmanuel, 32, 35, 41
Salvatori, Henry, 288
San Jose Mercury, 215
Savings and loan crisis (1980s), 258–59
Schedule C, and audit risk, 167
Schiff, Irwin, 201
Schlesinger, Sanford J., 10, 78, 265
Schwindt, Philip, 104
Secrecy rule
    Internal Revenue Service (IRS), 148–49,
        174, 251–52
    offshore tax havens, 309
Section 501(c)(3) deductions, 186
Securities and Exchange Commission
    (SEC), 49, 56
Seligman, R.A., 17
Senate Finance Committee, hearings on
    IRS (1997–1998), 145–56

September 11, 2001, 231, 236
Shah, Pallavi, 133
Shaye, Robert K., 271
Sheppard, Lee, 17, 224, 226
Short selling, 220–21, 268–69
Sidley Austin Brown & Wood, 272
Simkanin, Richard M., 206
Simon, William E., Jr., 271
Simonetti, Randal, 279
Sixteenth Amendment, 17
Skadden Arps Slate Meagher & Flom, 231
SLK Reinsurance, 188
Smith, Jerry E., 226
Snipes, Wesley, 195–96
Snow, John, 282
Social Security system
    Bush (George W.) on, 126–27
    crisis situation (1983), 121–22
    federal use of funds, 123
    offset of pension by benefits, 283–84
    redistribution scheme of, 125
Social Security taxes, 117–28
    ceiling for high-income earners, 40, 119,
        120, 125
    as double tax, 119–20
    raise in (1970–2000), 18, 40, 122–24
    as subsidy for tax cuts, 123–24, 127–28
Soldano, Patricia, 79–80, 88, 91
Sole proprietors, audit risk, decline of, 167
Soled, Jay, 82
Soros, George, support of estate tax,
    83–84
Sparrow, Malcolm, 213
Spear, Leeds & Kellogg, 186, 188
Spitz, William, 270
Sprint Corporation, 117–18, 270
Stallman, Bob, 74
Stanley Works, 236, 237–49
State taxation, 40
Stealth tax. *See* Alternative minimum tax
Steele Project, 297–98
Step-up basis, estate tax, 86
Steuerle, Eugene, 102–3
Stewart, Richard, 270
Stock
    delayed sale pitfall, 118
    exchange funds, 266–67
    in executive compensation package, 46,
        52
    legal versus economic ownership scheme,
        268–69
    open outcry and trade, 218
    pension plan contributions in, 280–81,
        285–87
    prearranged stock trades, 217–28
    short selling, 220–21
    step-up basis and estate tax, 86

Stock market
   decline (2001–2002), 29
   effect on pension plans, 284
Subchapter S corporations, audit risk, 167
Sullivan, Martin A., 112, 256
Sullivan & Cromwell, 226, 272
Sun Myung Moon, 235
Supplemental executive retirement plans
   (SERPs), 282–84
Supply-side economics
   basic concept, 32, 102, 120
   Reagan actions, 32, 102
Swap funds, 266–67
Sweet, Joe, 204
Swimmer, Gerald, 231
Symms, Douglas, 65–66

Tax avoidance
   corporate inversion scheme, 229–50
   and deferred compensation packages,
     46–50, 56–58, 117–18
   exchange funds, 266–67
   and executive compensation, 46–50,
     56–58
   expensing in U.S./profit taking overseas,
     251–61
   foreign-tax credits, 222–28
   intellectual property offshore, 255–57
   legal counseling for, 5–15
   life insurance trust, 263–66
   limited liability partnerships (LLPs),
     258–61
   and offshore tax havens, 207–14
   partnerships, 175–85
   private and corporate jets, 22, 63
   real estate partnerships, 176–79
   tax-exempt insurance companies, 186–93
   and tax protesters, 194–206
   Thirteenth Amendment as rationale,
     204
Tax credits
   child credit, 108–9, 140
   earned income tax credit, 129–44
Tax cuts
   Bush era, 17, 95–97, 99–100, 107–16,
     310
   Reagan era, 19, 102
   Social Security as subsidy for, 123–24,
     127–28
Tax-exempt insurance companies, 186–93
   capital investments loophole, 187
   operation and growth of, 187–93
   original intent for, 186–87
Tax gap, IRS measurement (1988–2003),
   296
Tax laws, technical correction laws, 139
Tax Notes, 17, 82, 98, 112, 156, 224, 256

Tax preferences
   and alternative minimum tax, 101–3
   and high-income earners, 101
Tax preparation
   and alternative minimum tax
     computation, 95
   profits from earned income tax credit,
     141–44
Tax protesters, 194–206
   arrests/indictments (2003), 206
   861 position, 194–95, 199, 202
   IRS passivity toward, 196–97, 199–200
   mass-marketed instruction, 201–5
   tax professionals involved in, 195, 198
   Thirteenth Amendment rationale, 204
Tax rebate, amounts, range of, 93
Tax reform, 292–317
   flat-tax proposal, 300–304, 310
   national retail sales tax proposal, 300
   Rossotti on IRS needs, 293–95
   tax code overhaul, 313–17
Tax Reform Act (1986), 102, 187
Tax refunds, refund anticipation loans
   (RALs), 142–43
Tax relief
   child credit (1997), 108–9
   versus tax cuts, 80
Tax Relief Act (1997), 165
Tax shelters
   defined, 220
   design and sale of, 219–20, 267–73, 298
   failed shelter lawsuits, 271–72
   and opinion letters, 272–73
Taxation
   alternative minimum tax, 95–116
   and democracy, 2–3
   estate tax, 71–91
   and federal control of prosperity, 10–11
   flat-tax proposal, 300–304, 310
   gift tax, 86–90
   and rich. *See* Wealth and taxation
   Social Security taxes, 117–28
Technical correction laws, 139
Telecommunications Act (1996), 275
Televisions, price reduction, 23
Tempalski, Jerry, 110–12
Tempesta, James J., 224
Ten Deadly Sins, 150–53
Thirteenth Amendment, and tax avoidance
   rationale, 204
Thompson, Al, 198–99
Thurell, Rae Ann, 200
Time, 293
Toth, Thomas and Cindy, 92–95, 100
Trade agreements, and U.S. price
   reductions, 23
Trani, John M., 238–49